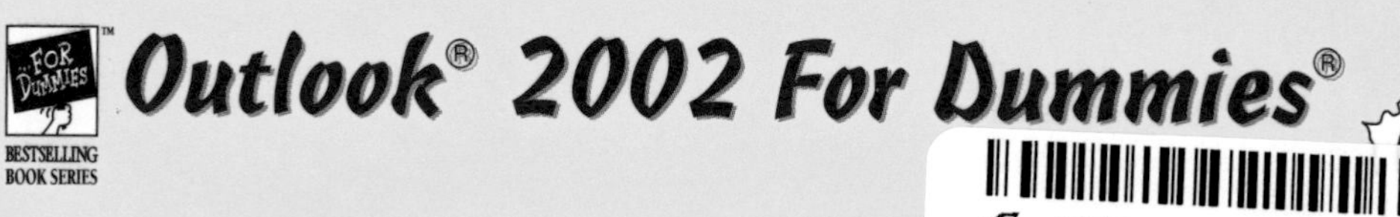

Outlook Toolbars

Clicking a button in a toolbar is a super-speedy way to do many jobs in Outlook. Many toolbar buttons disappear when they're not needed, so don't be surprised if your toolbars look different from these at times. If you want more tools to choose from, choose View⇨Toolbars⇨Advanced.

Message Tools — Standard toolbar buttons

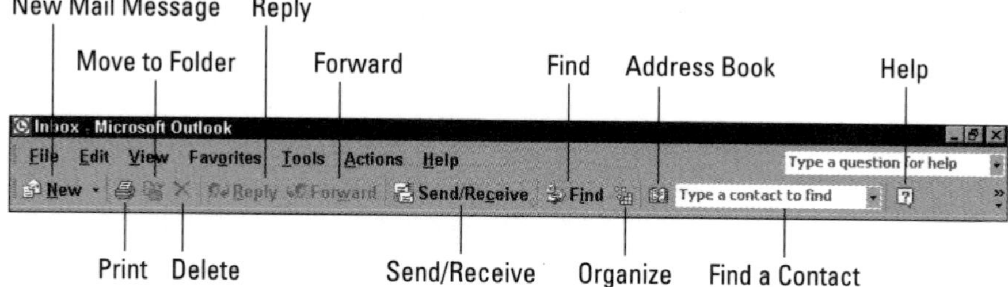

Calendar toolbar buttons

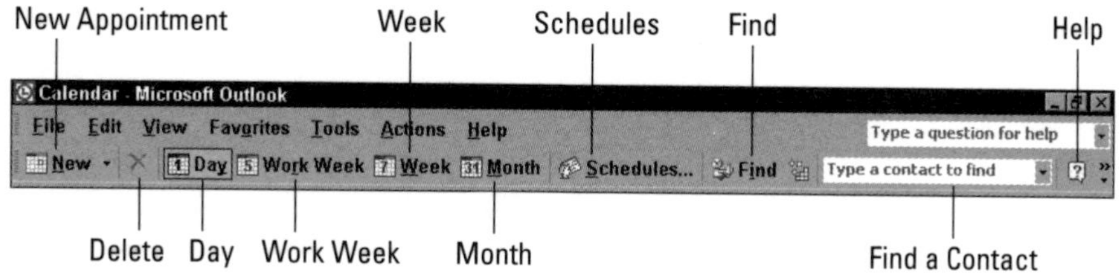

Contact toolbar buttons

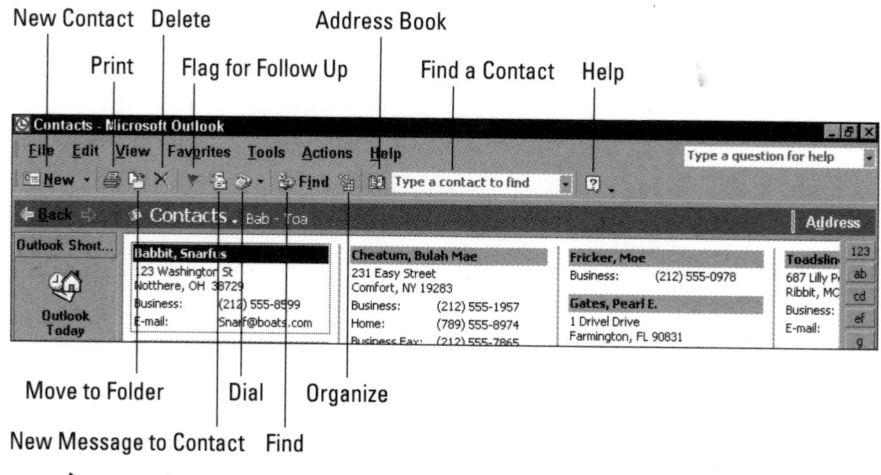

Outlook® 2002 For Dummies®

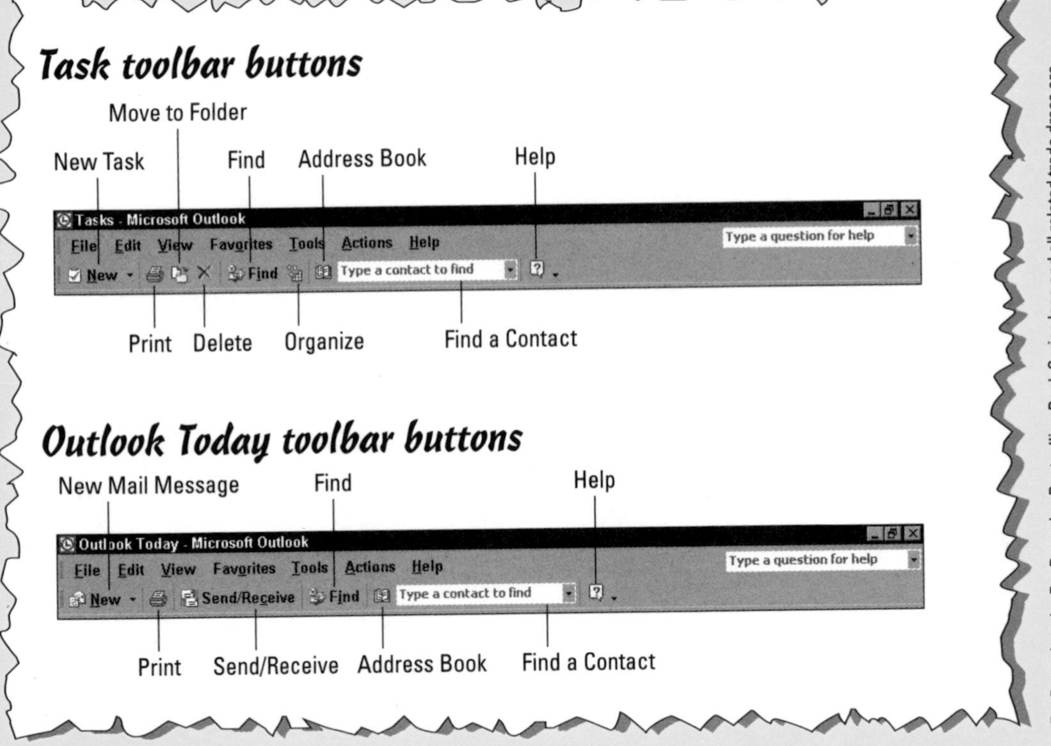

Cheat Sheet $2.95 value. Item 0828-8.
For more information about Hungry Minds, call 1-800-762-2974.

For Dummies: Bestselling Book Series for Beginners

Outlook® 2002 FOR DUMMIES®

by Bill Dyszel

Best-Selling Books • Digital Downloads • e-Books • Answer Networks • e-Newsletters • Branded Web Sites • e-Learning

New York, NY ◆ Cleveland, OH ◆ Indianapolis, IN

Outlook® 2002 For Dummies®

Published by
Hungry Minds, Inc.
909 Third Avenue
New York, NY 10022
www.hungryminds.com
www.dummies.com

Library of Congress Control Number: 2001089289

ISBN: 0-7645-0828-8

Printed in the United States of America

10 9 8 7 6 5 4

1B/RY/QV/QR/IN

Distributed in the United States by Hungry Minds, Inc.

Distributed by CDG Books Canada Inc. for Canada; by Transworld Publishers Limited in the United Kingdom; by IDG Norge Books for Norway; by IDG Sweden Books for Sweden; by IDG Books Australia Publishing Corporation Pty. Ltd. for Australia and New Zealand; by TransQuest Publishers Pte Ltd. for Singapore, Malaysia, Thailand, Indonesia, and Hong Kong; by Gotop Information Inc. for Taiwan; by ICG Muse, Inc. for Japan; by Intersoft for South Africa; by Eyrolles for France; by International Thomson Publishing for Germany, Austria and Switzerland; by Distribuidora Cuspide for Argentina; by LR International for Brazil; by Galileo Libros for Chile; by Ediciones ZETA S.C.R. Ltda. for Peru; by WS Computer Publishing Corporation, Inc., for the Philippines; by Contemporanea de Ediciones for Venezuela; by Express Computer Distributors for the Caribbean and West Indies; by Micronesia Media Distributor, Inc. for Micronesia; by Chips Computadoras S.A. de C.V. for Mexico; by Editorial Norma de Panama S.A. for Panama; by American Bookshops for Finland.

For general information on Hungry Minds' products and services please contact our Customer Care Department within the U.S. at 800-762-2974, outside the U.S. at 317-572-3993 or fax 317-572-4002.

For sales inquiries and reseller information, including discounts, premium and bulk quantity sales, and foreign-language translations, please contact our Customer Care Department at 800-434-3422, fax 317-572-4002, or write to Hungry Minds, Inc., Attn: Customer Care Department, 10475 Crosspoint Boulevard, Indianapolis, IN 46256.

For information on licensing foreign or domestic rights, please contact our Sub-Rights Customer Care Department at 212-884-5000.

For information on using Hungry Minds' products and services in the classroom or for ordering examination copies, please contact our Educational Sales Department at 800-434-2086 or fax 317-572-4005.

Please contact our Public Relations Department at 212-884-5163 for press review copies or 212-884-5000 for author interviews and other publicity information or fax 212-884-5400.

For authorization to photocopy items for corporate, personal, or educational use, please contact Copyright Clearance Center, 222 Rosewood Drive, Danvers, MA 01923, or fax 978-750-4470.

About the Author

Bill Dyszel writes frequently for leading magazines, including *PC Magazine, Success Magazine, Chief Executive Magazine,* and *Computer Shopper,* while also working as a consultant to many of New York's leading firms in the securities, advertising, and publishing industries. He appears regularly as a guest on national television programs on the CNNfn and the TechTV networks. An award-winning public speaker, he enjoys entertaining audiences with talks about the pleasures and pitfalls of using modern technology. He is also the author of *PalmPilot For Dummies* and *Handspring Visor For Dummies.*

The world of high technology has led Mr. Dyszel to grapple with such subjects as Multimedia (or how to make your $2,000 computer do the work of a $20 radio), Personal Information Managers (how to make your $3,000 laptop computer do the work of a $3.00 date book), and graphics programs (how to make your $5,000 package of computers and peripheral devices do the work of a 50-cent box of crayons). All joking aside, he has found that after you figure out the process, most of this stuff can be useful, helpful, and yes, even cool.

Like many public figures with skeletons in their closets, this author has a secret past. Before entering the computer industry, Mr. Dyszel sang with the New York City Opera and worked regularly on the New York stage as a singer, actor, and writer in numerous plays, musicals, and operas. His opera spoof — *99% ARTFREE!* — won critical praise from *The New York Times,* New York *Daily News,* and the Associated Press when he performed the show off-Broadway.

Acknowledgments

I'd like to thank all the wonderful people who helped me make this book entertaining and useful to the reader, especially Linda Morris, Stacee Ehman, Andy Cummings, and the whole staff of Hungry Minds, Inc. that make this series possible.

Publisher's Acknowledgments

We're proud of this book; please send us your comments through our Hungry Minds Online Registration Form located at www.dummies.com.

Some of the people who helped bring this book to market include the following:

Acquisitions, Editorial, and Media Development

Project Editor: Linda Morris

Acquisitions Editor: Stacee Ehman

Copy Editor: Nicole Laux

Technical Editor: Vince Averello

Editorial Manager: Constance Carlisle

Media Development Manager: Laura Carpenter

Media Development Supervisor: Richard Graves

Editorial Assistant: Amanda Foxworth

Production

Project Coordinator: Jennifer Bingham

Layout and Graphics: Amy Adrian, Jill Piscitelli, Brent Savage, Jacque Schneider, Julie Trippetti, Jeremey Unger

Proofreaders: John Greenough, Nancy Price, TECHBOOKS Production Services

Indexer: TECHBOOKS Production Services

General and Administrative

Hungry Minds Technology Publishing Group: Richard Swadley, Vice President and Executive Group Publisher; Bob Ipsen, Vice President and Group Publisher; Joseph Wikert, Vice President and Publisher; Barry Pruett, Vice President and Publisher; Mary Bednarek, Editorial Director; Mary C. Corder, Editorial Director; Andy Cummings, Editorial Director

Hungry Minds Manufacturing: Ivor Parker, Vice President, Manufacturing

Hungry Minds Marketing: John Helmus, Assistant Vice President, Director of Marketing

Hungry Minds Production for Branded Press: Debbie Stailey, Production Director

Hungry Minds Sales: Michael Violano, Vice President, International Sales and Sub Rights

Contents at a Glance

Cartoons at a Glance

By Rich Tennant

The 5th Wave
By Rich Tennant

"I like getting complaint letters by e-mail. It's easier to delete than to shred."

page 9

The 5th Wave
By Rich Tennant

"TELL THE BOSS HE'S GOT MORE FLAME MAIL FROM YOU-KNOW-WHO."

page 99

The 5th Wave
By Rich Tennant

"He saw your laptop and wants to know if he can check his Hotmail."

page 303

The 5th Wave
By Rich Tennant
Okay, enlarge the chicken bone by 900 percent and attach it to an email to the museum saying, "Getting close...send more money."

page 173

The 5th Wave
By Rich Tennant
It's an e-mail from my mother. She wants me to know how happy she is for us.

page 49

Cartoon Information:
Fax: 978-546-7747
E-Mail: richtennant@the5thwave.com
World Wide Web: www.the5thwave.com

Table of Contents

Introduction

Deep space adventurers have control panels on their spaceships, explorers in the Wild West had their faithful guides, and detectives have their little black books. Why? Because every adventurer knows how important it is to have good information. Knowing about the people with whom you're dealing, the things you need to do, and when you have to do those things can make the difference between triumph and failure.

Okay, maybe your daily adventures aren't exactly life-and-death struggles, but having a tool to help you keep a handle on whom and what you need to take care of from day to day is really nice. Even if your daily challenges are limited to dealing with a phone and a personal computer, having one place to look for all your daily details is convenient and timesaving.

Microsoft Outlook was designed to make organizing your daily information easy — almost automatic. You already have sophisticated programs for word processing and number crunching, but Outlook pulls together everything you need to know about your daily tasks, appointments, e-mail messages, and other details. More important, Outlook enables you to use the same methods to deal with many different kinds of information, so you have to learn only one program to deal with the many kinds of details that fill your life, such as

- Finding a customer's phone number
- Remembering that important meeting
- Planning your tasks for the day and checking them off after you're done
- Recording all the work you do so that you can find what you did and when you did it

Outlook is a Personal Information Manager (Microsoft calls it a Desktop Information Manager) that can act as your assistant in dealing with the flurry of small but important details that stand between you and the work you do. You can just as easily keep track of personal information that isn't business-related and keep both business and personal information in the same convenient location.

About This Book

As you read this book and work with Outlook, you discover how useful Outlook is, as well as new ways to make it more useful for the things you do most. If you fit any of the following categories, this book is for you:

- Your company just adopted Outlook as its e-mail program and you need to learn how to use it in a hurry.
- You're planning to purchase or have just purchased Outlook and want to know what you can do with Outlook and how to do it.
- You want an easier, more efficient tool for managing tasks, schedules, e-mail, and other details in your working life.

Even if you don't fall into one of these groups, this book gives you simple, clear explanations of how Outlook can work for you. It's hard to imagine any computer user who wouldn't benefit from the features that Outlook offers.

If all you want is a quick, guided tour of Outlook, you can skim this book; it covers everything that you need to get started. Getting a handle on most of the major features of Outlook is fairly easy — that's how the program is designed. You can also keep the book handy as a reference for the tricks that you may not need every day.

The first part of this book gives you enough information to make sense of the whole program. Because Outlook is intended to be simple and consistent throughout, when you've got the big picture, the details are fairly simple (usually).

Don't be fooled by Outlook's friendliness, though — you can find a great deal of power in it if you want to dig deeply enough. Outlook links up with your Microsoft Office applications, and it's fully programmable by anyone who wants to tackle a little Visual Basic script writing (I don't get into that in this book). You may not want to do the programming yourself, but finding people who can do that for you isn't hard; just ask around.

Foolish Assumptions

I assume that you know how to turn on your computer and how to use a mouse and keyboard. In case you need a brush up on Windows, I throw in reminders as I go along. If Windows and Microsoft Office are strange to you, I recommend picking up Andy Rathbone's *Windows For Dummies,* or Wally Wang's *Office 2002 For Dummies,* both published by Hungry Minds, Inc.

If all you have is a copy of this book and a computer running Outlook, you can certainly do basic, useful things right away, as well as a few fun ones. And after some time, you'll be able to do many fun and useful things.

How This Book Is Organized

To make it easier to find out how to do what you want to do, this book is divided into parts. Each part covers a different aspect of using Outlook. Because you can use similar methods to do many different jobs with Outlook, the first parts of the book focus on how to use Outlook. The later parts concentrate on what you can use Outlook to do.

Part I: Getting the Competitive Edge with Outlook

I learn best by doing, so the first chapter is a quick guide to the things that most people do with Outlook on a typical day. You find out how easy it is to use Outlook for routine tasks such as handling messages, notes, and appointments. You can get quite a lot of mileage out of Outlook even if you do only the things our fictional detective does in the first chapter.

Because Outlook allows you to use similar methods to do many things, I go on to show you the things that stay pretty much the same throughout the program: how to create new items from old ones by using drag-and-drop; ways to view items that make your information easy to understand at a glance; and the features Outlook offers to make it easier to move, copy, and organize your files.

Part II: Taming the E-Mail Beast

E-mail is now the most popular function of computers. Tens of millions of people are hooked up to the Internet, an office network, or one of the popular online services, such as The Microsoft Network or CompuServe.

The problem is that e-mail can still be a little too complicated. As I show you in Part II, however, Outlook makes e-mail easier. Computers are notoriously finicky about the exact spelling of addresses, correctly hooking up to the actual mail service, and making sure that the text and formatting of the message fit the software you're using. Outlook keeps track of the details involved in getting your message to its destination.

Outlook also allows you to receive e-mail from a variety of sources and manage the messages in one place. You can slice and dice your list of incoming and outgoing e-mail messages to help you keep track of what you send, to whom you send it, and the day and time you send it.

Part III: It's What You Know AND Who You Know: How to Succeed with Microsoft Outlook

Outlook takes advantage of its special relationship with your computer and your office applications (Microsoft Outlook with Microsoft Office, Microsoft Internet Explorer, and Microsoft Windows — notice a pattern emerging here?) to tie your office tasks together more cleanly than other such programs and make it easier for you to deal with all the stuff that you have to do. The chapters in Part III show you how to get the job done with Outlook.

Beyond planning and scheduling, you probably spend a great deal of your working time with other people, and you need to coordinate your schedule with theirs (unless you make your living doing something strange and antisocial, such as digging graves or writing computer books). Outlook allows you to share schedule and task information with other people (if you're on the same network) and synchronize with them. You can also assign tasks to other people if you don't want to do them yourself (now *there's* a timesaver). Be careful, though; other people can assign those tasks right back to you.

Part IV: Beyond the Basics: Tips and Tricks You Won't Want to Miss

Some parts of Outlook are less famous than others, but no less useful. Part IV guides you through the sections of Outlook that the real power users take advantage of to stay ahead of the pack.

If you've got yellow sticky notes covering your monitor, refrigerator, desktop, or bathroom door, you'll get a great deal of mileage out of Outlook's Notes feature. Notes are little yellow (or blue, or green) squares that look just like those handy paper sticky notes that you stick everywhere as reminders and then lose. About the only thing that you can't do is set your coffee cup on one and mess up what you wrote.

Sometimes, the "find-the-sticky-note" game takes a dark turn — you don't remember *what* you jotted down, you don't remember *where* you put the note, but you do remember *when* you wrote it. That's when Outlook's automatic Journal feature comes in handy. The Journal keeps track of every document that you create, edit, or print. In case it sounds too Big Brother-ish to have a computer recording everything you do, I tell you how to turn the Journal off.

Part V: The Part of Tens

Why ten? Why not! If you must have a reason, ten is the highest number you can count to without taking off your shoes. A program as broad as Outlook leaves a great deal of flotsam and jetsam that doesn't quite fit into any category, so I sum up the best of that material in groups of ten.

Conventions Used in This Book

Outlook has many unique features, but it also has lots in common with other Windows programs — dialog boxes, pull-down menus, toolbars, and so on. To be productive with Outlook, you need to understand how these features work, and you need to recognize the conventions I use for describing these features throughout this book.

Dialog boxes

Even if you're not new to Windows, you deal with dialog boxes more in Outlook than you do in many other Microsoft Office programs because so many items in Outlook are created with dialog boxes, which may also be called *forms*. E-mail message forms, appointments, name and address forms, and plenty of other common functions in Outlook use dialog boxes to ask you what you want to do. The following list summarizes the essential parts of a dialog box:

- **Title bar:** The title bar tells you the name of the dialog box.
- **Text boxes:** Text boxes are blank spaces into which you type information. When you click a text box, you see a blinking I-beam pointer, which means that you can type text there.
- **Control buttons:** In the upper-right corner of a dialog box, you find three control buttons:

   - The *Close button* looks like an X and makes the dialog box disappear.
   - The *Size button* toggles between maximizing the dialog box (making it take up the entire screen) and resizing it (making it take up less than the entire screen).
   - The *Minimize button* makes the dialog box seem to go away but really just hides it in the taskbar at the bottom of your screen until you click the taskbar to make the dialog box come back.

- **Tabs:** Tabs look like little file-folder tabs. If you click one, you see a new page of the dialog box. Tabs are just like the divider tabs in a ring binder; click one to change sections.

The easiest way to move around a dialog box is to click the part that you want to use. If you're a real whiz on the keyboard, you may prefer to press the Tab key to move around the dialog box; this method is much faster if you're a touch typist. Otherwise, you're fine just mousing around.

Links

Links are special pictures or pieces of text that you can click to change what you see on-screen. If you're used to surfing the Internet, you're used to clicking blue, underlined text to switch from one Web page to another. Outlook has some links that work just like links on the Internet. When you see underlined text, the text is most likely a link — click that text if you want to see where it leads.

Keyboard shortcuts

Normally, you can choose any Windows command in at least these three ways (and sometimes more):

- Choose a menu command or click a toolbar button.
- Press a keyboard combination, such as Ctrl+B, which means holding down the Ctrl key and pressing the letter B (you use this command to make text bold).
- Press the F10 key or the spacebar to pull down a menu, press an arrow key to choose a command, and press Enter (way too much trouble, but possible for those who love a challenge).

You often tell Outlook what to do by choosing from menus at the top of the screen. Each menu command has one letter underlined (such as File, Edit, Help), which means that you can hold the Alt key while pressing the underlined letter to open the menu. Press Alt+F to open the File menu, Alt+E to see the Edit menu, or Alt+H to see the Help menu.

I normally simplify menu commands by saying something like "Choose Yeah⇨Sure," which means "Choose the Yeah menu; then, choose the Sure command."

One rather confusing feature of Outlook is the way each menu appears in two different views. When you first click the name of a menu in the menu bar, a short menu appears to show the most popular choices from that menu. If you leave the menu open for about two seconds, the menu suddenly doubles in length, showing you every command available on that menu. Don't worry, your eyes aren't going bad — that's how the product was designed. Microsoft programmers believe that some people are more comfortable with shorter menus, whereas others prefer longer menus, so this "Jack-in-the-box" scheme will either make everyone equally happy or equally confused.

Icons Used in This Book

Sometimes the fastest way to go through a book is to look at the pictures — in this case, icons that draw your attention to specific types of information that's useful to know. Here are the icons I use in this book:

The Remember icon points out helpful information. (Everything in this book is helpful, but this stuff is even *more* helpful.)

A hint or trick for saving time and effort, or something that makes Outlook easier to understand.

The Warning icon points to something that you may want to be careful about in order to prevent problems.

The Technical Stuff icon marks background information that you can skip, although it may make good conversation at a really dull party.

The Time-Saver icon points out a trick that can save you time.

The Network icon points out information that applies primarily to people using Outlook on a computer network at the office.

The Internet icon points out a feature of Outlook that helps you connect to the Internet or use the Internet more effectively.

Getting Started

A wise person once said, "The best way to start is by starting." Okay, that's not all that wise, but why quibble? Plunge in!

Part I
Getting the Competitive Edge with Outlook

"I like getting complaint letters by e-mail. It's easier to delete than to shred."

In this part . . .

Outlook is an all-in-one information management system that lets you organize and manage your appointments, activities, e-mail, and office life with a few clicks of the mouse. In this part, I give you a basic vision of how Outlook works to improve the way you manage your days.

Chapter 1

Fundamental Features: How Did You Ever Do without Outlook?

In This Chapter

- Reading e-mail
- Answering e-mail
- Creating new e-mail
- Entering an appointment
- Adding a Contact
- Checking your calendar
- Taking notes
- Entering Tasks
- Marking Tasks complete
- Sending files by e-mail

Outlook is easier to use than you might think. It also does a lot more than you might realize. Even if you only use about 10 percent of Outlook's features, you'll be amazed at how this little program can streamline your life and spiff up your communications. People get pretty excited about Outlook — even if they only take advantage of a tiny fraction of the things the package can do. I'm kicking off this book with "Outlook's Greatest Hits," the things you'll want to do with Outlook every single day. The list sounds simple enough: sending e-mail, making appointments, and so on. But there's more here than meets the eye; Outlook does ordinary things extraordinarily well. I know you want to do the same, so read on.

The Easy Way to Do Anything with Outlook

If you learn a little, you can do a lot in Outlook — click an icon to do something, view something, or complete something. Using Outlook is so simple, I can sum it up in just a few sentences.

Here's how to do most common tasks in Outlook:

- **Open an item and read it:** Double click the item.
- **Create a new item:** Click an icon in the Outlook Bar, click the New button in the Toolbar at the top of the screen and fill out the form that appears. When you're done, click the button labeled Send or, alternatively, Save and Close.
- **Delete an item:** Click the item once to select it, and then click the Delete icon in the Toolbar at the top of the screen. The delete icon contains a black X.
- **Move an item:** Use your mouse to drag the item to where you want it.

Does that seem too simple? If you want to complicate things, I know you can find a way. Perhaps you can try to use Outlook while hopping on a pogo stick or flying the space shuttle, but in any case, these four tricks take you a long way.

Outlook can also do some very sophisticated tricks, such as automatically sorting your e-mail or creating automated form letters, but you'll need to learn a few details to take advantage of those tricks. The other 300 pages of this book cover the finer points of Outlook. If you only wanted the basics, I could've sent you a postcard.

The pictures that I show you in this book and the instructions that I give you assume that you're using Outlook the way it comes out of the box from Microsoft, with all the standard options installed. If you don't like the way the program looks or what things are named when you install Outlook, you can change nearly everything. If you change many things, however, some of the instructions and examples that I give you won't make sense, because the parts of the program that I talk about may have names that you gave them, rather than the ones that Microsoft originally assigned. The Microsoft people generally did a good job of making Outlook easy to use. I suggest leaving the general arrangement alone until you're comfortable using Outlook.

Reading E-Mail

E-mail is Outlook's most popular feature. I've run across people who only use the program for dealing with e-mail messages. It's a good thing that Outlook makes it so easy to read your e-mail.

When you start your computer and double-click the Outlook icon on the desktop, you'll see a list of messages. Usually you can see the first three lines of each unread message in the AutoPreview window (see Figure 1-1).

Here's how to see the entire message:

1. **Click Inbox in the Outlook Bar.**

   You don't need this step if you can already see the messages, but it doesn't hurt.

2. **Double-click the title of the message.**

   Now you can see the entire message.

3. **Press Esc.**

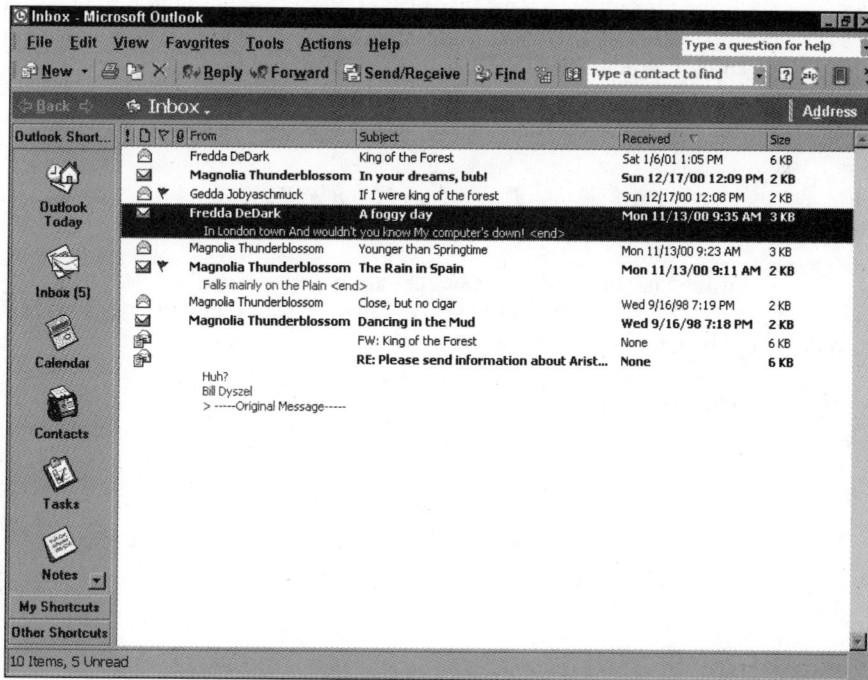

Figure 1-1: Double-click the message that you want to read.

If you want to read the next message in your Inbox, click the Next Item tool in the toolbar (the blue arrow that points downward), or press Ctrl+> to make the next message appear.

If you feel overwhelmed by the number of e-mail messages that you get each day, you're not alone. Billions and billions of e-mail messages fly around the Internet each day, and lots of people are feeling buried in messages. You discover the secrets to sorting and managing your collection of messages in Chapter 6.

Answering E-Mail

When you open an e-mail message in Outlook to read it, buttons labeled Reply and Reply to All appear at the top of the message screen. That's a hint. When you want to reply to a message you're reading, click the Reply button. That opens a new message form that's already addressed to the person who sent you the message. If you're reading a message that was sent to several people besides you, you also have the option of sending a reply to everyone involved by clicking the Reply to All button.

When you reply to a message, the text of the message that was sent to you is automatically included. Some people like to include original text in their replies, some don't. In Chapter 5, I show you how to change what Outlook automatically includes in replies.

Creating New E-Mail Messages

At its easiest, the process of creating a new e-mail message in Outlook is ridiculously simple. Even a child can do it. If you can't get a child to create a new e-mail message for you, you can even do it yourself.

To create a new e-mail message:

1. **Click Inbox in the Outlook Bar.**

   Your message list appears.

2. **Click the New button in the Toolbar.**

   The New Message form appears.

3. **Fill out the New Message form.**

   Put the address of your recipient in the To box, a subject in the Subject box, and type a message in the main message box.

4. **Click Send.**

   Your message is on its way.

To send a plain e-mail message, that's all you need to do. If you prefer to send fancy e-mail, you can do that too. You might want to send a High Priority message to impress some big shots. Or, you could send a Confidential message about certain hush-hush topics. Discover the mysteries of confidential e-mail in Chapter 4.

Sending a File

Call me crazy, but I suspect that you have more to do than exchange e-mail all day. You probably do lots of daily work in programs other than Outlook. You might create documents in Microsoft Word or build elaborate spreadsheets with Excel. When you want to send a file by e-mail, Outlook gets involved, although sometimes it works in the background.

To e-mail a document that you created in Microsoft Word, for example, follow these steps:

1. **Open the document in Microsoft Word.**

   The document appears on-screen.

2. **Choose File⇨Send To⇨Mail Recipient (as attachment).**

   The New Message form appears with your document listed on the Attachment line (see Figure 1-2).

3. **Type the e-mail address of your recipient on the To line.**

   The address you enter appears on the To line.

4. **Click Send.**

   Your file is now en route.

When you're just sending one Word file, this is the easiest way to go. If you're sending more than one file, I describe a more powerful way to attach files in Chapter 5.

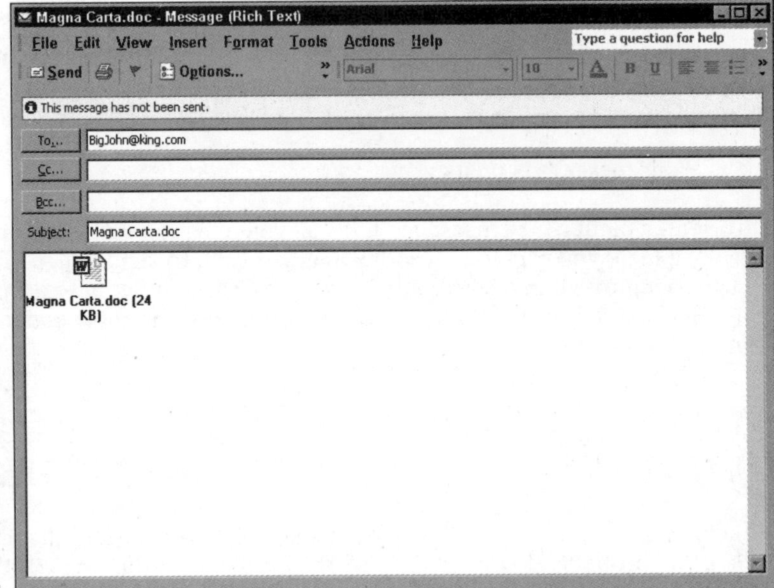

Figure 1-2: You can e-mail a document right from Microsoft Word.

Entering an Appointment

If you've ever used an old-fashioned paper planner, the Outlook Calendar will look familiar to you. When you click the Calendar icon, you see a grid in the middle of the screen with lines representing each half-hour of the day (see Figure 1-3). To enter an appointment at a certain time, just click the line next to the time when you want your appointment to begin, type a name for your appointment, and press Enter.

If you want to enter more detailed information about your appointment, such as ending time, location, category and so on, see Chapter 8 for the nitty-gritty about keeping your Calendar.

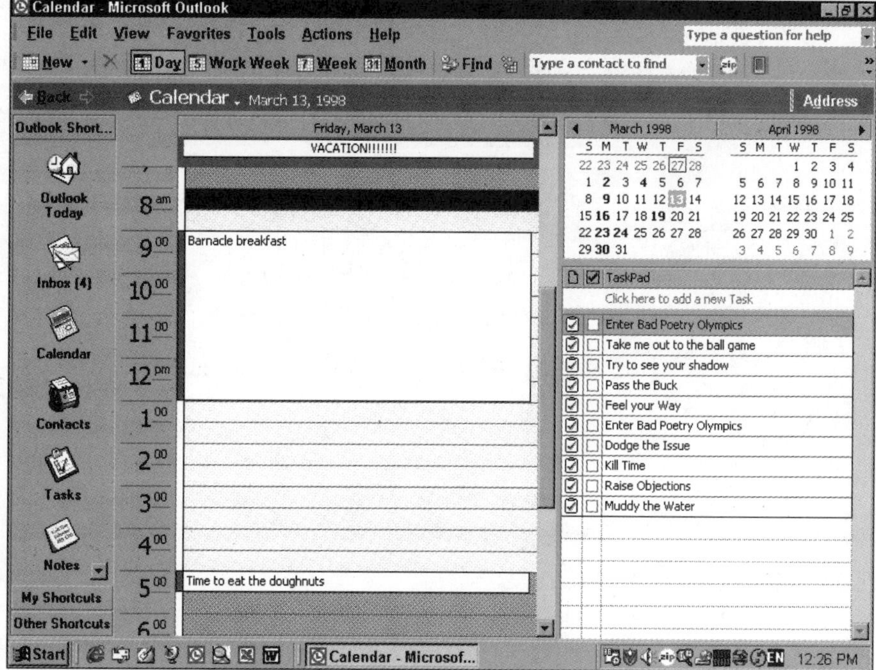

Figure 1-3: Track your busy schedule in the Outlook calendar.

Checking Your Calendar

Time management involves more than just entering appointments. If you're really busy, you want to manage your time by slicing and dicing your list of appointments to see when you're free enough to add even more appointments. You can choose from several different views of your calendar by clicking the Day, Week, and Month buttons at the top of the Calendar screen. If you need a more elaborate collection of calendar views, choose View⇨Current View, and then choose the view that suits you. To really master time management, see Chapter 8 to see the different ways that you can view your Outlook Calendar.

Adding a Contact

When it's not what you know but whom you know, you need a good tool for keeping up with who's who. Outlook is a great tool for managing your list of names and addresses and it's just as easy to use as your Little Black Book. To enter a new contact, click the New button on the toolbar to open the New Contact entry form, fill in the blanks on the form, and then click Save and Close (see Figure 1-4).

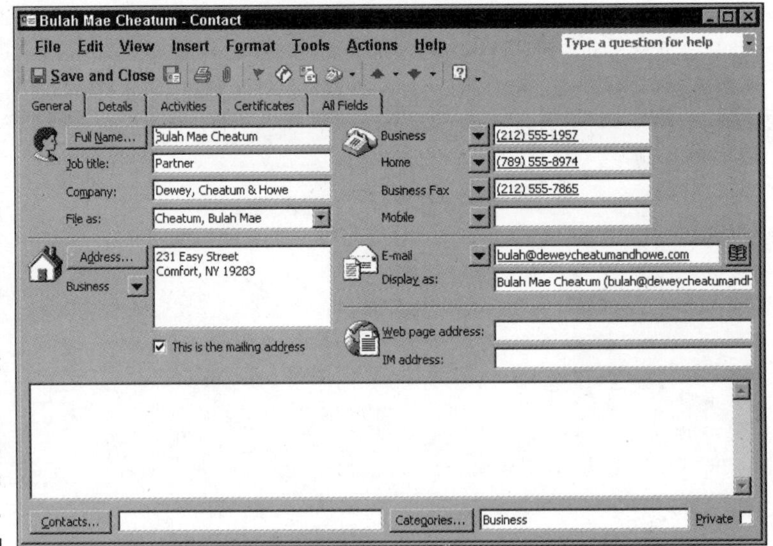

Figure 1-4: Keep detailed information about everyone you know in the Contacts list.

Outlook does a lot more than your little black book — if you know the ropes. Chapter 7 reveals the secrets of searching, sorting, and grouping your list of names and of using e-mail to keep in touch with all the important people in your life.

Entering a Task

Entering a Task in Outlook isn't much of a task itself. You can click either the Task icon or the Calendar icon to see a list of your tasks. If you see the words `Click here to add a new Task`, you've got a clue.

To enter a new task, follow these steps:

1. **Click the text that says** `Click here to add a new Task`**.**

   The words disappear, and you see the Insertion Point (a blinking line).

2. **Type the name of your task.**

   Your task appears in the block under the Subject line on the Tasks list (see Figure 1-5).

3. **Press the Enter key.**

   Your new task moves down to the Tasks list with your other tasks.

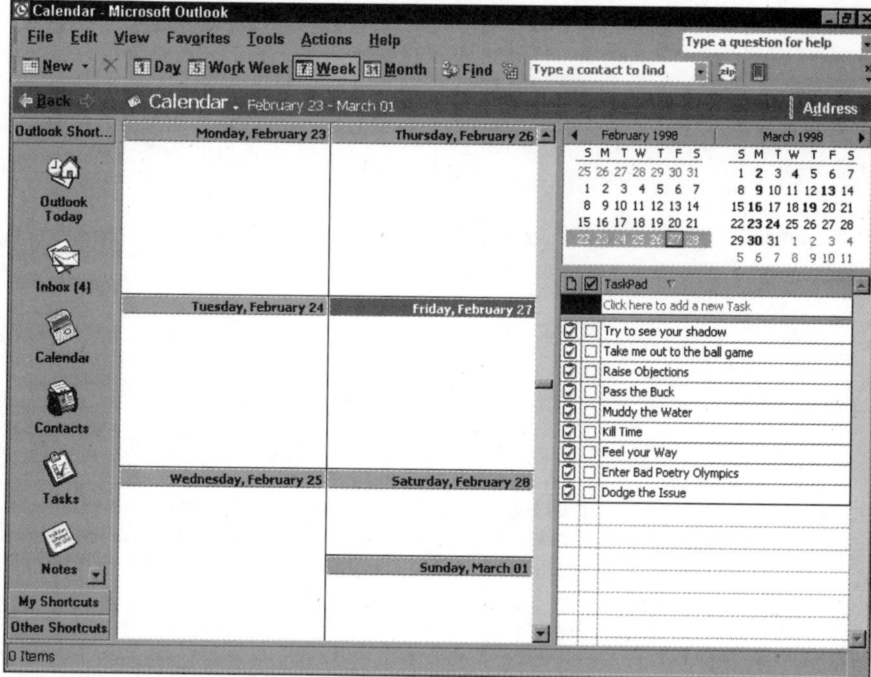

Figure 1-5: Entering your task in the TaskPad.

Outlook can help you manage anything from a simple shopping list to a complex business project. In Chapter 9, I show you how to deal with recurring tasks, regenerate tasks, and also how to mark tasks complete (and earn the right to brag about how much you've accomplished).

Taking Notes

I have hundreds of little scraps of information that I need to keep somewhere, but until Outlook came along, I didn't have a place to put them. Now all that written flotsam and jetsam that I need goes into my Outlook Notes collection where I can find it all again when I need it.

To create a new Note:

1. **Click the Notes icon.**

   Your list of Notes appears.

2. **Type the text you want to save.**

   The text you type appears in the note (see Figure 1-6).

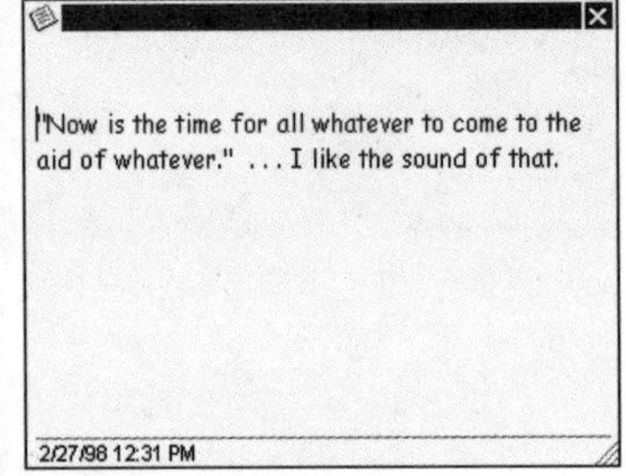
"Now is the time for all whatever to come to the aid of whatever." . . . I like the sound of that.
2/27/98 12:31 PM

Figure 1-6: Preserve your prose for posterity in an Outlook Note.

3. **Press Esc.**

   The note you created appears in your list of Notes.

An even quicker way to enter a note is to press Ctrl+Shift+N and type your note text. You can see how easy it is to amass a large collection of small notes. Chapter 10 tells you everything you need to know about Notes, including how to find the notes you've saved, as well as how to sort, categorize, and organize your collection of notes and even how to delete the ones you don't need anymore.

After you're in the habit of using Outlook to organize your life, I'm sure you'll want to move beyond the basics. That's what the rest of this book shows you. When you're ready to share your work with other people, send e-mail like a pro, or just finish your workday by 5 p.m. and get home, you'll find ways to use Outlook to make your job and your life easier to manage.

Chapter 2

Inside Outlook: Mixing, Matching, and Managing Information

In This Chapter

- Examining the many faces of Outlook
- Choosing menus: One from column A and one from column B
- Using the tools of the trade
- Taking the shortcut: Speedier keystrokes
- Getting the big picture from the Information Viewer
- Fine-tuning with the Folder List

Computer companies love new stuff. Every so often, they beef up their products with new names and new features and release them just before I've figured out how to use the old products. It's kind of confusing, but I can't deny that many of these newfangled features make my life easier after I get a handle on them.

In the old days B.C. (Before Computers), every task in an office required a different machine. You typed letters on a typewriter, calculated on an adding machine, filed names and addresses in a card file, and kept your appointments in a datebook. It would be very difficult to add up your monthly sales on the typewriter and even harder to type a letter on the calculator.

When computers started creeping in, each of these functions was taken over, one by one, by the computer. A different program replaced each machine. First, the word-processing program eliminated the typewriter; next, the spreadsheet replaced the calculator. After a brief flirtation with the giant record-keeping database, the frequent job of keeping track of names, addresses, and dates slowly (but not completely) gave way to a program called the Personal Information Manager (PIM). Microsoft claims to take the information manager concept one step further with Outlook.

Outlook and Other Programs

Outlook 2002 is a part of Office XP. Office XP is an Office *suite,* which means it's a collection of programs that includes everything you need to complete most office tasks. Ideally, the programs in a suite work together, enabling you to create documents that you couldn't create as easily with any of the individual programs. For example, you can copy a chart from a spreadsheet and paste it into a sales letter that you're creating in your word processor. You can also keep a list of mailing addresses in Outlook and use the list as a mailing list to address form letters (see Chapter 18).

Office XP includes six programs that cost less to buy together than you would pay to buy them separately. The concept is a little like buying an encyclopedia; it's cheaper to buy the entire set than it is to buy one book at a time. Besides, who wants just one volume of an encyclopedia (unless you're interested only in aardvarks)?

Outlook turns up in connection with several other Microsoft products, as well. Microsoft Exchange Server is the backbone of the e-mail system in many corporations, and Outlook is often the program that employees of those corporations use to read their company e-mail. Outlook's first cousin, Outlook Express, is included free when you install Internet Explorer and as a part of Windows 98, as well as all future versions of Windows. Outlook 2002 is also linked strongly to Internet Explorer, although technically they're separate programs. You don't need to worry about all this, though. You can start up Outlook and use it the same way no matter which other programs it's bundled with.

Enter the PIM

When it comes to the basic work of managing names, addresses, appointments, and e-mail, the word processing and spreadsheet programs just don't get it. If you're planning a meeting, you need to know with whom you're meeting, what the other person's phone number is, and when you can find time to meet.

Several small software companies recognized the problem of managing addresses and appointments long ago and offered Personal Information Managers (PIMs) to fill in the gap. PIMs, such as Lotus Organizer, SideKick, and Act!, specialized in names, addresses, dates, and tasks, leaving the word processing and number crunching to brawnier business applications, such as Microsoft Word and Excel.

The problem with PIMs before Outlook is that they must communicate with the word processors of the world, but they often can't. If you have a person's name and address stored in a PIM, such as SideKick, and you want to write a letter to that person in Microsoft Word, you have to copy and paste the address from the PIM into your letter, assuming that both programs allow you to do that. Even if they do allow that, however, the address is likely to be sliced up in the PIM in a way that doesn't work in Word. So the PIM that was supposed to make your life easier has, in fact, doubled your workload.

In designing Outlook, Microsoft took advantage of the fact that many people use Microsoft products for most of the work that they do. The company created a PIM that speaks a common language with Microsoft Word, Excel, and the rest of the Microsoft Office suite. Microsoft also studied what kind of information people use most often and tried to make sure that Outlook can handle most of it. The company also added the capability to move, copy, rename, and manage your files, using the same simple drag-and-drop techniques that you use for managing e-mail, tasks, appointments, and the like. The program also has enough customizability (what a tongue-twister — it just means that you can set it up however you need, after you know what you're doing) that Microsoft doesn't even call Outlook a PIM but rather a *Desktop Information Manager.* Yeah, that's right — it's a DIM. Microsoft doesn't always come up with the brightest names for things.

Above all, Outlook is easy to understand and hard to mess up. If you've used any version of Windows, you can just look at the screen and click a few icons to see what Outlook does. You won't break anything. If you get lost, going back to where you came from is easy. Even if you have no experience with Windows, Outlook is fairly straightforward to use.

There's No Place Like Home: Outlook's Main Screen

Outlook's appearance is very different from the other Microsoft Office applications. Instead of confronting you with a blank screen and a few menus and toolbars, Outlook begins by offering you large icons with simple names and a screen with information that's easy to use and understand. If you've spent much time surfing the Web, you'll find the Outlook layout pretty similar to many pages on the Web. Just select what you want to see by clicking an icon on the left side of the screen, and the information you selected appears on the right side of the screen.

Feeling at home when you work is nice. (Sometimes when I'm at work, I'd rather be at home, but that's something else entirely.) Outlook makes a home for all your different types of information: names, addresses, schedules, to-do lists, reminders, and even a list of all the files on your computer. You can customize the main screen as easily as you rearrange your home furnishings.

Although, to make it easier to find your way around at first, I recommend that you wait until you feel entirely at home with Outlook before you start rearranging the screen.

The Outlook main screen has all the usual parts of a Windows screen (see the Introduction if you're not used to the Windows screen), with a few important additions. At the left side of the screen, you see the Outlook Bar. Next to the Outlook Bar are the parts of the screen that take up most of the space: the Information Viewer and the Folder List (see Figure 2-1).

Outlook modules

All the work you do in Outlook is organized into *modules,* or sections. Each module performs a specific job for you: The Calendar stores and manages your schedule, the Tasks module stores and manages your to-do list, and so on. Outlook is always showing you one of its modules in the main screen or Information Viewer. Whenever you're running Outlook, you're always using a module, even if the module contains no information — the same way your television can be tuned to a channel even if nothing is showing on that channel. The name of the module you're currently using is displayed in large type at the top of the Information Viewer part of the screen, so you can easily tell which module is showing.

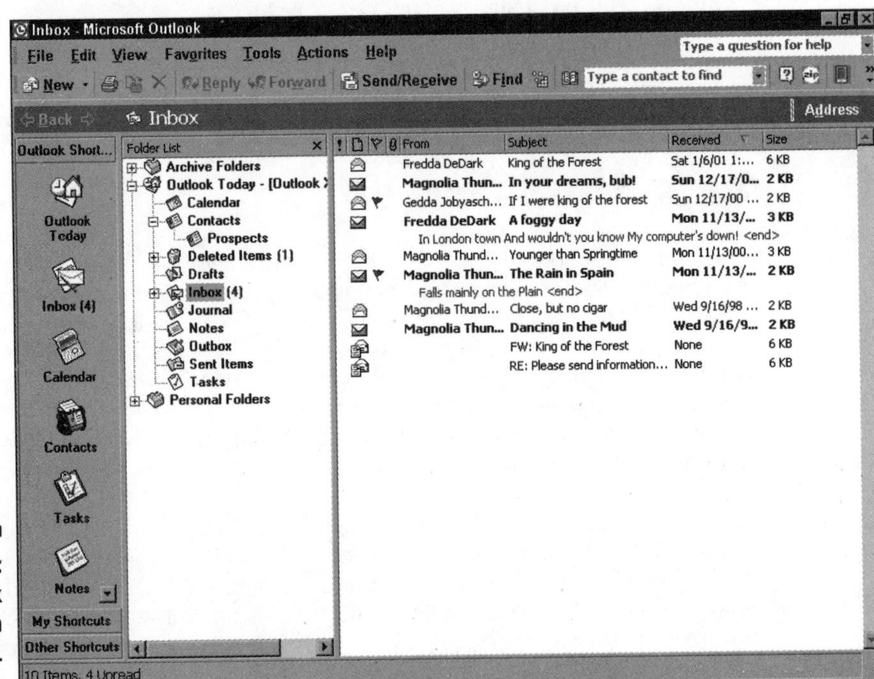

Figure 2-1: The Outlook main screen.

Each module has an *icon* (picture) in the Outlook Bar portion of the screen. Clicking the module's icon is a shortcut that takes you to a different module of Outlook. The Inbox collects your incoming e-mail. The Contacts module stores names and addresses for you. The Tasks module keeps track of all the work that you do. The Journal records all your activities. And the Notes module allows you to keep track of random tidbits of information that don't quite fit anywhere else.

To change Outlook modules, do either of the following things:

- Click View in the menu bar, and then click Go To to display the menu shown in Figure 2-2. Choose the module that you want.
- For faster action, simply click the module's icon in the Outlook Bar.

If you're using Outlook on your company network, your network's system administrator may have created a different set of icons for you to work with. You may have a few more or a few less than you see in this book, but the icons should work the same way.

After you're comfortable with Outlook, you may want to customize it to suit your taste. For example, you may want to add an icon for your floppy drive to make it easier to move or copy files onto a floppy disk. In Chapter 13, in which I show you how to create custom forms, you see how to create a new Outlook folder, which acts like a separate module. In Chapter 24, you can see how to add or remove tools and menu items. You can customize Outlook beyond recognition, if you want. What the heck — have it your way!

Beware, however — your local computer guru may get cranky if you keep deleting an icon installed expressly for you to use on your company's system.

Belly up to the Outlook Bar

Although James Bond never ordered a Martini at the Outlook Bar, it's still where the action is in Outlook. When you use Outlook, you see a column on the left side of the screen containing some icons (pictures) with names such as Calendar, Contacts, Tasks, Journal, and Notes — the basic Outlook modules. I explain these modules later, but the names alone already tell you the story.

Just click an icon, any icon, and you'll see what it sets in motion. Clicking the icon changes the stuff on the main screen to fit what the icon describes. Click the Calendar icon, and a Calendar screen shows up. Click Contacts, and you get a screen for names and addresses. The process is like changing the channels on the TV set. If you switch to a channel that you don't want, switch to another — no problem.

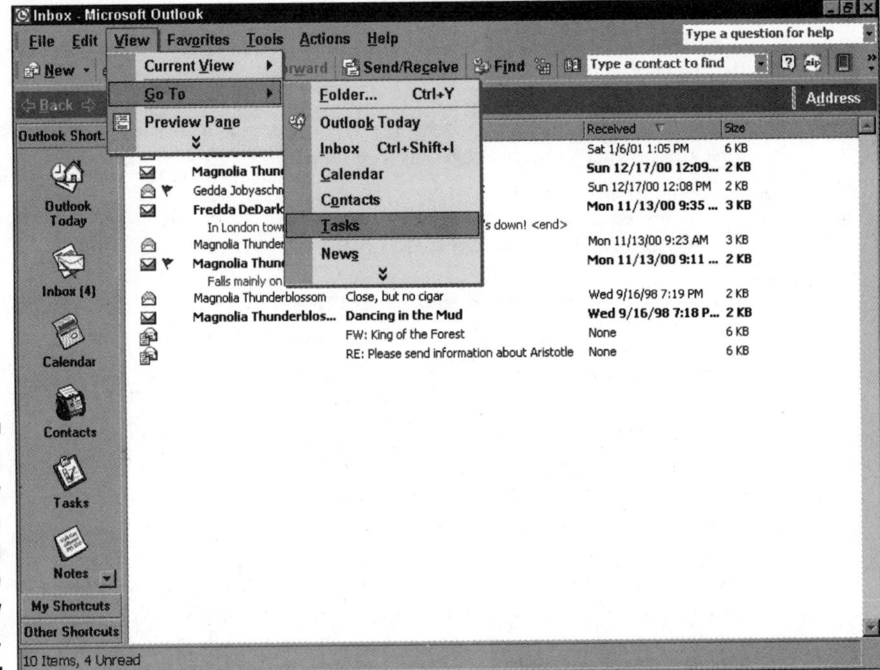

Figure 2-2: Click View and then Go To if you want to see a new module.

Although having the items that you use most often in the Outlook Bar is handy, finding them can be hard if you add too many things to that little bar. That's why the Outlook Bar is divided into groups. Each group is like a drawer in your file cabinet. You put different types of things in different file drawers so that you know right where to look when you want to find something. If you threw everything in one big box, finding anything would be harder. Outlook groups work the same way.

At the top and bottom of the Outlook Bar, you see little gray *separator bars* with names such as Outlook Shortcuts, My Shortcuts, and Other Shortcuts. Click each of these separator bars and you see the column slide up or down to reveal a different group of icons representing different things that you can do with Outlook. The technical term for one of these groups is . . . *group*. (That's easy.) Again, if you don't like the group that you chose, choose a different one.

Table 2-1 lists the icons that you can expect to see in each group when you use Outlook.

Table 2-1 The Groups in the Outlook Bar

Group	*Icons*
Outlook Shortcuts	Outlook Today, Inbox, Calendar, Contacts, Tasks, Notes, Deleted Items
My Shortcuts	Drafts, Outbox, Sent Items, Journal
Other Shortcuts	My Computer, My Documents, Favorites

To change Outlook groups, click the separator bar that has the name of the group you want, such as Outlook Shortcuts, My Shortcuts, or Other Shortcuts. You see the little bars slide up or down to reveal the group that you select. If nothing happens, the group that you selected was already selected.

Adding items to the Outlook Bar

The Outlook Bar comes set up with the icons that Microsoft thinks you'll use most often. You can add or remove icons if you don't like the ones that Microsoft gave you. You can also add or remove the separator bars that separate groups in the Outlook Bar, which I discuss in the following section, "Adding Outlook groups."

You can add nearly anything to the Outlook Bar — folders, documents, Web pages, network drives, and even icons that launch other programs.

To add an item to the Outlook Bar, follow these steps:

1. **Choose File⇨New⇨Outlook Bar Shortcut from the menu bar.**

   The Add to Outlook Bar dialog box appears. Your list of folders appears in the box at the bottom of the Add to Outlook Bar dialog box.

2. **Click the folder or drive that you want to add to the Outlook Bar.**

   The name of the folder or drive you clicked is highlighted.

3. **Click OK.**

   You see a new icon for the folder or drive you selected in the Outlook Bar. That icon comes in handy when you want to copy files between folders or drives that you use frequently. I get into that in Chapter 15 when I talk about file management.

The Look In text box enables you to choose between the two different types of folders that you can add to the Outlook Bar: Outlook folders that contain only Outlook items, or Windows file system folders that contain all the other types of files you create in Windows, as well as disk drives. For more about the two types of folders that you can use in Outlook, see the section

"Navigating the Folder List" later in this chapter. You need to install Integrated File Management tools before you can install an icon for a floppy drive or for any folder from the Windows file system. Chapter 15 talks about that, too.

Adding Outlook groups

Wouldn't it be nice if you could divide your filing cabinet into an unlimited number of file drawers? You can create as many Outlook groups as you want and name them whatever will make it easier for you to find things — on your computer, at least. Finding that lost sock in your dresser drawer is still a problem.

To add a group to the Outlook Bar, follow these steps:

1. **Right-click any group name in the Outlook Bar.**

   A menu appears with choices that pertain to items in the Outlook Bar.

2. **Choose Add New Group.**

   A new group divider, called New Group, appears at the bottom of the Outlook Bar, highlighted in blue.

3. **Type the name that you want to use for your new group (something like** Special Group**).**

4. **Press Enter.**

No matter what you do, the new group winds up at the bottom of the list. Sorry about that.

You can also change the name of any icon or group. You could rename the three original groups Larry, Curly, and Moe, for example, after the Three Stooges. Renaming the sections that way might make Outlook more fun, but harder to explain.

You can do most of your work in one Outlook group; that's okay. The main reason for having groups is to be able to keep all your icons visible on-screen. You can just as easily have a list of icons scrolling way below the screen; the icons will just be harder to use. You can also add icons for folders that pertain to different functions that you perform or different areas of interest. For example, you may have a group of icons relating to sales matters, another to production, and another to human resources.

The name of the group that's open appears in the separator bar at the top of the icons. If you click the name of the group that's already open, nothing happens. Don't worry — that's normal. You have to click a different group to see a change.

Making the most of Outlook Today

Outlook is designed to pull all your personal information into one handy package. The Outlook Today page pulls all the Outlook data that you likely need to see at any moment onto a single screen. All you really need to do is click the Outlook Today icon in the Outlook Bar. If you can't see the Outlook Today icon, just choose View⇨Go To⇨Outlook Today from the menu bar (see Figure 2-3).

The Outlook Today page is like a page on the Web. Most of the text on the page is made of something called *hypertext,* which means that if you click the text, the screen changes to show you the full text of the Outlook module or item it refers to. For example, if you click the word *Mail* in the Outlook Today page, the screen switches to a view of your Inbox and displays all the messages that are waiting for you.

I like to print Outlook Today each day to help remind me of what I need to do. That's the best way I know of to see a single summary of my most current appointments, tasks, and messages. If you want to print your Outlook Today page, click the Outlook Today icon in the Outlook Bar and then choose File⇨Print from the menu bar (or press Ctrl+P).

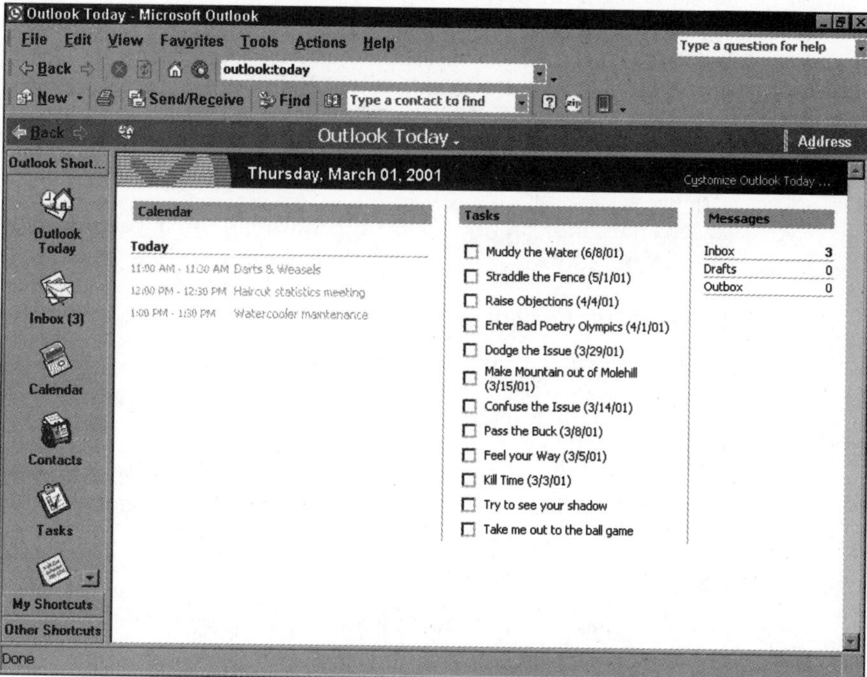

Figure 2-3: Outlook Today pulls together all the items you need right now.

The Information Viewer: Outlook's hotspot

The Information Viewer is where most of the action happens in Outlook. If the Outlook Bar is like the channel selector on your TV set, the Information Viewer is like the TV screen. When you're reading e-mail, you look in the Information Viewer to read your messages; if you're adding or searching for contacts, you see contact names here. The Information Viewer is also where you can do all sorts of fancy sorting tricks that each module in Outlook lets you perform. (I talk about sorting Contacts, Tasks, and so forth in the chapters that apply to those modules.)

Because you can store more information in Outlook than you want to see at any one time, the Information Viewer shows you only a slice of the information available. The Calendar, for example, can store dates as far back as the year 1601 and as far ahead as 4500. (Got any plans on Saturday night 2,500 years from now?) That's a lot of time, but Outlook breaks it down and shows it to you in manageable slices in the Information Viewer. The smallest Calendar slice you can look at is one day, and the largest slice is a month.

The Information Viewer organizes the items it shows you into units called *views.* You can use the views that are included with Outlook when you install it, or you can create your own views and save them. I go into more details about views in Chapter 16.

You can navigate between the slices of information that Outlook shows you by clicking different parts of the Information Viewer. Some people use the word *browsing* for the process of moving around the Information Viewer — it's a little like thumbing through the pages of your pocket datebook (that is, if you have a million-page datebook).

To see an example of how to use the Information Viewer, look at the Calendar module in Figure 2-4.

To browse the Calendar data in the Information Viewer, follow these steps:

1. **Click the Calendar icon in the Outlook Bar.**

   The Calendar appears.

2. **Choose View➪Current View➪Day/Week/Month.**

   The information in the Calendar appears in a form that looks like a conventional calendar.

3. **Choose View➪Week.**

   The weekly view of the Calendar appears, showing a small calendar in the upper-right corner of the Information Viewer and a larger calendar on the left half of the screen.

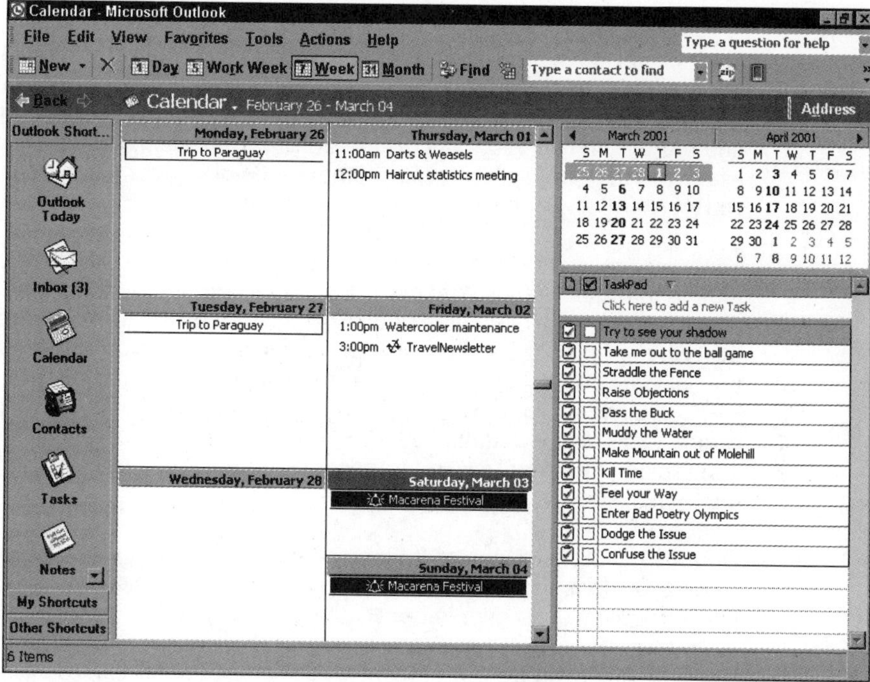

Figure 2-4: A calendar in the Information Viewer.

Try these tricks to see how the Information Viewer behaves:

- Click a date in the small calendar in the upper-right corner. Notice that the large calendar changes to a one-day view.
- Click the *W* for *Wednesday* at the top of one of the small calendars. Notice that the large calendar changes to a monthly view.

You can change the appearance of the Information Viewer an infinite number of ways to make the work that you do in Outlook make sense to you. For example, you may need to see appointments only for a single day or items that you've assigned to a certain category. Views can help you get a quick look at exactly the slice of information that you need.

Navigating the Folder List

If you want to navigate Outlook in a more detailed way than you can with the Outlook Bar, you can use the Folder List. If you think of the Outlook Bar as being like your car's radio buttons, which you use to pick your favorite stations, the Folder List is like the fine-tuning button, which you use to tune in any of the stations between your favorite ones. The Folder List simply shows you your folders — your Windows folders or your Outlook folders — which are where your files and Outlook items are stored.

A tale of two folders

Folders can seem more confusing than they need to be because, once again, Microsoft gave two different things the same name. Just as two kinds of Explorer (Windows and Internet) exist, more than two kinds of Outlook exist and more than two kinds of Windows (3.1, 95, 98, 2000, CE, NT, Me, and XP) exist. You may run across two different kinds of folders when you use Outlook, and each behaves differently.

You may be used to folders in Windows 95 or 98, which are the things you look in to organize files. You can copy, move, and delete files to and from folders on your disk drive. When you're using Outlook for file management, as I describe in Chapter 15, those are the kinds of folders you're dealing with. The part of Outlook that allows you to look at regular Windows files is optional in Outlook 2002, so your system administrator may not have installed it. If that option hasn't been installed in your copy of Outlook, you don't have to worry about using different types of folders in Outlook, because you get to use only one type.

Outlook has its own kind of folders for storing items that you create in the various Outlook modules: calendar items, contact names, tasks, and so on. Each module has its own folder that you can see in the Folder List.

If you're looking at an Outlook module, such as the Inbox, for example, and you turn on the Folder List by choosing View⇨Folder List, you see a list of folders that represent the other standard Outlook modules, such as the Tasks List, Contacts, Calendar, and so on.

Using the Folder List

The only times that you must use the Folder List are when you want to add a new icon to the Outlook Bar or when you want to create a new folder for a separate type of item (such as a special Contact list or a folder for filing e-mail). Using the Folder List is also a faster way to move, copy, or delete files when using Outlook.

You may quite possibly never use the Folder List at all. The Outlook Bar includes the folder choices that most people use most of the time. You may never need to get a different one. Fortunately, you can leave the Folder List turned off except when you really want it, if at all. I've run across people who leave the folder list on all the time and turn off the Outlook Bar to save space. It's a matter of taste, so take your pick.

Clicking Once: Outlook Toolbars

Tools are those little boxes with pictures in them that are all lined up in a row just below the menu bar. Together, they're called a *toolbar,* and they're even more popular than menus when it comes to running Windows programs. Outlook 2002 has three toolbars to choose from: the Standard toolbar, the Advanced toolbar, and the Web toolbar. If you don't do anything special, the Standard toolbar is the one you see, and it will probably do everything you need. If you want to get fancy and open another toolbar or customize any toolbar, see Chapter 24. Toolbars are great time-savers; one little click on a little picture, and voilà — your wish is granted and you're off to lunch.

Viewing ToolTips

Like menus, tools in Office XP programs get a little drop shadow when you hover the mouse pointer over them. The shadow tells you that if you click there, the tool will do what it's there to do: paste, save, launch missiles, whatever.

Another slick thing about tools is that when you rest the mouse pointer on them for a second or so, a little tag pops up to tell you the tool's name (see Figure 2-5). Tags of this sort, called *ToolTips,* are very handy for deciphering the hieroglyphics on those tool buttons.

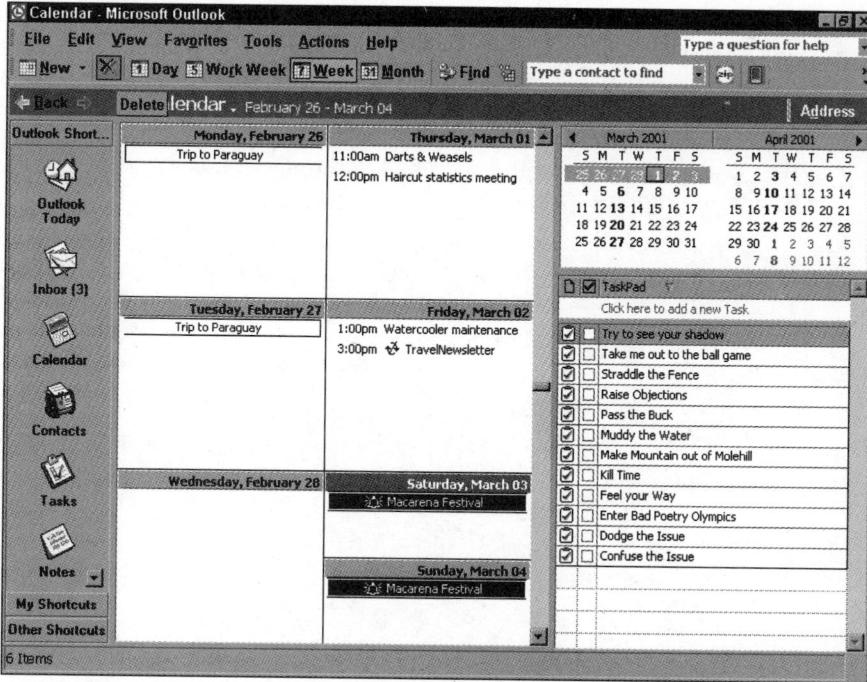

Figure 2-5: A ToolTip tells you the name of the tool that you're using.

To view a ToolTip, follow these steps:

1. **Place the mouse pointer on the word File in the menu bar.**
2. **Slide the mouse pointer straight down until it rests on the icon just below the word File.**

   After about half a second, you see a little tab that says "New Office Document" or "New *Something-or-Other.*" (The text changes, depending on what section of Outlook you're in.)

Some tools have a little down-pointing triangle to their right. This triangle means that the tool has a pull-down menu. The very first tool at the left end of any Outlook toolbar is the New tool. Click the triangle to pull down its menu and see all the new things that you can create — a new appointment, a new e-mail message, or even a new Office document.

Using the New tool

You can use the New tool, which is available in any module of Outlook, to create an item in any other module. Perhaps you're entering the name and address of a new customer who is also mentioned in an interesting article in today's paper. You want to remember the article, but it doesn't belong in the customer's address record. While you're still in the Contacts module (see Figure 2-6), you can pull down the New button's menu and create a quick note, which gets filed in the Note section. Using the New tool to create a new note when you're looking at the Contacts screen can get confusing. At first, you may think that the note isn't entered, but it is. Outlook just files it in the Notes module, where it belongs.

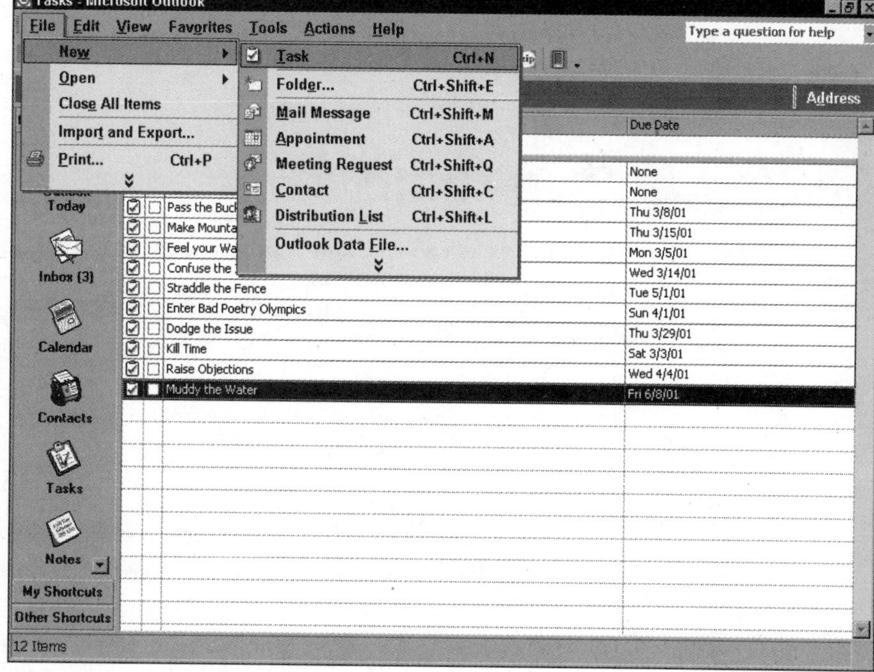

Figure 2-6: Use the New tool to create a note, request a meeting, or perform a variety of new tasks without switching to another Outlook module.

Turning Parts of the Outlook Screen On and Off

You can work with any part of the Outlook screen in any view, or you can turn parts of the screen off. The buttons near the bottom of the View menu allow you to change what you see. Sometimes, for example, you want to look at your Calendar in the largest possible view so that you can see a whole month and all its appointments clearly. In that case, you can switch to the Calendar module and then turn off the Outlook Bar, the Folder List, and possibly even the toolbar to make room for the Calendar. You also may need to turn on the Folder List when you're moving or copying files, but turn it off when you're scheduling tasks.

For example, to view the Folder List:

- Choose View➪Folder List.
- Alternatively, if you see a triangle below the title of the Information Viewer, click the title (such as Calendar), and the Folder List appears.

The View menu has icons for both the Outlook Bar and the Folder List; these icons allow you to turn those elements on or off. So, if you want to run

Outlook with just the Outlook Bar open, or just the Folder List, or both, or neither, it's up to you. I think that leaving the Outlook Bar open is the easiest way to go.

Getting Help in Outlook

Even though Outlook is as user-friendly a program as you could hope to find, at times you may want to take advantage of the efficient Windows online help system when you're temporarily stumped (of course, you can turn to this book for help, but sometimes online help is faster).

Using the Office Assistant

The Windows Help system was always helpful, but now it's downright sociable. A little animated character pops up and cavorts around when you ask for help; it even does little tricks when you do things, such as save a file or search for text. Try it!

You can change the type of character you use as your Office Assistant: You can use the Clippit character, shown in Figure 2-7. To use the Office Assistant, select Show the Office Assistant under the Help menu. The Dot character, Links the Cat, or others. All you have to do is right-click the Office Assistant character, choose a new character, and click OK. Microsoft Office includes a larger selection of Office Assistant characters than Outlook alone, so if you're an Office user, you're in luck.

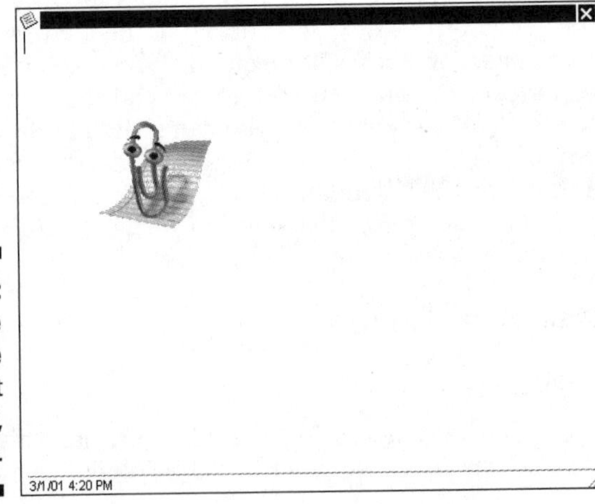

Figure 2-7: An adorable Office Assistant character, Clippit.

The Office Assistant character is included because research shows that people treat their computers as though they are other people. No kidding. Most people report more negative things about a computer to a second computer than they will to the computer that they're saying the bad things about; it's as though they're trying not to hurt the computer's feelings.

You don't have to worry about hurting the Office Assistant's feelings. Just press the F1 key any time; your Office Assistant pops up and invites you to ask a question (see Figure 2-8). Just type your question in plain English, and the Assistant scratches its head and returns with a list of help topics that are likely to answer your question. If you want to delete a message, for example, just press F1 and type **delete a message**. The list of choices includes everything that has to do with deleting messages.

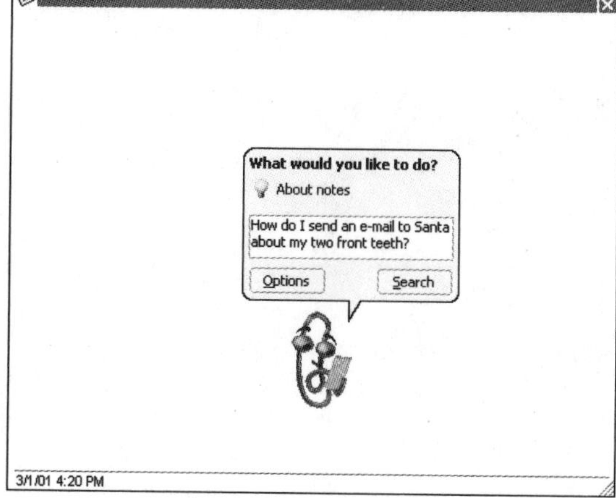

Figure 2-8: You can tell the Office Assistant what you need in plain English.

If you keep the Office Assistant open, some of the questions that you usually answer through dialog boxes are asked by the Assistant. Click the response that you want, just as you would in a regular dialog box.

The Office Assistant will get smarter with time; it's supposed to notice the things you do wrong repeatedly and chime in with suggestions about how to do them better. Microsoft calls this system the Social Interface; some people call it nagging. ***Remember:*** The Office Assistant only means to be helpful (just like your mother-in-law).

Getting rid of the Office Assistant

There are hard-nosed, no-nonsense people out there who find the Office Assistant annoying. Some of them don't even believe in Santa. If you're an Office Assistant hater, you can make the Office Assistant stay away (but don't make Santa stay away; I'm still waiting for my two front teeth). Just right-click the Office Assistant, choose Options, and then click the check box next to the words `Use the Office Assistant` to make the check disappear. If you get mushy and sentimental later on and want to bring the Office Assistant back, just choose Help⇨Show the Office Assistant.

After you turn off the Office Assistant, you still have the benefit of the Windows Help system whenever you press F1 (see Figure 2-9). The Windows Help system finds answers to any question that you type in the Answer Wizard text box. When you type a question in the Answer Wizard box and click the Search button, a list of possible answers appears in the box below the Answer Wizard text box. Click the answer that seems best related to your question and a full explanation appears in the box to the right of the Answer Wizard. The Help system includes lots of blue underlined text, just like you see in your Web browser, which you can click to make the Help System show you more information about the underlined topic.

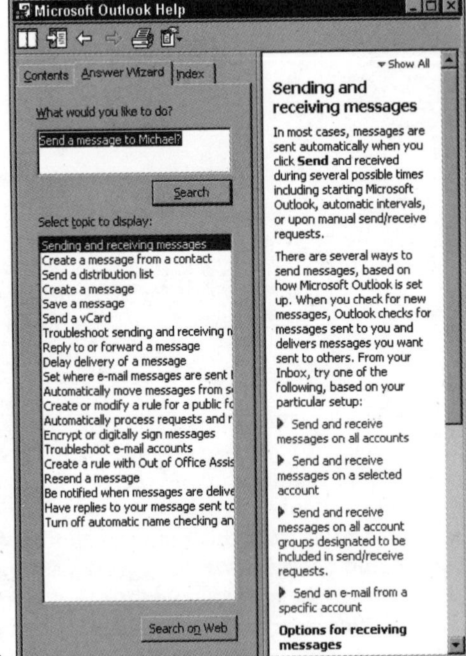

Figure 2-9: The Windows Help system gives no-nonsense answers to your questions.

Chapter 3

On the Fast Track: Drag 'til You Drop

In This Chapter

- Doing the drag-and-drop
- Creating and sending e-mail messages
- Creating Contact records
- Sending attachment files
- Deleting information

Typing — ugh! Who needs it? It's amazing to think that we still use a nineteenth-century device — the typewriter keyboard — to control our computers on the cusp of the twenty-first century. We appear to be stuck with the QWERTY keyboard (the standard keyboard we all know and love) for a while longer, but we can give our carpal tunnels a rest now and then by using the mouse, trackball, or glidepoint to drag and drop rather than hunt and peck.

How to Drag

When I say *drag,* I'm not referring to Monty Python's men in women's clothing. I mean the process of zipping items from one place to another with quick, easy mouse moves rather than slow, laborious menu choices. Throughout the rest of this book, I tell you how to do nearly everything in Outlook by the menu method only because it's the clearest way to explain how to do most things reliably. But if you want to work quickly in Outlook, drag-and-drop is the ticket to the simple and speedy completion of your tasks.

Before you can drag an item, you have to *select* it — which simply means to click the item once:

- *Dragging* means clicking your mouse on something and moving the mouse to another location while holding the mouse button down at the same time.
- *Dropping* means letting go of the mouse button.

When you drag an item, you see an icon hanging from the tail of the mouse pointer as you move the pointer across the screen. The icon makes the pointer look like it's carrying baggage, and to some degree, that's true; dragging your mouse between Outlook modules "carries" information from one type of item to another.

When you drag and drop items between different Outlook modules, you can keep creating new types of items from the old information, depending on what you drag and where you drop it.

Everything that you can do by using the drag-and-drop method can also be done through menu choices or keystroke shortcuts, but you lose the advantage of having the information from one item flow into the new item, so you have to retype information. I'm too lazy for that, so I just drag and drop.

Because I'm using this chapter to extol the benefits of drag-and-drop, I describe every action in terms of a drag-and-drop movement rather than through menu choices or keyboard shortcuts. Throughout the rest of the book, I describe how to do things in terms of menu choices because the menus never change, whereas you can change the names of the icons in the Outlook Bar if you customize them. So when you read other parts of the book, don't think that I'm discouraging you from trying drag-and-drop; I'm just trying to offer you the clearest explanation I can. (Whew! I'm glad that's off my chest.)

Creating E-Mail Messages

Anything that you drag to the Inbox becomes an outgoing e-mail message. If the thing that you drag to the Inbox contains an e-mail address, such as a contact, Outlook automatically creates the message with that person's e-mail address filled in.

If the item that you drag to the Inbox contains a subject, such as a task, Outlook automatically creates the message with that subject filled in.

From a name in your Address Book

Addressing messages is one of the most useful drag-and-drop techniques in Outlook. E-mail addresses can be cumbersome and difficult to remember, and if your spelling of an e-mail address is off by even one letter, your message won't go through. It's best to just keep the e-mail addresses of the people to whom you sent messages in your Contact list and use those addresses to create new messages.

To create an e-mail message from your Contact list:

1. **Click the Contacts icon.**

   The Contact list appears, as shown in Figure 3-1. You can use any view, but Address Cards view is easiest, because you can click the first letter of the person's name to see that person's card. For more about viewing your Contact list, see Chapter 7.

2. **Drag a name from your Contact list to the Inbox icon.**

   The Message form appears, with the address of the contact filled in.

3. **Type a subject for your message.**

   Keep it simple; a few words will do.

4. **Click in the text box and type your message.**

   You can also format text with bold type, italics, and other effects by clicking the appropriate buttons on the toolbar.

5. **Click Send.**

   The display returns to the Contact list and your message is sent.

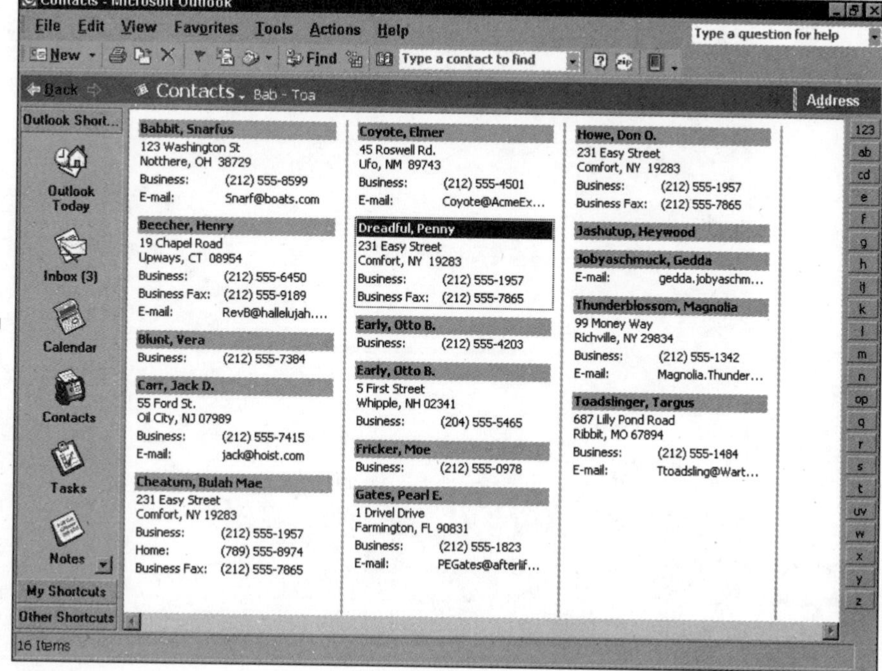

Figure 3-1: Dragging a contact to your Inbox creates a new message addressed to that person.

From an appointment

After you enter the particulars about an appointment, you may want to send that information to someone to tell that person what the appointment is about, where it occurs, and when it occurs.

To send an e-mail message with information about an appointment:

1. **Click the Calendar icon.**

   The Calendar appears.

2. **Drag the appointment you're interested in from the Calendar to the Inbox icon (see Figure 3-2).**

   The Message form appears. The subject of the message is already filled in.

3. **In the To text box, type the name of the person to whom you want to send a copy of the appointment.**

   Alternatively, you can click the To button and choose the person's name from the Address Book. If you use the Address Book, you have to click To again and then click OK.

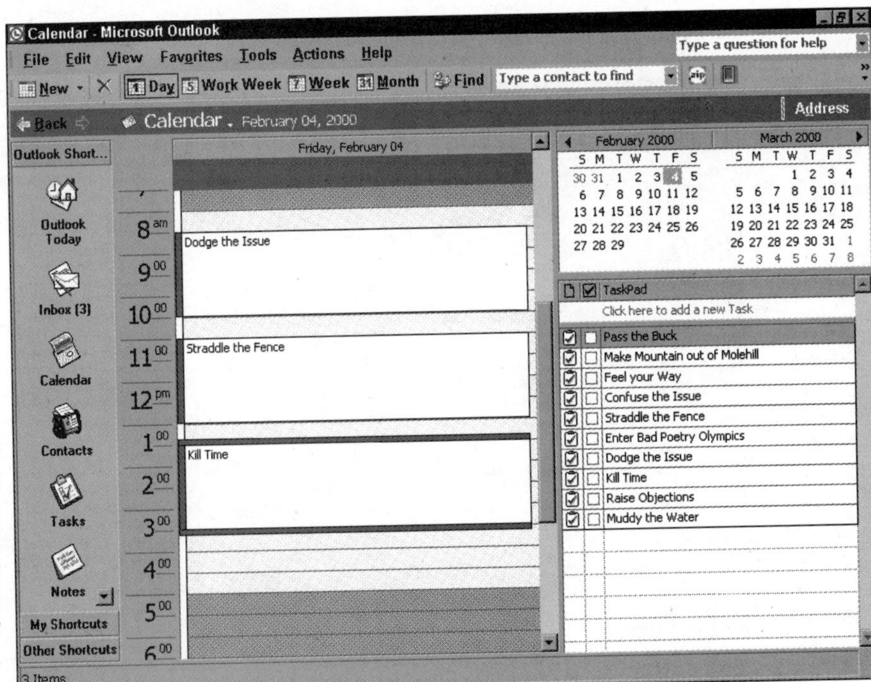

Figure 3-2: Dragging an appointment to the Inbox creates a new message.

4. **Click the Send button.**

   Your recipient gets an e-mail message with details about the meeting. You can add additional comments in the text box.

If you plan to invite other people in your organization to a meeting, and you want to check their schedules to plan the meeting, you can also use the Attendee Availability tab of the Appointment form. For this method to work, the people whom you plan to invite to the meeting must be sharing their schedules through Microsoft Exchange Server.

Sending a File by E-Mail

Sometimes, you don't need to type a message; you just want to send a file by e-mail — that Excel spreadsheet with sales figures, for example, or your new book proposal in Word.

When you send someone a file (or when someone sends you a file), the file, called an *attachment,* travels as a part of the message. When you attach a file to your e-mail message, the recipient gets a copy of the file, and you still have one, too. The process is like sending a fax, except that no paper is involved, and it's better than a fax because the person who gets the file can make changes in the file.

Dragging a file to the Inbox is a tiny bit more complicated than dragging contacts or appointments because you locate files using the My Computer icon, which is in a different section of the Outlook Bar from the Inbox. Also, some people remove the My Computer section when they install Outlook, so that icon may not be available. But when everything's installed and you're accustomed to the different groups in the Outlook Bar, it's a breeze to drag and drop files anywhere you want them.

To send a file using e-mail:

1. **Click the words *Other Shortcuts* in the Outlook Bar.**

   The My Computer icon appears.

2. **Click the My Computer icon in the Outlook Bar.**

   The list of your computer's disk drives appears.

3. **Double-click the icon for the C: drive (or whatever drive contains the file that you want to send).**

   The list of folders on your disk drive appears.

4. **Click the My Documents icon (or the icon for whatever folder contains the file you want to send).**

   The list of files in the folder you selected appears.

5. **Click the name of the file that you want to send.**

   The file darkens, indicating that you've selected it (see Figure 3-3).

6. **Click the Outlook Shortcuts group divider in the Outlook Bar.**

   The Inbox icon appears, along with all the usual Outlook icons.

7. **Drag the file that you selected to the Inbox icon.**

   The New Message form appears with an icon in the message space (see Figure 3-4).

8. **In the To text box, type the name of the person to whom you want to send a copy of the file.**

   Alternatively, you can click the To button and choose the person's name from the Address Book. If you use the Address Book, you have to click To again and then click OK.

9. **Click the Send button.**

   Your file is on its way.

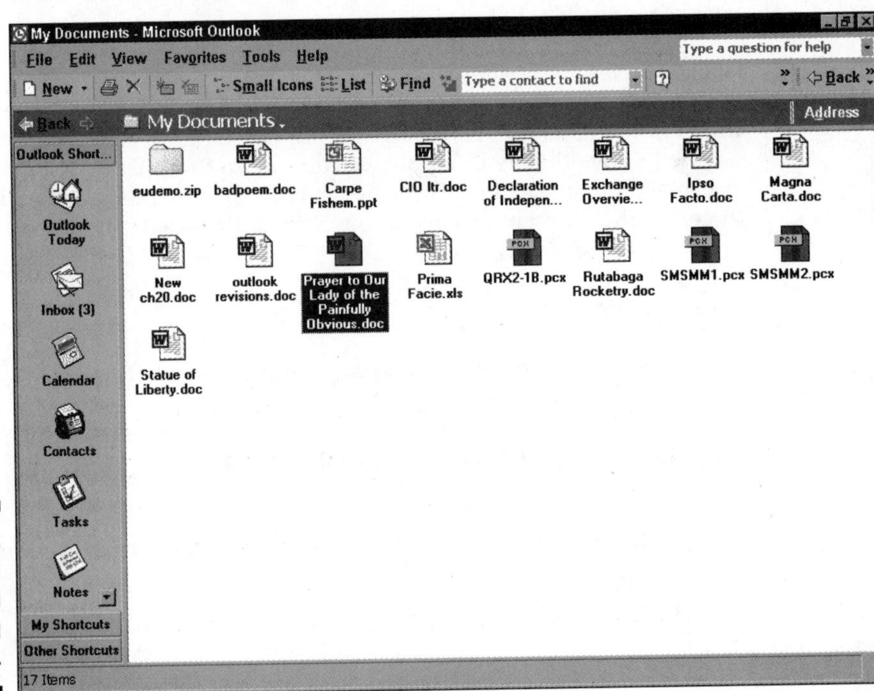

Figure 3-3: Select the file that you want to drag to the Inbox.

Look out for heavy files!

When it comes to sending e-mail, all files are created equal, but some are much bigger than others. You can e-mail all files, big and small, but the big ones can take a long time to send and receive. If you and the person to whom you're sending a file are on the same network, the size of the file isn't such a big problem. If you're sending the file to someone who gets e-mail from an online service over a regular telephone line, however, it's a good idea to check with that person to see whether he or she is willing to accept a file that could take 10 to 15 minutes, or more, to download. Not all online services let your recipient know the size of the files he or she is getting.

Think about that when you send a file. If the size of the file that you're sending is measured in megabytes, it could take some time for the person to whom you're sending the file to receive it. Some people think that you broke their machine because the file took so long to receive. You can't break someone's machine by sending a file, but there are people to whom you don't want to give that impression. You can use compression programs such as PKZIP or WinZip to reduce the size of your files before you send them, but it's still possible to create files that take a long time to send through a phone line even when you compress them.

Isn't that easy? There's actually an even easier way: When you're working on a file in Word, Excel, or PowerPoint, choose File➪Send To➪Mail Recipient and then perform Steps 8 and 9 of the preceding list.

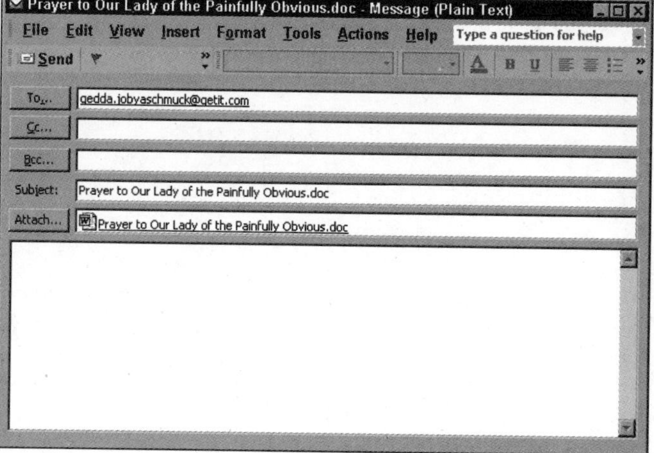

Figure 3-4: Your attached file is ready to be sent in an e-mail message.

Creating Contact Records from E-Mail

You can drag an item from any other Outlook module to the Contacts icon, but the only item that makes sense to drag is an e-mail message in order to create a Contact record that includes the e-mail address. You not only save work by dragging a message to the Contacts icon, but also eliminate the risk of misspelling the e-mail address.

To create a new Contact record:

1. **Click the Inbox icon.**

   A list of your current incoming e-mail messages appears. Select the message for which you want to make a Contact record (see Figure 3-5).

2. **Drag the selected message to the Contacts icon.**

   The New Contact form opens, with the name and e-mail address of the person who sent the message filled in.

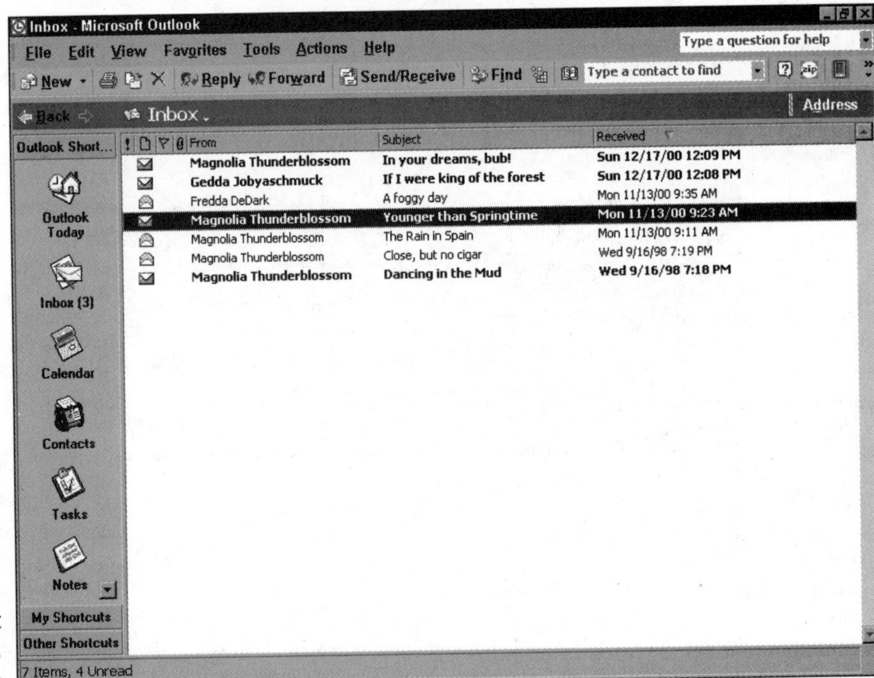

Figure 3-5: Somebody is about to receive a Contact record.

3. **If you want to include more information than the e-mail address of the contact, type that information in the appropriate box on the Contact form.**

   You can change existing information or add information — the company for whom the person works, the postal mail address, other phone numbers, and so on.

   If the body of the e-mail message contains information that you want to use as contact information, select that information and drag it to the appropriate box of the New Contact form.

4. **Click the Save and Close button.**

   You now have the e-mail address and any other information for the new contact stored for future reference.

Another quick way to capture an e-mail address from an incoming message is to right-click the name of the sender in the From line of the incoming message block. The From line is not a normal text box, so you may not think that right-clicking it would do anything, but it does. A shortcut menu appears. Click Add to Contacts to open the New Contact dialog box and then follow the last two steps of the preceding list.

Drag and Drop Dead: Deleting Stuff

If in doubt, throw it out. You know the drill.

Here's how to delete an item using drag-and-drop:

1. **Click the Notes icon in the Outlook Bar.**

   Your list of notes appears. You can click any icon that has items you want to delete. (I'm just using notes as an example.)

2. **Click the down arrow on the Outlook Bar until you see the Deleted Items icon.**

   The icon looks like a trash can.

3. **Drag a note to the Deleted Items icon in the Outlook Bar.**

   Kiss it goodbye — it's gone.

If you change your mind after deleting something, just click the Deleted Items icon. The folder opens and a list of everything that you've deleted is there. It's like being a hit man in the afterlife — you get another chance to see everyone you've disposed of. Except in this case, you can bring items back to life. Just drag them back to where they came from. Even Don Corleone couldn't do that.

Right Button Magic

So far I've talked about holding down your mouse button as if your mouse has only one button. But most PC mice have two buttons and some have even more. Many people use only the left button and they get along just fine. (Just to confuse matters, you can change your mouse into a left-handed mouse by adjusting some settings in Windows. When you do that, the left and right buttons exchange functions.)

When you right-drag an item, or drag it by holding down the right button instead of the left button, something different happens when you drop the item off: A menu appears asking you exactly what result you want. For example, if you right-drag a contact to the Inbox, a menu with a half-dozen choices appears. The choices are

- Copy here as message with text
- Copy here as message with shortcut
- Copy here as message with attachment
- Move here as message with attachment

I don't always remember what's going to happen when I drag an item and drop it off, so I like to use the right-drag feature just to be sure.

Part II

Taming the E-Mail Beast

The 5th Wave
By Rich Tennant
RICHTENNANT
It's an e-mail from my mother. She wants me to know how happy she is for us.

In this part . . .

E-mail . . . everybody's doing it, but not everybody's doing it well. In this part, you learn to harness the power of Outlook to dress up your e-mail, stay in touch with your contacts, and span the globe through the Internet without leaving your desk.

Chapter 4

The Essential Secrets of E-Mail

In This Chapter

- Sending messages
- Opening and replying to messages
- Previewing message contents
- Forwarding messages
- Deleting messages
- Saving an unfinished message
- Saving messages as files
- Setting message sensitivity and importance

If you're as lazy as I am, electronic mail — e-mail — is a dream. I love getting mail — fan mail, junk mail, official mail, anything except bills. But regular paper mail stacks up in ugly piles, and I always lose the important stuff. E-mail is quick to read, easy to find, and simple to answer. Outlook makes e-mail even easier to read, create, and answer. You don't even have to organize your e-mail in Outlook; it organizes itself!

Front Ends and Back Ends

You need two things to send and receive e-mail:

- A program that helps you create, save, and manage your messages
- A program that actually transports the messages to or from the other people with whom you exchange messages

Some technical people call these two parts the front end and the back end, respectively. Outlook is a front end for e-mail; it helps you create, format, store, and manage your messages, but it has very little to do with actually getting your messages to your destination. That work is done by a back-end service (such as Microsoft Exchange Server in your office), by your Internet Service Provider (ISP), or by an online service such as CompuServe or The Microsoft Network (MSN).

If you feel that you're the last person on earth without Internet e-mail capability, you've got that capability now with Outlook. Microsoft has made it fiendishly simple to sign up for several online services through the Windows desktop. Remember, though, your easiest choice isn't always your best choice. Literally hundreds of companies are out there ready to give you Internet access, so it pays to shop around. I tell you more about online services in Chapter 12.

You may already be set up on an office e-mail system, such as Microsoft Exchange. If so, I assume that you have a computer guru around to set you up, because that stuff can get kind of messy. You can definitely use Outlook to exchange e-mail via nearly any regular Internet Service Provider. Usually the ISP's technical support people can help you set up Outlook.

In many ways, electronic mail is better than regular paper mail (also known as snail mail). E-mail is delivered much faster than paper mail — almost instantaneously. I find that speedy delivery is really handy for last-minute birthday greetings. E-mail is also incredibly cheap; in fact, it's free most of the time.

Creating Messages

Creating a new message is insanely easy. You can probably figure it out without my help, but here's a hint: Start Outlook, click the New button, enter an address in the To box, a subject in the Subject box, a message in the message box, and click Send. See you figured it out! Isn't it easy?

Hut! Just in case you prefer more detailed directions, here's the entire recipe for sending a message:

1. **Click the Inbox icon in the Outlook Bar.**

   The e-mail Inbox appears.

2. **Choose File⇨New⇨Mail Message (or press Ctrl+N).**

   The New Message form appears (see Figure 4-1).

3. **Click the To text box and type the e-mail address of the person to whom you're sending your message.**

   You can also click the To button itself, find the name of the person to whom you're sending the message in the Address Book, and then click OK. Or you can use the AutoName feature, which I describe in the "What's in a name? AutoName!" sidebar in this chapter.

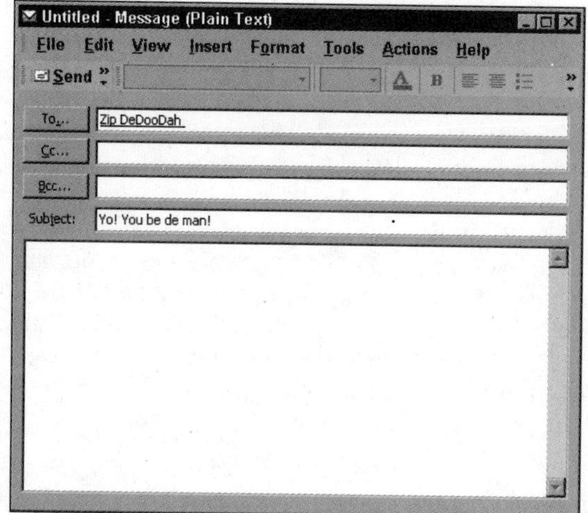

Figure 4-1: The New Message form.

4. **Click the Cc text box and type the e-mail addresses of the people to whom you want to send a copy of your message.**

   If you're sending messages to multiple people, separate their addresses with either a comma or a semicolon.

5. **Type the subject of the message in the Subject box.**

   Your subject can be up to 256 characters long, but keep it shorter. A snappy, relevant subject line makes someone want to read your message; a long or weird subject line doesn't. (Well, you never know with a weird subject line — but don't send weird e-mail at the office unless everybody does.)

6. **Type the text of your message in the text box.**

   If you use Microsoft Word as your word processor, you can also set up Outlook to use Word as your e-mail editor. You can include formatting, graphics, tables, and all the tricks available in Word to make your e-mail more attractive. When you use Word as an e-mail editor, you don't do anything different — you just see the Word toolbars in the Outlook e-mail form when you're creating e-mail. You can use all the tools you see to add formatting to your e-mail. I've listed a few formatting tricks you can use in Chapter 20. You can also read Dan Gookin's *Word 2002 For Dummies* (Hungry Minds, Inc.) for more complete information about using Microsoft Word. If you're completely at home with Microsoft Word, you can just create messages in Word and send them right out without even opening Outlook. Simply type a message in Word by choosing File➪Send To➪Mail Recipient, type an address and subject, and then click Send.

What's my e-mail address?

When you have an e-mail account, you want to tell other people your e-mail address so that they can send stuff to you. E-mail addresses are a little like long-distance telephone numbers. If you live in Chicago, and you're calling someone in New York, you tell that person that your number is (312) 555-9780; if the other person lives in Chicago, you leave off the (312) and just tell him or her to call you at 555-9780. If you work in the same office, you say that you're at extension 9780; the other person knows the rest.

Likewise, your e-mail address comes in short, medium, and long versions for different people, depending on how much of the address they share with you. If you use The Microsoft Network and your account name is Jane_Doe, your e-mail address to the world at large is Jane_Doe@msn.com. (Don't_forget_that_punctuation; computers still aren't smart enough to know that Jane_Doe with the underscore and Jane Doe with no underscore are the same person.) Other members of The Microsoft Network address mail to you as Jane_Doe. (The underscore isn't required; I'm just using it as an example of things that stop a computer cold but that you and I wouldn't notice.)

The same is true if you're on an office e-mail system. If you work for International Widgets Corporation, you may be Jdoe@widgets. com. (Check with your company's computer guru about your corporate e-mail address.) Your coworkers can send you messages at Jdoe.

Be careful how you format e-mail to send to people on the Internet. Not all e-mail systems can handle graphics or formatted text, such as boldface or italics, so the masterpiece of correspondence art that you send to your client on the Internet may arrive as gibberish. If you don't know what the other person has on his or her computer, go light on the graphics. When you're sending e-mail to your colleagues in the same office, or if you're sure that the person you're sending to also has Outlook, the formatting and graphics should look fine.

7. **Click the Send button.**

   Your mail is sent to the Outbox. If you're on an office network, your mail automatically goes from your Outbox to the Inbox of the person to whom you're sending the message. If you're using an online service such as MSN or CompuServe, you need to press F5 to send the e-mail message along.

Setting the priority of a message

Some messages are more important than others. The momentous report that you're sending to your boss demands a different level of attention than the wisecrack that you're sending to your friend in the sales department. Setting the importance level to High tells the person getting the message that your message requires attention.

What's in a name? AutoName!

One neat feature of Outlook is that you can avoid memorizing long, confusing e-mail addresses of people to whom you send mail frequently. If the person to whom you're sending a message is entered in your Contact list (see Chapter 7 for more information about contacts) and you've included an e-mail address in the Contact record, all you have to type in the To box of your e-mail form is the person's name or even just a part of the person's name. Outlook helps you fill in the rest of the person's name and figures out the e-mail address. You know that you got it right when Outlook underlines the name with a solid black line after you press the Tab key or click outside the To box. If Outlook underlines the name with a red wavy line, Outlook thinks that it knows the name you're entering, but the name isn't spelled quite right, so you need to correct the spelling. If Outlook doesn't put any underline below the name, it's telling you that it has no idea to whom you're sending the message but that it will use the name that you typed as the literal e-mail address. So you have to be doubly sure that the name is correct.

Here's how you set the priority of a message:

1. **While composing your message, click the Options button in the toolbar.**

   The Message Options dialog box appears (see Figure 4-2). You can also open the Message Options dialog box by choosing View ⇨ Options if you're not using Microsoft Word as your e-mail editor. The Message Options dialog box allows you to define qualities about your message that are optional (clever name, eh?).

2. **Click the triangle at the right end of the Importance box.**

   A menu appears (see Figure 4-3).

3. **Choose High, Normal, or Low.**

   Usually, Importance is set to Normal, so you don't have to do anything. Putting a Low importance on your own messages seems to be silly, but you can also assign importance to messages that you receive in your Inbox, to tell yourself which messages can be dealt with later, if at all.

4. **To close the Message Options dialog box, click Close (or press Esc).**
5. **If the Office Assistant asks "Do you want to save changes?" click Yes.**

An even quicker way to set the priority of a message is to use the buttons in the message toolbar. The button with the red exclamation point marks your message as a High importance message. The button with the arrow pointing downward marks your message as a Low importance message. You might wonder why anyone would mark a message as a Low importance message. After all, if it's so unimportant, why send the message in the first place?

Apparently, some bosses like their employees to send in routine reports with a Low importance marking so that the bosses know to read that stuff after the exciting new things that they read every day.

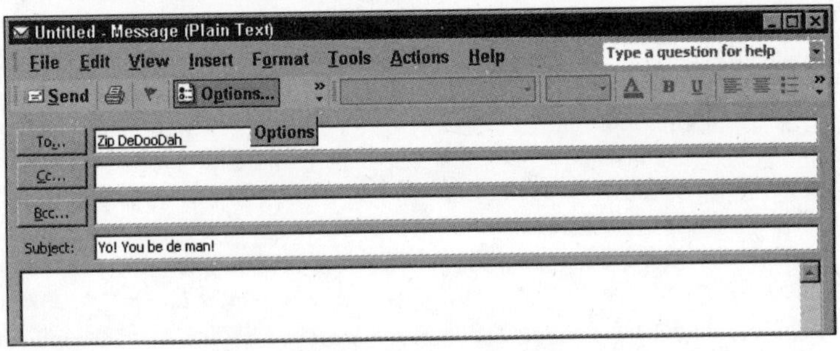

Figure 4-2: The Options button appears on the message toolbar.

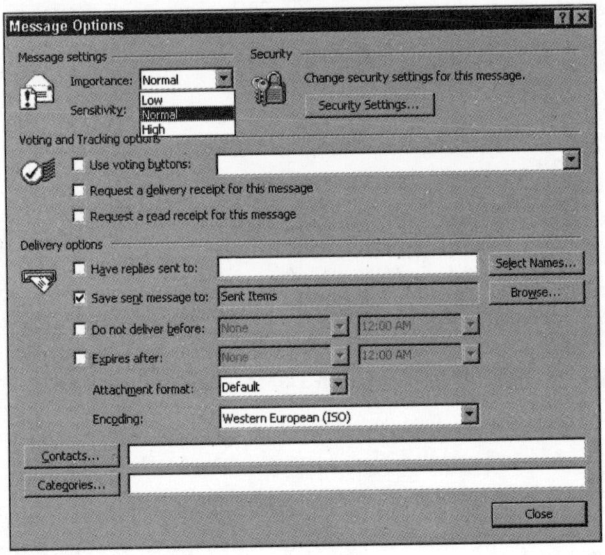

Figure 4-3: Use the Message Options dialog box to set the priority of your message.

Setting the sensitivity of a message

You may want your message to be seen by only one person, or you may want to prevent your message from being changed by anyone after you send it. Sensitivity settings allow you to restrict what someone else can do to your message after you send it and who that someone else can be.

To set the sensitivity of a message:

1. **While composing your message, click the Options button in the toolbar.**

   The Message Options dialog box appears (see Figure 4-4).

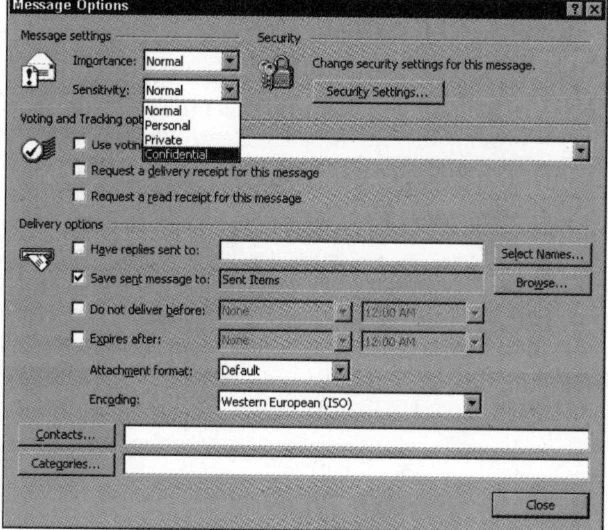

Figure 4-4: Click the Options button to set the sensitivity of your message.

2. **Click the scroll-down button (the triangle) at the right end of the Sensitivity box.**

   A menu scrolls down with the words Normal, Personal, Private, and Confidential (refer to Figure 4-4). Most messages you send will have Normal sensitivity, so that's what Outlook uses if you don't say otherwise. The Personal and Confidential settings only notify the people getting the message that they may want to handle the message differently from a Normal message. Some organizations even have special rules for dealing with Confidential messages. Marking a message Private means that no one can modify your message when forwarding or replying to it.

3. **Choose Normal, Personal, Private, or Confidential.**
4. **To close the Message Options dialog box, click Close.**
5. **When you finish composing your message, click Send (or press Alt+S).**

   Outlook sends your message off.

Setting the sensitivity of a message to Private or Confidential doesn't make the message any more private or confidential than any other message; it just notifies the recipient that the message contains particularly sensitive information. Many corporations are very careful about what kind of information can be sent by e-mail outside the company. If you use Outlook at work, check with your system administrators before presuming that the information you send by e-mail is secure.

Setting other message options

When you click the Options button and open the Options page the way I describe in the previous section, you may notice a number of strange-sounding options. The other options include Request Read Receipt (which notifies you when your recipient reads your message) and Expires After (which makes a message disappear if your recipient doesn't open it before a time you designate). Those are very handy options, but if you want to use them, there's a catch: Both your e-mail system and your recipient's mail system must support those features or they won't work at all. If you and your recipient are both on the same network using Microsoft Exchange Server, everything should work just fine. If you're not using Outlook on an Exchange Network, it's a gamble. See Chapter 14 for more about how to use the features of Outlook that work only on Exchange Server.

Adding an Internet link to an e-mail message

All Microsoft Office programs automatically recognize the addresses of items on the Internet. If you type the name of a Web page, such as `www.outlookfordummies.com`, Outlook changes the text color to blue and underlines the address, making it look just like the hypertext you click to jump between different pages on the Web. That makes it easy to send someone information about an exciting Web site; just type or copy the address into your message. If the recipient is also an Outlook user, he or she can just click the text to make the Web browser pop up and open the page you told that user about.

Reading and Replying to E-Mail Messages

Outlook has a couple of ways to tell you when you receive an e-mail message. In the Outlook Bar, a number in parentheses next to the Inbox icon tells you how many unread e-mail messages you have (see Figure 4-5). The word *Inbox* in the Folder List changes to boldface type when you have unread e-mail, and when you look in the Inbox, you see titles of unread messages in bold as well.

To open and read an e-mail message, follow these steps:

1. **Choose View➪Go To➪Inbox (or press Ctrl+Shift+I).**

   The Inbox screen opens, showing your incoming mail.

2. **Double-click the title of the message that you want to read.**

   The message opens, and you can see the text of the message (see Figure 4-6). If the message is really long, press the down-arrow key or the PgDn key to scroll through the text.

3. **To close the Message screen, choose File➪Close (or press Alt+F4).**

   The Message screen closes, and you see the list of messages in your Inbox.

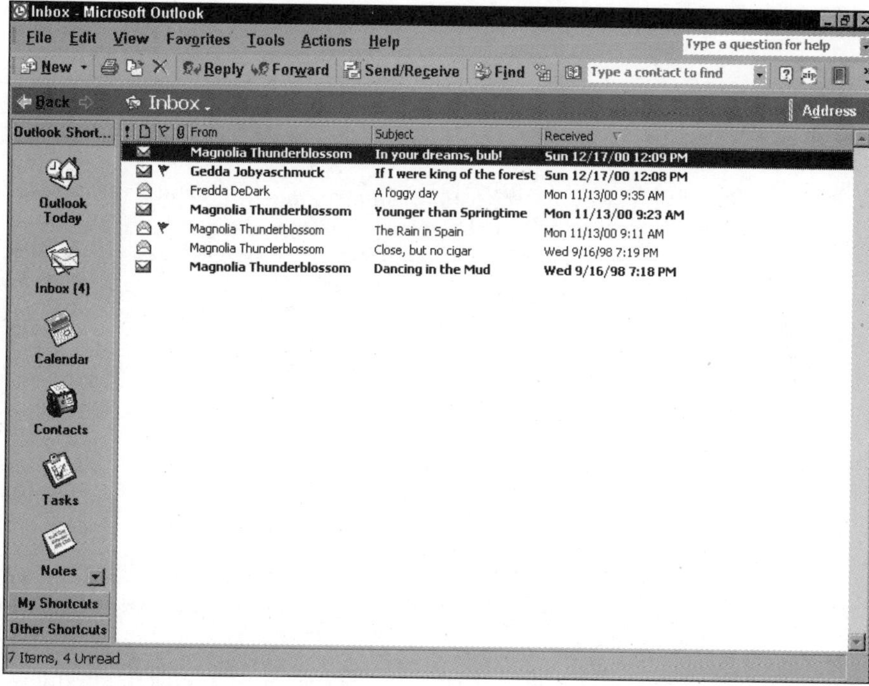

Figure 4-5: Numbers next to your Inbox icon tell you how many unread messages are there.

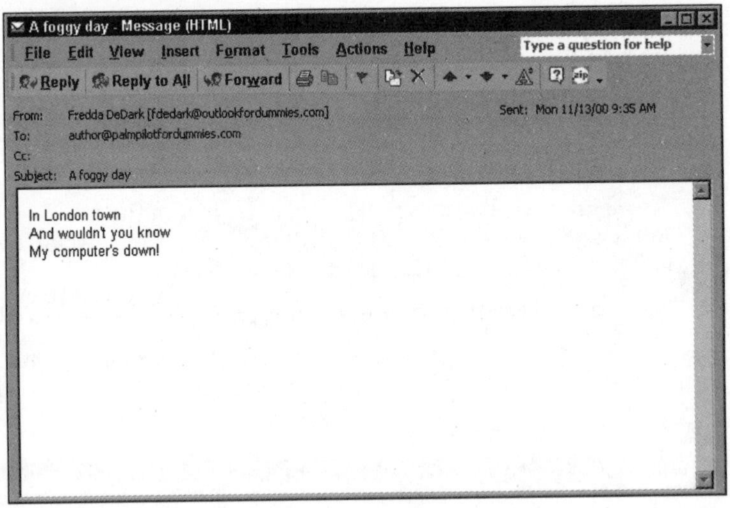

Figure 4-6: Double-click a message to open it and read the contents.

Previewing message text

When you start getting lots of e-mail, some of it will be important, but some of it will be relatively unimportant — if not downright useless. When you first see the mail in your Inbox, it's nice to know which messages are important and which are not so that you can focus on the important stuff. You can't count on the people who send you e-mail to say, "Don't read this; it's unimportant" (although a Low priority rating is a good clue). Outlook tries to help by allowing you to peek at the first few lines of a message so that you know right off the bat whether it's worth reading.

To see previews of your unread messages:

1. **Choose View⇨Go To⇨Inbox (or press Ctrl+Shift+I).**

   The Inbox screen opens, showing your incoming mail.

2. **Choose View⇨Current View⇨Messages with AutoPreview (see Figure 4-7).**

   The list of messages in your Inbox appears with the first few lines of each unread message displayed in blue.

Every module in Outlook has a collection of views that you can use to make your information easier to use. The view called Messages with AutoPreview is the best way to look at your incoming e-mail. In Chapter 16, I show you some of the other views that can make your collection of e-mail messages more useful.

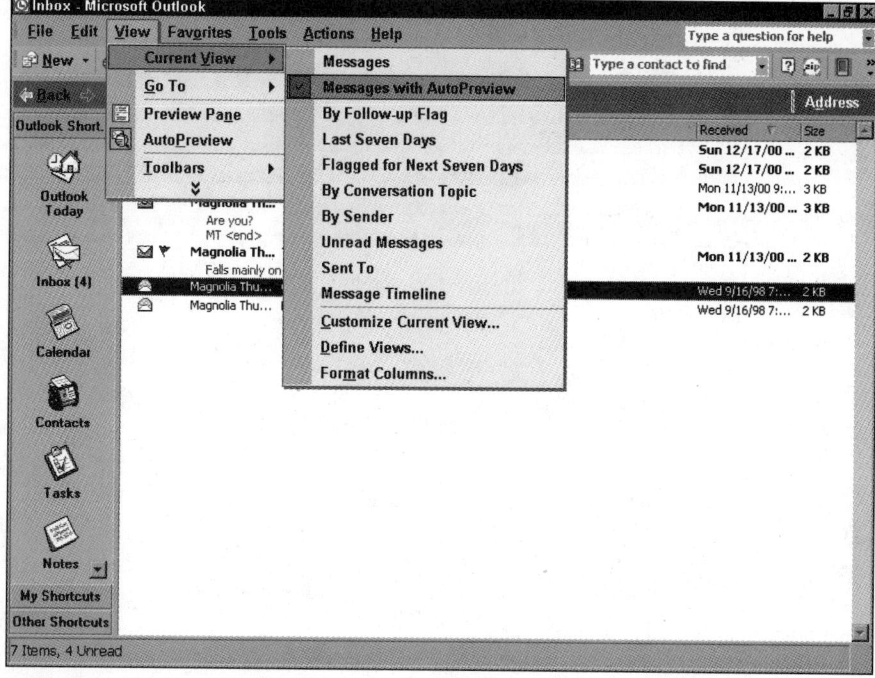

Figure 4-7: You can see a preview of your messages with AutoPreview.

Sending a reply

The thing I love about e-mail is that sending a reply is so easy. You don't even need to know the person's address when you're sending a reply; just click the Reply button and Outlook takes care of it for you.

Here's how you reply to a message:

1. **Choose View➪Go To➪Inbox (or press Ctrl+Shift+I).**

   The Inbox screen opens, showing your incoming mail.

2. **Double-click the title of the message to which you want to reply.**

   The message you double-clicked opens, and you can see the contents of the message.

   If the message is already open, you can skip the first two steps and go directly to Step 3.

3. **To reply to the people who are named in the From line, click the Reply button.**

4. **To reply to the people who are named in the Cc line as well as the From line, click the Reply to All button.**

   The Reply screen appears (see Figure 4-8).

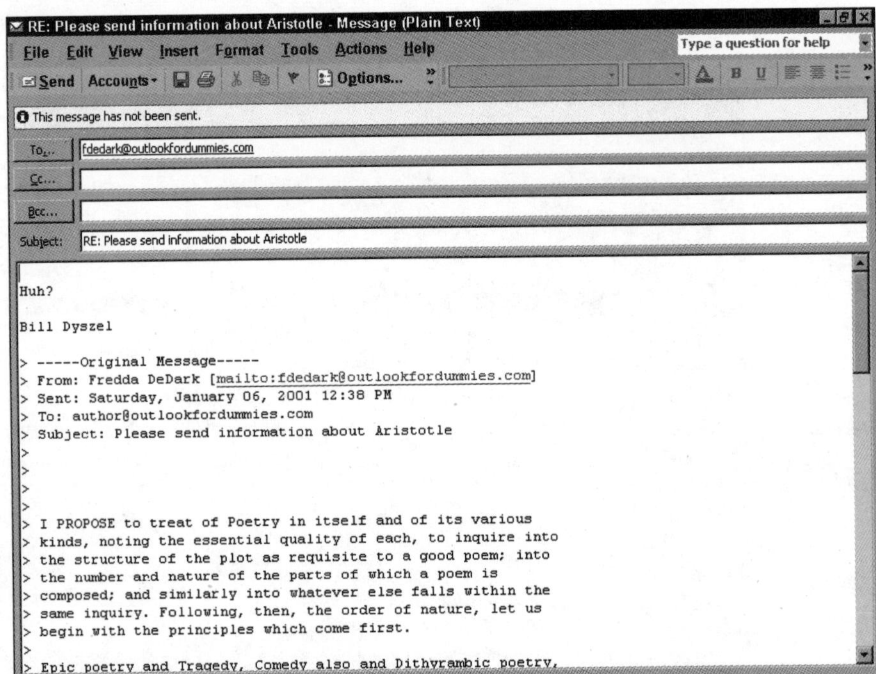

Figure 4-8: The Reply screen.

You may get (or send) e-mail that's addressed to a whole bunch of people all at one time. At least one person must be named in the To line; more than one person can be in the Cc line, which is for people to whom you're sending only a copy. Very little difference exists between what happens to mail that's going to people in the To line and mail that's going to the people in the Cc line — all of them can reply to, forward, or ignore the message. You don't always need to reply to the people on the Cc line, or you may want to reply to only some of them. If you do that, you must click the Reply button (not Reply to All) and add them again to the Cc line.

5. **Type your reply in the Message box.**

   Don't be alarmed that text is already in the text box — that's the text of the message to which you're replying. Your blinking cursor is at the top of the screen, so anything that you type precedes the other person's message. (This arrangement means that the person who gets your message can review the original message as a memory jogger when your reply comes back.)

6. **Click the Send button.**

   NETWORK

   On your office network, clicking Send speeds the message to its intended recipient.

If you're a stand-alone user who's sending mail on an online service, such as The Microsoft Network or CompuServe, you must also choose Tools⇨Send or press F5 to send your message out over the Internet. See Chapter 12 for more about sending e-mail from your home computer with Outlook.

7. **Choose File⇨Close (or press Esc) to close the Message screen.**

   The Message form disappears and your Inbox reappears.

Using a link to the Web from your e-mail

When you open a message, sometimes you see blue, underlined text with the name of a Web page or other Internet resource, such as `www.outlookfordummies.com`. If you want to look at that page, all you have to do is double-click the text and, if everything is installed correctly, your Web browser pops up and opens the Web page whose name you've clicked.

After you open the page, you can save the page to your Favorites folder to allow you to find it again easily.

That's Not My Department: Forwarding E-Mail

You may not always have the answer to every e-mail message that you get. You may need to pass a message along to somebody else to answer, so pass it on.

To forward a message:

1. **Choose View⇨Go To⇨Inbox (or press Ctrl+Shift+I).**

   The Inbox screen opens, showing your incoming mail.

2. **Double-click the title of the message that you want to forward.**

   The Message screen opens (see Figure 4-9). You can forward the message as soon as you read it. If you've already opened the message, you can skip the first two steps.

3. **Click the Forward button.**

   The Forward screen appears (see Figure 4-10). The subject of the original message is now the subject of the new message, except that the letters *FW:* (for Forward) are inserted at the beginning.

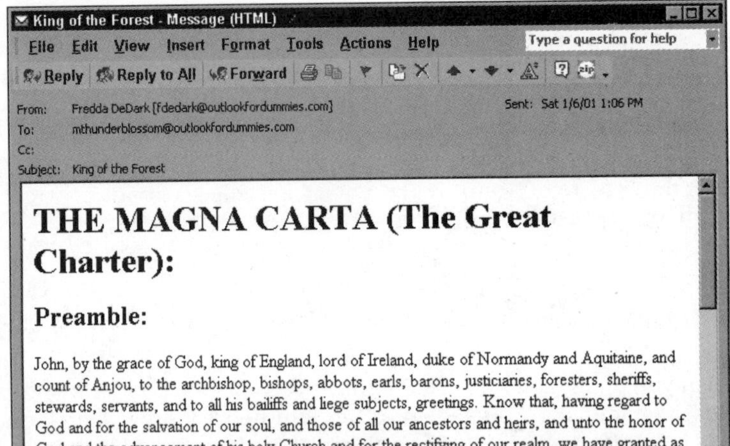

Figure 4-9: The message you want to forward is opened.

Figure 4-10: The Forward screen.

4. **Click the To text box and type the e-mail address of the person to whom you're forwarding the message.**

   If the person to whom you're forwarding is entered in your Contact list, just type the person's name — Outlook figures out the e-mail address for you.

5. **Click the Cc text box and type the e-mail addresses of the people to whom you want to forward a copy of your message.**

   Many people forward trivia, such as jokes of the day, to scads and scads of their friends by e-mail. Most recipients are included as Cc addresses.

   Remember, business e-mail etiquette is very different from home e-mail etiquette. Many employers have strict policies about appropriate use of their corporate e-mail systems. If you work for such a company, be aware of your company's policies.

   If you want to pester your friends by sending silly trivia from your home computer to their home computers (as I do), that's your own business.

6. **In the text box, type any comments that you want to add to the message.**

   The text of the original message appears in the text box, preceded by the words Original Message and a couple of blank lines. You can preface the message that you're forwarding if you want to give that person a bit of explanation — for example, **This is the 99th message I've had from this person.**

7. **Click the Send button.**

   Your message is on its way.

Deleting Messages

You can zap an e-mail message without a second thought; you don't even have to read the thing. As soon as you see the Inbox list, you know who's sending the message and what it's about, so you don't have to waste time reading Burt's Bad Joke of the day. Just zap it.

If you accidentally delete a message you didn't want to lose, click the Deleted Items icon; you find all the messages you've deleted in the last few months. To recover a deleted message, just drag it from the Deleted Items list to either the Inbox icon or the Outbox icon.

Here's how you delete a message:

1. **Choose View➪Go To➪Inbox (or press Ctrl+Shift+I).**

   The Inbox screen opens, showing your incoming mail.

2. **Click the title of the message that you want to delete.**

   You don't have to read the message; you can just delete it from the list.

3. **Choose Edit➪Delete (or press Delete).**

When you delete messages, Outlook doesn't actually eliminate deleted items; it moves them to the Deleted Items folder. If you have unread items in your Deleted Items folder, Outlook annotates the Deleted Items icon with the number of unread items, the same way that it annotates the Inbox with the number of unread items. You can get rid of the annotation by choosing Tools➪Empty Deleted Items Folder. Or you can just ignore the annotation. After you empty your Deleted Items folder, the messages that were in it disappear forever.

Saving Interrupted Messages

If you get interrupted while writing an e-mail message, all is not lost. You can just save the work that you've done and return to it later. Just choose File➪Save (or press Ctrl+S), and your message is saved to the Drafts folder, as shown in Figure 4-11 (unless you had reopened the message from the Outbox, in which case Outlook saves the unfinished message to the Outbox).

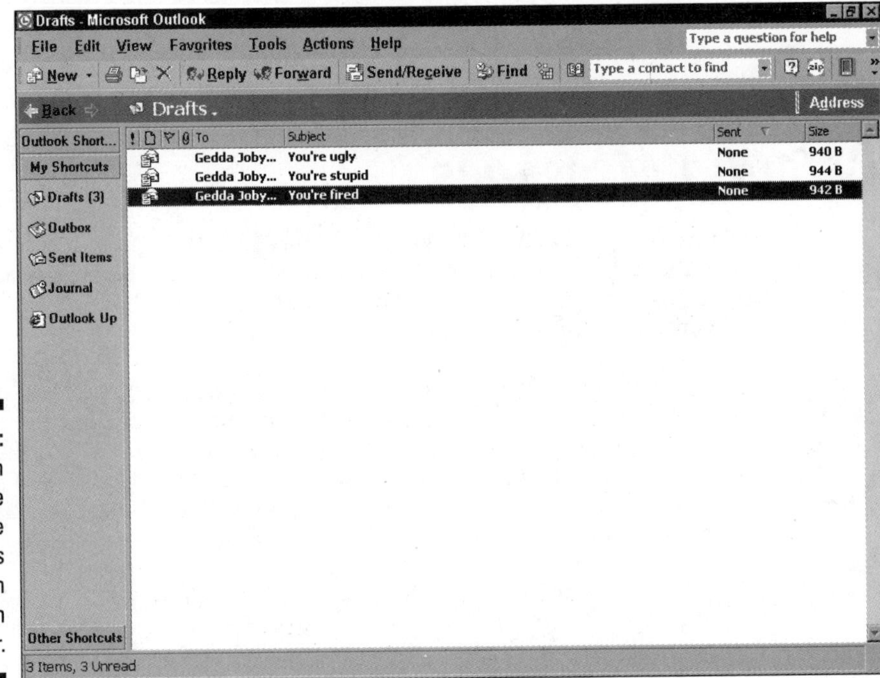

Figure 4-11: You can save incomplete messages and return to finish them later.

When a message is ready to be sent, its name appears in the Outbox in italics. If you've saved it to work on later, its name appears in normal text, not italics. If you're not finished with the message and plan to return to it later, save it (press Ctrl+S). If the message is ready for prime time, send it (press Alt+S).

Saving a Message as a File

You may create or receive an e-mail message that's so wonderful (or terrible) that you just have to save it. You may need to print the message and show it to someone else, save it to a floppy disk, or export it to a desktop-publishing program.

To save a message as a file, follow these steps:

1. **Choose File⇨Save As (or press F12).**

   The Save As dialog box appears.

2. **Click the triangle at the end of the Save In box (called the scroll-down button) to choose the drive to which you want to save your file.**

   If you do all your work on drive C, Outlook chooses drive C first, so you don't have to do anything. To save to a floppy disk, choose the A drive.

3. **Click the name of the folder in which you want to save the file.**

   A list appears of all files in the folder that you select.

4. **Click the File Name text box and type the name that you want to give the file.**

   Type any name you want, up to 256 characters.

5. **If you want to change the type of the file, click the triangle at the end of the Save as Type box and choose a file type.**

   If you're using Word as your e-mail editor, you see the entire range of file types that you can create in Word. If not, the list offers text, the Outlook message format, Outlook Template, and the Internet standard format, HTML (see Figure 4-12). Use HTML. The Outlook Template format is for a message you want to use repeatedly in Outlook.

6. **Click Save (or press Enter).**

   The message is saved to the file and folder you specified in Steps 2 through 4.

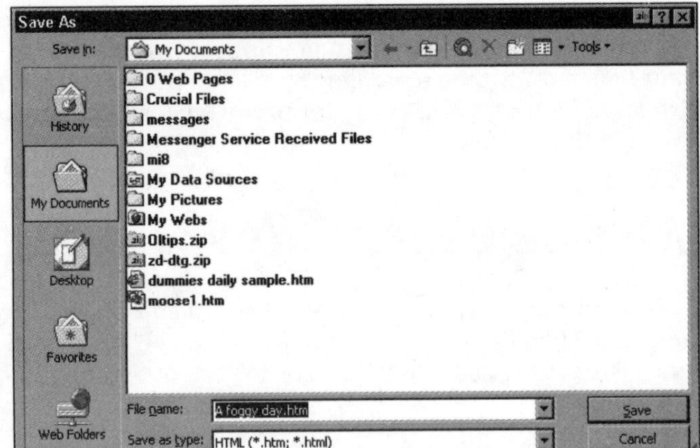

Figure 4-12: The Save As dialog box.

Postscript

Sending e-mail is simple. Keeping track of all the tens of millions of people to whom you want to send e-mail is a bigger task. Fortunately, Outlook does both things, so you can go to one program to get the names of the people you know, find the things that you know about them, and send them e-mail asking them to tell you more.

Chapter 5

E-Mail Tools You Can't Do without

In This Chapter

- Using flags with messages
- Saving copies of messages you send
- Including your name with your remarks in replies
- Setting options for replies
- Attaching files to messages
- Setting up a signature

Outlook can do all sorts of tricks with the mail you send out, as well as with the messages you receive. You can flag messages with reminders, customize your messages with a signature, or add special formatting to the messages you send as replies.

As the automobile ads say, "Your mileage may vary." Outlook is just the pretty face on an elaborate arrangement of other items that makes e-mail work. Outlook is like the dashboard of your car; you can use the dashboard to make the car do what you want it to do, but the things that your car can do depend more on what's under the hood than what's on the dashboard. In the same way, some features of Outlook work only if the system that's backing it up supports those features, too. Some features work only if the person to whom you're mailing uses a system that supports advanced features as well.

Microsoft Exchange Server is the name of a program that runs on many corporate networks and adds a number of features to Outlook, such as delaying delivery of messages or diverting messages to someone else. In this chapter, I don't discuss features you may not have, but if you want to know more about the features that you may have on a corporate network with Microsoft Exchange Server, see Chapter 14. If you're not among the fortunate ones who have Exchange Server, don't worry — Outlook can do plenty all by itself.

Nagging by Flagging

Over time, flags have become my favorite Outlook feature. Back when I received only a few dozen e-mail messages a week, flags didn't matter that much. Now that I get thousands of messages each week, I need help remembering to get back to important messages that otherwise might get lost in the shuffle. If I can't respond to an important message right away, I like to flag that message as soon as I read the message. Then I'm sure to get back to it. You can also plant a flag in a message you send to others to remind them of a task that they have to do if both you and the other person are on an Exchange network.

Adding a flag to an e-mail message

You can add flags to e-mail messages for the same reason that you add reminders to tasks and appointments — to help you remember to do something. Reminders can be set for a specific time of day, whereas flags are set by day but not by time of day.

To attach a flag to your e-mail messages (ones you send and ones that you're sent):

1. **Click the Inbox icon in the Outlook Bar (or press Ctrl+Shift+I).**

   The Inbox screen opens, showing your incoming mail (see Figure 5-1).

2. **Click the message that you want to flag.**

   The message appears highlighted to show that you selected it.

3. **Choose Actions ⇨ Follow Up.**

   The Flag for Follow Up dialog box appears (see Figure 5-2). At this point, if you click OK (or press Enter), your message is flagged. You can set more detailed options by using the following steps.

4. **Click the triangle at the right end of the Flag To text box and choose one of the menu items or type your own choice.**

   A handy flag is "Follow Up," to remind you to confirm an appointment or other arrangement.

5. **Click the Reminder box and type the date on which you want the reminder flag to appear.**

   You can type the date **3/3/99**; Outlook understands. You can type **first wednesday of march**; Outlook understands. You can type **a week from Wednesday**; Outlook understands that to mean "seven days after the

Wednesday that comes after today." You don't even have to worry about capitalization. Don't type **I hate mondays**, though; Outlook doesn't understand that. (But I do.)

If you'd rather just pick a date from a calendar, you can click the little down arrow next to the Reminder box to reveal a calendar, and then just click the date you want.

6. **Click OK.**

When the date you entered in the Flag for Follow Up dialog box arrives, a reminder dialog box pops up to help jog your memory.

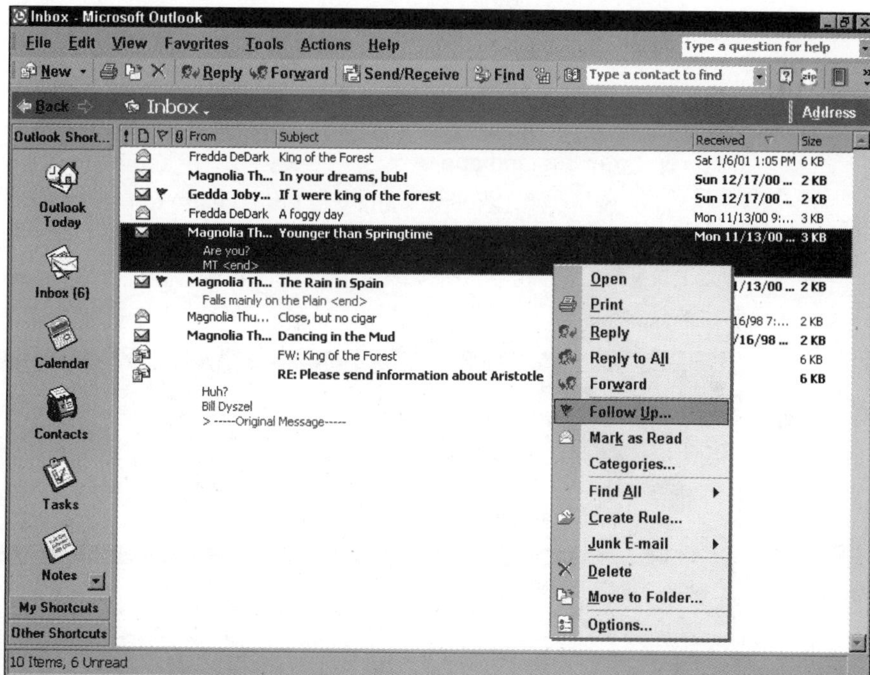

Figure 5-1: The Inbox screen with your mail.

Flag for Follow Up

Flagging marks an item to remind you that it needs to be followed up. After it has been followed up, you can mark it complete.

Flag to: Follow up — Clear Flag

Due by: next friday — 5:00 PM

Completed

OK — Cancel

Figure 5-2: Need to add a flag?

Changing the date on a flag

Procrastination used to be an art; Outlook makes it a science. When someone nags you with flags, you can still put it off. Yes, dear, you *can* do it later.

To change the date on a flag:

1. **Click the Inbox icon in the Outlook Bar (or press Ctrl+Shift+I).**

   The Inbox screen opens, showing your incoming mail (see Figure 5-3).

2. **Double-click the message with a flag that you want to change.**

   The Message dialog box appears.

3. **Choose Actions⇨Follow Up (or press Ctrl+Shift+G).**

   The Flag for Follow Up dialog box appears (see Figure 5-4).

4. **Click the Reminder box and type the new date when you want the reminder flag to appear.**

   Type the date when you think you'll feel ready to be flagged again. Typing **999 years from now** will work — really!

5. **Click OK.**

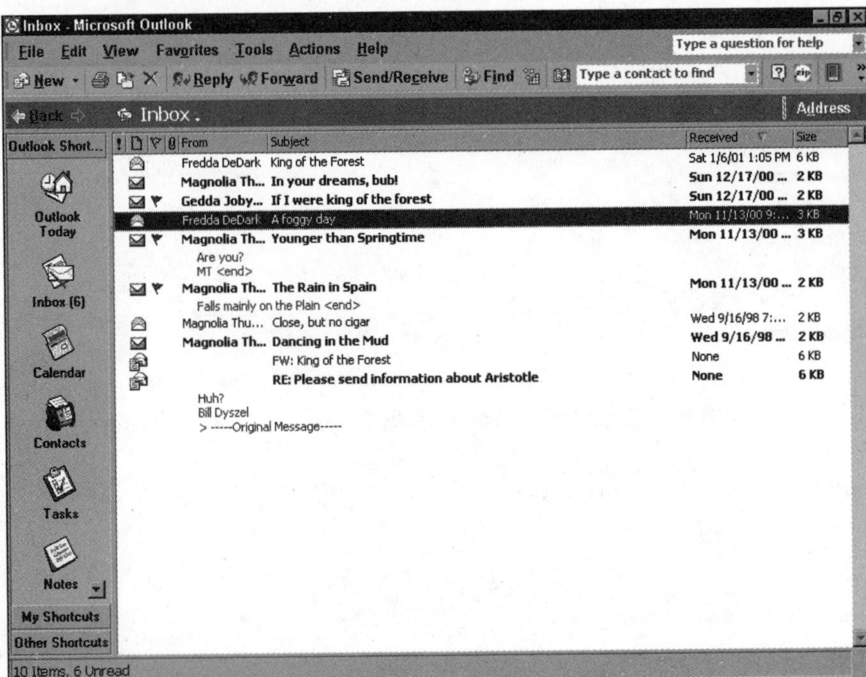

Figure 5-3: A mass of messages, waiting for flags.

Of course, there's a catch. You can always change the date on the flags that you've set, but if someone sends you a message, flags it, and marks it "Private," you can't change the contents of the flag. Rats!

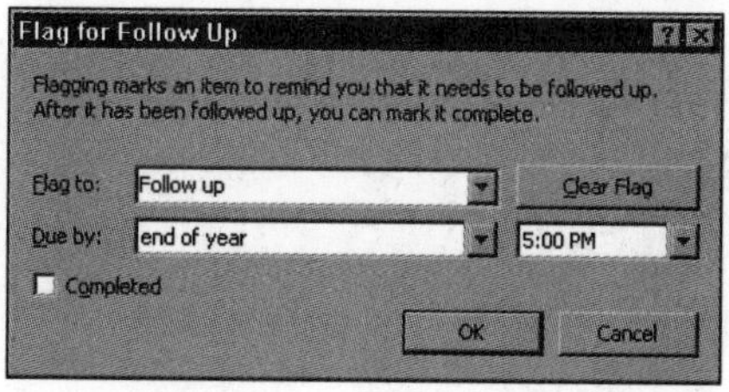

Figure 5-4: The Flag for Follow Up dialog box.

Saving Copies of Your Messages

Nothing is handier than knowing what you've sent and when you sent it. You can save all your outgoing mail in Outlook so that you can go back and look up the messages you've sent. Outlook starts saving sent items when you first install the program, but you can turn this feature on and off. So before you go changing your options, look in your Sent Messages folder to see whether it contains messages.

To save copies of your messages:

1. **Choose Tools⇨Options.**

   The Options dialog box appears.

2. **Click the E-mail Options button.**

   The E-mail Options dialog box appears (see Figure 5-5).

3. **Click the Save Copies of Messages in Sent Items Folder check box.**

   If the box already contains a check mark, leave it alone. (That's the way Outlook is set up when you first install it.) If you click the box when it's already checked, you turn off your option for saving messages. Don't worry if you make a mistake; you can always change it back. Just make sure a check appears in the box if you want to save messages.

4. **Click OK.**

Outlook saves two months' worth of saved messages and sends older messages to an archive file to save disk space on your computer.

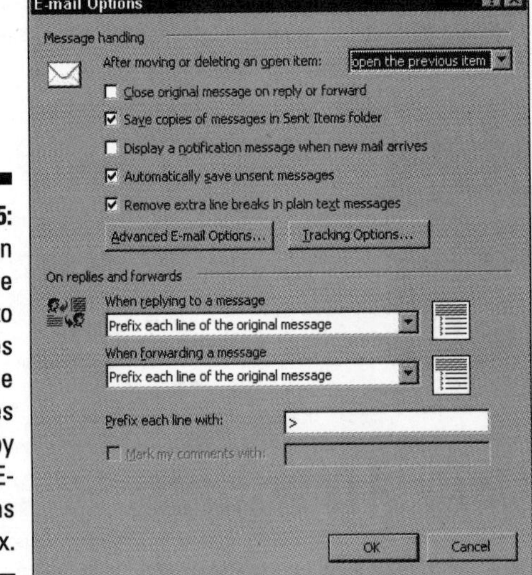

Figure 5-5: You can decide whether to save copies of the messages you send by using the E-mail Options dialog box.

Automatically Adding Your Name to a Reply

When you reply to a message, it helps to include parts of the original message that you're replying to so that the person reading your message knows exactly what you're responding to. The trick is, how will the reader know which comments are his or hers and which are yours?

Outlook allows you to preface your comments with your name or any text that you choose. If you want to be understood, it's best to use your name. If you want to confuse the issue, use a phrase, such as "Simon says."

To tag your replies with your name

1. **Choose Tools⇨Options.**

   The Options dialog box appears.

2. **Click the E-mail Options button.**

   The E-mail Options dialog box appears (see Figure 5-6).

3. **Click the Mark My Comments With check box.**

   Be sure that the check box isn't already checked or you'll remove the check.

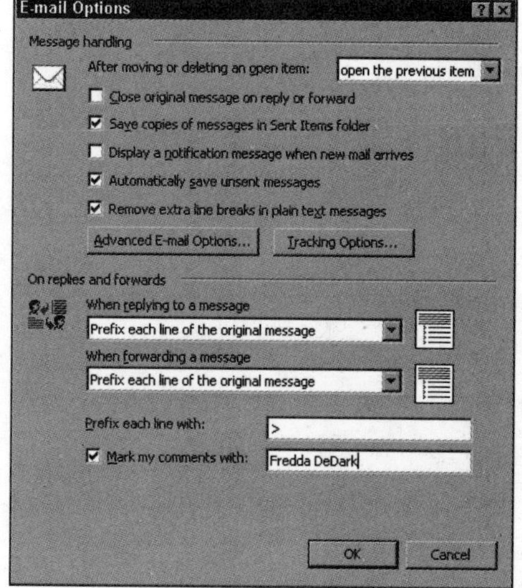

Figure 5-6: Preface your replies with your name by checking the box at the bottom of the E-mail Options dialog box.

4. **In the Mark My Comments With text box, type the text that you want to accompany your annotations.**

   Your best bet is to enter your name here. Whatever you enter will be used as the prefix to all text you type when replying to messages.

5. **Click OK.**

You can select and delete the text of the original message when you create a reply, but including at least a part of the message you're replying to makes your response easier to understand. You also have the option of selecting and deleting the parts of the original text that aren't relevant to your reply.

Setting Your Options

You can control the appearance of the messages that you forward, as well as your replies. If all your e-mail stays in your office among other Microsoft Office users, you can make your text look pretty incredible in messages you send to one another by adding graphics, wild-looking fonts, or special effects, such as blinking text. If you're sending mail to poor ol' Internet users or to people on an online service, such as CompuServe (see Chapter 12 for more about sending e-mail to online services and the Internet), you need to pay attention to how messages look to those people.

To set your options:

1. **Choose Tools➪Options.**

   The Options dialog box appears.

2. **Click the E-mail Options button.**

   The E-mail Options dialog box appears (see Figure 5-7).

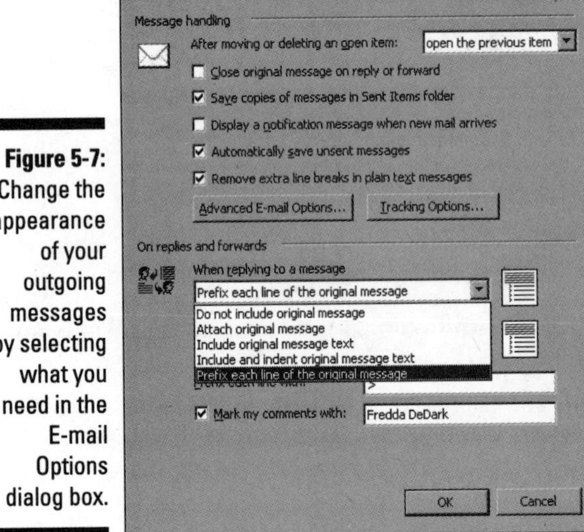

Figure 5-7: Change the appearance of your outgoing messages by selecting what you need in the E-mail Options dialog box.

3. **Click the scroll-down button (triangle) at the right end of the When Replying to a Message box.**

   A menu of options drops down. When Outlook is first installed, Include and Indent Original Message Text is the default option. The diagram to the right of the scroll-down menu illustrates how the message will be laid out when you choose each option.

4. **Choose the style that you prefer to use for replies.**

   The little diagram to the right of the menu changes when you make a choice to show you what your choice will look like. If you don't like the choice that you've made, try another and see how it looks in the diagram.

5. **Click the triangle at the right end of the When Forwarding a Message box.**

   The When Forwarding a Message box has one choice fewer than the When Replying to a Message box does, but the two menus work the same way, and they both have that little diagram of the page layout off to the right.

6. **Choose the style that you prefer to use for forwarding messages.**

   Just pick one; you can always change it.

7. **Click OK.**

You can do all sorts of fancy, exciting, and even useful tricks with e-mail by taking advantage of Outlook's options. If the advanced options seem confusing, you can easily ignore them. Just click Reply and type your answer.

Sending Attachments

If you've already created a document that you want to send to somebody, you don't have to type the document all over again in a message; you just send the document as an attachment to an e-mail message. You can attach any kind of file — word-processing documents, spreadsheet files, and presentations from programs, such as PowerPoint. Any kind of file can be sent as an attachment. The easiest way to send a file from a Microsoft Office program, such as Microsoft Word, is to open that file in Word and choose File⇨Send To. But if you'd rather not do that, you can send a file attachment straight from Outlook.

To send an attachment:

1. **Click the Inbox icon in the Outlook Bar (or press Ctrl+Shift+I).**

   The Inbox screen opens, showing your incoming mail.

2. **Choose File⇨New⇨Mail Message (or press Ctrl+N).**

   The New Message form appears.

3. **Choose Insert⇨File or click the paper-clip button in the Message Form toolbar.**

   The Insert File dialog box appears (see Figure 5-8). It looks just like the dialog box that you use for opening files in most Windows 95 programs, and it works like opening a file, too. Just click the name of the file you want to send and press Enter.

4. **In the list of files, click the name of the file that you want to send.**

   An icon appears in your text representing the file you attached to your message.

5. **Click OK.**

   Your Message form now contains an icon. The name of the icon is the same name as the file that you selected, which means that the file is attached. When you send this e-mail message, a copy of the file that you selected will go to your recipient.

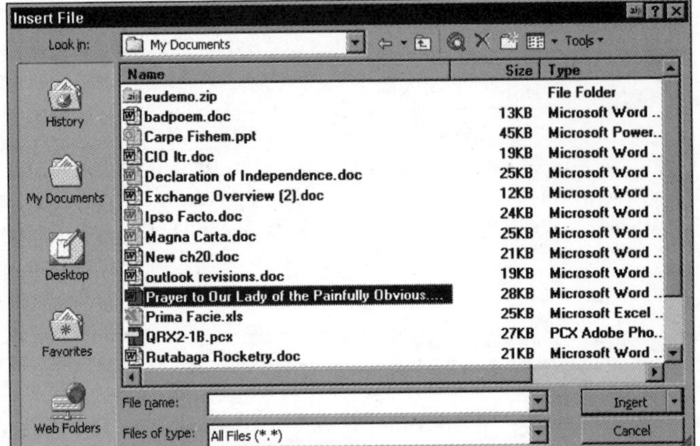

Figure 5-8: The Insert File dialog box.

6. **Type your message (if you have a message to send).**

   You may not have a message; perhaps you want to send only the attachment. If what you want to say is in the attachment, that's fine, but remember that the contents of an attachment don't show up on the recipient's screen until he or she double-clicks to open the attachment.

7. **Click the To button.**

   The Select Names dialog box appears.

8. **Select a name from your address book.**

   If the name of the person to whom you want to send your message isn't in the list, you can click the Cancel button and return to the Message form. Then just type the person's e-mail address in the To text box.

9. **Click the To button.**

   The name of the selected person appears in the Message Recipients box of the Select Names dialog box.

10. **Click OK.**

    The name of the selected person is now in the To box of the message.

11. **Click the Subject text box and type a subject for your message.**

    A subject is optional, but if you want somebody to read what you send, including a subject helps.

12. **Click the Send button.**

    Your message and its attachment are sent.

Those are just a few of the tricks that you can do with the mail you send. You can also do tricks with the mail you get; I cover those tricks in Chapter 9.

Creating Signatures for Your Messages

Many people like to add something called a *signature* to the end of every message they send. A signature is usually a small piece of text that identifies you to everyone reading your message and tells something you want everyone to know. Many people include their name, the name of their business, their motto, a little sales slogan, or some squib of personal information.

You can tell Outlook to add a signature automatically to all your outgoing messages, but first you must create a signature file. Here's how to create your signature file:

1. **Choose Tools⇨Options.**

   The Options dialog box appears.

2. **Click the Mail Format tab.**

   The Mail Format dialog box appears.

3. **Click the Signature button.**

   The Create Signature dialog box appears (see Figure 5-9).

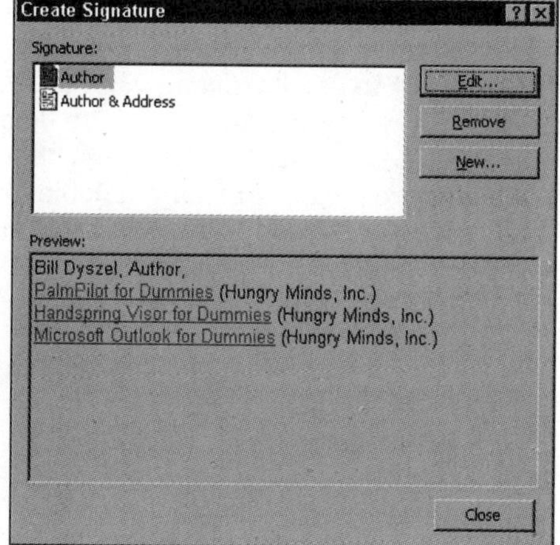

Figure 5-9: The Create Signature dialog box.

4. **Click the New button.**

   The Create New Signature dialog box appears.

5. **Type a name for your new signature.**

   The name you type appears in the Signature box. You can name a signature anything you want.

6. **Click the Next button.**

   The Edit Signature dialog box appears.

7. **Type the text of the signature you want to create.**

   The text you type appears in the Signature text box. You can put anything you want in a signature, but try to be brief. You don't want your signature to be longer than the message to which it's attached.

8. **Click the Finish button.**

   The Signature Picker dialog box appears.

9. **Click OK.**

   The Mail Format dialog box appears.

10. **Click OK.**

    The Options dialog box appears.

11. **Click OK.**

    Your new signature will now appear on every message you send. If you create more than one signature, you can switch between signatures by following Steps 1 and 2 and then choosing the signature you want from the scroll-down menu next to the words *Use this signature by default.*

I like to change the signature I use depending on the addressee of the message. Business messages need to be more formal; personal messages can be, well, more personal. Often I don't want to send a signature at all. My solution is to create a blank signature, name it Blank and make that the default signature. Then, when I want to add a signature to a message, I just choose Insert⇨Signature and pick the signature I want for that particular message. Outlook 2000 also features a Signature button on the toolbar that displays a list of available signatures.

Chapter 6

Conquering Your Mountain of Messages

In This Chapter

- Setting up a new mail folder
- Filing messages in folders
- Using and customizing stationery
- Looking at your messages
- Previewing your messages
- Using the Rules Wizard
- Sorting junk e-mail
- Using Remote Mail

I have good news and bad news about e-mail. The good news is that e-mail is free; you can send as much as you want for virtually no cost. The bad news is that e-mail is free; anybody can easily send you more e-mail than you can possibly read. Before long, you need help sorting it all out so that you can deal with messages that need immediate action.

Outlook has some handy tools for coping with the flood of electronic flotsam and jetsam that finds its way into your Inbox. You can create separate folders for filing your mail, and you can use Outlook's view feature to help you slice and dice your incoming messages into manageable groups.

Even better than the view feature is the Rules Wizard, which automatically responds to incoming messages according to your wishes. You can move all messages from certain senders to the folder of your choice, send automatic replies to messages about certain subjects, or delete messages that contain certain words that offend you.

An even more effective way to deal with offensive messages is to use the new junk e-mail filters that are built into Outlook. You need to turn the filters on only once — after you do, you'll have a lot less junk mail cluttering up your Inbox.

Creating a New Mail Folder

The simplest way to manage incoming mail is just to file it. Before you file a message, you need to create at least one folder in which to file your messages. You have to create a folder only once; it's there for good after you create it. You can create as many folders as you want; you may have dozens or just one or two.

I have folders for filing mail from specific clients, for example. All the e-mail I've received in connection with this book is in a folder called Outlook For Dummies (clever title, eh?). Another folder called Personal contains messages that aren't business-related.

To create a folder for new mail:

1. **Click the Inbox icon.**

   The list of messages in your Inbox appears.

2. **Choose View⇨Folder List.**

   The Folder List appears.

3. **Right-click the word Inbox in the Folder List.**

   A shortcut menu appears.

4. **Choose New Folder from the shortcut menu.**

   The Create New Folder dialog box appears (see Figure 6-1).

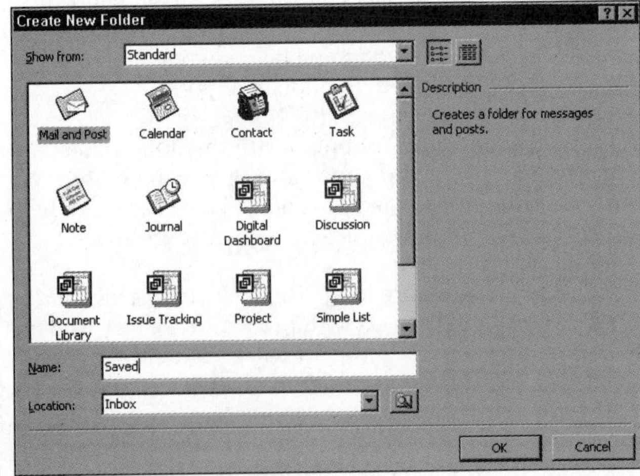

Figure 6-1: The Create New Folder dialog box.

5. **In the Name text box, type a name for your new folder, such as** Personal.

   You can name the subfolder anything you like. You can also create many folders for saving and sorting your incoming e-mail. Leaving all your mail in your Inbox gets confusing. On the other hand, if you create too many folders, you may be just as confused as if you had only one.

6. **Click OK.**

   The Add Shortcut to Outlook Bar dialog box appears.

7. **Click Yes if you want to add an Outlook Bar icon for your new folder.**

   You're not obligated to add an Outlook Bar icon for every folder, but if you plan to use a folder frequently, an Outlook Bar icon makes the folder easier to find.

You now have a new folder named Personal (or whatever name you entered) for filing messages you want to save for future reference. I like to use three or four mail folders for different types of mail to make finding what I'm looking for easier.

Moving messages to another folder

Filing your messages is as easy as dragging them from the folder they're in to the folder where you want them. Just click the Inbox to look at your messages when they arrive, and then drag each message to the folder where you want your messages to stay.

To move messages to another folder:

1. **Click the Inbox icon in the Outlook Bar (or press Ctrl+Shift+I).**

   Your list of incoming mail messages appears.

2. **Click the title of the message that you want to move.**

   The message is highlighted.

3. **Drag the message to the icon on the Outlook Bar for the folder in which you want to store it.**

   Your message is moved to the folder to which you dragged it. If you created a folder named Personal (or anything else) in the preceding section of this chapter, you can drag the message there.

The Outlook toolbar has a button called *Move to Folder* that you can click to move a selected message to the folder of your choice. The best thing about the Move to Folder button is that it remembers the last ten folders to which you moved messages. That feature makes it easy to move messages to folders that may not even appear on your Outlook Bar.

Using stationery

It has been only a few centuries now since preprinted stationery came into fashion for paper mail, so I suppose it's not too early for the same idea to catch on for electronic mail.

Stationery is designed to convey a visual impression about your message. With the right choice of stationery, you can make your message look uniquely important, businesslike, or just plain fun.

Unlike paper stationery, you have an unlimited selection of stationery for your e-mail messages without spending any money on printing and paper. Just pick the design you want from a menu, and there you are! Correspondence Art!

To use stationery:

1. **Choose Actions⇨New Mail Message Using⇨More Stationery.**

   The Select a Stationery dialog box appears, containing a list of each type of stationery you can choose (see Figure 6-2). Each time you click the name of a type of stationery, you see what that stationery looks like in the Preview window.

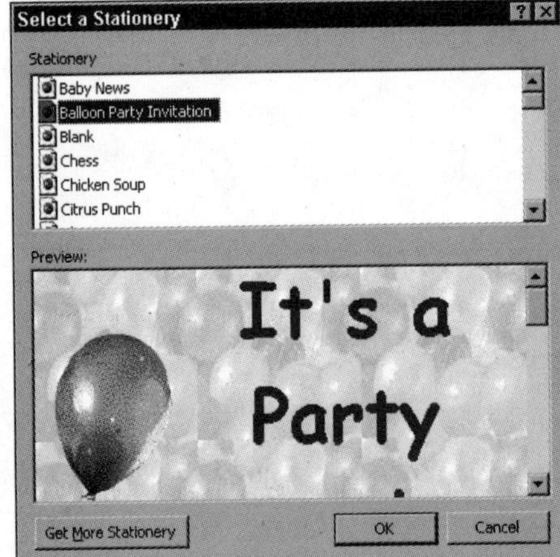

Figure 6-2: The Select a Stationery dialog box.

If the New Mail Message Using command on the Actions menu isn't black and doesn't work when you click it, you need to turn the feature on. Choose Tools⇨Options, click the Mail Format tab, and choose HTML from the scroll-down menu at the top of the Mail Format page.

2. **Double-click the stationery that you want.**

   The stationery you choose appears. For this example, I chose the Balloon Party Invitation Stationery (see Figure 6-3).

Figure 6-3: The Balloon Party stationery.

3. **Fill in the information in the form.**

   You can customize stationery to fit any need. Just click any box where you can put information and type your desired text. You can replace any existing text on a piece of stationery; just select the text you want to replace by dragging the mouse pointer over the text and then type the text you want.

4. **Click the To button.**

   The Select Names dialog box appears (see Figure 6-4).

5. **Select the name of the person to whom you want to send the message.**

   The name you click is highlighted to show that you've selected it.

6. **Click the To button.**

   Yes, I know, you clicked the To button before. This one enters the person's name in your e-mail message.

7. **Click OK.**

   The Select Names dialog box disappears and the stationery reappears.

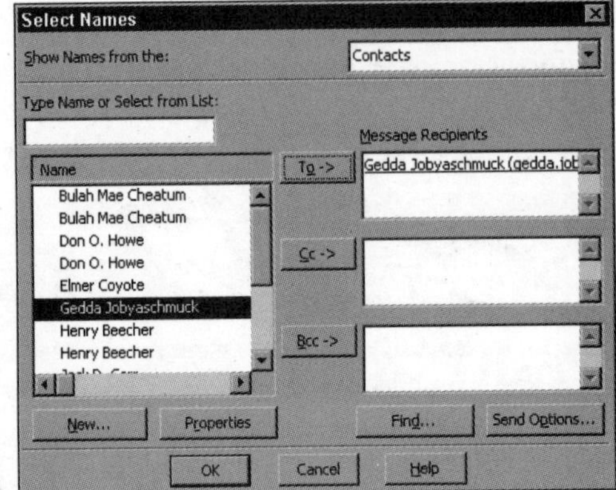

Figure 6-4: The Select Names dialog box.

8. **Click Send.**

   If your computer is on a network at your office, your message is on its way. If you're using Outlook at home, you have to send your message by choosing Tools⇨Check for New Mail. (I know that "Check for New Mail" doesn't sound like what you'd do to send mail, but that's the name for the command.) You can also press F5.

Not everyone uses Outlook to read his or her e-mail, which means that the beauty of your stationery may be lost on some of the people to whom you send messages. Don't be offended if your stationery design is lost in shipment as long as the text of your message arrives.

Using the Preview Pane

If you need to skim through a whole bunch of messages quickly, the Preview Pane can help. When you choose View⇨Preview Pane, the Inbox screen divides into two sections. The top section shows your list of messages; the bottom shows the contents of the message you've selected in the top section (see Figure 6-5). To move from one message to the next, just press the down-arrow key. You can also view any message in your Inbox by clicking the title of the message.

The difference between looking at messages in the Preview Pane and looking at them in AutoPreview mode is that you can see graphics and formatting in the Preview Pane, but you can see only the text of a message in the AutoPreview mode. If your friends send you messages using Outlook Stationery, for example, you can appreciate their graphic genius by viewing their messages in the Preview Pane.

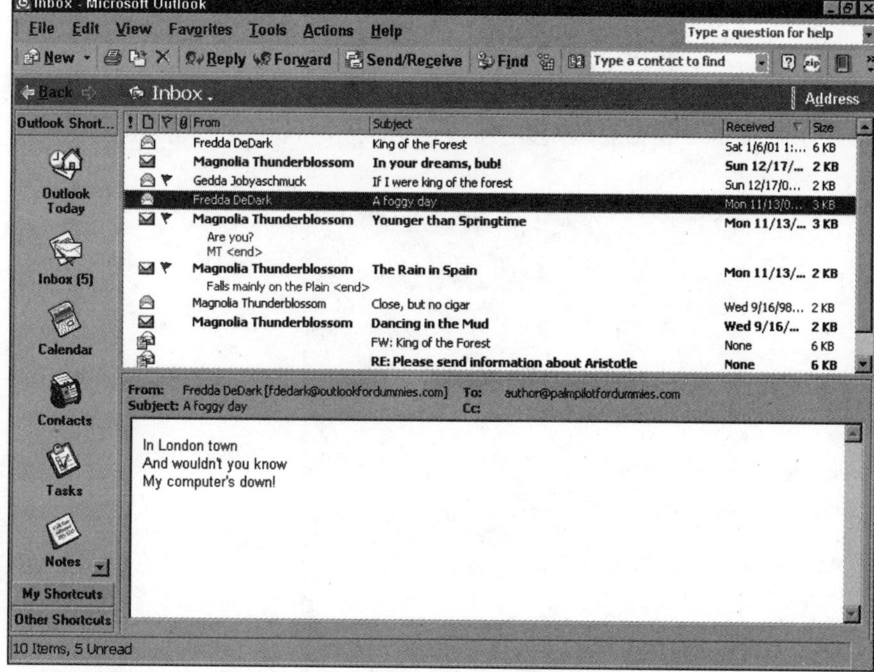

Figure 6-5: The Preview Pane displays the list of messages along with the contents of one message.

Using Rules

Rules are probably my favorite feature in Outlook. The rules feature lets you make Outlook act on certain kinds of e-mail messages automatically. For example, I get tons of e-mail messages, and I can easily waste the whole day sorting through them. So, I set up rules in Outlook to automatically sort my incoming mail into different folders so that I can waste a little less time wading through all the messages.

I don't know exactly how many different rules you can create with the Rules Wizard, but I'm sure that you can create more rules than you and I will ever need.

Creating a rule

The Rules Wizard is called a wizard because of the way the program leads you step by step to create each rule. The process is pretty simple. Here's how you create a simple rule to move an incoming message from a certain person to a certain folder:

1. **Click the Inbox icon in the Outlook Bar (or press Ctrl+Shift+I).**

   The list of messages in your Inbox appears.

2. **Choose Tools➪Rules Wizard.**

   The Rules Wizard dialog box appears (see Figure 6-6).

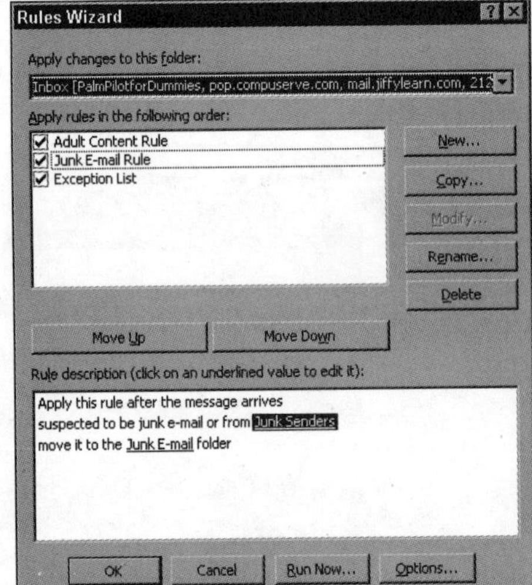

Figure 6-6: The Rules Wizard dialog box lets you make the rules.

3. **Click the New button.**

   A dialog box for creating new rules appears. The dialog box contains a list of the types of rules you can create.

4. **Choose the type of rule you want to create.**

   The Rules Wizard offers several common types of rules that you may want to create, such as Move new messages from someone, Assign categories to sent messages, or Notify me when important messages arrive (see Figure 6-7). For this example, I suggest choosing Move new messages from someone. The words Apply this rule after the message arrives from people or distribution list move it to the specified folder appear in the Rule Description box at the bottom of the dialog box.

5. **Click the first piece of underlined text in the Rule Description box, which says people or distribution list.**

   The Rules Address dialog box appears.

6. **Double-click the name of each person whose messages you want to move to a new folder.**

   The name of each person you choose appears in the right column of the Rules Address dialog box.

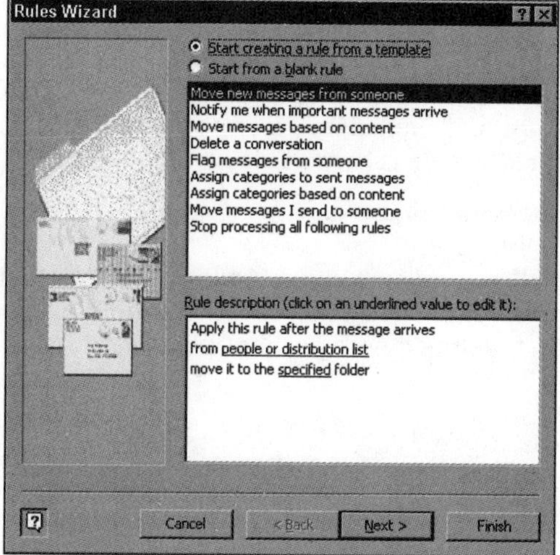

Figure 6-7: Choose the type of rule you want to create.

7. **Click OK when you've chosen all the people whose messages you want to move.**

   The Rules Address dialog box closes and the names you've selected replace the words people or distribution list.

8. **Click the next piece of underlined text in the Rule Description box, which is the word specified.**

   Another dialog box opens to let you choose the folder to which you want to move the message (see Figure 6-8).

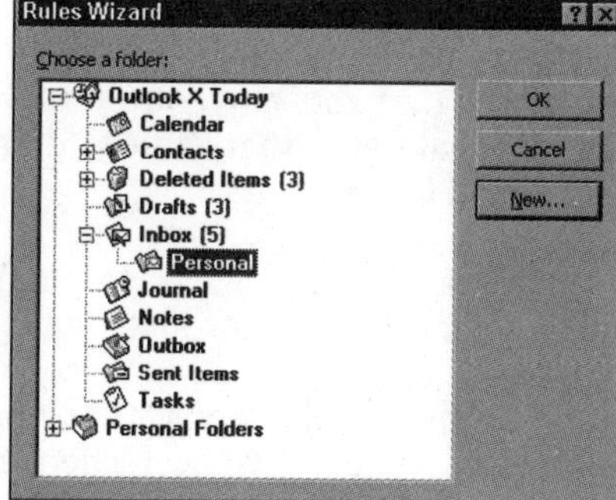

Figure 6-8: Choose the folder to which your messages will go.

9. **Double-click the name of the folder to which you want to move messages.**

   The dialog box closes, and the name of the folder you choose appears in the sentence in the Rule Description box.

10. Click Finish.

The first Rules Wizard dialog box appears with a list of all your rules. Each rule has a check box next to it. You can turn rules on and off by clicking the check boxes. If a check mark appears next to a rule, it's turned on; otherwise, the rule is turned off.

11. Click OK to close the Rules Wizard.

Rules can do much more than just sort incoming messages. You can create rules that automatically reply to certain messages, flag messages with a particular word in the subject, delete messages about specific topics . . . the sky's the limit.

Running a rule

Normally, rules go into action when messages arrive in your Inbox. When you create a rule to move messages from a certain person to a certain folder, the messages that arrive after you create the rule get moved, but the messages sitting in your Inbox keep sitting there. If you want to apply a rule to the messages that are already sitting in your Inbox, use the Run Now button at the bottom of the Rules Wizard dialog box. When the Run Rules Now dialog box appears, check the rule you want to run and then click the Run Now button at the bottom of the dialog box.

Filtering Junk E-Mail

The Junk E-mail filter is a special kind of rule that looks over all your incoming mail and automatically moves anything that looks like junk e-mail to a special folder. You can delete everything that gets moved to your Junk E-mail folder now and again after checking to make sure that Outlook didn't mistakenly move real e-mail to your Junk E-mail folder.

I don't entirely know how Outlook figures out which messages are junk and which are real. I find that some junk e-mail still gets through, but Outlook catches more than half of the junk messages I get. Once or twice I've seen it dump items from real people into the Junk E-mail folder. Outlook once sent a message from my father to the Junk E-mail folder; I've been checking the Junk E-mail folder regularly ever since.

You need to turn Junk E-mail filtering on so that Outlook knows that you want the junk e-mail moved. You also need to make separate choices about whether you want to get rid of plain junk mail and adult-oriented junk mail. Some folks like junk mail; who's to say?

To turn on Junk E-mail filtering:

1. **Choose Tools⇨Organize (or click the Organize button on the toolbar).**

   The Organize window appears.

2. **Click the Junk E-mail link in the Organize window.**

   The text in the right portion of the Organize window changes to reveal controls related to Junk E-mail.

3. **Click the scroll-down button next to the word *Automatically* in each line of the Organize window and choose Move from the list.**

   The word Move appears in the scroll-down menus (see Figure 6-9).

4. **Click the top Turn on button to the right of the scroll-down menu that says Junk E-mail.**

   If you've never created a Junk E-mail folder before, a dialog box appears, asking whether you want to create one.

5. **Click Yes.**

   The Turn on button that you clicked changes to a button called Turn off.

6. **Click the lower Turn on button.**

   Both buttons now say Turn off.

7. **Choose Tools⇨Organize (or click the Organize button on the toolbar).**

   The Organize window closes.

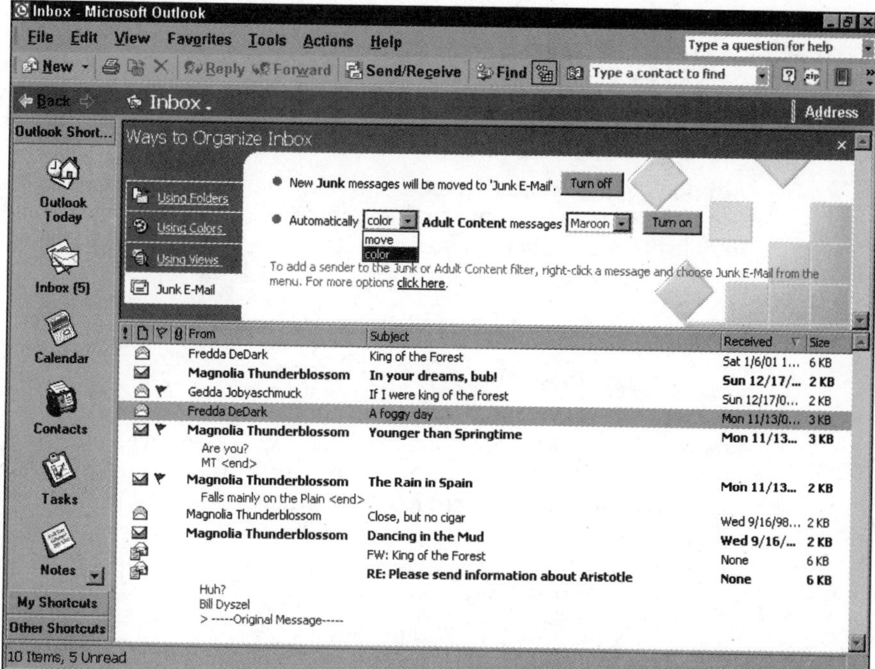

Figure 6-9: Junk e-mail filters let you assign a color to off-color messages.

Archiving

It doesn't take long to accumulate more messages than you can deal with. Some people just delete messages as they read them. Others hold on to old messages for reference purposes. I hold onto all the messages I've ever sent or received in Outlook because I never know when I'll need to check back to see what someone said to me or what I said.

The problem is, Outlook slows down when you store lots of e-mail messages. Besides, a huge collection of messages is cumbersome to manage. Also, if you're on a corporate e-mail system, your system administrators may not let you store more than a certain amount of e-mail because it clogs up the system.

Archiving is a feature built right into Outlook to help you store messages and other Outlook items that you don't need to look at right now, but you still might want to refer to in the future. If you use Outlook on an Exchange network at work, Archiving makes it easy for you to get along with your system administrators by slimming down the number of messages you're storing in the e-mail system.

Even if you don't want to use the Archiving feature right now, you'll want to understand how it works. Outlook sometimes archives things automatically, which may look to you like your Outlook items are disappearing. In this section, I show you how to find the items that Outlook has archived for safekeeping.

If the AutoArchive feature seems scary and complicated to you, try not to worry. I agree that Microsoft hasn't done a very good job of making the Archive feature understandable. Once you get the hang of it, however, AutoArchiving could become very valuable to you.

Although e-mail messages are the things that people archive most often, all Outlook items can be sent to the archive; appointments, tasks, everything. People don't usually archive Contacts and Notes, but you can even archive those if you want.

Setting up AutoArchive

You don't have to do anything to make Outlook archive your items; the program is set up to archive items automatically. If you want to see how Outlook is set up to archive your old items, or change the way Outlook does the job, follow these steps:

1. **Choose Tools➪Options.**

   The Options dialog box appears.

2. **Click the Other tab.**

   The Other options page appears.

3. **Click the AutoArchive button.**

   The AutoArchive dialog box appears (see Figure 6-10).

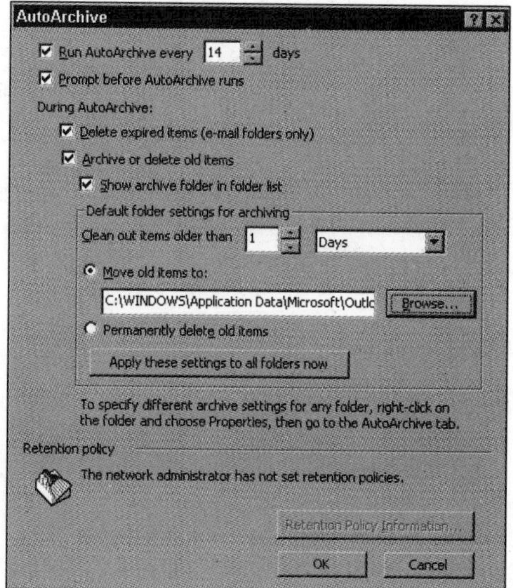

Figure 6-10: The AutoArchive dialog box.

Don't go barging ahead and changing things in the AutoArchive dialog box until you look to see what's set up already. Four important things that the AutoArchive dialog box tells you are as follows:

- How often Outlook archives items
- How old items have to be for Outlook to send them to the archive
- The name and location of the archive file
- Whether or not the AutoArchive feature is turned on

When you first install Outlook, the program automatically archives items every fourteen days, sending items that are over six months old to the archive file listed in the AutoArchive dialog box. For most people, those settings are just fine. Some people prefer to turn off the AutoArchive feature and run the Archive process manually, as I describe in the next section. You can turn off the AutoArchive process by clicking the check box labeled "Run AutoArchive every 14 days" at the top of the AutoArchive dialog box.

Activating the Archive process manually

You can archive messages any time you want by choosing File⇨Archive from the Outlook menu and following the prompts. The advantage of running the Archive process manually is that you get slightly better control of the process; you can give Outlook a cutoff date for archiving items, say the first of the year. You can also tell Outlook which folders to archive and where to send the archived items. You can even archive different Outlook folders to different archive files. The disadvantage to all this control is that it's possible to make an innocent mistake and send archived items to a place that you can't find again easily. Try not to change the name or location of the files to which your archived items are sent, because it's surprisingly easy to lose track of what went where, and Outlook doesn't help you keep track of archived files very easily.

Finding and viewing archived items

Sometimes AutoArchive seems like magic. Older items are mysteriously filed away without any action on your part. Isn't that easy? It's easy until you need to find one of those items that moved magically to your archive. Then you need to figure where it went and how to get at it again.

I usually like to talk up the good points of Outlook, but honestly, this is one place where the Outlook developers fell down on the job. Although it's easy to move items into your Archive, it's pretty confusing to get them back. What's the point of archiving items if you can't find them again?

Anyway, when you want to take another look at the items you've archived, you need to open the archive folder, which Outlook also refers to as a *data file.*

To open a data file containing your archive items, follow these steps:

1. **Choose File⇨Open⇨Outlook Data File.**

   The Create or Open Outlook Data File dialog box appears.

2. **Type the name of the file you want to open in the File Name box.**

   The name you enter appears in the File Name box.

3. **Click OK.**

   The name of the data file you opened appears in the Folder Banner in large letters.

4. **Choose View⇨Folder List.**

   Your folder list appears, showing two sets of folders: Your normal folders and your Archive folders.

Simple enough, right? Yes, but there's a fly in the ointment. You probably don't know the name of the archive file you want to open, and it doesn't usually show up in the list in the Create or Open Outlook Data File dialog box.

To find out the name of the archive file you need to open, choose File⇨Archive and look in the box labeled "Archive File." Be *very* careful not to change anything about the information in that box; otherwise, Outlook may start sending your archived items someplace else. The information in the Archive File box is usually complex gobbledygook with colons and slashes and all sorts of stuff that normal people can't remember. My favorite trick for capturing a long name in a dialog box is to copy the information. Do this by clicking the name once, pressing Tab, pressing Shift+Tab, and pressing Ctrl+C, then click Cancel. After you copy the file name, you can follow the previous steps, except that you can paste the name you want into the File Name box by pressing Ctrl+V, and you don't have to remember that long, crazy file name.

Closing the Archive file

You can keep your Archive file open in the Outlook Folder list as long as you want, but most people prefer to close it after they find what they need. Outlook runs a little faster when you close any unnecessary data files.

To close a data file:

1. **With the Folder List open, right-click the name of your Archive folder.**

   A shortcut menu appears.

2. **Choose Close Folder from the shortcut menu.**

   Your archive folder disappears from the Folder List.

The way that folders are named in Outlook is odd. You may find that something called "Personal Folders" appears several times in your folder list. To make Outlook run as quickly as possible, close as many of them as you can. Your main set of folders — the set you use every day — won't close, so you don't have to worry about closing the folders you use every day.

Viewing Your Messages

You can use at least ten sets of views to see your messages, beginning with the set that comes with Outlook. You can modify each view by sorting on any column of information in any view; you simply click the title of the column by which you want to sort. Any of these views works in any mail folder, and the mechanics of using views of your mail are the same as the mechanics of using views in other Outlook modules. For an overview of views in Outlook, see Chapter 16.

To change your view of your messages, choose View⇨Current View, and then choose one of the following views from the menu:

- **Messages.** This is the no-frills picture of your Inbox — From, To, Subject — just the basics. Messages that you haven't read yet are listed in boldface type; the others are listed in plain type.

  I like to leave my Inbox in the Messages view or the AutoPreview view. Because I've set up folders for sorting other personal mail, I normally move incoming messages to other folders, where I manage them by applying different views.

- **Messages with AutoPreview.** When you don't have time to read all the messages you get, a preview is helpful. The first few lines give you a hint as to which messages you want to read. AutoPreview shows you these first few lines.

  Normally, you see previews only of messages that you haven't read yet. You see only the titles of messages that you have read. Actually, Outlook assumes that you've read any message you've opened. You can also mark a message read or unread by right-clicking it and choosing Mark as Read or Mark as Unread. I sometimes mark messages as Read and then delete them when I've judged from their preview or return address that I'm not interested in reading them. Sometimes I mark a message Unread after I read it if it's a long message that I'd like to devote more time to later. Marking a message unread makes the blue AutoPreview text appear, which helps jog my memory.

- **By Follow-Up Flag.** You can flag incoming messages to help you keep track of what you have to do in response to each message. Flagged view groups your messages according to whether flags are set on the messages, and lists what kinds of flags are set and when they're due. For more about flagging, refer to Chapter 5.

  Some experts say that the most efficient way to deal with all your incoming messages is to file them according to what you need to do with them and then act upon them according to each message's priority and timing. Message flags are one handy way of getting a handle on what you have to do with the messages that you get. By Follow-Up Flag view automatically organizes your messages according to the action that they demand, making you instantly efficient, right?

- **Last Seven Days.** When you're asked to take immediate action on a message you received a few days ago, it's not always easy to find the message that told you what to do, especially if you get lots of e-mail. Last Seven Days view shows you only the messages that you got within the past week. Finding an item in a short list is easier than in a long one.

  The Last Seven Days list limits your view to messages that arrive in a seven-day time period. It does not sort messages according to what's in them or who sent them. You can sort your messages according to the name of the sender or the subject of the message by clicking the titles at the top of the columns in the view.

- **Flagged for Next Seven Days.** If you're flagging messages that are really important, the messages that you flagged to get your attention in the next few days are likely to require your attention first. For a quick look at the hottest of the hot items, use Flagged for Next Seven Days view.

  Like Flagged view, Flagged for Next Seven Days view cuts to the essentials: who sent the message, what the subject of the message is, and when action is due on the message that's marked.

- **By Conversation Topic.** You should always include a subject line that's easy to understand so that the person who gets your message will know at first glance the topic of your message and what to do about it. With any luck, other people will do the same thing for you. Then you can really get some mileage from your messages by sorting them in By Conversation Topic view.

- **By Sender.** When the boss calls and asks, "Did you get the e-mail message about bonuses that I sent you three weeks ago?" you probably don't want to spend a great deal of time sorting through everybody else's messages from the past three weeks. The quickest way to answer the boss's question promptly is to switch to By Sender view.

  You can instantly find the boss's name in By Sender view. Double-click the message titled Bonuses. Then you can tell the boss, "I certainly did; it's right here in front of me." You'll be able to reply so quickly that the boss will be glad to give you that bonus.

- **Unread Messages.** You don't have to read every message that comes across your screen, but Murphy's Law says that the most important information will be in a message that you haven't read yet. The Unread Messages view gives you a quick peek at the things you haven't taken a quick peek at yet.

  Don't leave your Inbox in the Unread Messages view all the time because messages will seem to vanish when you finish reading them. It's easier to use Messages view most of the time and switch to Unread Messages view now and then as a strategy for finding things.

- **Sent To.** It may seem silly to have a view of your Inbox sorted according to the name of the person each message is sent to. After all, it's your Inbox; everything should be sent to you, or it wouldn't be here, right?

  You have two reasons for using Sent To view. Some messages that come to you are addressed to everybody at your company, for example, so it's good to know that certain messages shouldn't be taken personally. The second reason is that the same set of views is available in the Inbox and the Sent Items folder. The Sent Items folder is where Outlook keeps copies of messages that you've sent to other people. Knowing what you sent to whom can come in very handy.

  Sent To view is only sorted, not grouped, which means that the messages appear in order of the names of the people who sent them. A grouped view would display as the heading of a group the name of each person who has sent you mail. If you click the Subject column, you lose the benefit of having the list sorted by sender. If your Sent To list appears to be sorted incorrectly, just click the word To at the top of the To column.

- **Message Timeline.** The Message Timeline view is one of the most interesting views in Outlook; it draws a graph of all your messages according to when they arrived. Message Timeline view is designed to help you find messages when you can remember when they arrived but not why they arrived or who sent them.

  The little icons that represent the messages are actually shortcuts to the messages that they represent. You can open a message by double-clicking the icon for that message. You can also right-click the message icon to reply to a message, delete a message, or move a message to another folder.

Part III

It's What You know AND Who You Know: How to Succeed with Outlook

"TELL THE BOSS HE'S GOT MORE FLAME MAIL FROM YOU-KNOW-WHO."

In this part . . .

You can send messages to nearly anyone, anytime, but what are the messages about? Business — all those things that keep us off the streets, out of trouble, and best of all, paid! Meetings and deadlines, schedule conflicts, and too many tasks — all crying out for your expert attention. In this part, you see how Outlook makes it easy to keep your business in line.

Chapter 7

Your Little Black Book: Creating Contact Lists

In This Chapter

- Storing names and addresses
- Checking out the view
- Sorting and rearranging views
- Using grouped views
- Finding names in your Contact lists
- Sending a vCard

Hardly anybody works alone. Even if you work at home, you always have people you need to keep track of — people you sell things to, buy things from, have lunch with, or any of dozens of things you need to do with other people. All that personal information can be hard to store in a way you can find and use again quickly when you need it. And you need to know different things about people in different parts of your life. So you need a tool that's flexible enough to let you organize names, addresses, and all that other information in ways that make sense in different contexts.

For example, I work as a computer consultant and write for computer magazines. The information I need to keep about consulting clients (systems, software, hours, locations, and networks) differs from the information I need for dealing with people in the publishing business (editors, deadlines, topics, and so on). I'm also still active as a professional singer and actor, and my contacts in those businesses are two entirely different kettles of fish. But when someone calls on the phone, or when I want to do a mailing to a group from one world or another, I need to be able to look up the person right away, regardless of which category the person fits in.

Outlook is flexible enough to let me keep all my name and address information in a single place but sort, view, find, and print it differently, depending on what kind of work I'm doing. You can also keep lists of family and friends stored in Outlook right alongside your business contacts and still distinguish them from one another quickly when the need arises.

Storing Names, Numbers, and Other Stuff

Storing lots of names, addresses, and phone numbers is no big trick, but finding them again can take magic unless you have a tool like Outlook. You may have used other programs for storing names and related numbers, but Outlook ties the name and number information together more tightly with the work you do that uses names, addresses, and phone numbers, such as scheduling and task management.

If you've ever used a little pocket address book, you pretty much know how to use the Outlook Contacts feature. Simply enter the name, address, phone number, a few juicy tidbits, and there you are!

The quick and dirty way to enter Contacts

Entering a new name to your Contact list is utterly simple. Click the New button on the toolbar to open the New Contact entry form, fill in the blanks on the form, and then click Save and Close. That's really all there is to it. If you don't enter every detail about a contact right away, it's okay — you can always add more information later.

The slow, complete way to enter Contacts

If you want, you can enter scads of details about every person you enter in your Contact list and choose from literally dozens of options, but if all you do is enter the essentials and move on, that's fine. If you're more detail-minded, here's the way to enter every jot and tittle for each contact record:

1. **Click the Contacts icon in the Outlook Bar.**

   The Contact list appears (see Figure 7-1).

2. **Choose File⇨New⇨Contact.**

   The New Contact form appears.

   TIME-SAVER: To be really quick about it, press Ctrl+Shift+C instead to see the form shown in Figure 7-2.

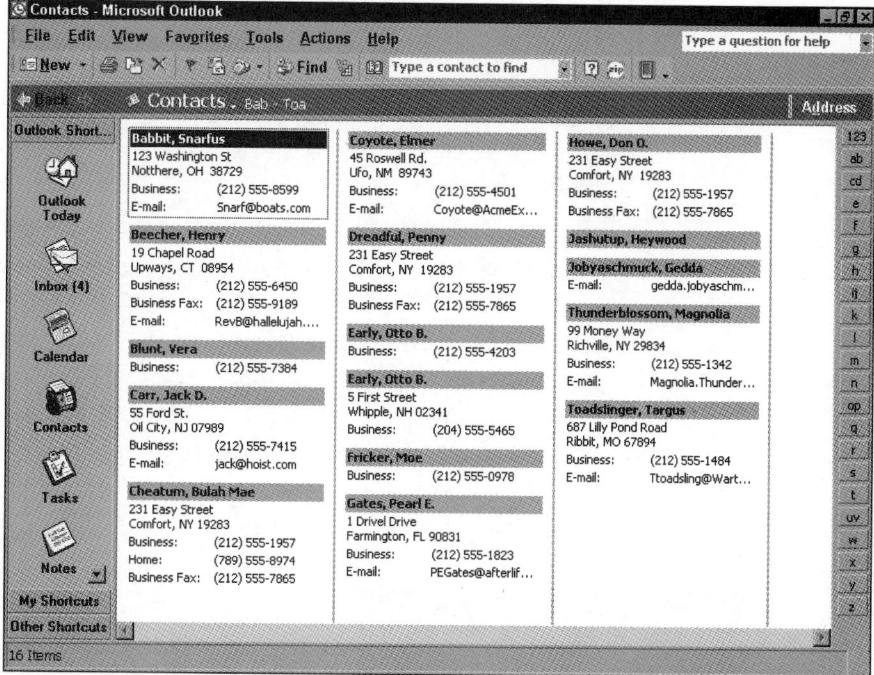

Figure 7-1: The Contacts list.

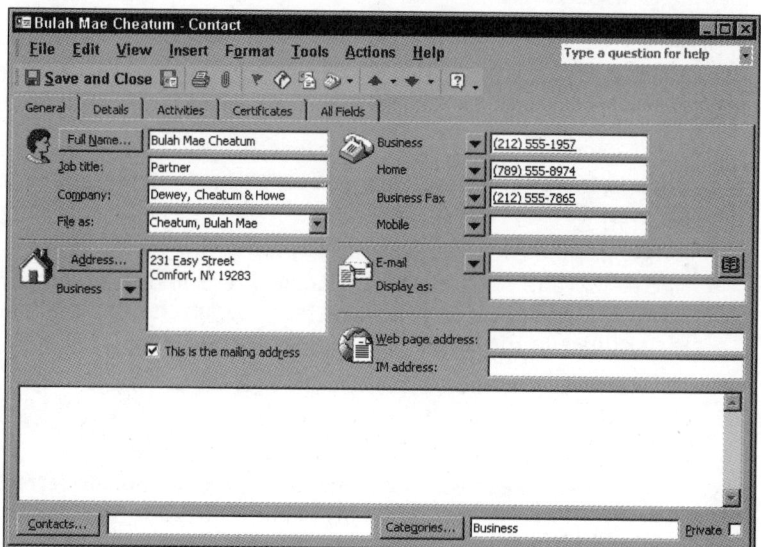

Figure 7-2: The New Contact form.

3. **Click the Full Name button.**

   The Check Full Name dialog box appears (see Figure 7-3):

   - Click the triangle (called the scroll-down button) on the right edge of the Title text box and choose a title from the list that drops down, such as Mr., Ms., or Dr., or type one in, such as **Rev.**, **Ayatollah**, or whatever.
   - Click in the First text box and type the contact's first name.
   - Click in the Middle text box and type the contact's middle initial (if any). If there's no middle initial, you can leave this box blank.
   - Click in the Last text box and type the contact's last name.
   - Click in the Suffix drop-down list and choose a suffix, such as Jr., III, or type one in the box, such as **Ph.D.**, **D.D.S.**, or **B.P.O.E.**
   - Click OK. The Check Full Name dialog box closes, and you're back in the New Contact form, where the name you entered is now shown in both the Full Name and File As text boxes.

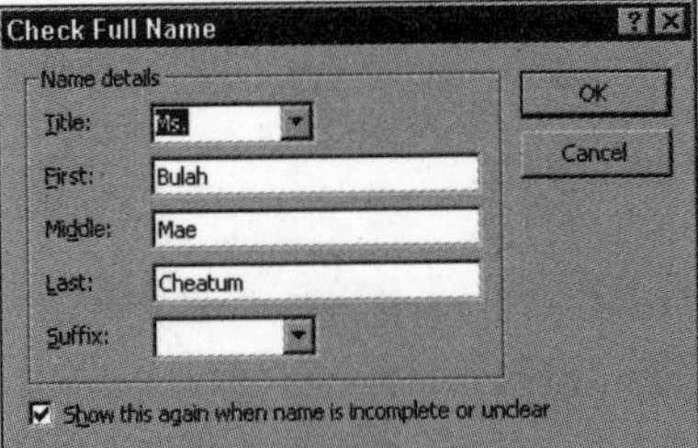

Figure 7-3: The Check Full Name dialog box.

4. **Click in the appropriate box and enter the information requested on the New Contact form.**

   If the information isn't available — for example, if the contact has no job title — leave the box blank. A triangle after the box indicates a drop-down list with choices you can select. If your choice isn't listed, type your choice in the box.

   - If you've entered a name in the Full Name box, the File As box will already contain that name.

   - If you want this person filed under something other than his or her name, click in the File As box and type in your preferred designation. For example, you may want to file your dentist's name under the term *Dentist* rather than by name. If you put Dentist in the File As box, the name turns up under Dentist in the alphabetical listing rather than under the name itself. Both the Full Name and the File As designation exist in your Contact list. That way, for example, you can search for your dentist either by name or the word *Dentist.*

5. **Click the Address button to open the Check Address dialog box.**

- Click the Street text box and type in the contact's street address.
- Click the City text box and type in the contact's city.
- Click the State/Province text box and type in the contact's state.
- Click the ZIP/Postal Code box and type in the contact's postal code.
- Click the triangle at the right end of the Country box and choose the contact's country if Outlook hasn't already chosen the correct one.

See Figure 7-4 for a look at a completed Check Address dialog box.

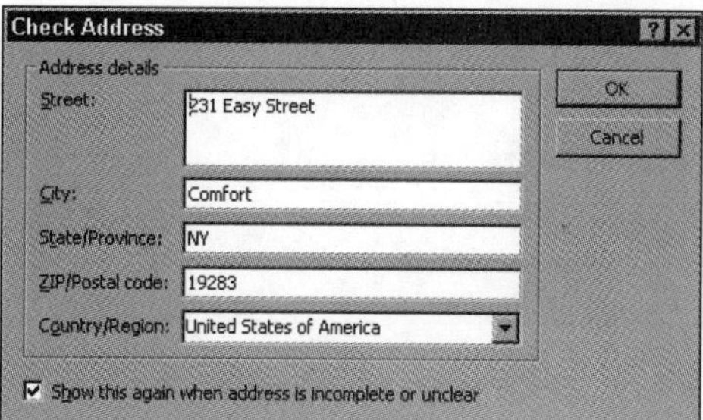

Figure 7-4: The Check Address dialog box.

6. **Click OK.**

   The Check Address dialog box closes.

7. **Click the check box on the New Contact form next to** This Is the Mailing Address **if the address you just entered is the address you plan to use for sending mail to the contact.**
8. **Click in the text box to the right of the Business phone box and type in the contact's business phone number.**
9. **Click in the text box to the right of the Home phone box and type in the contact's home phone number.**

   For numbers other than Business and Home phones, click the triangle to the right of the phone number type block and choose the kind of number you're entering. Then enter the number.

   The New Contact form has four phone number blocks. Any of them can be used for any of the nineteen phone number types that are available in the drop-down list. You can also add custom fields so that you can include more than four phone numbers for a single contact. For the person who has everything, you can create custom fields for that person's Ski Phone, Submarine Phone, Gym Phone — as many as you want. For more about Custom Fields, see Chapter 24.

   You can choose any of nineteen phone number types to enter, depending on what types of phone numbers your contacts have (see Figure 7-5).

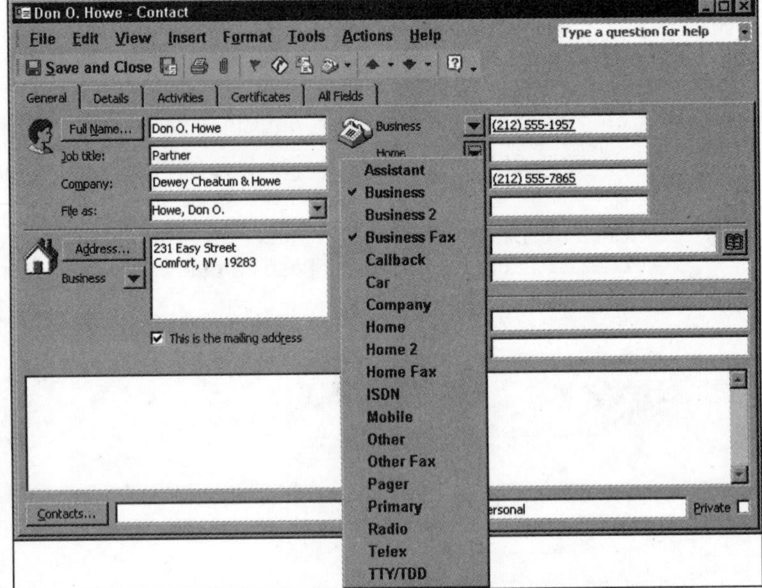

Figure 7-5: You can always reach your contact at one of these phone numbers.

10. **Click in the E-mail text box and enter your contact's e-mail address.**

    If your contact has more than one e-mail address, click the triangle at the left edge of the E-mail box (see Figure 7-6), select E-mail 2, and then click in the text box and enter the second address.

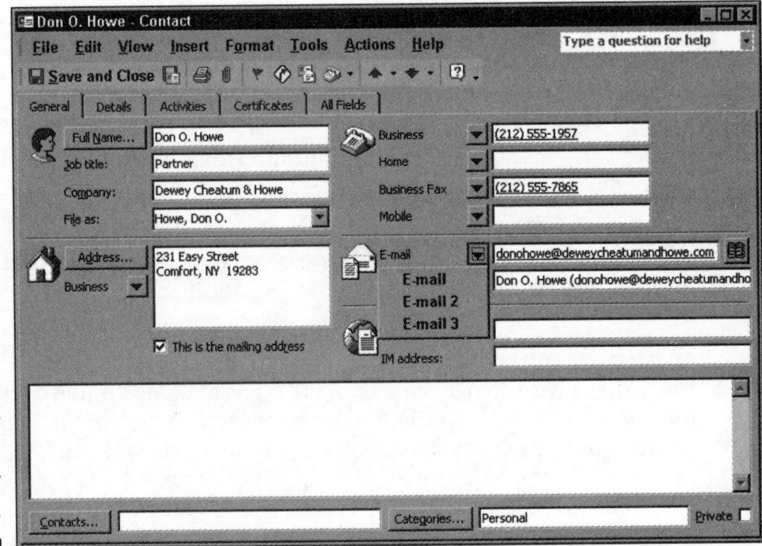

Figure 7-6: You can enter more than one e-mail address for each person in your Contact list.

11. **Click in the Web Page text box if the contact has a Web page, and type the URL address for that page if you want to be able to link to that page directly from the Address Card.**

    URL is a fancy name for the address of a page on the World Wide Web. When you see ads on TV that refer to `www.discovery.com` or `www.dummies.com`, what you're seeing is a *Uniform Resource Locator,* or URL. You can view a Web page by entering the URL for the page in the Address box of your Web browser. If a person or company in your Outlook Contact list has a Web page, you can enter the URL for that page in the Web Page box. To view the Web page for a contact, open the contact record and choose Actions➪Explore Web Page (or press Ctrl+Shift+X); your Web browser opens and loads the contact's Web page.

12. **Click in the large text box at the bottom of the form and type in anything you want.**

    You can enter directions, details about meetings, the Declaration of Independence — anything you want (preferably something that can help you in your dealings with the contact).

Format the text in the big text box (see Figure 7-7) by using the buttons on the formatting toolbar, if you want. The tools on the formatting toolbar are just like the ones all the other word-processing programs use: font, point size, bold, italic, justification, and color. Select the text you want to format and change the formatting. You can change the formatting of a single letter or the whole text box. You can't format the text in the smaller data text boxes in the other parts of the Contact form — only that in the big text box at the bottom of the form. If your formatting toolbar isn't showing, choose View➪Toolbars➪Formatting from the Contact form menu.

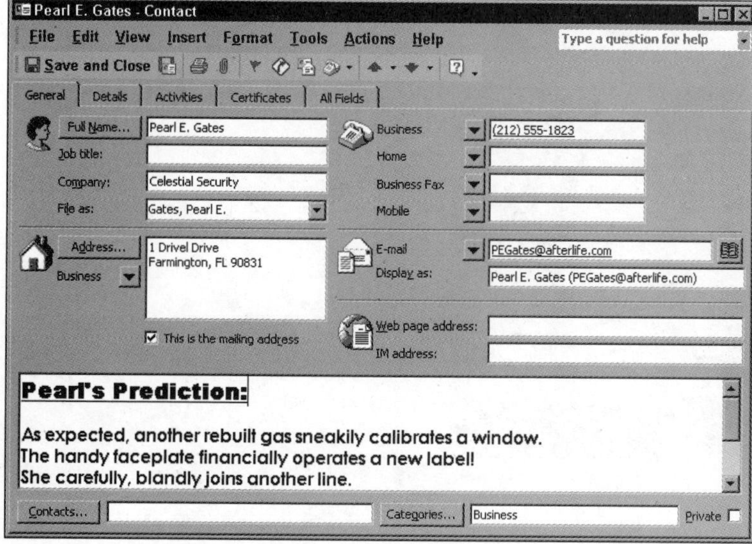

Figure 7-7: Have fun with formatting in the Contact text box.

13. Click the Categories button at the bottom center of the screen to assign a category to the contact, if you want.

Assigning categories is another trick to help you find things easily. For an example of how to use categories with any Outlook item, see Chapter 8. After you assign categories to Outlook items, you can easily sort or group the items according to a category that you've assigned.

Choose one of the existing categories if one suits you, and then click OK (see Figure 7-8).

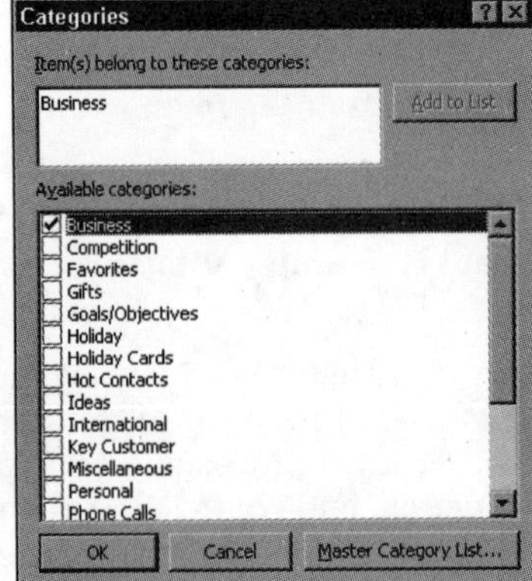

Figure 7-8: Put your contact in a category for easy reference.

14. If none of the existing categories suits you, click Master Category List in the lower-right corner to see the Master Category List box.

Type a category of your choice in the New Category box (see Figure 7-9). Be sure not to add too many new categories because doing that could make it hard to find things.

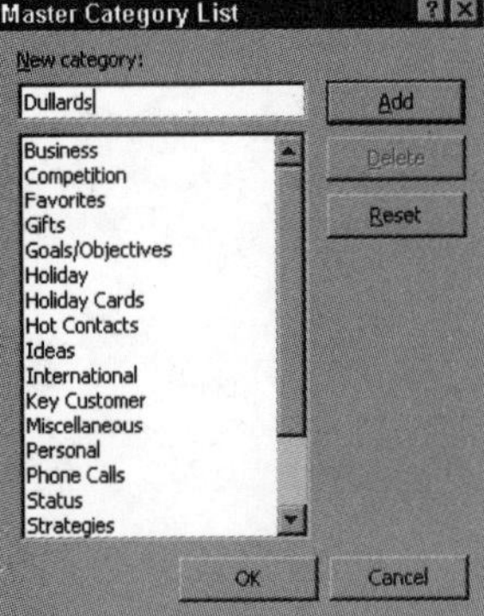

Figure 7-9: Create your own category in the Master Category List.

15. **Click Add and then click OK to return to the Categories list.**

    Choose the new category from the list if you want. You can choose more than one category at a time.

16. **Click the Private box in the lower-right corner of the New Contact form if you're on a network and you don't want others to know about this contact.**

    I'm not suggesting that you get all paranoid and secretive here, but you may want to keep contact information confidential.

17. **When you're done, click Save and Close.**

After you enter anything you want or need (or may need) to know about people you deal with at work, you're ready to start dealing.

Viewing Contacts

After you enter your contact information, Outlook lets you see the information arranged in many different and useful ways, called *views*. Viewing your contact information and sorting the views are quick ways to get the big picture of the data that you've entered (see Chapter 16 for more information on views). Outlook comes with anywhere from five to twelve predefined views in each module. You can easily alter any predefined view. Then you can name and save your altered view and use it just like the predefined views that come with Outlook.

To change the view of your Contact list:

1. **Click the Contacts icon in the Outlook bar.**

   The Contact list box appears.

2. **Choose View⇨Current View and pick the view you want.**

   You can shift between views as you can switch television stations, so don't worry about changing views and changing back. Figure 7-10 shows the Current View menu and its list of views for Contacts with the Detailed Address Cards view selected.

3. **Choose By Location from the drop-down menu (or whatever other view you want).**

   You can also choose Address Cards, Detailed Address Cards, Phone List, By Category, By Company, By Location, or whatever other views are listed.

4. **You see the By Location view as shown in Figure 7-11 (or whatever other predefined view you select).**

To use one of the other views, repeat the preceding steps and choose the view you want.

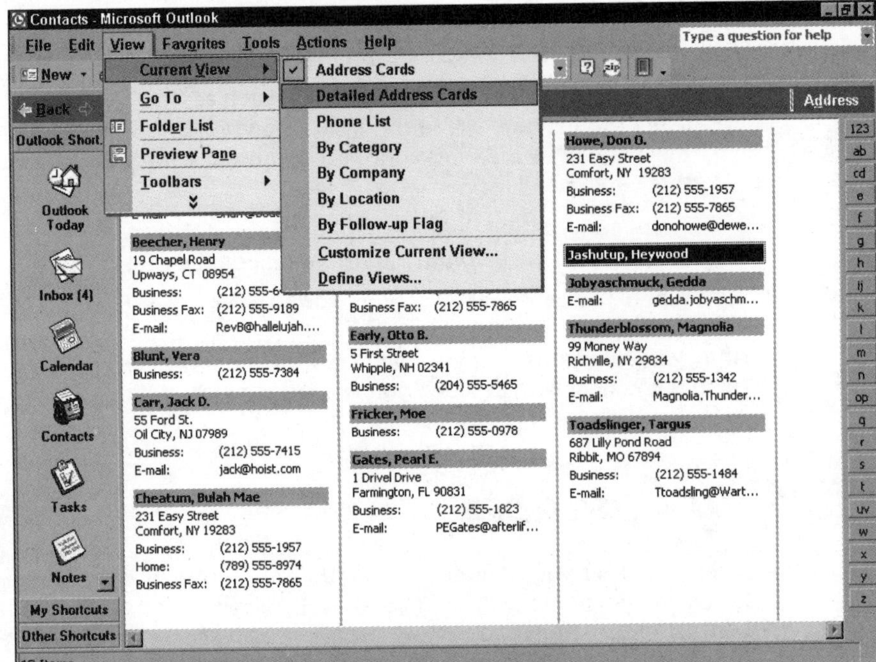

Figure 7-10: The Detailed Address Cards view.

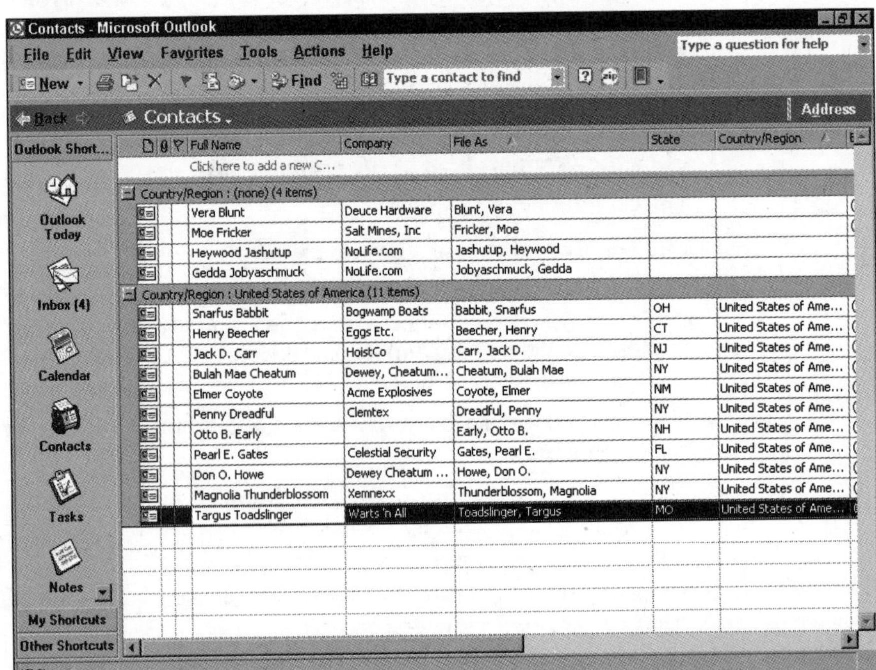

Figure 7-11: Your contacts in the By Location view.

Sorting a view

Some views are organized as simple lists, such as the Phone List view of the Contacts module. Figure 7-12 shows the Phone List: a column of names on the left, followed by a column of company names, and so on.

If you're missing one view that is arranged in columns, all you have to do to sort that column is click once on the title of the column. For example, suppose you want to see the names of the people who work for IBM who are entered in your Contact list. One easy way to see all their names simultaneously is to sort on the Company column:

1. **Choose View⇨Current View.**

   The list of views appears.

2. **Choose the Phone List view.**

   Your list of contacts appears in the Phone List view.

3. **Click the head of the Company column.**

   You see a little icon with the letters AFZ and an arrow. That tells you that Outlook is sorting the column in alphabetical order. If you have only a few items to sort, the icon may flash by so quickly that you don't notice it. When you have a really long list to sort, the icon may stay there for several seconds as Outlook sorts your list.

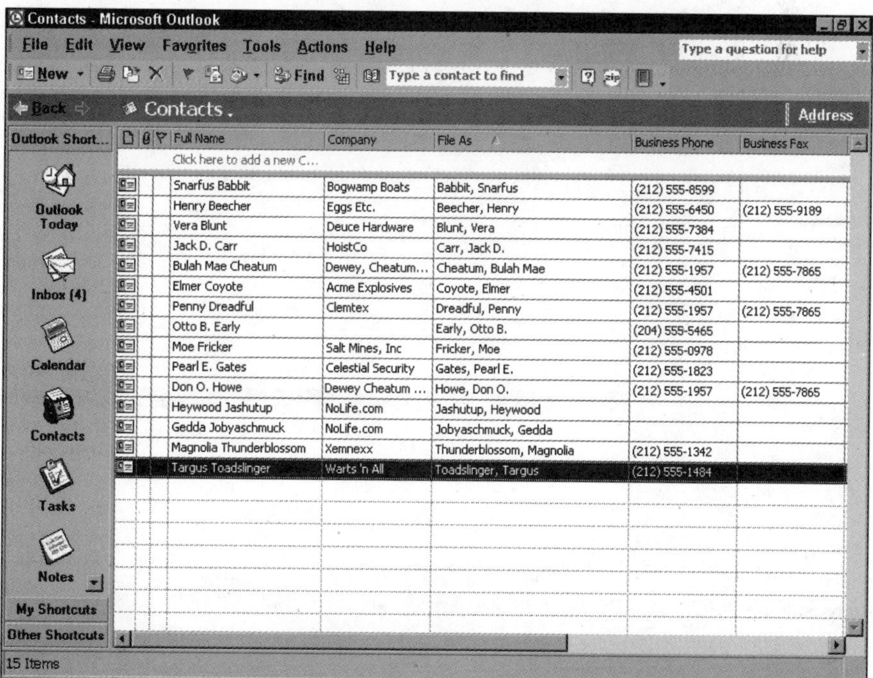

Figure 7-12: The Phone List view.

After you sort your list, it's easier to find the name of somebody by scrolling down to that part of the alphabet. If you sort by company, all the contacts line up in order of company name, so you can scroll down to the section of your list where all the people from a certain company are listed.

Rearranging Views

You can rearrange views simply by dragging the column title and dropping the title where you want it. For example, to move the Business Phone column in the Phone List view:

1. **Choose View⇨Current View⇨Phone List.**

   The Phone List view of your contacts appears.

2. **Click the Business Phone heading and drag it on top of the column to its left.**

   You see a pair of red arrows pointing to the border between the two columns to the left of the Business Phone column. The red arrows tell you where Outlook will drop the column when you release the mouse button (see Figure 7-13).

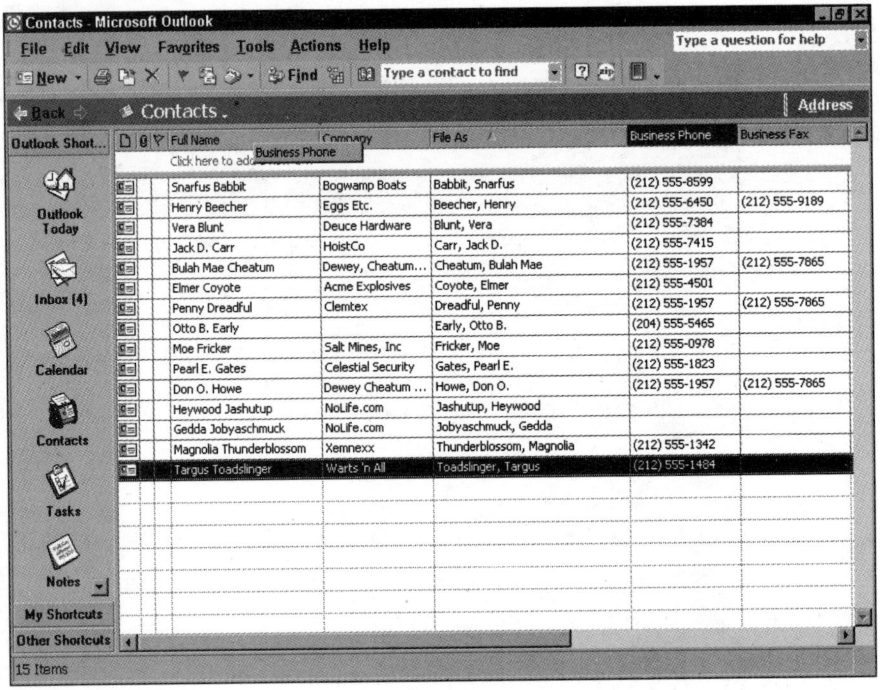

Figure 7-13: You can rearrange the columns in an Outlook Table view by dragging the column heading to the location you desire.

3. **Release the mouse button.**

   The Business Phone column is now to the left of the File As column rather than to the right. If it makes more sense to you to have File As to the right of Business Phone, you can set up your view in Outlook to put it there.

You can use the same process to move any column in any Outlook view. Because the screen is not as wide as the list, you may need to move columns around at times to see what you really want to see. For example, the Phone List in Figure 7-13 shows eight columns, but the list in that view really has twelve columns. You must use the scroll bar at the bottom of the list to scroll to the right to see the last column, Categories. If you want to see the Categories column at the same time as the Full Name column, you have to move the Categories column to the left.

Using grouped views

Sometimes sorting just isn't enough. Contact lists can get pretty long after awhile; you can easily collect a few thousand contacts in a few years. Sorting a list that long means that if you're looking for stuff starting with the letter *M*, the item you want to find will be about three feet below the bottom of your monitor screen, no matter what you do.

Groups are the answer, and I don't mean Outlook Anonymous. Outlook already offers you several predefined lists that use grouping.

You can view several types of lists in Outlook: A sorted list is like a deck of playing cards laid out in numerical order, starting with the deuces, then the threes, then the fours, and so on up through the picture cards. A grouped view is like seeing the cards arranged with all the hearts in one row, then all the spades, then the diamonds, and then the clubs. Outlook also has several other view types that don't apply to contacts, such as Timeline and Address Cards.

Gathering items of similar types into groups is handy for tasks such as finding all the people on your list who work for a certain company when you want to send congratulations on a new piece of business. Because grouping by company is so frequently useful, the By Company view (see Figure 7-14) is set up as a predefined view in Outlook.

To use the By Company view:

1. **Click the Contacts icon in the Outlook Bar.**

   The Contacts module opens with its current view displayed.

2. **Choose View⇨Current View⇨By Company.**

   Each gray bar labeled Company: (name of company) has a little box at the left with a plus or minus sign on it. Click a plus sign to see additional names in that category; a minus sign indicates that no more entries are available.

3. **Click the plus icon to see entries for the company listed on the gray bar.**

This grouping thing gets really handy if you've been assigning categories to your contacts as you've created items. If you're clever about how you use and add categories that fit the work you do, grouping by category can be a huge timesaver.

If the predefined group views don't meet your needs, you can group items according to just about anything you want, assuming that you've entered the data.

To see the By Category view:

1. **Click the Contacts icon in the Outlook bar.**

   The Contacts view appears.

2. **Choose View⇨Current View⇨By Category.**

   If you've made changes to the current Contacts view, a dialog box appears, asking you to Discard, Save, or Update the Current View. Choose Discard.

   Each gray bar has an icon on the left side with a plus or a minus, followed by Category: *name of Category.* A minus indicates that no entries are hidden under that company's heading; a plus indicates that more entries are available (see Figure 7-15).

3. **Click a plus icon to see more entries for the Category listed on the gray bar.**

Grouping is a good way to manage all Outlook items, especially contacts. After you get a handle on using groups, you'll save a lot of time when you're trying to find things.

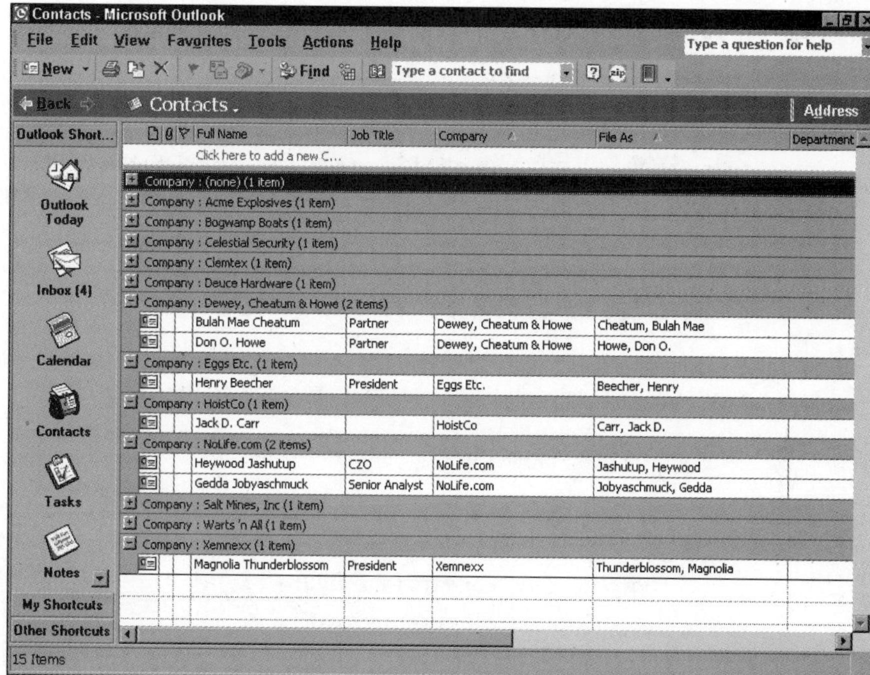

Figure 7-14: The By Company view.

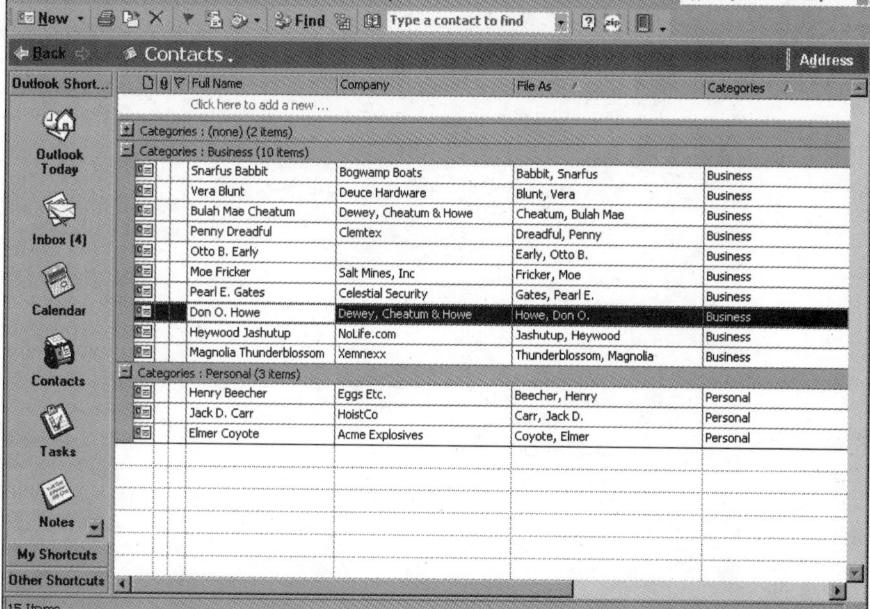

Figure 7-15: In the By Category view, if a plus sign is to the left, you need to click it see more entries.

Flagging Your Friends

Sometimes you need a reminder to do something involving another person. For example, if you promise to call someone a month from now, the best way to help yourself remember is to flag that person's name in the Contact list. A reminder will pop up on the appointed date and prompt you to make the call.

Adding a flag to a contact

E-mail messages aren't the only items that you can flag. You can add reminders to tasks and appointments to achieve the same effect.

To attach a flag to a contact:

1. **With the Contacts screen open, right-click the contact that you want to flag.**

   A shortcut menu appears (see Figure 7-16).

2. **Choose Follow Up.**

   The Flag for Follow Up dialog box appears (see Figure 7-17).

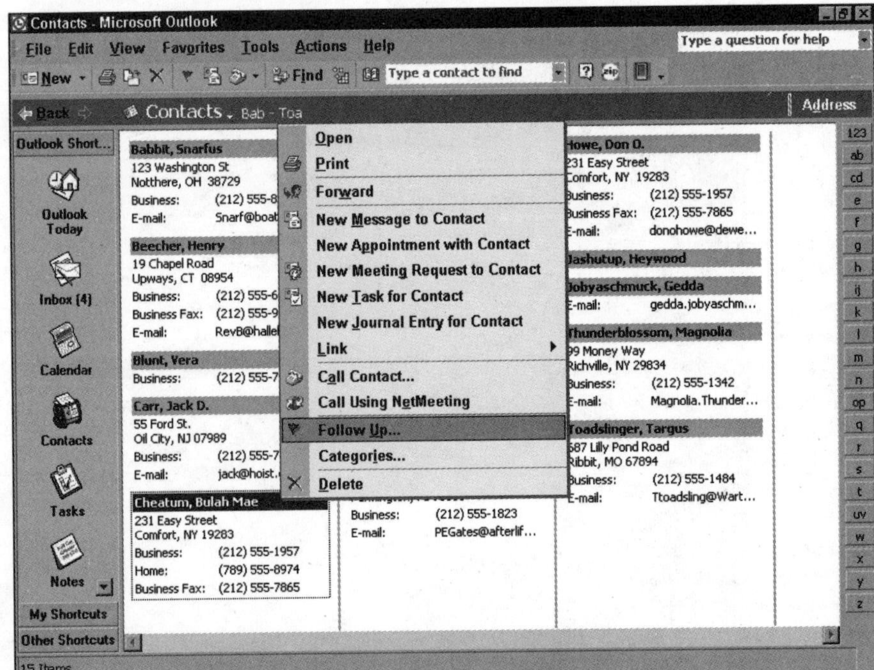

Figure 7-16: Right-click any contact to add a flag.

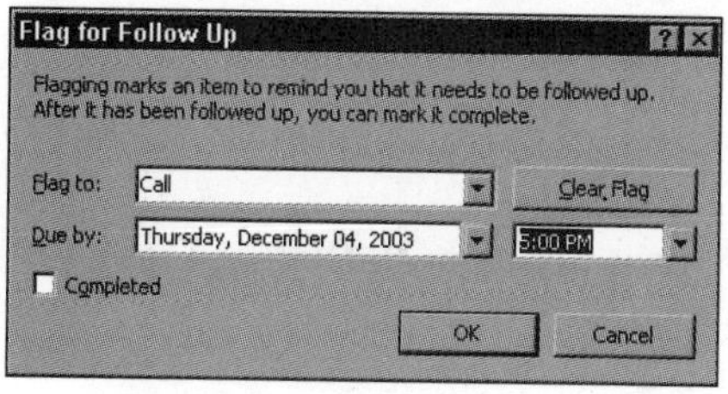

Flag for Follow Up

Flagging marks an item to remind you that it needs to be followed up. After it has been followed up, you can mark it complete.

Flag to: Call — Clear Flag

Due by: Thursday, December 04, 2003 — 5:00 PM

Completed

OK — Cancel

Figure 7-17: Want to flag a friend?

3. **Click the triangle at the right end of the Flag to text box and choose one of the menu items or type your own choice.**

   "Follow up" is a handy flag to remind you to confirm an appointment or other arrangement.

4. **Click the Due by box and type the date on which you want the reminder flag to appear.**

   You can either enter the exact date by typing something like **11/12/98**, or you can type **12 days from now** or **the first Friday of February**. Outlook can even figure out some holidays. If you type **Christmas** or **Valentine's Day**, it knows what you mean and substitutes the date. If you type **Thanksgiving** or **Bastille Day**, Outlook doesn't understand. (Maybe Outlook only remembers holidays that involve gifts. I know people like that.)

5. **Click the box to the right of the Due by box and enter the time of day when you want to be reminded.**

   The time you enter appears in the box.

6. **Click OK.**

When the date you entered in the Flag for Follow Up dialog box arrives, a reminder dialog box pops up to help jog your memory.

Hitting the Snooze button

Even after you instruct Outlook to nag you to pieces with flags and reminders, you can always wait just a teeny bit longer by hitting the Snooze button when your flag pops up. If you usually hit the Snooze button on your alarm clock a few dozen times each morning, you'll understand just how satisfying this feature can be. Unfortunately, Outlook can't play the radio for you while you snooze.

To set a flag to snooze:

1. **Click the scroll-down menu that says "Remind me again in" on the Reminder dialog box.**

   The range of available choices appears, starting at 5 minutes and ending at 1 week (see Figure 7-18).

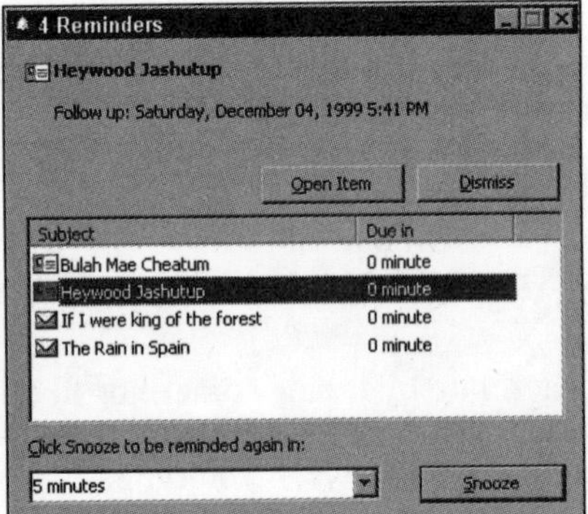

Figure 7-18: A flag reminder popping up to remind you to do something.

2. **Choose the length of time by which you want to delay the reminder.**

   The time you choose appears in the text box.

3. **Click the Snooze button.**

   The Reminder dialog box disappears.

It may seem silly to set a flag to remind you to do something and then put the job off by hitting Snooze. I find it helpful to keep things on the agenda, even while I'm putting them off. I don't really know whether it helps me get more done. I'll check it out and get back to you . . . later.

Using Contact Information

Call me crazy, but I bet that when you enter all that contact information, you plan to use the information some time. I'm sure you'll indulge me while I show you a few ways to dig up and exploit the valuable nuggets you've stashed in your Contacts list.

Finding a contact from any Outlook module

A box on the toolbar with the words "Type a contact to find" can help you dig up a contact record in a jiffy from any Outlook module. Just click the box, type the name of a contact, and press Enter to make Outlook open the record for that contact. If you just type in a fragment of a name, Outlook displays a list of names that contain that fragment and lets you choose which contact you had in mind. For example if you type **Wash**, you'll get George Washington and Sam Washburn and anyone else in your list whose name includes Wash. Double-click the name of the contact record that you want to see.

The Find a Contact box has a scroll-down button (triangle) at the right side. If you click the button, you see a list of the last dozen people you looked up, which is handy when you look for the same people repeatedly. When the list appears, just click the name of the contact you want to see.

Finding contacts in the Contacts module

The whole reason for entering names in a Contact list is so that you can find them again. Otherwise, what's the point of all this rigmarole?

Finding names in the Outlook Contacts module is child's play. The easiest way is to look in the Address Cards view under the last name.

To find a contact by last name:

1. **Click the Contacts icon in the Outlook Bar.**

   Your list of contacts appears.

2. **Choose View⇨Current View⇨Address Cards.**

   The Address Cards view appears (see Figure 7-19).

The Address Cards view has a set of lettered tabs along the right edge. You can click a tab to go to that lettered section, but you can use an easier way: Simply type the first letter of the name you're looking for. For example, if you're looking for Magnolia Thunderblossom (and you've let Outlook make her File As name Thunderblossom, Magnolia), type the letter **T**. You see the names that start with T.

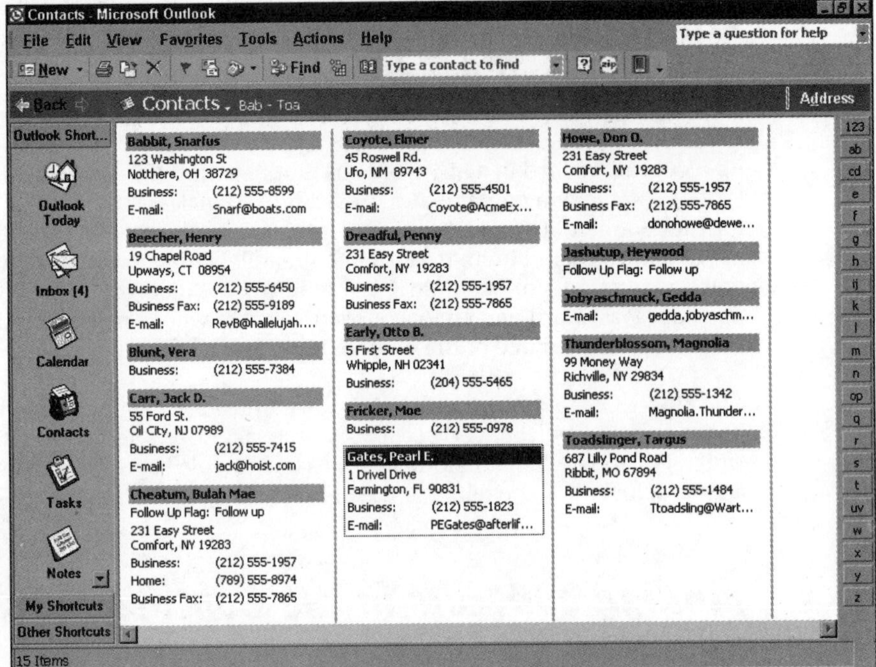

Figure 7-19: The Address Cards view.

Of course, you may need to search for a contact name based on something like the company the contact works for. Or you may want to find all the people on your list who live in a certain state. Or people who put you in a certain state of mind (if you've included that in their Contact record). To do this, use the Find Items tool.

To search for a contact using the Find Items tool:

1. **Click Tools⇨Find on the menu bar (or click the Find button on the Toolbar).**

   The Find window appears (see Figure 7-20).

2. **Type the text that you want to find.**

   If you're looking for your friend George Washington's phone number, type **Washington**.

3. **Press Enter.**

   If your search is successful, a list of contacts that match the text you entered appears below the Find window.

4. **Double-click the name of the contact in the list at the bottom of the screen to see the Contact record.**

   If you get nothing, check to see whether the thing you're searching for is spelled exactly right.

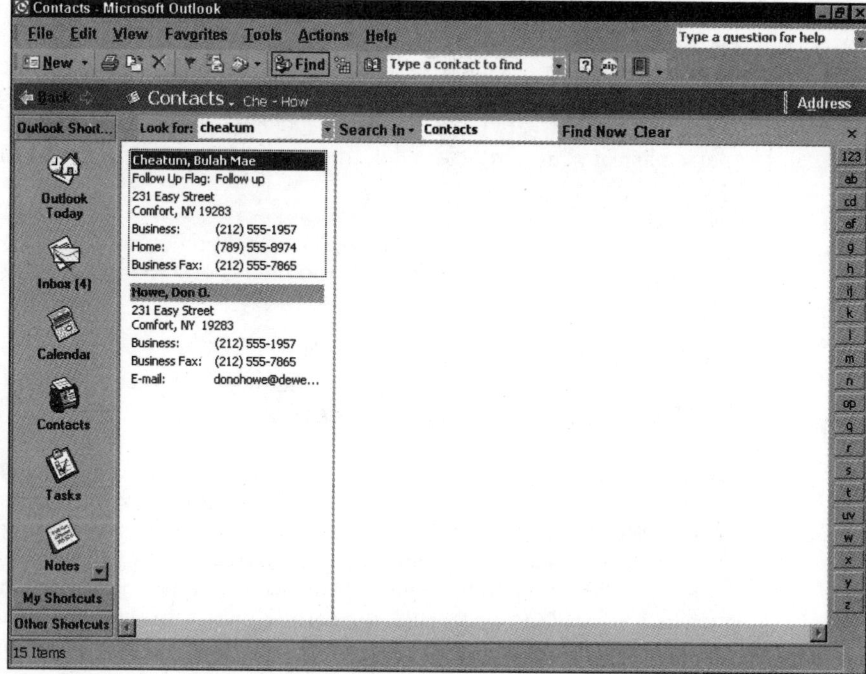

Figure 7-20: Choose what kind of item you're looking for with the Find tool.

Remember, it's hard to be as stupid as computers — close doesn't count with them. If you see Grge Wshngtn, you know to look for George Washington. Not a computer; George would have to have his vowels removed before a computer would see those two words the same way.

On the other hand, if you have only a scrap of the name you're looking for, Outlook can find that scrap wherever it is. A search for "Geo" would turn up George Washington as well as any other Georges in your Contact list, including Phyllis George and George of the Jungle (if they're all such close, personal friends of yours that they're in your Contact list).

Linking contacts to other items

You can attach the name of a contact to any Outlook item (except Notes) so that you can keep track of what you do and for whom you do it. For example, you might want to set up an appointment and include the contact record for the person with whom you're meeting, just in case there's a last-minute change. You can even attach a contact to another contact for situations when two people are related in a way that you need to know. For example, you may want to keep track of who referred each of your active customers so that you can remember to return the favor.

To link a contact to another item, just open the item you want to link and click the Contacts button at the bottom of the form. (If you're linking a contact to an e-mail message, you'll need to choose View➪Options because the Contacts button is located on the Options page of an e-mail message.) When you click the Contacts button, the Select Contacts dialog box opens and displays a list of your contacts. Click the name of the contact you want to add and click OK (see Figure 7-21).

When you open an item to which you've attached contact records, you can jump right to the contact record by double-clicking the name in the Contacts text box.

Using the Activities tab

When you open a contact record, you see a tab named Activities. That's the place to look for a summary of every Outlook item you've associated with that person. When you click the Activities tab, Outlook starts a search for all items linked with your contact. If you have a large collection of Outlook items, the search can take some time. If you're sure you want to find something specific, such as an e-mail message, click the scroll-down button (triangle) next to the word Show and choose the type of item you want. That way Outlook looks only at the kind of items you've specified, and your search will go faster.

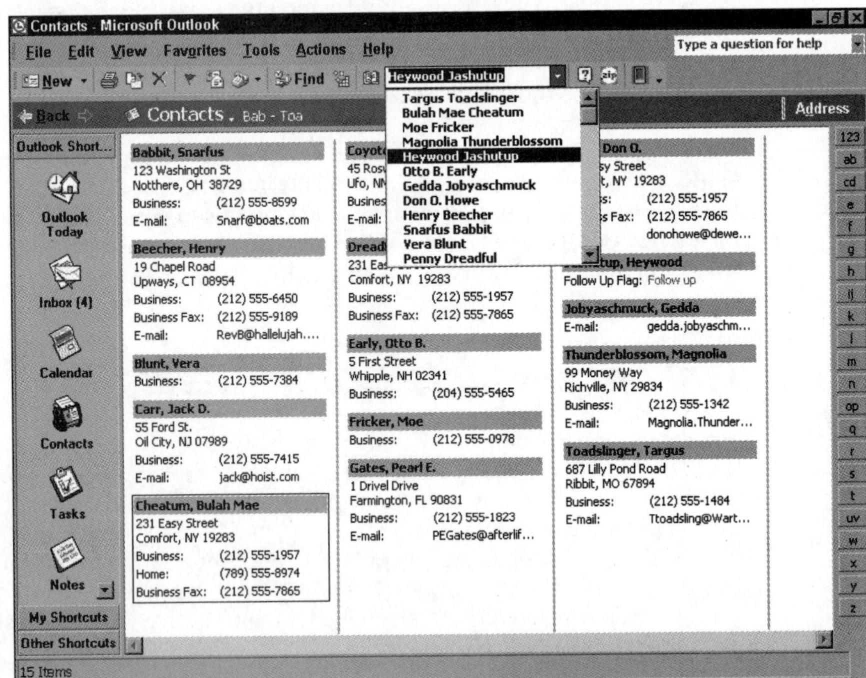

Figure 7-21: The Select Contacts list saves the names you've found most recently.

Sending a business card

Outlook also has the capability to forward an electronic "business card," or *vCard,* to any other person who uses Outlook or any other program that understands how to use a vCard. You can easily send any contact record in your list to anybody by e-mail.

The most obvious thing you may want to send this way is your own contact information. All you need to do is create a contact record for yourself that contains all the information you want to send someone. Then, follow these steps:

1. **Click the Contacts icon in the Outlook Bar.**

   Your list of contacts appears.

2. **Double-click the contact record containing the information you want to send.**

   The contact record you double-clicked opens.

3. **Choose Actions⇨Forward as vCard.**

   A new message form opens with a vCard file attached to the message.

4. **Type the address of the person to whom you want to send the message in the To text box.**

   You can also click the To button and pick a name from the Address Book.

5. **Click the Send button (or press Alt+S).**

   Your message and the attached vCard are sent to your recipient.

When you receive a vCard in an e-mail message, you can add the vCard to your Contact list by double-clicking the icon in the message that represents the vCard to open a new contact record, and then choosing Save and Close to add the name to your Contacts list.

Distribution Lists

You can create a Distribution List in your Contacts module that includes the name of more than one person for those times when you need to send a message to several people simultaneously. You can also assign categories to your Distribution Lists (just as you can with individual contacts), and you can send a Distribution List to other people as an attachment to an e-mail message so that they can use the same list that you do if they also use Outlook 2002.

Creating a Distribution List

Creating a Distribution List is a simple matter of making up a name for your list and choosing from the collection of names you've stored up on your system. A Distribution List doesn't keep track of phone numbers and mailing addresses, just e-mail addresses.

To create a Distribution List in your Contacts module:

1. **Choose File⇨New⇨Distribution List (or press Ctrl+Shift+L).**

   The Distribution List dialog box appears.

2. **Type the name that you want to assign to your Distribution List.**

   The name you type appears in the Name text box.

3. **Click the Select Members button.**

   The Select Members dialog box appears, displaying a list of available names on the left side and a blank box on the right side.

4. **Double-click the name of each person you want to add to your Distribution List.**

   Each name that you double-click appears in the Add to Distribution List column on the right side of the dialog box.

5. **When you're done picking names, click OK.**

   The Select Members dialog box closes.

6. **Click Save and Close (or press Alt+S).**

   The Distribution List dialog box closes and your Distribution List appears in your list of contacts.

When you're creating a Distribution List, you may also want to include the e-mail addresses of people who aren't included in your Contacts list or any of your other Outlook Address books. To do that, click Add New rather than Select Members in Step 4. Enter the name and e-mail address of the person you want to add in the Add New Members dialog box, click OK, and follow the rest of the steps exactly the same way.

Editing a Distribution List

People come and people go in Distribution Lists, just like everywhere else. It's a good thing that you can edit the lists. Just click the Contacts icon in the Outlook Bar and double-click the name of one of your Distribution Lists. Distribution Lists are the entries with a little two-headed icon to the right of their name. When you open a Distribution List entry, you see the same screen you saw when you first created the list. To remove a member of the list, click that name and click the Remove button. To select a new member from the names that are already in your Contact list or Global Address list, click Select Members and follow the same routine you used when you created the list. If you want to add a person whose e-mail address isn't listed in any of your address books, click the Add New button, fill in the person's name and e-mail address, and click OK.

Using a Distribution List

Distribution Lists show up as items in your Contact list just like a person's name, so, as you'd guess, you can use a Distribution List to address an e-mail message just as you would with any contact. You can drag the card for a Distribution List to your Inbox to create a new e-mail message to that list. You can also type the name of the Distribution List in the To line of an e-mail message and click the Check Names button in the toolbar. When Outlook adds an underline to the name in the To box, you know that your message will go to the people on your Distribution List.

Chapter 8

The Calendar: How to Unleash Its Power

In This Chapter

- Using the Date Navigator
- Finding a date (the number kind)
- Making and breaking dates
- Viewing in Calendar
- Printing your appointments

All those precious minutes, and where do they go? Outlook makes your computer the perfect place to solve the problem of too little time in the day. Although Outlook can't give you any extra hours, you can use it to get a better grip on the hours you've got, and it can free those precious minutes that can add up to more hours spent in productive work. If only Outlook could solve the problem of having to do productive work in order to earn a living.

No doubt you've been looking at calendars your whole life, so the Outlook Calendar will be pretty simple for you to understand because it looks like a calendar: plain old rows of dates, Monday through Friday plus weekends, and so on. You don't have to learn to think like a computer to understand your schedule.

If you want to see more information about something in your calendar, most of the time all you have to do is click the calendar with your mouse. If that doesn't give you enough information, click twice. If that doesn't give you everything you're looking for, read on; I fill you in on the fine points. I suspect that the Outlook Calendar will be so easy that you won't need much special training to find it useful.

The Date Navigator: Really Getting Around

The Date Navigator is actually the name of this feature, but don't confuse it with Casanova's chauffeur. The Date Navigator is a trick you can use in Outlook to change the part of the Calendar you're seeing or the time period you want to look at (see Figure 8-1).

Believe it or not, that unassuming little two- or three-month calendar scrap is probably the quickest way to change how you look at the Calendar and make your way around in it. All you have to do is click the date you want to see, and it opens in all its glory. It couldn't be simpler.

To use the Date Navigator:

1. **Choose View⇨Go To⇨Calendar.**

   The Calendar appears.

2. **Choose View⇨Current View⇨Day/Week/Month.**

   The Date Navigator appears as a small calendar in the upper-right corner.

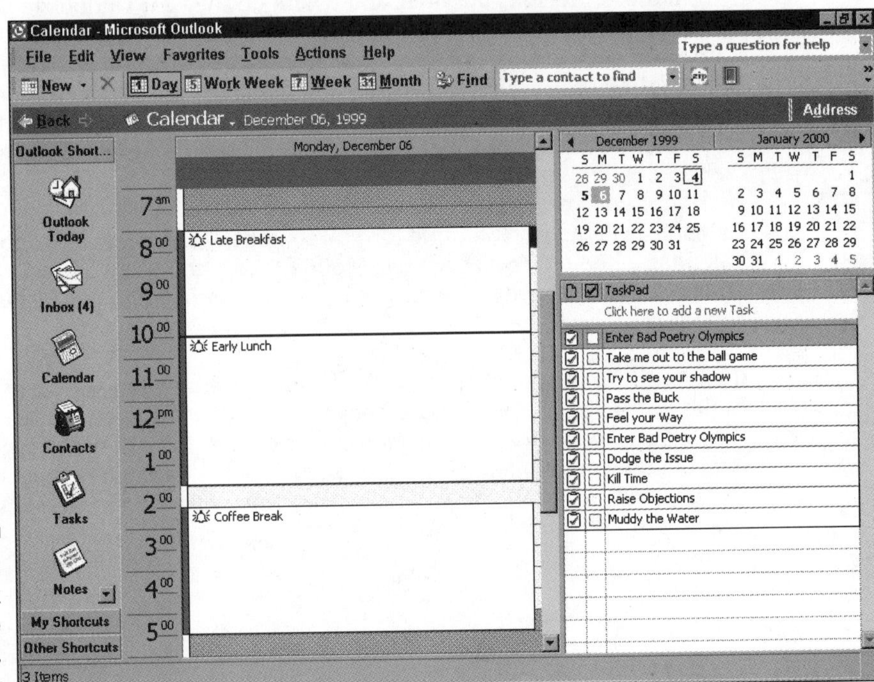

Figure 8-1: The Outlook Date Navigator.

- To see details of a single date, click that day in the Date Navigator. You see the appointments and events scheduled for the day you clicked.
- To see a full-month view, click one of the letters (SMTWTFS) at the top of the months.
- To see a week's view, move the mouse pointer just to the left of the week you want to see. When the arrow points up and to the right rather than up and to the left, click it.
- As time goes by (so to speak), you'll find that you gravitate to the Calendar view that suits you best. I like the Seven Day view because it includes both Calendar and Task information in a screen that's pretty easy to read. You can leave Outlook running most of the time in order to keep the information you need handy.

Time travel isn't just science fiction. You can zip around the Outlook calendar faster than you can say "Buck Rogers." Talk about futuristic; the Outlook calendar can schedule appointments for you well into the year 4500! Think about it: Between now and then are more than 130,000 Saturday nights! That's the good news. There are also more than 130,000 Monday mornings. Of course, in our lifetimes, you and I have to deal with only about 5,000 Saturday nights at most, so we have to make good use of them. Better start planning.

So when you need to find an open date fast:

1. **Choose View⇨Go To⇨Go To Date (or press Ctrl+G).**

   A dialog box appears with a date highlighted.

2. **To go to another date, type the date you want as you normally would, such as** January 15, 1998, **or** 1/15/98.

   A really neat way to change dates is to type something like **45 days ago** or **93 days from now** (see Figure 8-2). Try it. Outlook understands simple English when it comes to dates. Don't get fancy, though — Outlook doesn't understand **Four score and seven years ago**. But who does?

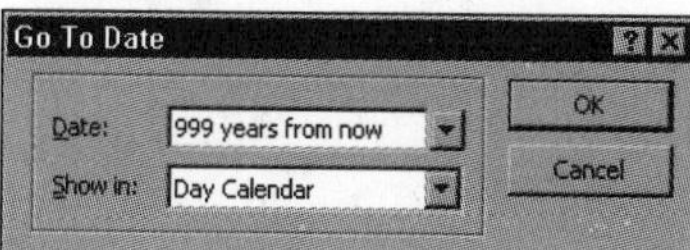

Figure 8-2: The Go To Date dialog box.

If you want to go to today's date, choose View⇨Go To⇨Go To Today. No matter which date you land on, you can plunge right in and start scheduling. You can double-click the time and date of when you want an appointment to occur and then enter the particulars, or you can double-check details of an appointment on that date by double-clicking the date and making changes to the appointment if necessary. You can also do something silly like find out what day of the week your birthday falls on 1,000 years from now. Mine's on Saturday. Don't forget.

Meetings Galore: Scheduling Appointments

Many people live and die by their datebooks. The paper type of datebook is still popular, being the easiest to put stuff in (although after it's in, the stuff can be a pain to find). Outlook makes it easier to add appointments than most computer calendars do, and Outlook makes it a whole lot easier to find things after you've entered them. It also warns you when you've scheduled two dates simultaneously. (Very embarrassing!)

The quick and dirty way to enter an appointment

Some appointments don't need much explanation. If you're having lunch with Mom on Friday, there's no reason to make a big production out of entering the appointment. When you're looking at a view of your Calendar that shows the hours of the day in a column, such as the Workweek view, just click the starting time of your appointment and type a description, such as **Lunch with Mom**, and press Enter. Your appointment is now part of your official schedule faster than you can say "Waiter!"

The complete way to enter an appointment

Appointments that you set up at work often require you to include a little more information than you'd need for your lunch date with Mom. You might want to add details about the location of a meeting and some notes about the meeting agenda; you might also want to assign a category to a meeting so that you can show the boss how much time you spend with your clients. When you want to give an appointment the full-Monty treatment, use the complete method.

To schedule an appointment the complete way:

1. **Choose File⇨New from the menu bar.**

   The New Item menu appears (see Figure 8-3).

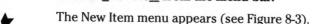

   You may notice Ctrl+N next to the word *Appointment.* If you press Ctrl+N in any section of Outlook, a dialog box appears to let you create a new item in that section.

   Press Ctrl+Shift+A from any section of Outlook to create an appointment. The catch is that you won't see the appointment on the calendar until you switch to the Calendar view.

2. **Choose Appointment.**

   The Appointment form opens (see Figure 8-4).

3. **Click in the Subject box and type something there to help you remember what the appointment's about.**

   Type **Dentist appointment** or **Receive Oscar** or whatever. This text shows up on your calendar.

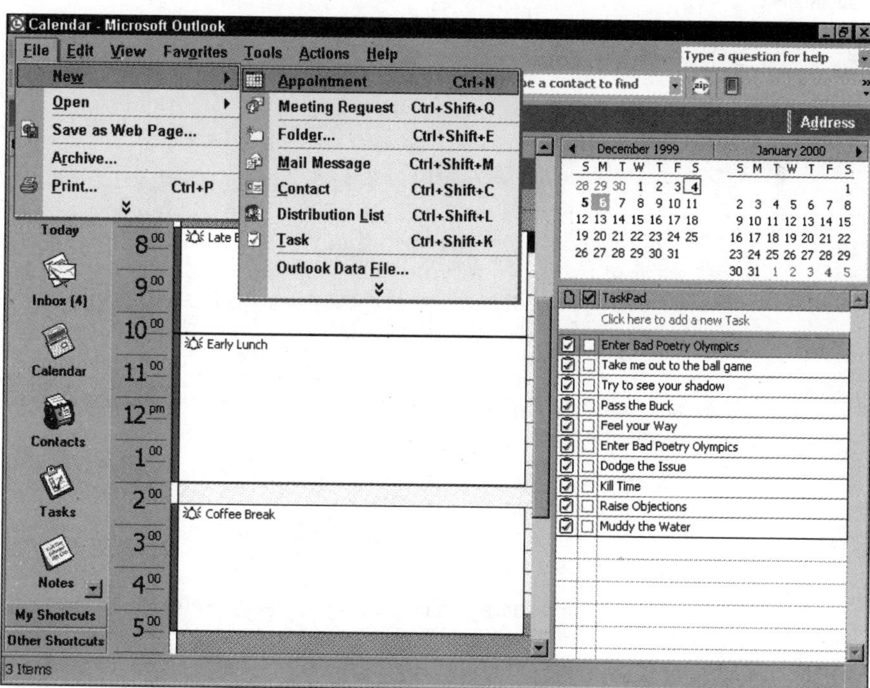

Figure 8-3: Creating a new appointment.

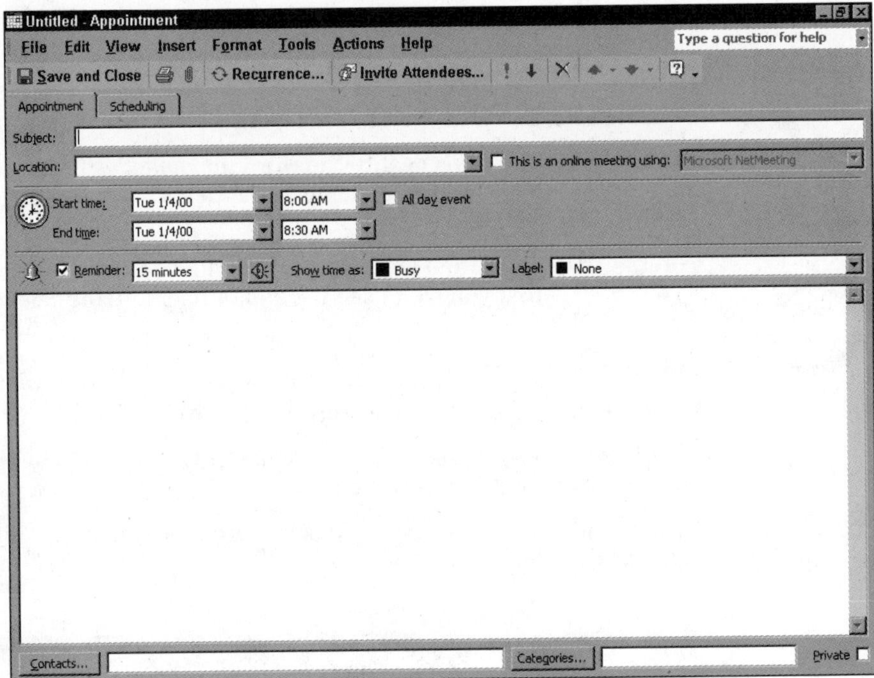

Figure 8-4: The Appointment form.

4. **Click in the Location box and enter the location.**

   Notice the little triangle (scroll bar button) at the right side of the box. If you click the triangle, you see a list of the last few locations where you scheduled appointments so that you can use the same places repeatedly without having to retype them. Another advantage to having this recallable list of locations is that it makes entering locations easy. That way, you can sort your list of appointments according to location to see, for example, whether conference rooms are free.

5. **If you want Outlook to remind you of your appointment, click the Reminder box.**

   Choose how far in advance you want Outlook to notify you of an upcoming appointment. You can set the amount yourself by typing it in, or you can click the scroll-down button and choose a predetermined length from the Reminder box.

   - If you want a sound to play as a reminder, click the sound icon next to the Reminder box to see the Reminder Sound dialog box, as shown in Figure 8-5. (If you don't have a sound card, you won't be able to hear a sound.)
   - If the appointment is tentative, click the scroll-down button to the right of the Show Time As menu and choose Tentative.

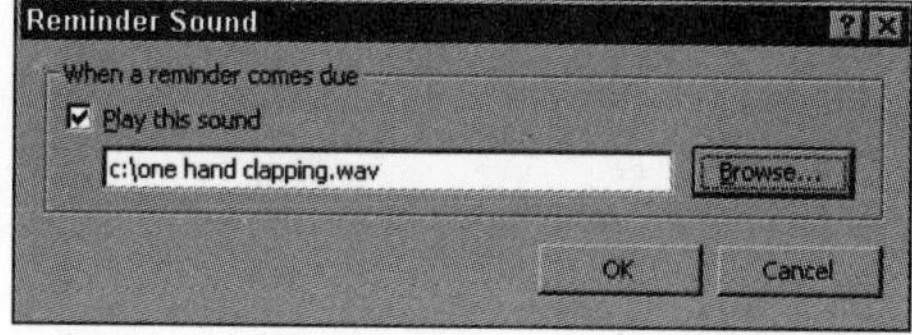

Figure 8-5: Pick a sound.

- You can also mark the appointment as Free, Busy, or Out of Office. (Out of Mind is not an option yet.)

If you're using Outlook on an office network, other people may be able to see your schedule in order to plan meetings with you. Designations, such as Free, Busy, or Out of Office, let coworkers who can view your schedule know whether you're available for a meeting.

- If you need to remember more information about this appointment, type the information in the text box at the bottom of the dialog box: directions to a new client's office, books for school, the Declaration of Independence, whatever turns you on.

6. **Click the Categories button at the bottom to assign a category to the appointment if you like.**

   Using the Categories dialog box (see Figure 8-6) is another trick for finding things easily.

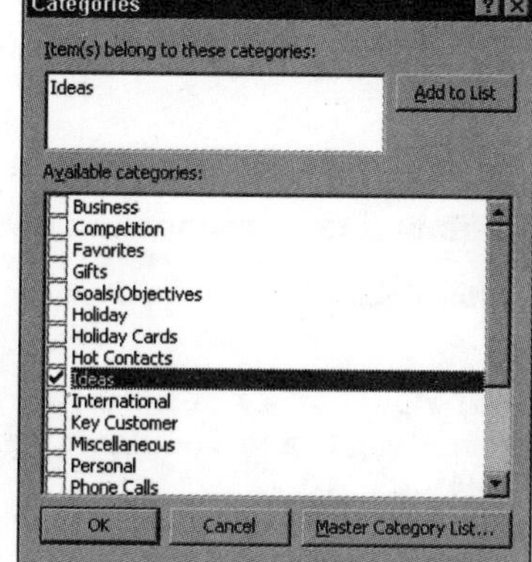

Figure 8-6: The Categories dialog box.

7. **Choose an existing category, if one suits you, and then click OK.**

8. **If none of the existing categories suits you, click the Master Category List button at the bottom right of the Categories dialog box.**

   The Master Category List dialog box appears (see Figure 8-7).

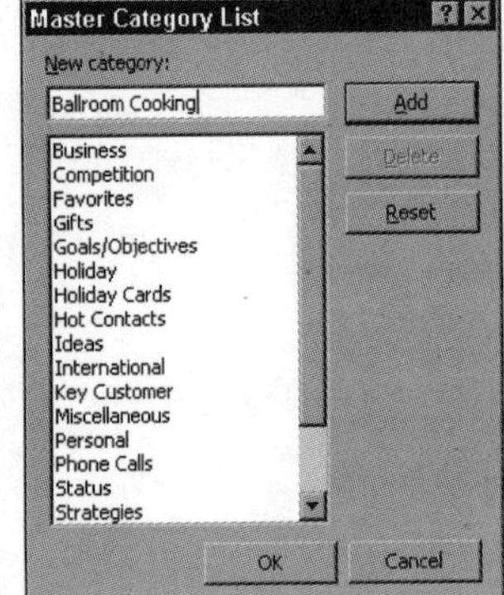

Figure 8-7: The Master Category List dialog box.

9. **Type a category of your choice in the New category box.**

   Be sure not to add too many new categories, because you could have a hard time finding things.

10. **Click Add and click OK.**

    You're now back in the Categories dialog box, with the new category added to the list.

11. **Select the new category from the Available Categories list and then click OK.**

    You can select more than one category at a time.

12. **Click the Contacts button if you want to link your appointment to a specific name in your Contacts list.**

    The Select Contacts dialog box appears.

13. **Double-click the name you want to link to your appointment.**

    The Select Contacts dialog box closes, and the name you chose appears in the Contacts text box.

14. **Click the Private box in the lower-right corner of the New Appointment form if you're on a network, and you don't want others to know about your appointments.**

15. **Click Save and then Close.**

    The appointment you created appears in the Active Appointments view (see Figure 8-8).

You may have to change your view of the Calendar by clicking the Date Navigator on the date the appointment occurs so that you can see your new appointment.

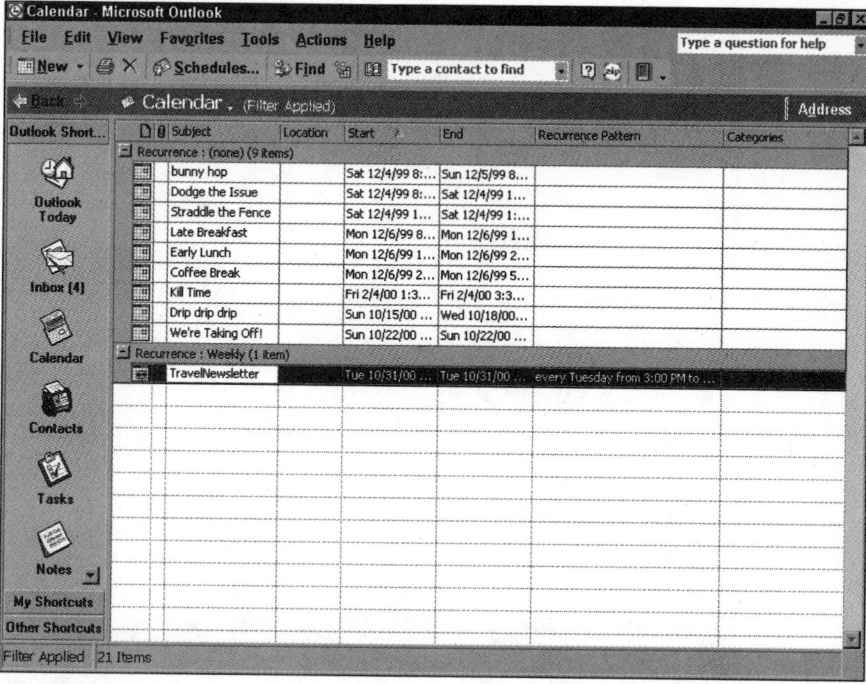

Figure 8-8: The Active Appointments view of the Calendar module.

If you're using reminders for all your important appointments, you must have Outlook running so that the reminder pops up. You can keep Outlook running in the background if you start up a second program, such as Microsoft Word. When the reminder time arrives, you either see a dialog box or a message from the Office Assistant like the one in Figure 8-9.

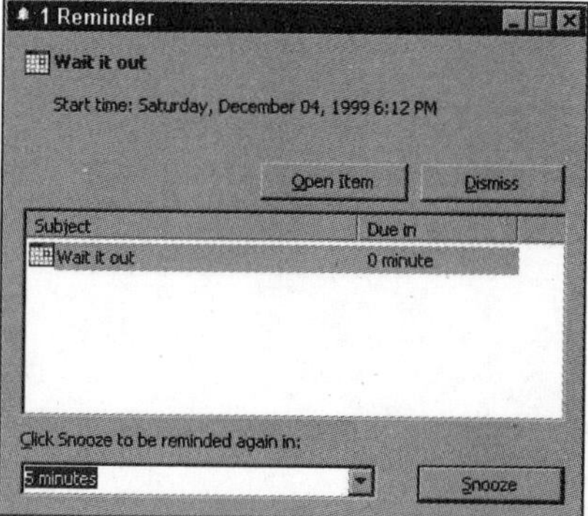

Figure 8-9: A dialog box pops up to remind you of your appointment.

Not this time: Changing dates

You can be as fickle as you want with Outlook. In fact, to change the time of a scheduled item, all you do is drag the appointment from where it is to where you want it to be (see Figure 8-10). Or back again . . . maybe . . . if you feel like it. . . .

To change an appointment:

1. **Click the appointment in the Calendar view.**

   A blue bar appears at the left edge of the appointment.

2. **Place the mouse pointer over the blue bar.**

   The mouse pointer turns into a little four-headed arrow.

3. **Drag the appointment to the time or date where you want it to be.**

   If you're in the One-Day view, drag an appointment to a different date on one of the small calendars in the upper right.

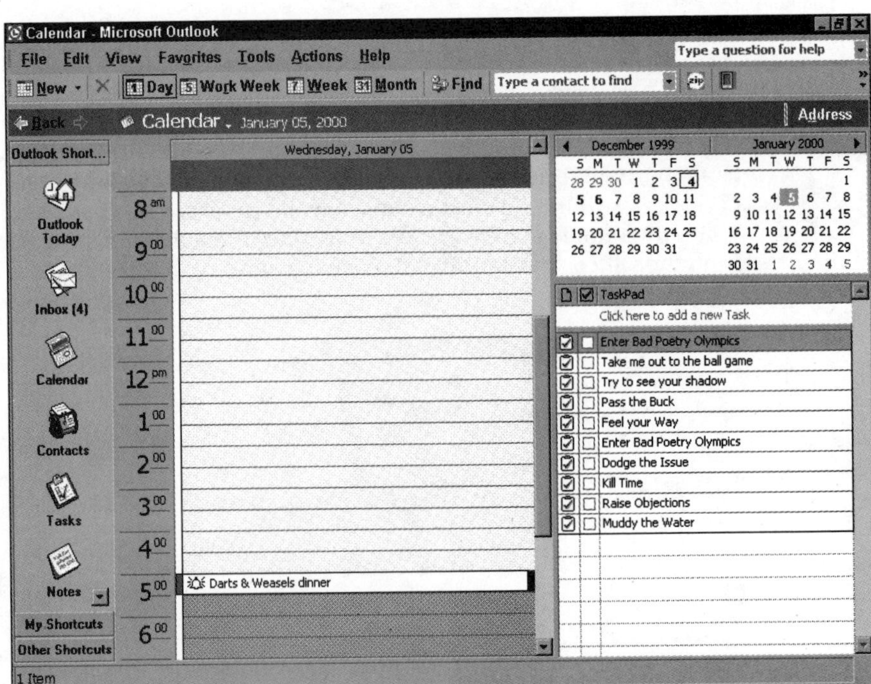

Figure 8-10: If your appointment is a drag, drop it in a new time slot.

If you want to create a copy of an appointment for another time, hold down the Ctrl key while you use the mouse to drag the appointment to another time or date. For example, if you're scheduling a Summer Intern Orientation from 9 a.m. to 11 a.m. and 1 p.m. to 3 p.m., you can create the 9 a.m. appointment and then copy it to 1 p.m. by holding Ctrl and dragging the appointment. Then you have two appointments with the same subject, location, and date, but different hours.

If you copy an appointment to a different date by dragging the appointment to a date on the Date Navigator, you retain the hour of the appointment but change the date.

If you want to change an appointment to a date you can't see on the Calendar:

1. **Double-click the appointment.**

   The Appointment dialog box opens.

2. **Click in the leftmost Start time block and then click the scroll-down button to the right of the date to pull down a calendar (see Figure 8-11).**

3. **Pick the month by clicking one of the triangles beside the month's name.**

   Clicking the left triangle moves you one month earlier; clicking the right triangle moves you one month later.

4. **Click the day of the month you want.**

5. **Click in the rightmost Start Time text box and enter the appointment's new time, if needed.**

6. **Make any other changes you need in the appointment by clicking on the information you want to change and typing the revised information over it.**

7. **Click Save and Close.**

To change the length of an appointment:

1. **Click the appointment.**

2. **Move the mouse pointer over the lines at the top or bottom of the appointment.**

   When it's in the right place, the mouse pointer turns into a two-headed arrow that you can use to drag the lines of the appointment box.

3. **Drag the bottom line down to make the appointment time longer; drag the bottom line up to make the appointment shorter.**

   You can change an appointment's length only by dragging in multiples of 30 minutes (see Figure 8-12).

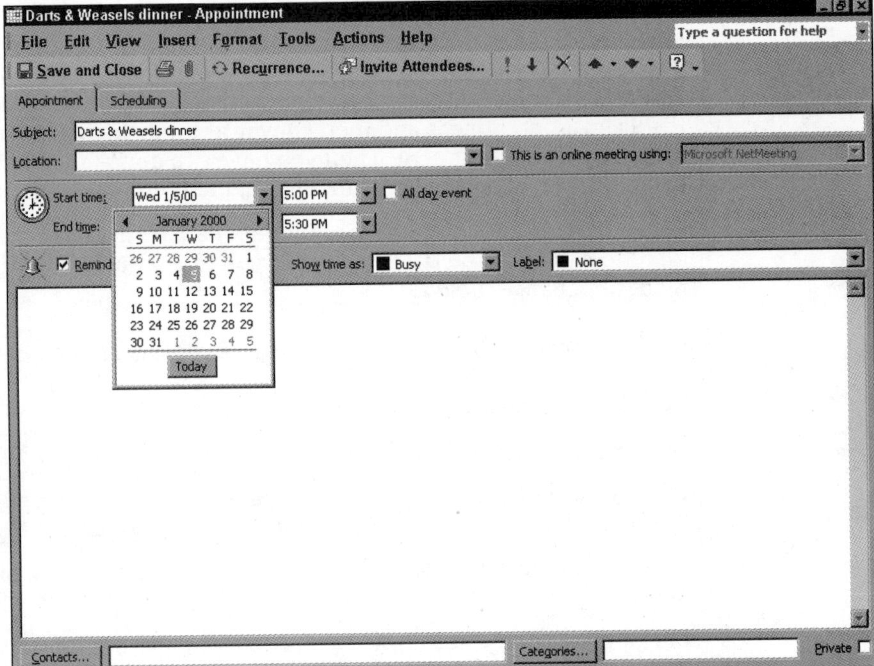

Figure 8-11: The pull-down Calendar in the Appointment form.

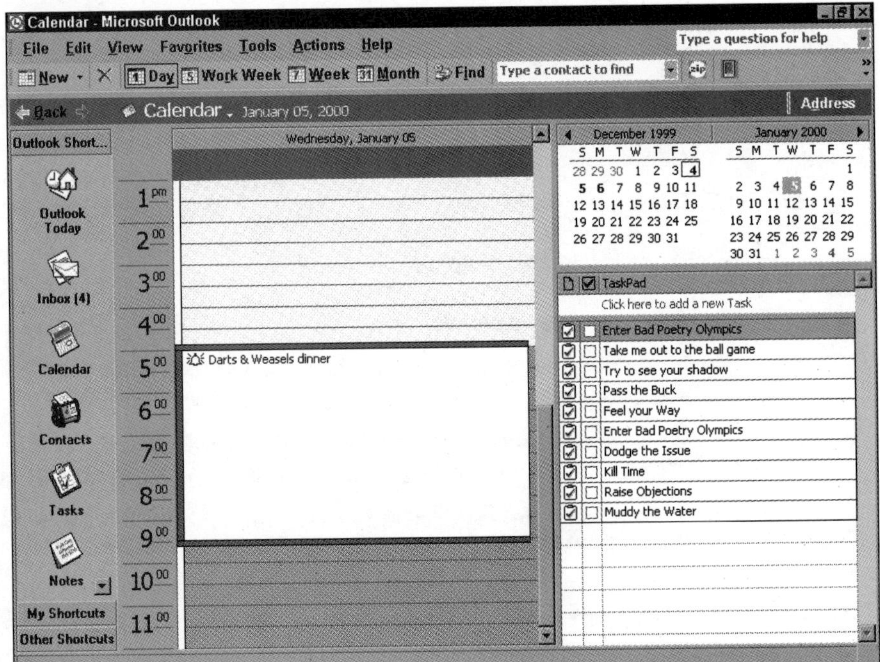

Figure 8-12: The thick, dark line shows an appointment being lengthened.

To shorten an appointment to less than 30 minutes:

1. **Double-click the appointment and click the End Time box.**
2. **Type the ending time.**
3. **Click Save and Close.**

You can enter times in Outlook without adding colons and often without using a.m. or p.m. Outlook translates **443** as 4:43 p.m. If you plan lots of appointments at 4:43 a.m., just type **443A**. Just don't call *me* at that hour, okay?

Not ever: Breaking dates

Well, sometimes things just don't work out. Sorry about that. Even if it's hard for you to forget, with the click of a mouse Outlook deletes dates that you otherwise fondly remember. Okay, two clicks of a mouse. *C'est la vie, c'est l'amour, c'est la guerre.* (Look for my next book, *Tawdry French Clichés.*)

To delete an appointment (after you've called to break it, of course):

1. **Right-click the appointment (that is, click with the right mouse button).**
2. **Click Delete.**

   Your appointment has been canceled.

The Ctrl+D combination you see next to the Delete command means that you can delete the appointment in just one keystroke. How cold.

We've got to keep seeing each other: Recurring dates

Some appointments are like a meal at a Chinese restaurant; as soon as you're done with one, you're ready for another. With Outlook, you can easily create an appointment that comes back like last night's spicy Szechwan noodles.

To create a recurring appointment (that is, an appointment that's regularly scheduled):

1. **Choose View⇨Go To⇨Calendar.**

   The Calendar appears.
2. **Click the New tool icon at the left end of the toolbar (see Figure 8-13).**

   The Appointment form appears (refer to Figure 8-4). Yeah, I know. I do it differently earlier in the chapter when I tell you how to create an appointment the first time. This way is the *really* easy way to create a new appointment.

3. **Click the Subject box and enter the subject.**
4. **Click the Location box and enter the location.**
5. **If you want Outlook to remind you, click the Reminder box.**
   - Choose how far in advance you want Outlook to remind you.
   - If you want a sound to play as a reminder, click the sound icon.
6. **Click the Actions menu.**

   The Actions menu drops down (see Figure 8-14).

7. **Choose Recurrence.**

   The letters Ctrl+G next to the Recurrence command mean that you can also create the recurring appointment with just that one keystroke.

   The Appointment Recurrence dialog box appears (see Figure 8-15).

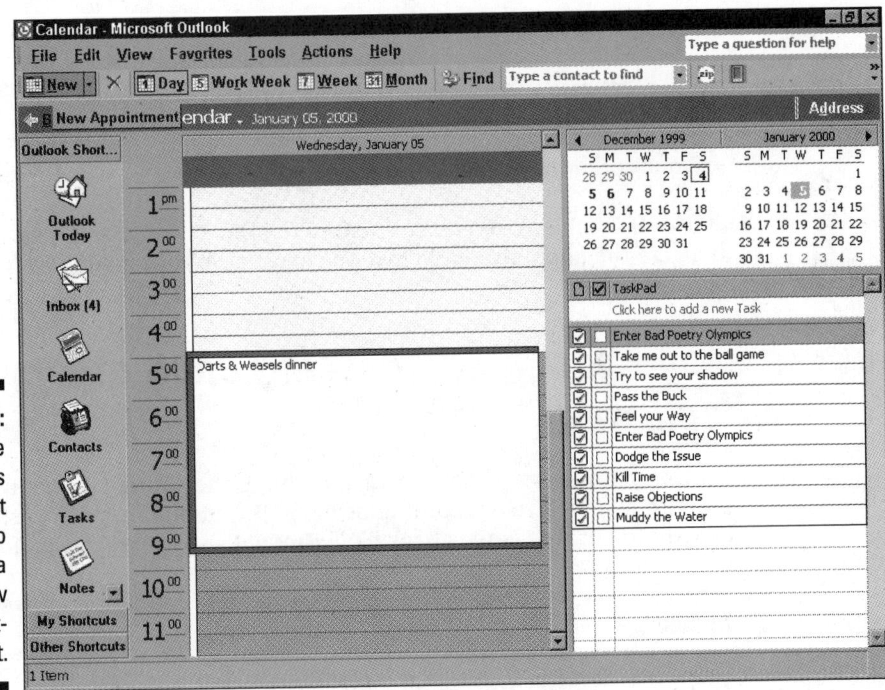

Figure 8-13: Clicking the New tool is the easiest way to create a new appointment.

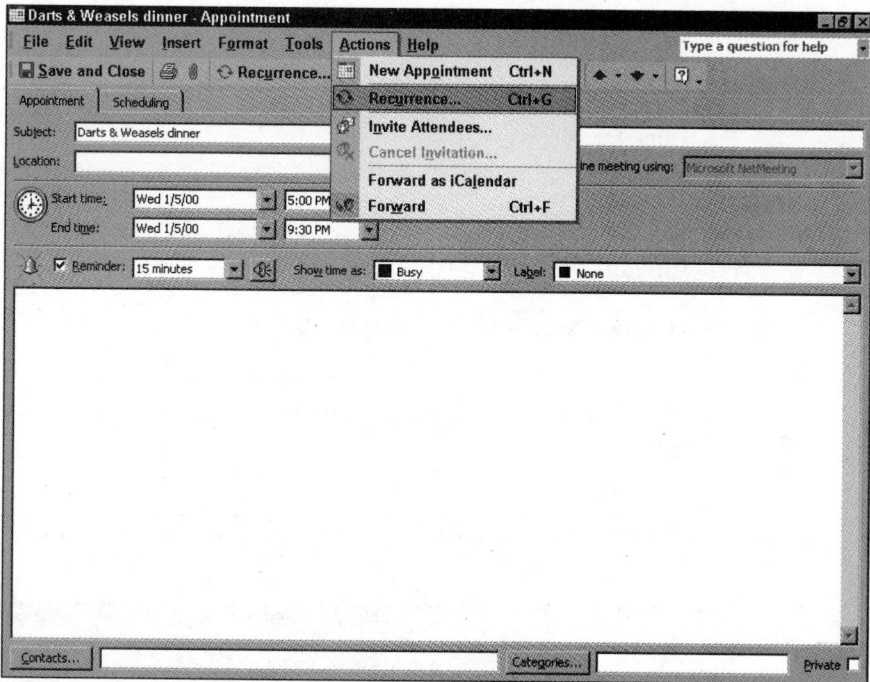

Figure 8-14: The Actions menu.

Figure 8-15: The Appointment Recurrence dialog box.

8. **Click the End text box and enter the ending time.**

9. **In the Recurrence Pattern box, click the Daily, Weekly, Monthly, or Yearly option button to select how often the appointment recurs.**

10. **In the next part of the Recurrence Pattern box, choose how often the appointment occurs.**

11. **In the Range of Recurrence box, enter the first occurrence in the Start box.**

12. **Choose when the appointments will stop.**

    You can select No End Date, End After a certain number of occurrences, or End By a certain date.

13. **Click OK.**
14. **Click Save and Close.**

Even a recurring appointment gets changed once in awhile. To edit a recurring appointment:

1. **Double-click the appointment you want to edit.**

   The Open Recurring Item dialog box appears.

2. **Choose whether you want to change just the occurrence you clicked or the whole series.**
3. **Click OK.**

   The Recurring Appointment dialog box appears (see Figure 8-16).

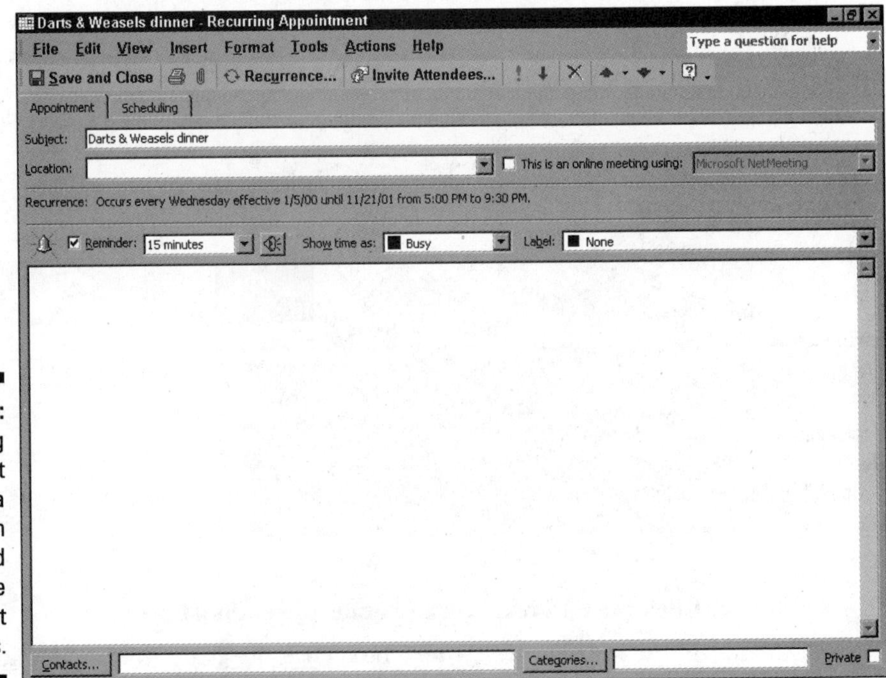

Figure 8-16: A Recurring Appointment includes a description of how and when the appointment recurs.

4. **Edit the details of the appointment.**

   To change the recurrence pattern, click Actions➪Recurrence. Then change the recurrence pattern and click OK.

5. **Click Save and Close.**

I find it helpful to enter regular appointments, such as classes or regular recreational events, even if I'm sure I won't forget them. Entering all my activities into Outlook prevents me from scheduling conflicting appointments.

Getting a Good View of Your Calendar

Outlook lets you slice and dice the information in every section nearly any way you can imagine, using different views. You could easily fill a cookbook with different views you can create, but I'm going to stick to the standard ways of looking at a calendar that most people are used to. If you want to cook up a calendar arrangement that nobody's ever thought of before, Outlook will probably let you. That's okay; if you accidentally create a Calendar view you don't like, you can delete it.

The basic Calendar views are the Daily view, shown in Figure 8-17, the Weekly view, shown in Figure 8-18, and the Monthly view, shown in Figure 8-19.

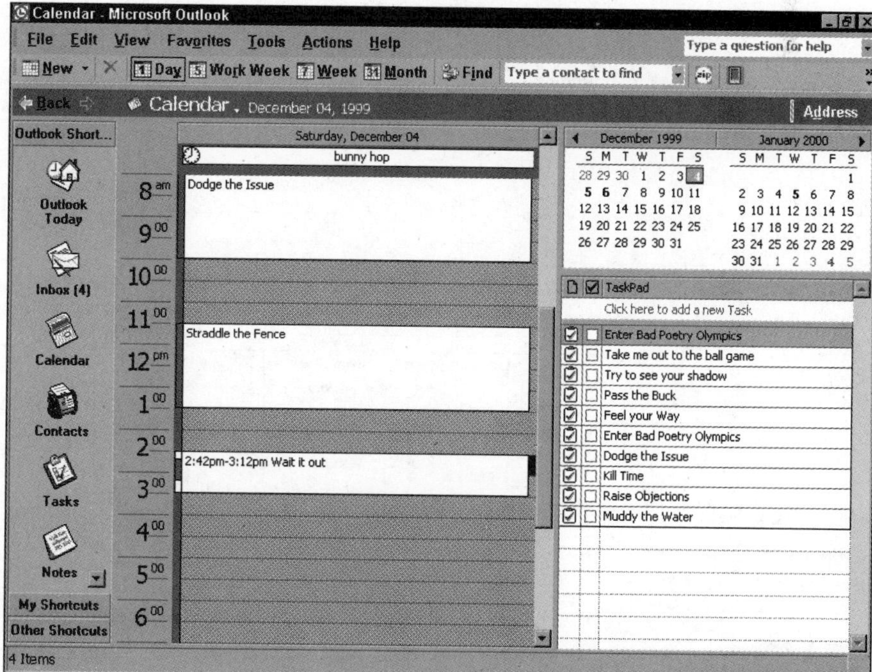

Figure 8-17: The Daily view.

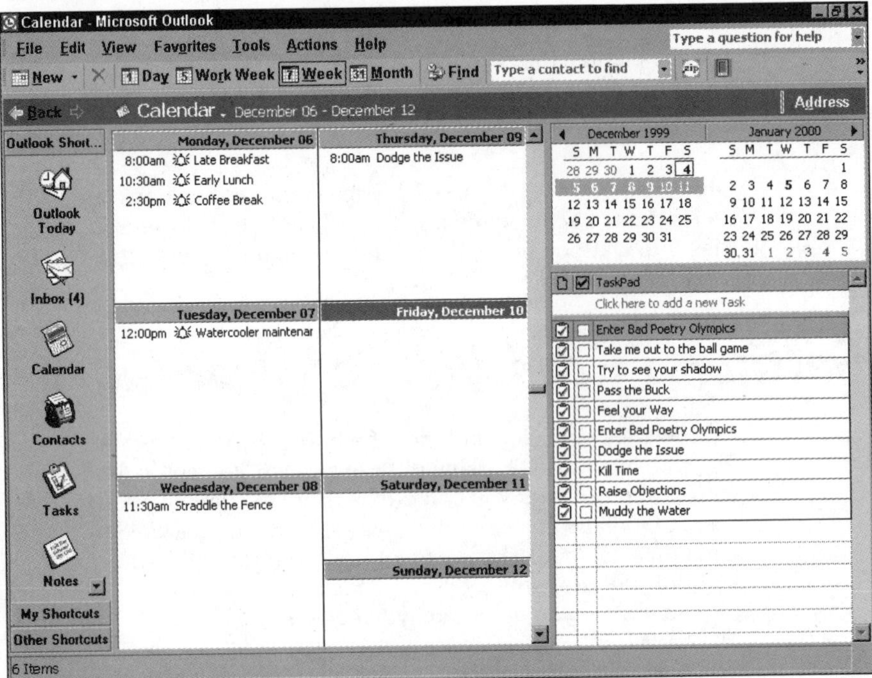

Figure 8-18: The Weekly view

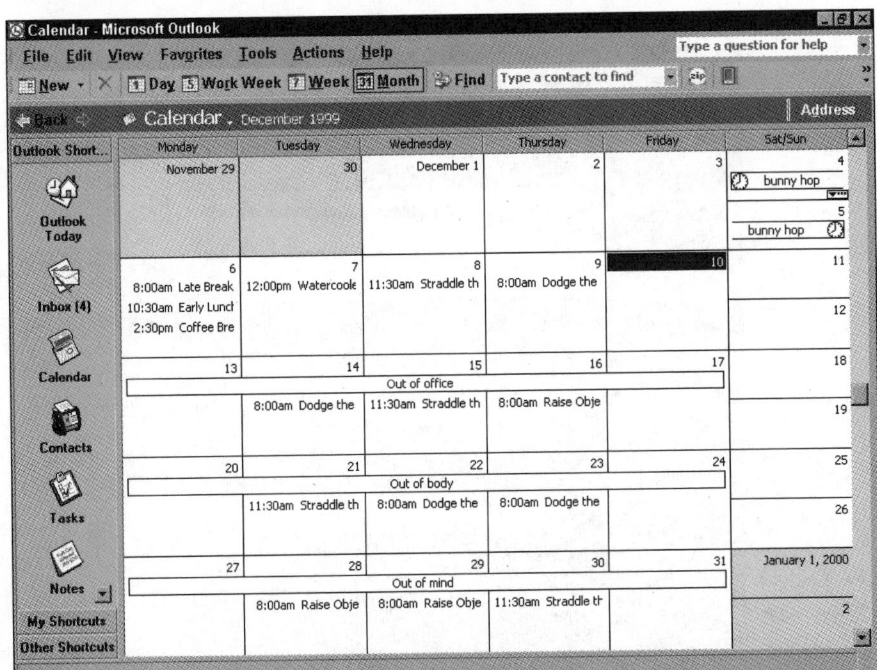

Figure 8-19: The Monthly view.

Other views of the Calendar, such as the Active Appointments view, are helpful when you're trying to figure out when you did something or when you will do something.

To view Active Appointments:

1. **Choose View⇨Current View.**

   The View menu appears.

2. **Choose Active Appointments.**

   You see a list of appointments yet to come.

In Active Appointments view (see Figure 8-20), you can see details of appointments that you have coming up in a list that's easy to read. You can also sort the view on any column, such as Location, Subject, or Start date, by clicking the column's title.

The Active Appointments view is only one of a half-dozen preprogrammed views that come with Outlook. Pull down the menu and try each of the other choices: You've seen the Daily/Weekly/Monthly view, which lets you look at your schedule in the familiar calendar layout. Events view shows you items that last more than a day. Annual Events shows the list of items that last more than a day and return at the same time each year. Recurring is the view of appointments that you've set up to repeat themselves. By Category view groups your appointments according to the category that you assigned them to.

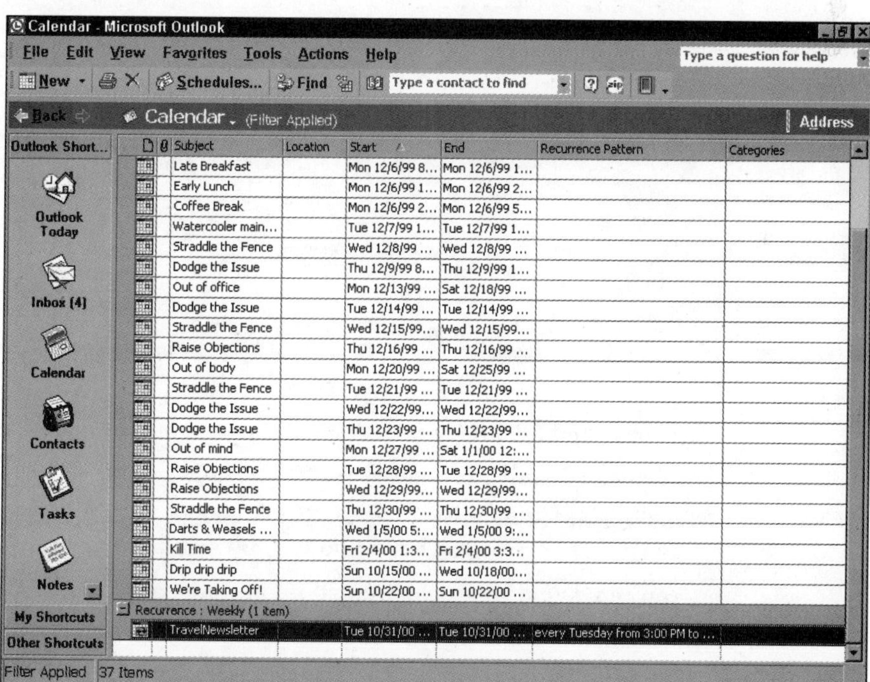

Figure 8-20: The Active Appointments view.

Printing Your Appointments

Plain old paper is still everybody's favorite medium for reading. No matter how slick your computer organizer is, you may still need old-fashioned ink-on-paper to make it really useful. You use the same basic steps to print from any module in Outlook. Here's how to print your appointments:

1. **Click a date within the range of dates you want to print.**

   If you want to print a single day, click just one day (see Figure 8-21). If you want to print a range of dates, click the first date and then hold the Shift key and click the last date in the range. The whole range is then highlighted to show which dates you've selected.

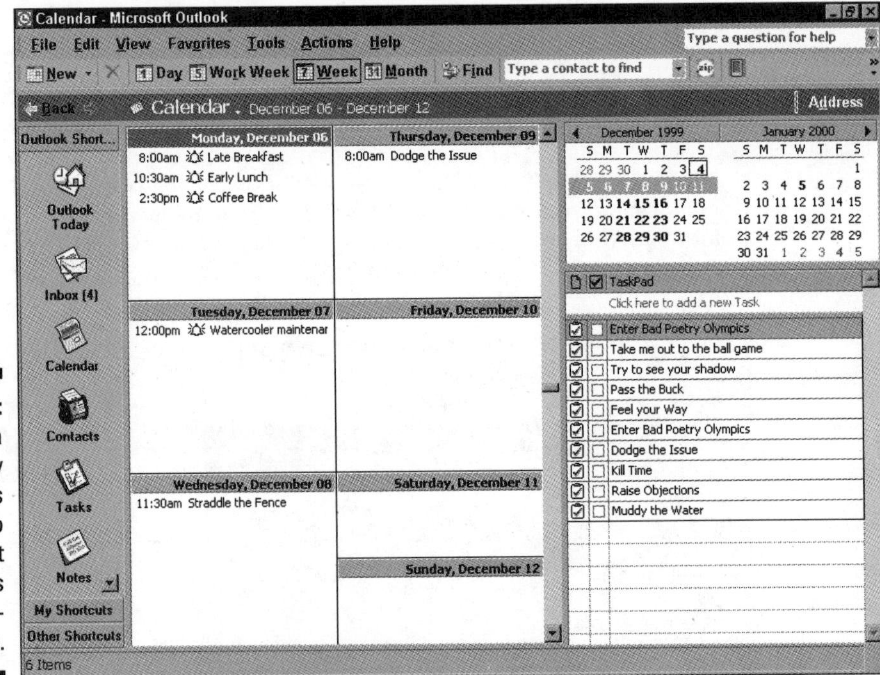

Figure 8-21: Click a single day and press Ctrl+P to print that day's appointments.

2. **Choose File➪Print (or press Ctrl+P).**

   The Print dialog box appears (see Figure 8-22).

3. **In the Print Style group, choose Daily, Weekly, Monthly, Trifold, Memo, or any other style you want that may be available in your Style box.**

   You can define your own print styles in Outlook, so you may eventually have quite a collection of choices here.

Scheduling your main events

You can enter more than just appointments in your calendar. You can also add events by clicking the All Day Event check box in the Appointment form, or you can begin by choosing Actions⇨New All Day Event and follow the same steps you use to create an appointment. (Refer to the section "Meetings Galore: Scheduling Appointments," earlier in this chapter.)

Events allow you to add things to your calendar, such as business trips or conferences that last longer than an appointment, while still letting you quickly enter routine appointments that may take place at the event. For example, you can create an event called "2005 Auto Show" and then add appointments to see General Motors at 9 a.m., Chrysler at noon, and Ford at 3 p.m.

4. **In the Print Range box, set the range of dates you want to print.**

   Because you began by clicking a date in that range, it should already be correct. If it's not correct, you can change the range in the Print dialog box to the print range you want.

5. **Click OK.**

   Your dates are sent to the printer.

Clicking the Print icon on the toolbar is another handy way to start the print process. The icon looks like a tiny printer.

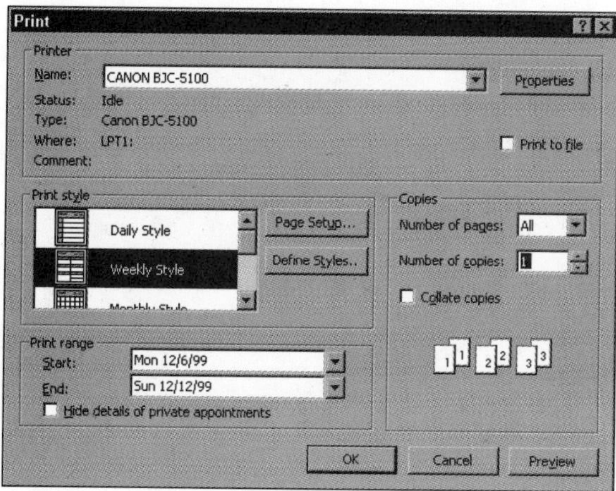

Figure 8-22: The Print dialog box.

Chapter 9

Task Mastery: Discovering All the Bells and Whistles

In This Chapter

- Entering a new task
- Changing, copying, and deleting tasks
- Creating recurring and regenerating tasks
- Completing tasks
- Using views

You can store and manage more information about your daily tasks in Outlook than you may have wanted to know, but you'll certainly find that Outlook makes it easy to remember and monitor your daily work. Organizing your tasks doesn't have to be a task in itself.

Some people say that work expands to fill the available time, and chances are that your boss is one of those people. Who else would keep expanding your work all the time? One way of saving time is to keep a list of the tasks that are filling your time. That way, you can avoid getting too many more tasks to do.

I used to scrawl a to-do list on paper and hope I'd find the list in time to do the things I had written down. Now Outlook pops up and reminds me of the things I'm trying to forget to do just before I forget to do them. It also keeps track of when I'm supposed to have done my daily tasks and when I actually did them. That way, I can use all the things I was supposed to do yesterday as an excuse not to do the things I'm supposed to do today. (Outlook still won't do the stuff for me — it just tells me how far I'm falling behind. Be forewarned.)

Using the Outlook Tasks List

The Outlook Tasks list is easy to recognize as an electronic version of the good old plain-paper, scribbled to-do list. It's every bit as simple as it looks: a list of tasks and a list of dates for doing the tasks (see Figure 9-1).

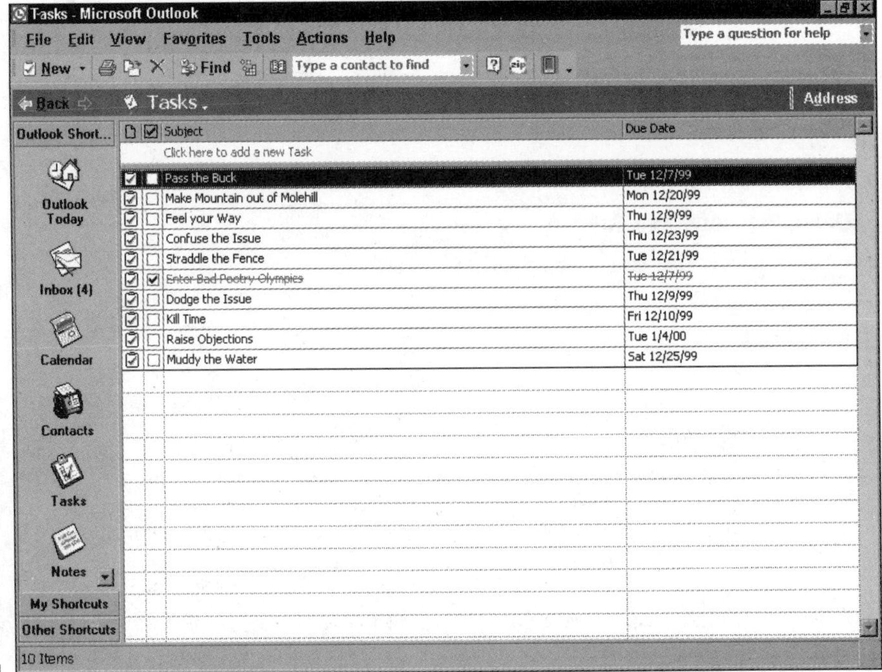

Figure 9-1: Your Tasks lists — more than you'll ever want to do.

The Tasks list actually turns up in more than one section of Outlook. Of course, it's in the Tasks module, but it also turns up in certain views of the Calendar. Seeing your Tasks list in Calendar view is very handy for figuring out when you need to do things as well as what you need to do (see Figure 9-2).

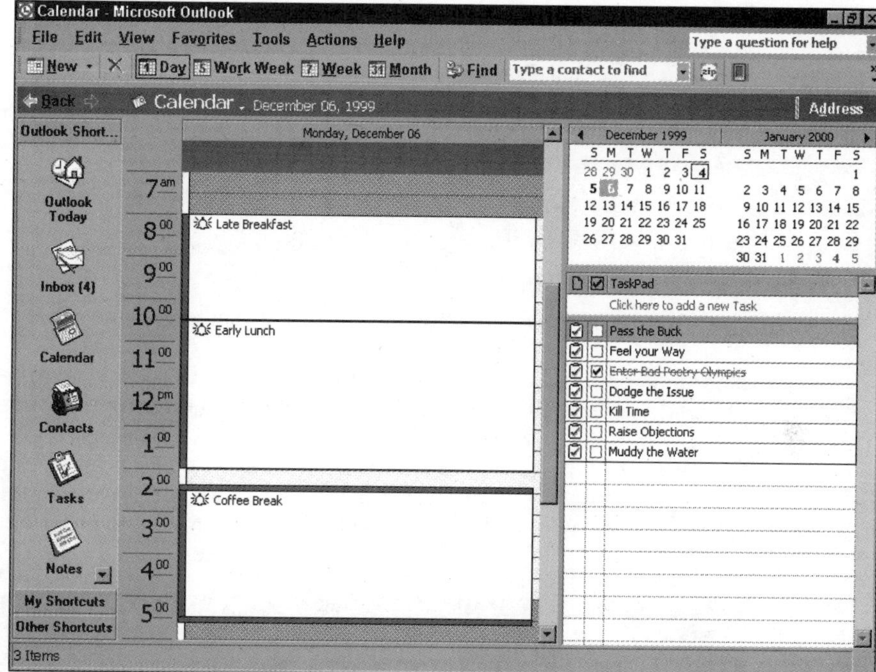

Figure 9-2: A list of tasks in your Calendar view.

Entering New Tasks

I don't mean for you to add work to your busy schedule; you already have plenty of that. But adding a task to your Tasks list in Outlook isn't such a task. Even though you can store gobs of information about your tasks in Outlook, you have both a quick way and a really quick way to enter a new task.

The quick-and-dirty way to enter a task

If you're in one of the views that appear in Figure 9-1 and Figure 9-2, a little box at the top of the list says `Click here to add a new Task`. Do what the box says. (If you can't see the box, go on to the following section to discover the regular, slightly slower way to enter the task.)

To enter a task by using the quick-and-dirty way:

1. **Click the text that says** `Click here to add a new Task.`

   The words disappear, and you see the Insertion Point (a blinking line).

2. **Type the name of your task.**

   Your task appears in the block under the Subject line on the Tasks list, as shown in Figure 9-3.

3. **Press the Enter key.**

   Your new task moves down to the Tasks list with your other tasks.

Isn't that easy? If only the tasks themselves were that easy to do. Maybe in the next version of Outlook, the tasks will get easier, too (in my dreams).

Of course, all you have is the name of the task — no due dates, reminders, or any of the cool stuff. If you want that information, you have to enter the task the regular way. See the next section, "The regular way to enter a task."

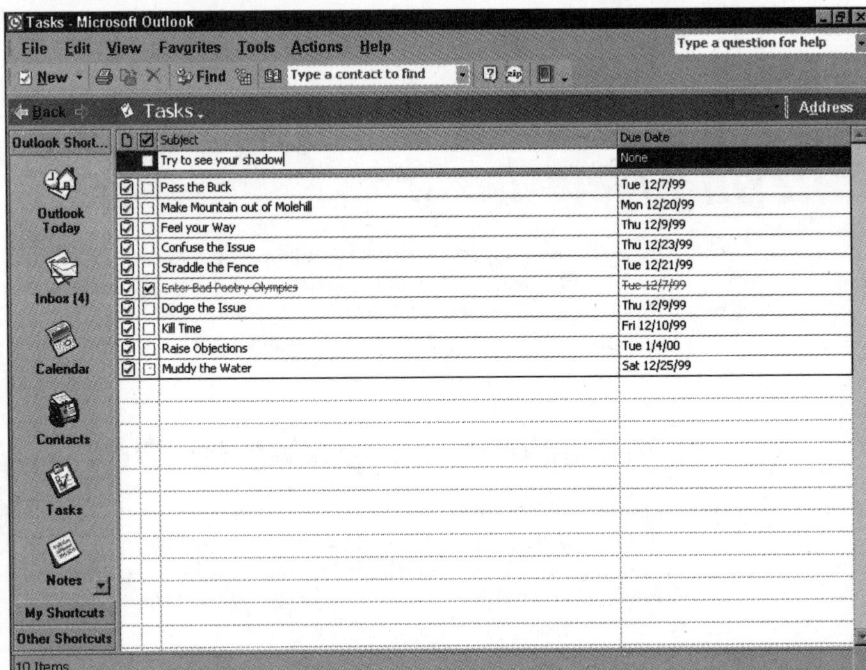

Figure 9-3: Entering your task in the Tasks list.

The regular way to enter a task

The regular way to enter a task is through the Task form, which looks like more work, but it's really not. As long as you enter a name for the task, you've done all that you really must. If you want to go hog-wild and enter all sorts of due dates or have Outlook remind you to actually *complete* the tasks that you've entered (heaven forbid!), you just need to put information in a few more boxes.

To add a task to your Tasks list, follow these steps:

1. **Click the Tasks icon in the Outlook Bar.**

   Your Tasks list appears.

2. **Choose File⇨New⇨Task (or press Ctrl+N).**

   The Task form appears (see Figure 9-4).

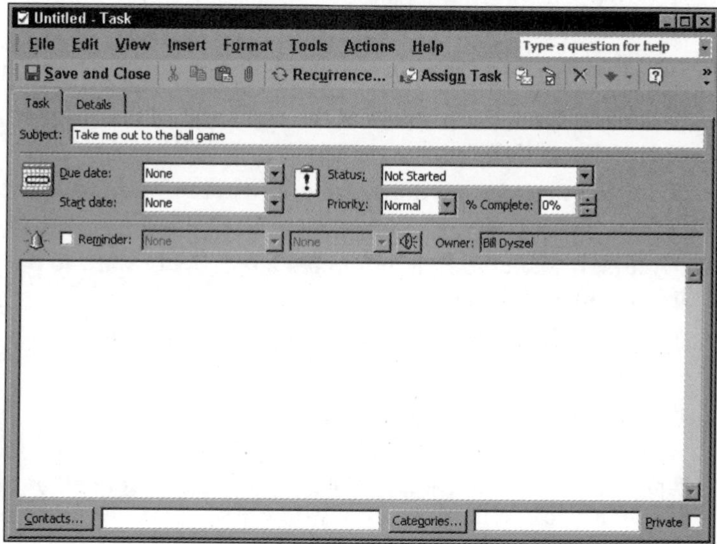

Figure 9-4: Enter your new task in the Task form.

3. **Type the name of the task in the Subject box.**

   Use a subject that will help you remember what the task is. The main reason to create a task is to help you remember to do the task.

   You can finish at this point by jumping to Step 24 (choose Save and Close or press Alt+S) if you want to add only the name of the task to your list. If you want to note a due date, start date, reminders, and so on, you have more to do. All the rest of the steps are optional; you can skip the ones that don't interest you.

4. **(Optional) To assign a due date to the task, click the Due Date box.**

5. **(Optional) Enter the due date in the Due Date box.**

   You can enter a date in Outlook in several ways. You can type **7/4/97**, **the first Friday of July**, or **Three weeks from Friday**. You can also click the scroll-down button (triangle) at the right end of the Due Date text box and choose the date you want from the drop-down calendar.

6. **(Optional) To assign a start date to the task, click the Start Date box and enter the start date.**

   If you haven't started the task, you can skip this step. You can use the same tricks to enter the start date that you use to enter the due date.

   When you're entering information in a dialog box such as the Task form, you can press the Tab key to move from one text box to the next. You can use the mouse to click each text box before you type, but pressing the Tab key is a bit faster. I've written the directions in the order that you follow if you use the Tab key to move through the dialog box.

7. **(Optional) Click the triangle at the right end of the Status box to choose the status of the task.**

   If you haven't begun, leave Status set to Not Started. You can also choose In Progress, Completed, Waiting on Someone Else, or Deferred.

8. **(Optional) Click the triangle at the right end of the Priority box to choose the priority.**

   If you don't change anything, the priority stays Normal. You can also choose High or Low.

9. **(Optional) Click the Reminder check box if you want to be reminded before the task is due.**

   If you'd rather forget the task, forget the reminder. But then, why enter the task at all?

10. **(Optional) Click the date box next to the Reminder check box and enter the date when you want to be reminded.**

    If you entered a due date, Outlook has already entered that date in the Reminder box. You can enter any date you want (see Figure 9-5). If you choose a date in the past, Outlook lets you know that it won't be setting a reminder. If you open the scroll-down menu by clicking the triangle on the right of the date box, a calendar appears. You can click the date you desire in the calendar.

11. **(Optional) Enter the time you want to activate the reminder in the time box.**

    The easiest way to set a time is to type the numbers for the time. You don't need colons or anything special. If you want to finish by 2:35 p.m., just type **235**. Outlook assumes that you're not a vampire, and it schedules your tasks and appointments during daylight hours unless you say otherwise. If you are a vampire, type **235a**; Outlook translates that to 2:35 a.m. If you simply *must* use correct punctuation, Outlook can handle that, too.

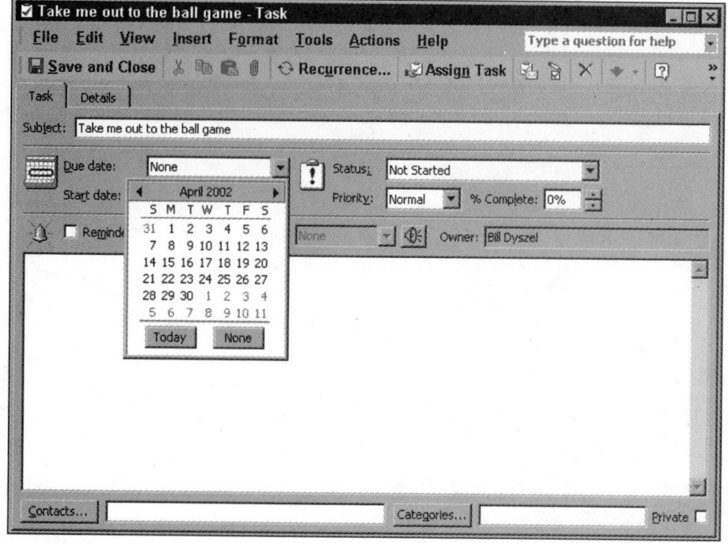

Figure 9-5: A calendar drops down to show the date your task is due.

12. **(Optional) In the text box, enter miscellaneous notes and information about this task.**

    If you need to keep directions to the appointment, a list of supplies, or whatever, it all fits here.

13. **(Optional) Click the Categories button to assign a category to the appointment, if you want.**

    (Using the categories setting is another trick for finding things easily.) The Categories dialog box appears (see Figure 9-6).

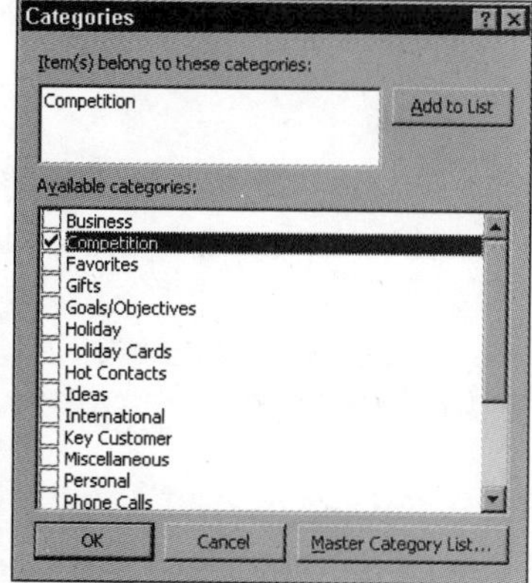

Figure 9-6: The Categories dialog box.

14. **(Optional) Choose one of the existing categories, if one suits you, and then click OK.**

15. **(Optional) If none of the existing categories suits you, click Master Category List.**

    The Master Category List dialog box appears (see Figure 9-7).

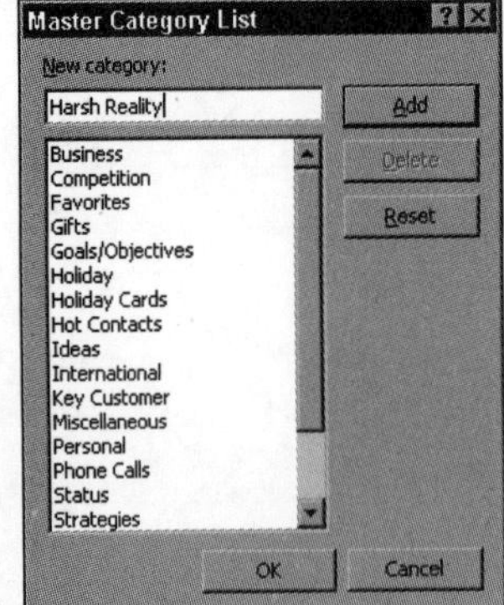

Figure 9-7: The Master Category List.

16. **(Optional) Type a category of your choice in the New Category box.**

    Be sure not to add too many new categories; if you do, finding things may be difficult.

17. **(Optional) Click Add.**
18. **(Optional) Click OK.**
19. **(Optional) Select the new category from the categories list.**

    You can choose more than one category at a time.

20. **(Optional) Click OK.**
21. **(Optional) Click the Contacts button if you want to link your task to a specific name in your contacts list.**

    The Select Contacts dialog box appears.

22. **(Optional) Double-click the name you want to link to your task.**

    The Select Contacts dialog box closes and the name you chose appears in the Contacts text box.

23. **(Optional) Click the Private box, in the lower-right corner of the Task form, if you're on a network and you don't want other users to know about your tasks.**
24. **Click the Save and Close button to finish.**

    Your new task is now standing at the top of your task list, waiting to be done.

Adding an Internet link to a Task

If you type the name of a Web page, such as `www.pcstudio.com`, in the text box at the bottom of the Task form, Outlook changes the text color to blue and underlines the address, making it look just like the hypertext you click to jump between different pages on the World Wide Web. That makes it easy to save information about an exciting Web site; just type or copy the address into your task. To view the page you entered, just click the text to make your Web browser pop up and open the page.

Editing Your Tasks

No sooner do you enter a new task than it seems that you need to change it. Sometimes, I enter a task the quick-and-dirty way and change some of the particulars later — add a due date, a reminder, an added step, or whatever. Editing tasks is easy.

The quick-and-dirty way to change a task

For lazy people like me, Outlook offers a quick-and-dirty way to change a task, just as it has a quick-and-dirty way to enter a task. You're limited in the number of details you can change, but the process is fast.

If you can see the name of a task, and if you want to change something about the task you can see, follow the steps that I describe in this section. If you can't see the task or the part that you want to change, use the regular method, which I describe in the next section of this chapter.

To enter a task the quick-and-dirty way:

1. **Click the thing that you want to change.**

   You see a blinking line at the end of the text, a triangle at the right end of the box, or a menu with a list of choices.

2. **Select the old information.**

   The old text is highlighted to show you that it's selected (see Figure 9-8).

3. **Type the new information.**

   The new information replaces the old. If you click the Status box, a menu drops down and you can choose from the list.

4. **Press the Enter key.**

Isn't that easy? If all you want to change is the name, status, or due date, the quick-and-dirty way will get you there.

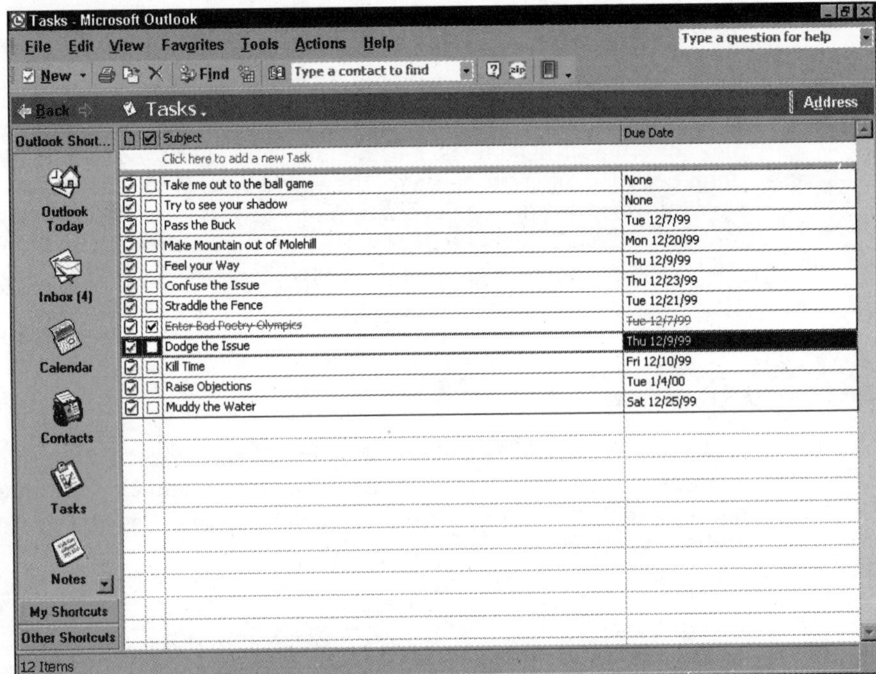

Figure 9-8: A task highlighted in the Tasks list.

The regular way to change a task

If you don't want to be quick and dirty, or if the information that you want to change about a task isn't on the list you're looking at, you have to take a slightly longer route. The regular way is a little more work, but not much.

To make changes to a task the clean-and-long way (also known as the regular way), follow these steps:

1. **Click the Tasks icon in the Outlook Bar.**

   The Tasks module opens.

2. **Choose View⇨Current View⇨Simple List.**

   You can choose a different Current View if you know that the view includes the task you want to change. The Simple List is the most basic view of your tasks; it's sure to include the task you're looking for.

3. **Double-click the name of the task that you want to change.**

   The Task form appears (see Figure 9-9). Now you can change anything you can see in the box. Just click the information you want to change, type the new information, and click Save and Close (or press Alt+S).

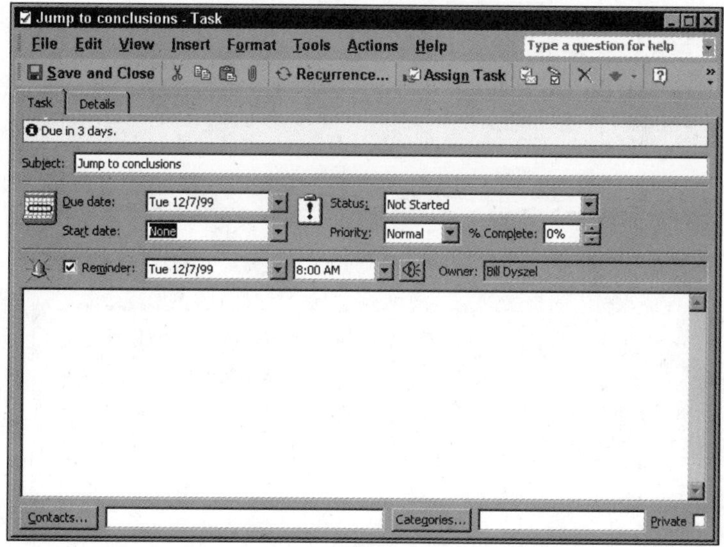

Figure 9-9: The Task form.

4. **Change the name of the task.**

   The name is your choice. Remember to call the task something that helps you remember the task. There's nothing worse than a computer reminding you to do something that you can't understand.

5. **To change the due date, click the Due Date box.**

6. **Enter the new due date in the Due Date box.**

   Plenty of date styles work here — **7/4/97**, **the first Friday in July**, **Six weeks from now**, whatever. Unfortunately, **the 12th of Never** isn't an option. Sorry.

7. **Click the Start Date box and enter the new start date.**

   If you haven't started the task, you can skip this step. You don't absolutely need a start date; it's just for your own use.

8. **Click the scroll-down button (triangle) at the right end of the Status box to see a menu that lets you change the status of the task.**

   If you're using Outlook at work and you're hooked up to a network, the Status box entry is one way of keeping your boss informed of your progress. You'll need to check with your boss or system administrator if this is the case.

   If you're using Outlook at home, chances are that nobody else will care, but you may feel better if you know how well you're doing. You can't add your own choices to the Status box. I'd like to add, "Waiting, hoping the task will go away." No such luck. Figure 9-10 shows the Task box with the Status line highlighted.

9. **Click the scroll-down button (triangle) at the right end of the Priority box to change the priority.**

   Switch the priority to High or Low, if the situation changes (see Figure 9-11).

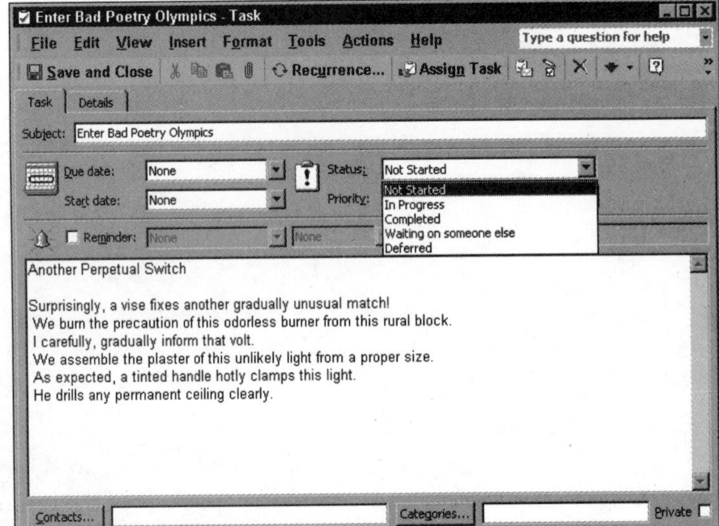

Figure 9-10: This task hasn't been started yet.

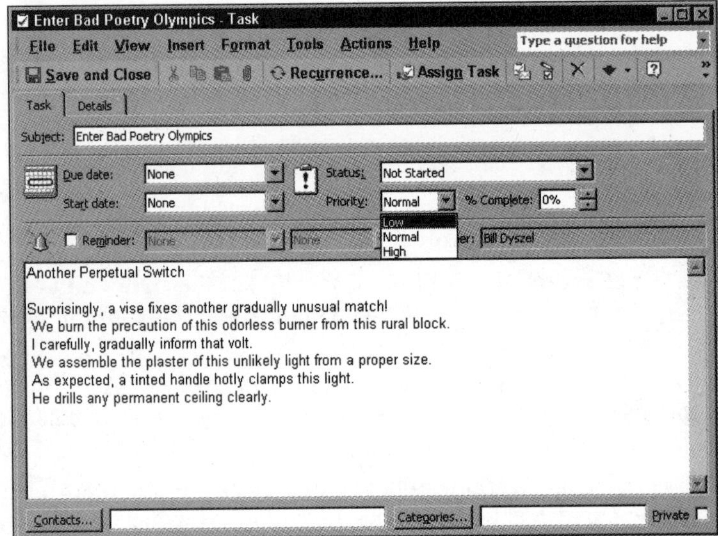

Figure 9-11: Let's hear it for a lower priority.

10. **Click the Reminder check box if you want to turn the reminder on or off.**

    Reminders are easy and harmless, so why not? If you didn't ask for one the first time, do it now.

11. **Click the date box next to the Reminder check box to enter or change the date when you want to be reminded.**

    You can enter any date you want. Your entry doesn't have to be the due date; it can be much earlier, reminding you to get started. You can even set a reminder after the task is due, which isn't very useful. You should make sure that the reminder is before the due date. The default date for a reminder is the date the task is due.

12. **Change the time you want to activate the reminder in the time box.**

    When entering times, keep it simple. The entry **230** does the trick when you want to enter 2:30 p.m. If you make appointments at 2:30 a.m. (I'd rather not know what kind of appointments you make at that hour), you can type **230a**.

13. **Click the text box to add or change miscellaneous notes and information about this task.**

    You can add detailed information here that doesn't really belong anywhere else in the Task form (see Figure 9-12). You see these details only when you open the Task form again; they don't normally show up in your Tasks list.

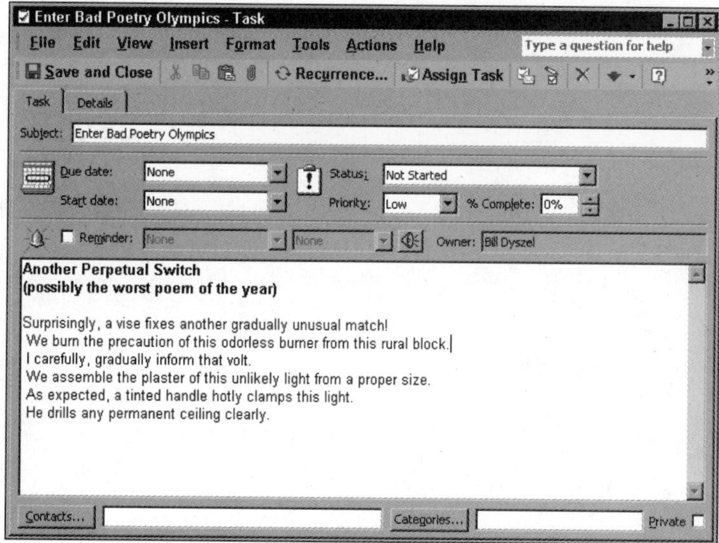

Figure 9-12: Details, details. Add 'em in the text box.

14. **Click the Save and Close button to finish.**

    There! You've changed your task.

Copying a task

By now, you're probably saying, "I had so much fun setting up a task for myself, I'd like to set up another one." If it's the same task on a different day, the easiest approach is to copy the task.

To copy a task, follow these steps:

1. **Select the task that you want to copy.**

   The selected task is highlighted in blue (see Figure 9-13).

2. **Choose Edit⇨Copy (or press Ctrl+C).**
3. **Choose Edit⇨Paste (or press Ctrl+V).**

   A new, identical copy of your task appears just below the old one. The problem is that it's exactly the same task. You don't need Siamese-twin tasks, so you probably want to change the date of the new task. Double-click the new task and change the date.

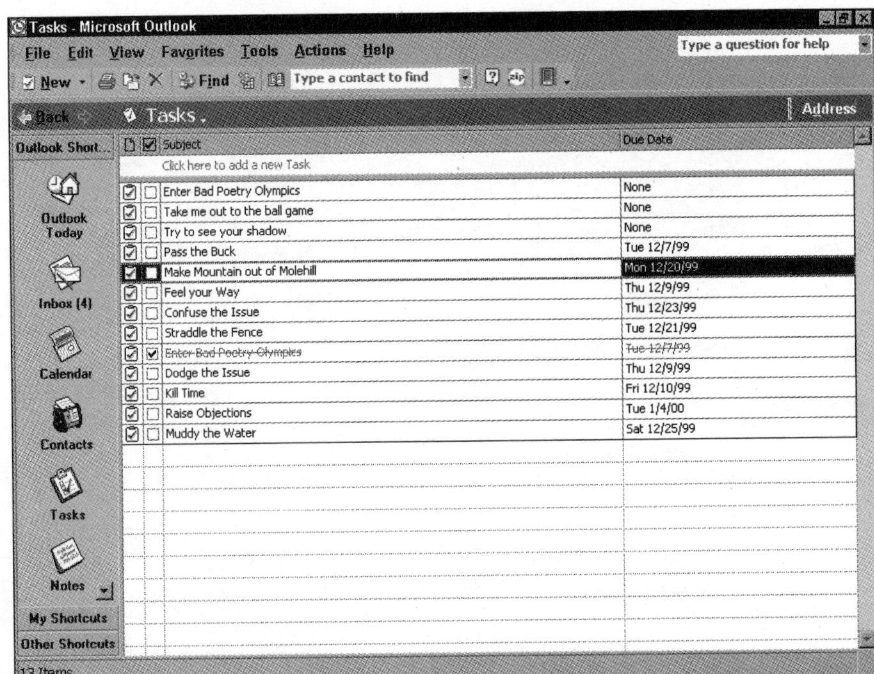

Figure 9-13: Your selected task is highlighted.

For creating tasks that recur every day, copying the task is pretty laborious. That's why you can set up a task as a recurring task the way I describe in the section "Managing Recurring Tasks," later in this chapter.

Deleting a task

The really gratifying part about tasks is getting rid of them, preferably by completing the tasks that you entered. You may also delete a task you changed your mind about. Of course, nothing is stopping you from deleting tasks you just don't want to bother with; this version of Outlook can't really tell whether you've actually completed your tasks. Rumor has it that the next version of Outlook will know whether you've finished your tasks and report to Santa. Don't be naughty!

To delete a task, follow these steps:

1. **Select the task.**
2. **Choose Edit⇨Delete (or press Ctrl+D, or click the Delete button in the toolbar).**

   Poof! Your task is gone.

Managing Recurring Tasks

Lots of tasks crop up on a regular basis. You know how it goes — same stuff, new day. To save you the effort of entering a task, such as a monthly sales report or a quarterly tax payment over and over again, just set it up as a recurring task. Outlook can then remind you whenever it's that time again.

To create a recurring task, follow these steps:

1. **Open the task by double-clicking it.**

   The Task form appears (see Figure 9-14).
2. **Click the Recurrence button in the Task Form toolbar (or press Ctrl+G).**

   The Task Recurrence dialog box appears (see Figure 9-15).
3. **Choose the Daily, Weekly, Monthly, or Yearly option to specify how often the appointment occurs.**

   Each choice you make — Daily, Weekly, or Monthly — changes the types of exact choices available for when the task recurs. For example, a daily recurring task can be set to recur every day or every five days or whatever. A monthly recurring task can be set to recur on a certain day of the month, such as the 15th of each month, or on the second Friday of every month.

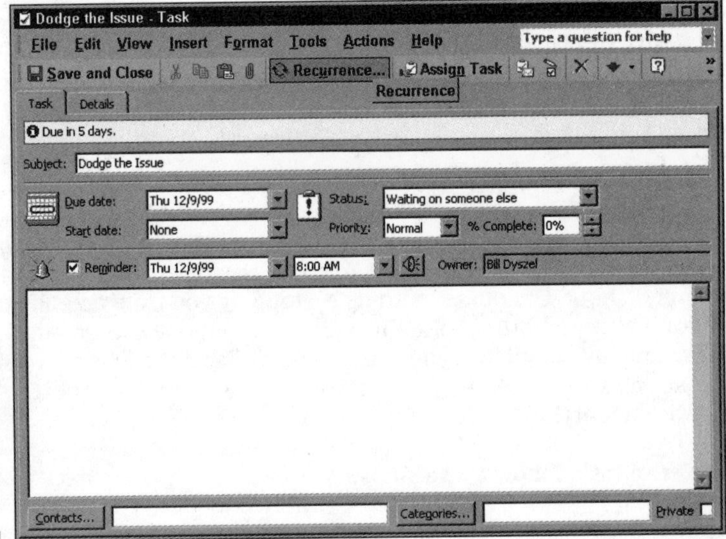

Figure 9-14: Getting a handle on recurring tasks.

4. **In the next box to the right, specify how often the appointment occurs, such as every third day or the first Monday of each month.**

   If you choose to create a monthly task, for example, you can click the scroll-down buttons (triangles) to choose "First" then "Monday" to schedule a task on the first Monday of each month.

5. **In the Range of Recurrence box, enter the first occurrence in the Start box.**

6. **Choose when you want the appointments to stop (no end date, after a certain number of occurrences, or at a certain date).**

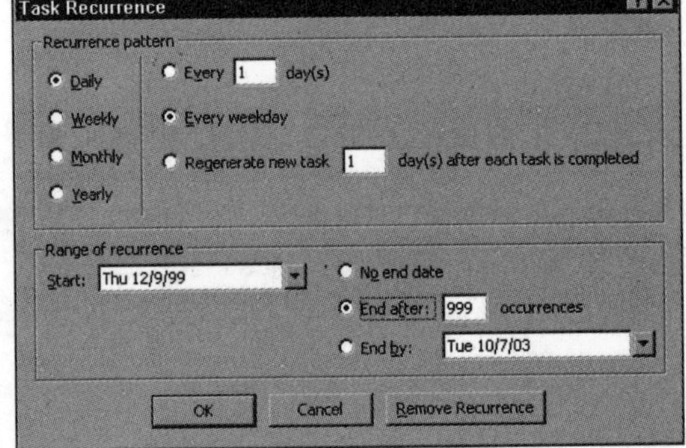

Figure 9-15: How often should this task be done?

7. **Click OK.**

   A banner appears at the top of the Task form describing the recurrence pattern of the task.

8. **Click Save and Close.**

Your task appears in the list of tasks once, but it has a different type of icon than nonrecurring tasks so that you can tell at a glance that it's a recurring task.

Creating a regenerating task

A *regenerating task* is like a recurring task except that it recurs only when a certain amount of time passes after the last time you completed the task. Say that you mow the lawn every two weeks. If it rains for a week and one mowing happens a week late, you still want to wait two weeks for the next one. If you schedule your mowings in Outlook, you use the Regenerating Task feature to enter your lawn-mowing schedule.

To create a regenerating task:

1. **Open the task by double-clicking it.**

   The Task form appears.

2. **Click the Recurrence button in the toolbar in the Task form (or press Ctrl+G).**

   The Task Recurrence dialog box appears.

3. **Click Regenerate New Task (see Figure 9-16).**

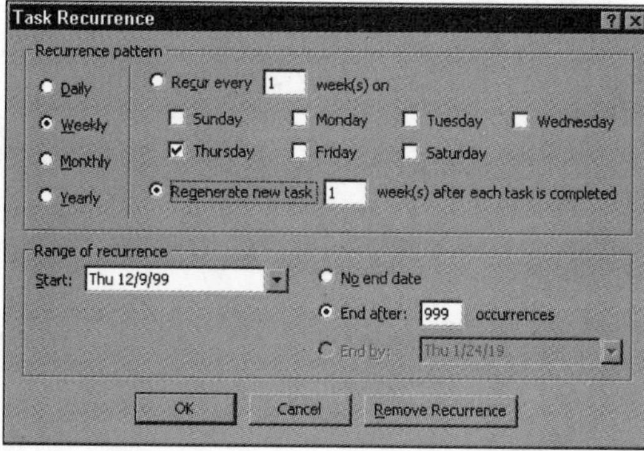

Figure 9-16: You can regenerate a task in the Task Recurrence box.

4. **Enter the number of weeks between regenerating each task.**
5. **Click OK.**

   A banner appears in the Task form describing the regeneration pattern you've set for the task.
6. **Click Save and Close.**

Your task appears in the list of tasks once, but it has a different type of icon than nonrecurring tasks have so that you can tell at a glance that it's a regenerating task.

Skipping a recurring task once

When you need to skip a single occurrence of a recurring task, you don't have to change the recurrence pattern of the task forever; just skip the occurrence you want to skip and leave the rest alone.

To skip a recurring task:

1. **Click the Tasks icon in the Outlook Bar.**

   Your list of tasks appears.
2. **Choose View⇨Current View⇨Simple List.**

   It doesn't matter which view you use, as long as you can see the name of the task that you want to skip. I suggest the Simple List because it's . . . well, simple.
3. **Double-click the name of the task that you want to change.**

   The Task form appears.
4. **Choose Actions⇨Skip Occurrence.**

   The due date changes to the date of the next scheduled occurrence.
5. **Click Save and Close.**

   Your task remains in the list with the new scheduled occurrence date showing.

Marking Tasks Complete

Marking off those completed tasks is even more fun than entering them, and it's much easier. If you can see the task that you want to mark complete in your Tasks list, just click the check box next to the name of the task. Nothing could be simpler.

To mark a task complete, follow these steps:

1. **Click the Tasks icon in the Outlook Bar.**

   The Tasks module opens.

2. **Choose View➪Current View➪Simple List.**

   Actually, you can choose any view you want, as long as the task that you're looking for shows up there. If the task that you want to mark complete isn't in the view you chose, try the Simple List, which contains everything.

3. **Click the box next to the name of the task that you want to mark complete.**

   The box in the second column from the left is the one that you want to check (see Figure 9-17).

   When you check the box, the name of the task changes color and gets a line through it. You're finished.

Outlook has more than one place for marking tasks complete. You can look at the Task list that I just described, as well as certain views of your Calendar, and also the list of tasks in Outlook Today.

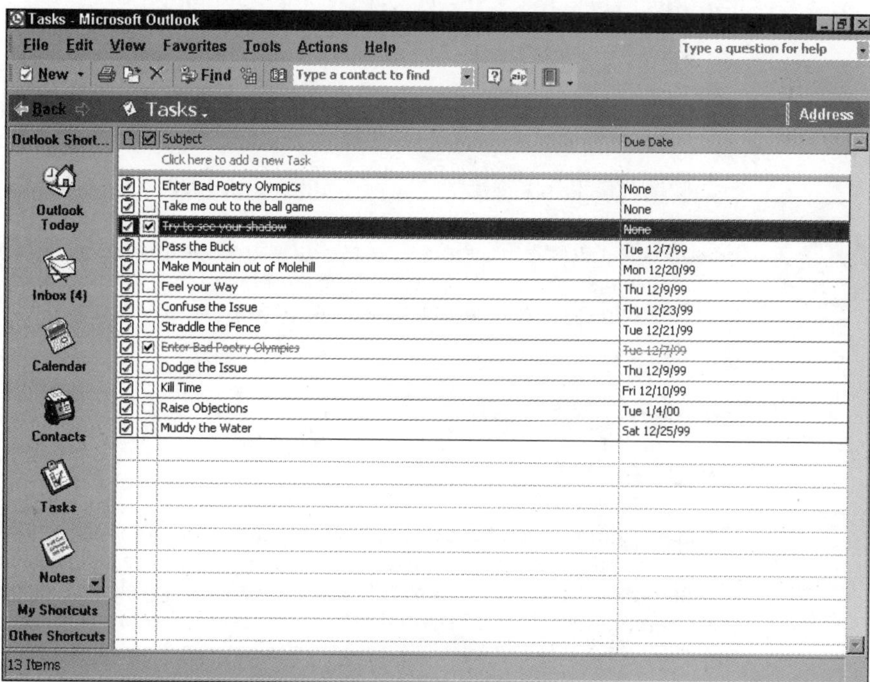

Figure 9-17: A check marks the task complete.

Marking several tasks complete

Perhaps you don't race to your computer every time you complete a task. Marking off your completed tasks in groups is faster than marking them one by one. Outlook allows you to do that by making a multiple selection.

To mark several tasks complete, follow these steps:

1. **Click the Tasks icon in the Outlook Bar.**

   The Tasks module opens.

2. **Choose View⇨Current View⇨Simple List.**

   Again, I'm just suggesting Simple List view because it's most likely to show you all your tasks. You can pick any view that allows you to see the tasks that you want to mark.

3. **Click the first task that you want to mark.**
4. **Hold down the Ctrl key and click each of the other tasks that you want to mark.**

   All the tasks you clicked are highlighted, showing that you've selected them.

5. **Right-click one of the tasks that you highlighted.**

   A menu appears (see Figure 9-18).

6. **Choose Mark Complete.**

   The tasks you selected are marked complete.

There are two good reasons for recording your tasks and marking them complete. One is so that you remember everything you have to do; the second reason is to tell other people everything you've done, like your boss at raise time, for instance. It pays to toot your own horn, and keeping a completed task list helps you remember what to toot your horn about.

Picking a color for completed or overdue tasks

When you complete a task or when it becomes overdue, Outlook changes the color of the text for the completed tasks to gray and the overdue tasks to red, which makes it easy for you to tell at a glance which tasks are done and which tasks remain to be done. If you don't like Outlook's color choices, you can pick different colors.

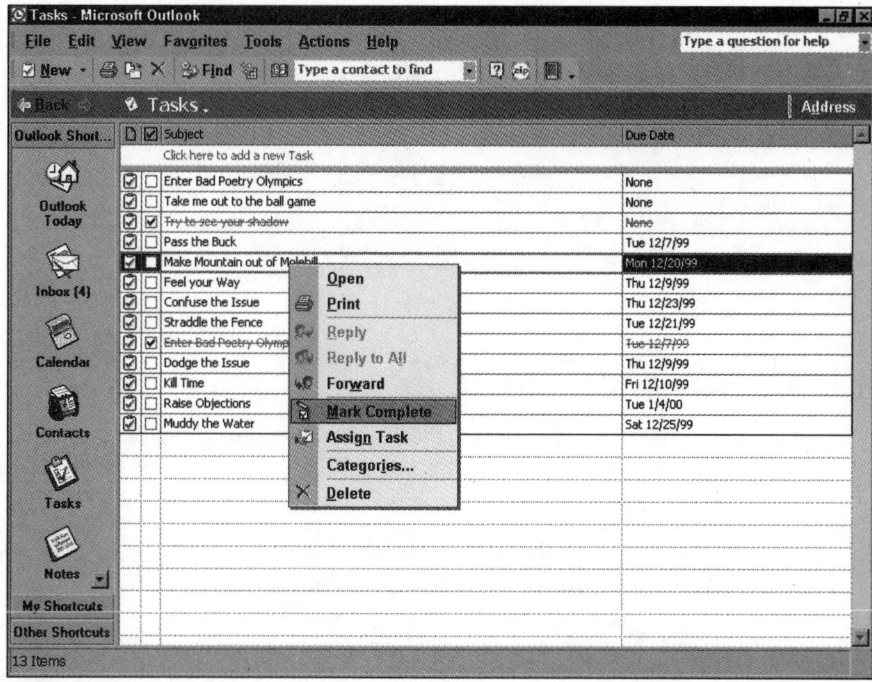

Figure 9-18: A shortcut in the Tasks list.

Here's how to change the color of completed and overdue tasks:

1. **Choose Tools⇨Options.**

   The Options dialog box appears.

2. **Click the Task Options button.**

   The Task Options page appears (see Figure 9-19).

3. **Click the scroll-down button (triangle) at the right end of the Overdue Tasks box.**

   A list of colors drops down.

4. **Choose a color for overdue tasks.**

5. **Click the scroll-down button (triangle) at the right end of the Completed Tasks box.**

   A list of colors drops down.

6. **Choose a color for completed tasks.**

7. **Click OK.**

Your completed and overdue tasks will appear on your list in the colors you chose.

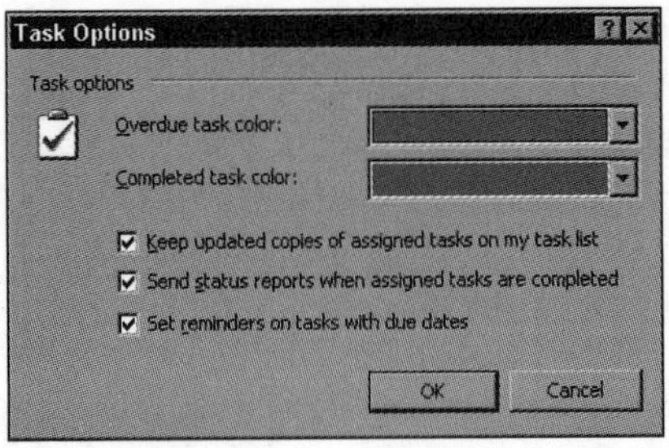

Figure 9-19: The Task Options page.

Viewing Your Tasks

Outlook comes with several ways to view your Tasks list and allows you to invent and save as many custom views as you like. The views that come with Outlook take you a long way when you know how to use them.

To change your view of your tasks, choose View⇨Current View, and then choose one of the following views from the menu:

- **Simple List** view presents just the facts — the names you gave each task and the due date you assigned (if you assigned one). The Simple List view makes it easy to add new tasks and mark old ones complete. However, you won't see any extra information. If you want details. . . .
- **Detailed List** view is a little more . . . uh, detailed than the Simple List view. It's really the same information, plus the status of the tasks, the percentage of each task complete, and whatever categories you may have assigned to your tasks.
- **Active List** view shows you only tasks that you haven't finished yet. After you mark a task complete, zap! Completed tasks vanish from the Active List view, which helps keep you focused on the tasks remaining to be done.
- **Next Seven Days** view is even more focused than the Active List view. The Next Seven Days view shows only uncompleted tasks scheduled to be done within the next seven days. It's just right for those people who like to live in the moment, or at least within the week.
- **Overdue Tasks** view means that you've been naughty. These are the tasks that needed doing yesterday but are still hanging around today.
- **By Category** view breaks up your tasks according to the category that you've assigned each task. You can open and close categories to focus on the type of tasks you're looking for. For example, you may assign a category of Sales to the sales-related tasks in your list. When you want to focus on sales, use the By Category view and click the Sales category.

- **Assignment** view lists your tasks in order of the name of the person upon whom you dumped, er, I mean delegated, each task.
- **By Person Responsible** view contains the same information as the Assignment view, but the list is grouped to let you see the assignments of only one person at a time.
- **Completed Tasks** view shows (you guessed it) tasks you've marked complete. You don't need to deal with completed tasks anymore, but looking at the list gives you a warm, fuzzy feeling, doesn't it?
- **Task Timeline** view draws a picture of when each task is scheduled to start and end. Seeing a picture of your tasks gives you a better idea of how to fit work into your schedule sensibly.

Part IV

Beyond the Basics: Tips and Tricks You Won't Want to Miss

In this part . . .

When you finally get ahead in the rat race, what do you find? Faster rats, of course. This part shows you how to stay ahead of those rascally rodents without getting lost in a maze of work by using Outlook's secret power tools.

Chapter 10

A Sticky Subject: Using Notes

In This Chapter

- Composing a note
- Locating a note
- Opening and reading a note
- Deleting a note
- Resizing a note
- Changing your colors
- Taking a look at your notes
- Putting your notes in categories
- Printing notes
- Changing your options for new notes
- Forwarding a note

The simple, dopey features of a program are often my favorites — the features that I end up using all the time, such as Outlook Notes. There's really nothing earth-shattering about Notes and certainly nothing difficult. This feature is just there when you need it, ready to record whatever strange, random thoughts are passing through your head while you're doing your work. (As you can tell from my writing, strange, random thoughts are a common occurrence for me. That's why I love using Notes.)

A note is the only type of item you can create in Outlook that doesn't use a normal dialog box with menus and toolbars. Notes are easier to use but somewhat trickier to explain than other Outlook items, because I can only describe the objects you're supposed to click and drag. No name appears on the Note icon, and no name exists for the part of the note that you drag when you want to resize the note (see Figure 10-1).

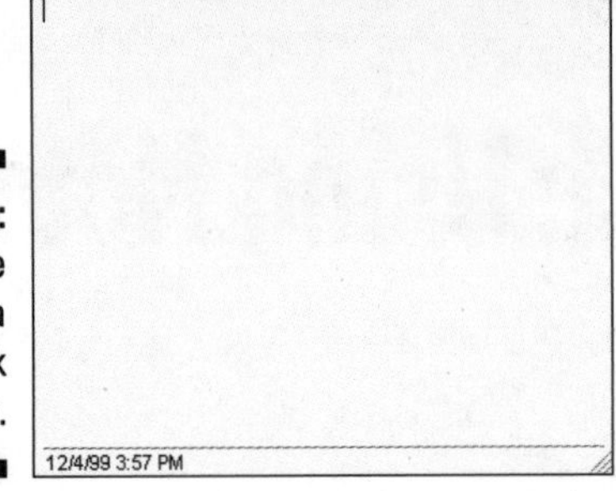

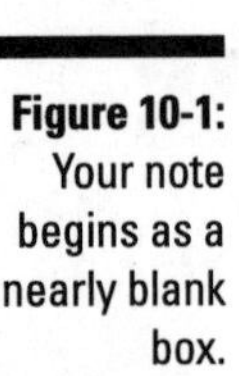

Figure 10-1: Your note begins as a nearly blank box.

Writing a Note

How did we ever live without those little yellow stick-on notes? They're everywhere! The funny thing about stick-on notes is that they came from an inventor's failure. A scientist was trying to invent a new formula for glue, and he came up with a kind of glue that didn't stick very well. Like the computer scientists who came later, he said, "That's not a bug; that's a feature!" Then he figured out how to make a fortune selling little notes that didn't stick too well. It's only natural that an invention like this would be adapted for computers.

Here's how to take notes while doing your work:

1. **Click the Notes icon in the Outlook Bar.**

   The Notes list appears.

   You don't actually have to go to the Notes module to create a new note; you can go right to Step 2. I suggest going to the Notes module first only so that you can see your note appear in the list of notes when you finish. Otherwise, your note seems to disappear into thin air (but it doesn't). Outlook automatically files your note in the Notes module unless you make a special effort to send it somewhere else.

2. **Choose File⇨New⇨Note (or press Ctrl+N).**

   The blank Note box appears.

3. **Type what you want to say in your note (see Figure 10-2) and click the Note icon in the upper-left corner of the note.**

4. **Click Close (or press Alt+F4).**

   An even quicker way to create a note is to press Ctrl+Shift+N in any Outlook module. You don't see your note listed with all the other notes until you switch to the Notes module, but you can get that thought entered.

Tricks with Notes

Each time you start a program, the Windows taskbar at the bottom of the screen adds an icon. That way, you know how many programs you're running. If you click an icon for a program in the taskbar, you switch to that program. If you start Word and Excel, for example, you see two icons in the taskbar. You can have two or more documents open in Word or Excel, but you see only one icon for each program.

When you choose File⇨New to create a new item in Outlook, you see a second icon open in the taskbar for the item that you're creating. The icon remains until you close and save the item. It's like having two or more programs open in Windows simultaneously. The advantage of this arrangement is that you can leave something like a note open for a long time and keep switching to it to add comments. The disadvantage is that if you don't look at the taskbar to see how many notes you have open, you may be creating a clutter of notes when you may prefer just one.

Another advantage is that you can have two notes open at the same time, or a note and an e-mail message, and drag text from one to the other.

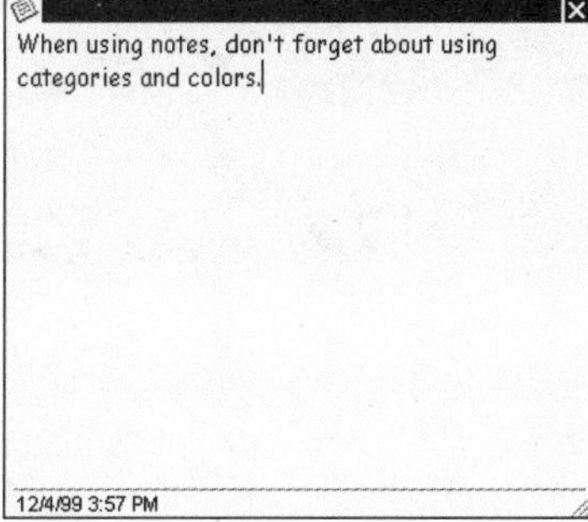
When using notes, don't forget about using categories and colors.
12/4/99 3:57 PM

Figure 10-2: You can write a note to remind yourself of something.

Finding a Note

Unlike paper stick-on notes, Outlook Notes allows you to always find the things you write — or at least your computer can find them. As a matter of fact, you can find any item you create in Outlook just by using the Find tool. (I wish I had a Find tool to help me round up all my lost galoshes and umbrellas.)

Here's how to find a misplaced note:

1. **Click the Notes icon in the Outlook Bar.**

   Your list of notes appears.

2. **Choose Tools⇨Find (or click the Find button in the toolbar).**

   The Look For box appears (see Figure 10-3). The Look For box contains a blinking bar, the insertion point, which shows you where the next thing you type will go.

3. **In the Look For box, type the word or phrase you're looking for.**

   Don't worry about capitalization. Outlook doesn't worry about capitalization; it just looks for the string of letters you entered.

4. **Press Enter.**

   A list of notes that contain the text you typed appears in the Outlook screen.

5. **If the note you're looking for turns up, double-click the Note icon to read what the note says.**

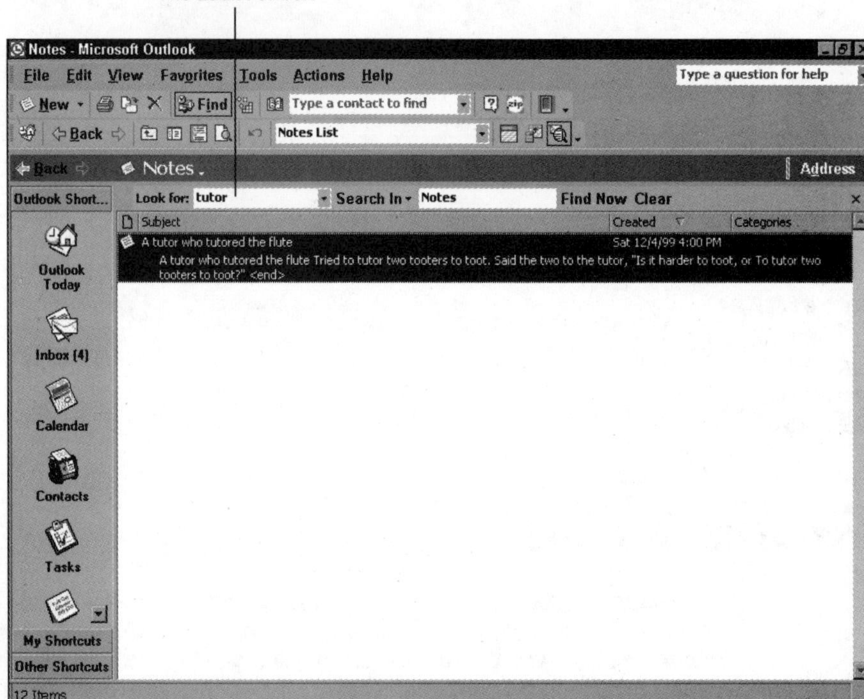

Figure 10-3: The Look For box.

Reading a Note

When you write a note, no doubt you plan to read it sometime. Reading notes is even easier than writing them. To read a note:

1. **Click the Notes icon in the Outlook Bar.**

   Your list of notes appears.

2. **Double-click the title of the note that you want to open.**

   The note appears on-screen (see Figure 10-4). You can close the note when you're done by pressing Esc.

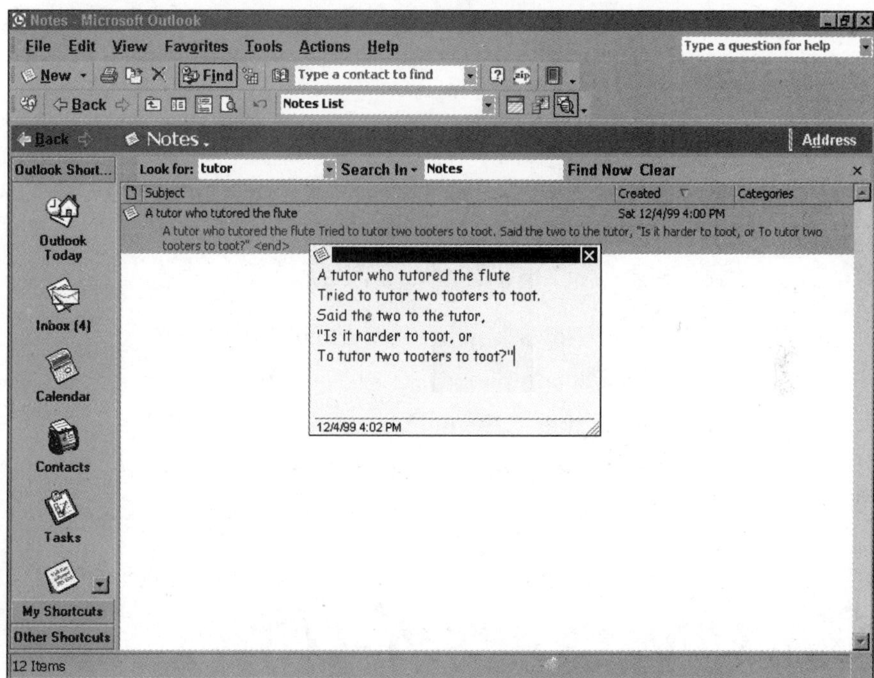

Figure 10-4: Aha! The missing note is found.

Funny how notes look the same when you're reading them as they do when you're writing them.

Taking your pick: Multiple selections

When you're sorting your notes or assigning them to categories, one way to work a little faster is to select several notes simultaneously. If you want to select a group of notes that you can see one right after another in a list, click the first one and then hold down the Shift key while clicking the last one. That action selects both of the notes that you clicked and all the notes in between.

If you're selecting several items that aren't arranged next to one another, hold down the Ctrl key while clicking each item. The notes that you click are highlighted and the others stay plain. Then you can open, move, delete, or categorize the entire group of notes that you selected in a single stroke. To view several notes, right-click any notes you've selected and choose Open.

Deleting a Note

Notes don't have to be forever. You can write a note this morning and throw it out this afternoon. What could be easier?

Here's how to delete a note:

1. **Click the Notes icon in the Outlook Bar.**

   Your list of notes appears.

2. **Click the title of the note that you want to delete.**
3. **Choose Edit⇨Delete (or press Delete).**

   You can also click the Delete button in the Outlook toolbar.

Changing the Size of a Note

You may be an old hand at moving and resizing boxes in Windows. Notes follow all the rules that other Windows boxes follow, so you'll be okay. If you're new to Windows and dialog boxes, don't worry — notes are as easy to resize as they are to write and read.

To change the size of a note:

1. **Click the Notes icon in the Outlook Bar.**

   Your list of notes appears.

2. **Double-click the title of the note that you want to open.**

   The note pops up.

3. **Move your mouse pointer to the bottom-right corner of the note until the mouse pointer changes into a two-headed arrow pointed on a diagonal.**

   Use this arrow to drag the edges of the note to resize it. Don't be alarmed. Resizing boxes is much easier to do than to read about. After you resize one box, you'll have no trouble resizing another.

4. **Drag with your mouse until the note is the size you want it to be.**

   As you drag the mouse pointer around, a gray box appears, showing you what size the note will be when you release the mouse button (see Figure 10-5). Don't worry if the size doesn't come out right the first time; you can change the note size again by dragging the mouse again.

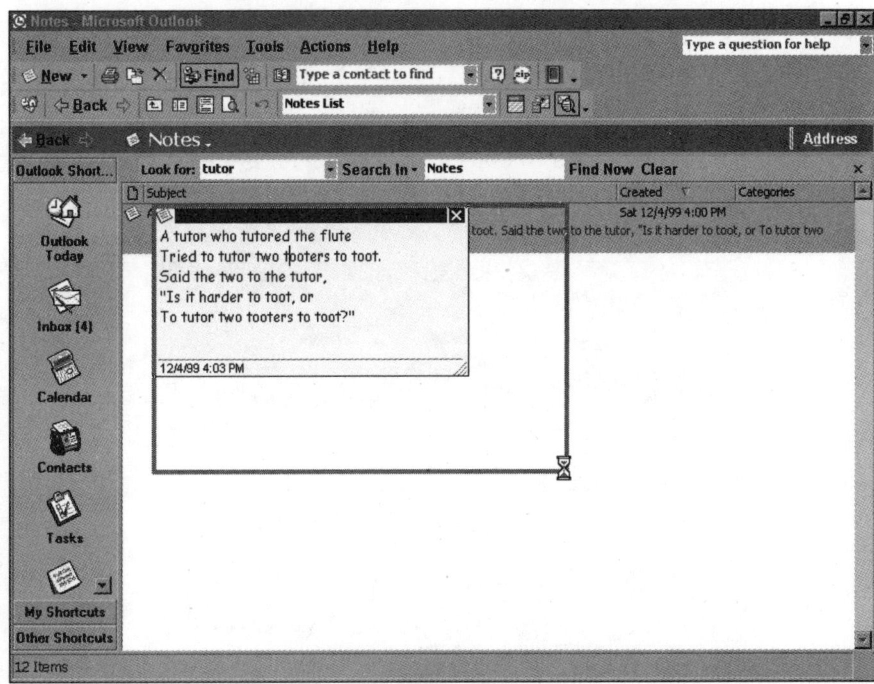

Figure 10-5: A gray box appears around your note when you're resizing it.

Changing Your Colors

Color may seem to be a trifling issue, but it can help you keep track of your notes. You can assign a color to a level of importance, for example, or to a specific task, so that you can quickly see the note you want among the many notes in your list. Later in the chapter, I explain how you can sort your list of notes according to color. Sorting is useful, so spending your entire day changing the colors of your notes isn't just aesthetic; it's also productive.

Here's how to change your note's color:

1. **Open the note and click the Note icon in the top-left corner of the note.**

   I wish there were a better way to describe this icon than "the little thingy up on the left," but that's what it is. The icon is easy to see; it's the only little thingy in the top-left corner of your note. Anyway, when you do click the thingy, the Note menu appears.

2. **Choose Color.**

   A menu of colors appears (see Figure 10-6). Currently, the only choices are Blue, Green, Pink, Yellow, and White. I hope you like pastels, because those are your only options at the moment. Perhaps Burgundy and Off-Mauve notes will be in next season for more color-conscious computer users.

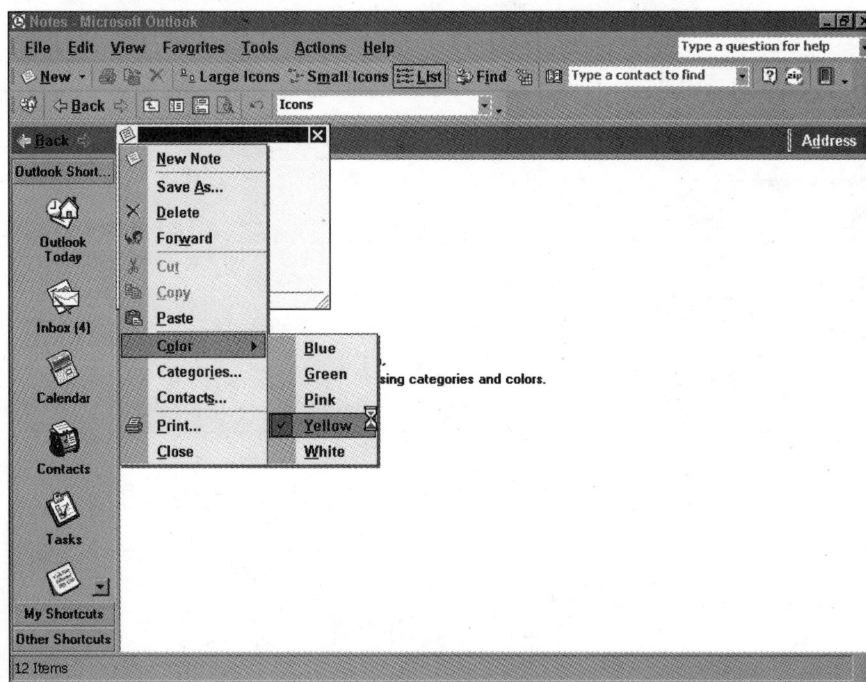

Figure 10-6: The Color menu.

3. **Pick a color.**

You can also change the colors of notes when viewing a list of notes; just right-click the icon for a note and choose a color from the menu that appears.

Viewing Your Notes

Notes are handy enough to be able to stash tidbits of information any way you want, but what makes Notes really useful is what happens when you need to get the stuff back. You can open your notes one by one and see what's in them, but Outlook's Notes module offers even handier capabilities for arranging, sorting, and viewing your notes in a way that makes sense for you.

Icons view

Some folks like Icons view — just a bunch of notes scattered all over, as they are on my desk. Because I can already see a mess of notes any time I look at my desk, I prefer organized lists for viewing my notes on my computer, but you may like the more free-form Icons view.

To use Icons view:

1. **Click the Notes icon in the Outlook Bar.**

   The Notes list appears.

2. **Choose View⇨Current View.**

   The Current View menu appears.

3. **Choose Icons.**

   The screen fills with a bunch of icons and incredibly long titles for each icon (see Figure 10-7).

Outlook uses the entire text of your message as the title of the icon, so the screen gets cluttered fast. If you prefer creative clutter, this view is for you. If not, keep reading.

Notes List view

The Notes list is as basic as basic gets. Just the facts, ma'am. The Notes list shows the subject and creation date of each note, as well as the first few lines of text.

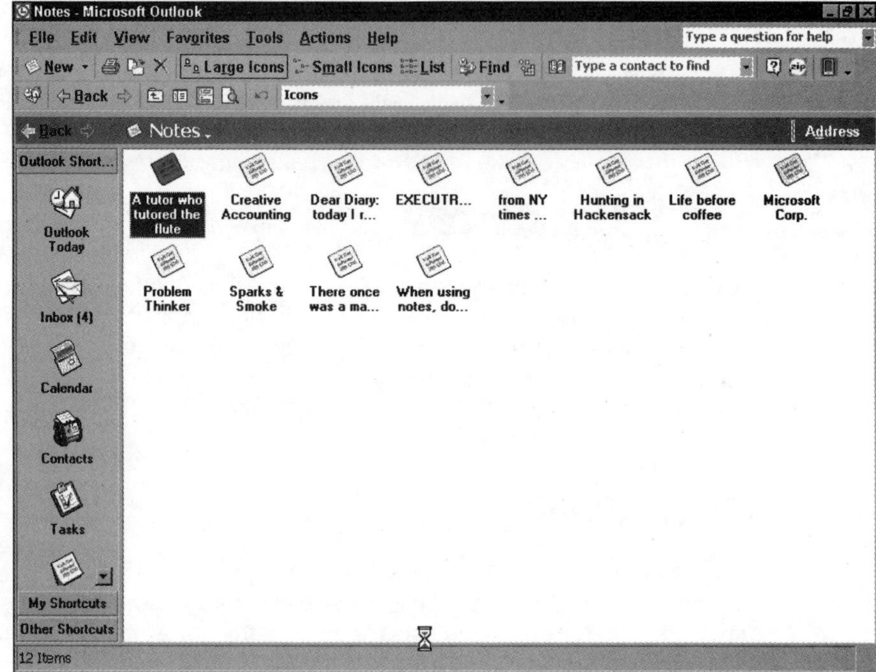

Figure 10-7: The Icons view — a clutter of notes.

To use Notes List view:

1. **Click the Notes icon in the Outlook Bar.**

   The Notes list appears.

2. **Choose View➪Current View.**

   The Current View menu appears.

3. **Choose Notes List.**

   A listing of your notes appears (see Figure 10-8).

I usually recommend Notes List view for opening, forwarding, reading, and otherwise dealing with notes because it's the most straightforward. Anything you can do to a note in Notes List view, you can do in the other Notes views. The difference is that the other views don't always let you see the note that you want to do things to.

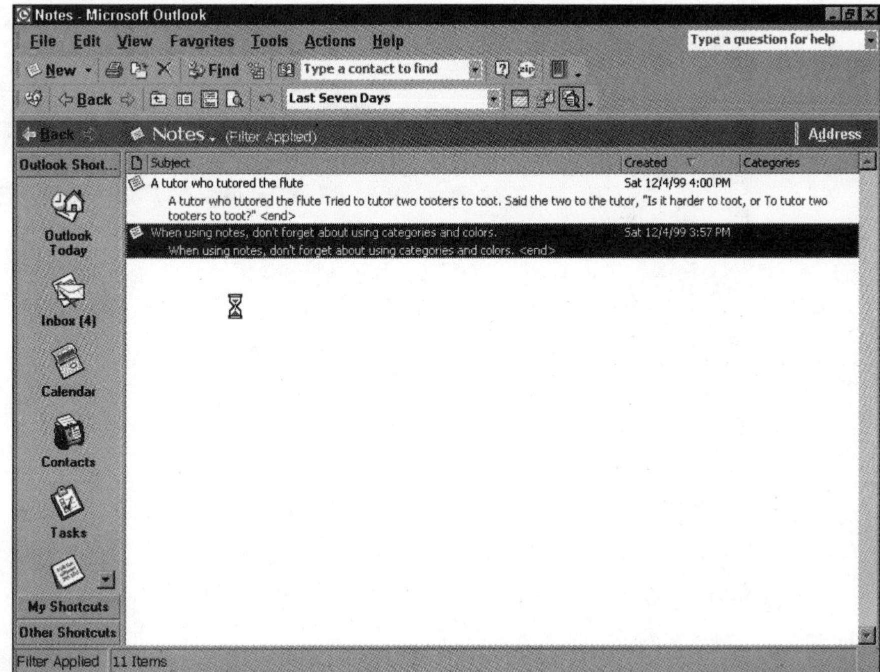

Figure 10-8: Your Notes List view.

Last Seven Days view

The notes that you dealt with in the last few days are most likely to be the notes that you'll need today. So, Outlook includes a special view of the notes that you modified in the last seven days. You're more likely to quickly find what you're looking for in the seven-day view.

To see your notes for the last seven days:

1. **Click the Notes icon in the Outlook Bar.**

   The Notes list appears.

2. **Choose View⇨Current View.**

   The Current View menu appears.

3. **Choose Last Seven Days.**

   You see seven days' worth of notes (see Figure 10-9).

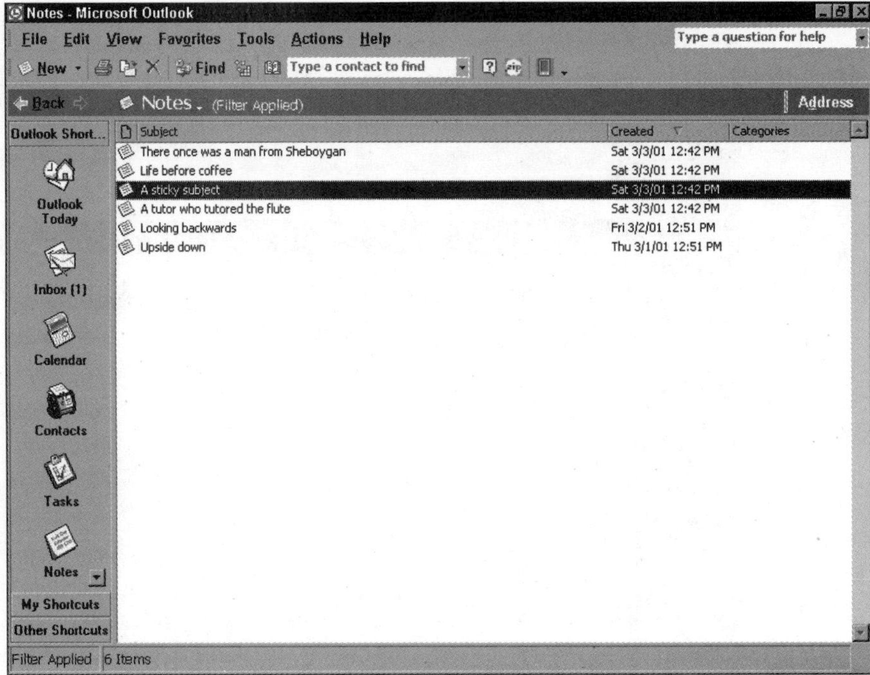

Figure 10-9: Your notes for the past week, in all their glory.

If you haven't modified any notes in the past seven days, Last Seven Days view will be empty. If having an empty view bothers you, create a note. That'll tide you over for a week.

By Category view

Every item that you create in Outlook can be assigned to a category. You use the same category list for all items, and you can create your own categories. With categories, you have another useful way to organize your views of Outlook items. I explain how to assign categories to a note in the section "Assigning a Category to Your Notes" later in this chapter.

To see your notes arranged by category, follow these steps:

1. **Click the Notes icon in the Outlook Bar.**

   The Notes list appears.

2. **Choose View➪Current View.**

   The Current View menu appears.

3. **Choose By Category.**

   Your notes are arranged by category (see Figure 10-10).

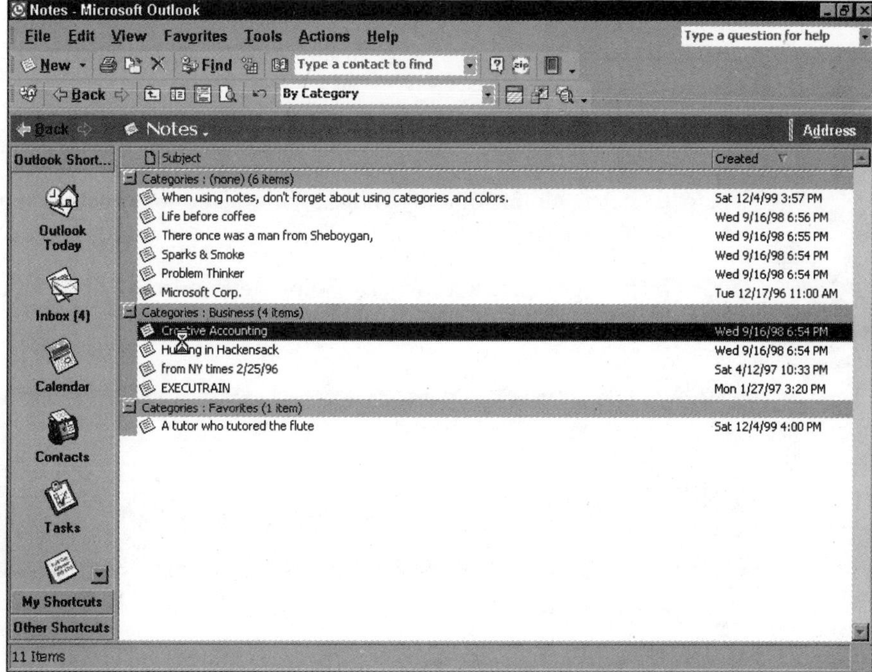

Figure 10-10: Your notes in By Category view.

By Category view is a *grouped view,* meaning that the notes are collected in bunches, according to the categories that you've assigned. You can just look at the category of notes that you're interested in to organize the information that you've collected.

By Color

Color coordination means more than making sure your socks match. The fact that you can group notes by color means that you can create a system of organizing your notes that tells you something important about your notes at a glance. If sales representatives call asking you to buy merchandise, you may want to create and color code a note for each request: green for requests that you're approving, yellow for requests that you're considering, and pink for requests that you're turning down, for example.

To view your notes by color:

1. **Click the Notes icon in the Outlook Bar.**

   The Notes list appears.

2. **Choose View➪Current View.**

   The Current View menu appears.

3. **Choose By Color.**

   You see a color-coded list of your notes (see Figure 10-11).

You can choose among only five colors for an Outlook note, so you can have only that many groups by color.

You can also right-click a note in By Color view and change the color for sorting.

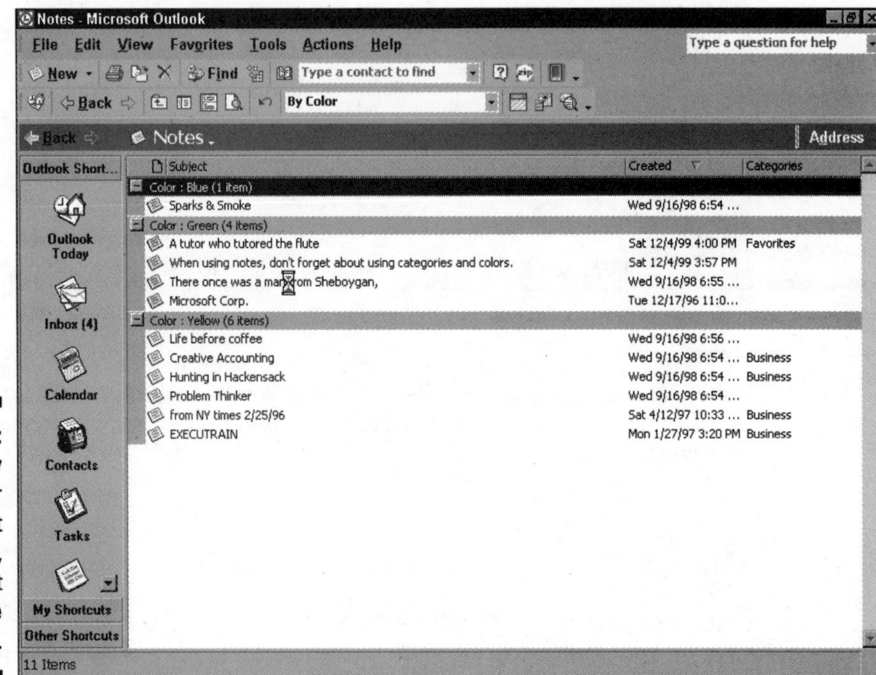

Figure 10-11: The By Color view — not Technicolor, but attractive nonetheless.

Assigning a Category to Your Notes

If you really want to get yourself organized, you can assign categories to all the items that you create in Outlook. That way, all your items can be sorted, grouped, searched, and even deleted according to the categories that you assigned them to.

To categorize your notes:

1. **Click the Note icon in the upper-left corner of the Note.**

   The Note menu drops down (see Figure 10-12).

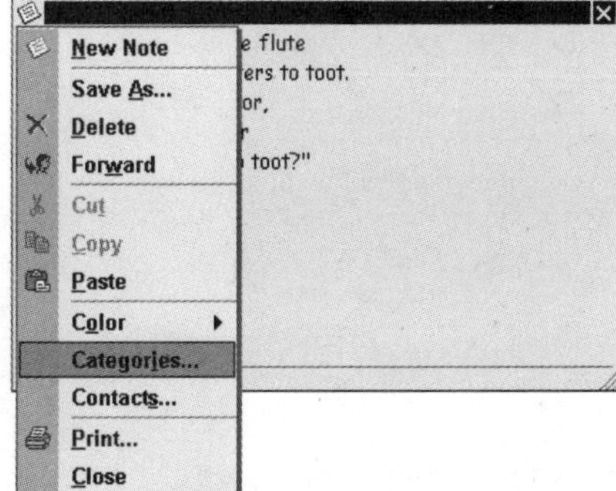

Figure 10-12: The Note menu.

2. **Choose Categories.**

   The Categories dialog box appears, as shown in Figure 10-13.

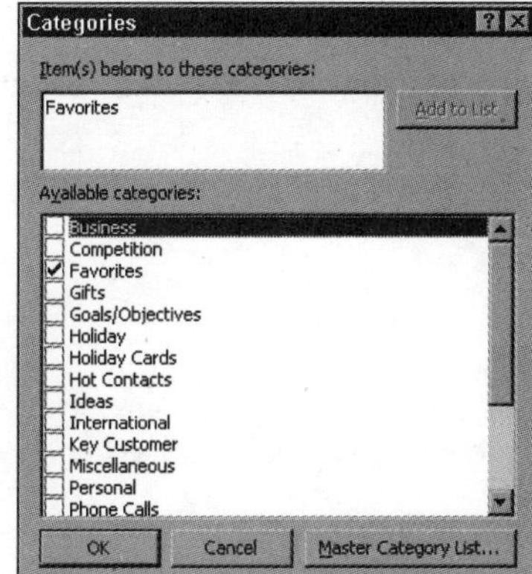

Figure 10-13: The Categories dialog box.

3. **Choose one of the existing categories, if one suits you, and then click OK.**

   You can also enter your own category in the Item(s) Belong to These Categories dialog box.

4. **If none of the existing categories suits you, click Master Category List.**

   From the Master Category List, you can add or delete categories (see Figure 10-14).

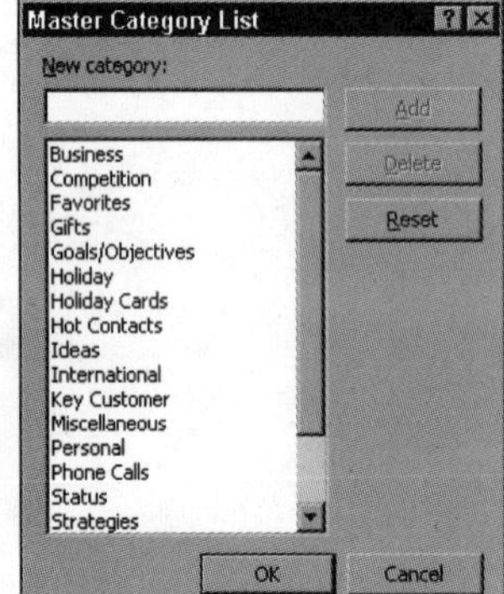

Figure 10-14: The Master Category List.

5. **Type a category of your choice in the New Category box.**

   Be sure not to add too many new categories, or else finding things could get hard.

6. **Click Add.**

   Your new category is part of the Categories list.

7. **Click OK.**

Whenever you see the Categories list, your new category will be among the categories that you can choose.

Printing Your Notes

You can organize and view your notes in so many clever ways that you'll also want to print what you can see, or at least the list of what you can see.

Printing a list of your notes

To print a list of your notes:

1. **Click the Notes icon in the Outlook Bar.**

   The Notes list appears.

2. **Choose File➪Print (or press Ctrl+P).**

   The Print dialog box appears (see Figure 10-15).

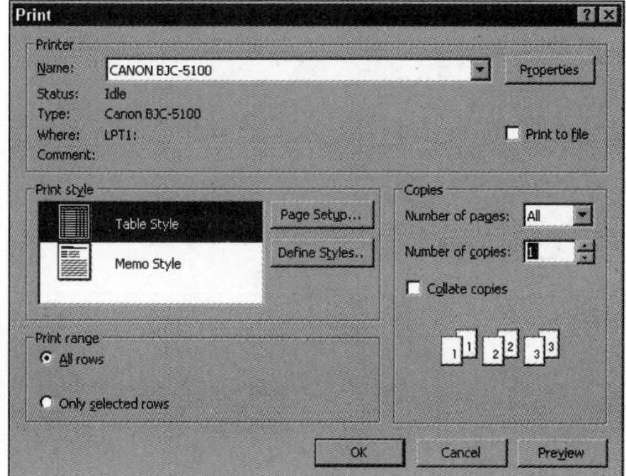

Figure 10-15: The Print dialog box.

3. **In the Print Style box, choose Table Style.**

   If you choose Memo Style, you print the contents of a note rather than a list of notes.

4. **Click OK.**

If you want to print only a portion of your list of notes, click the first note that you want listed and then hold down the Shift key while clicking the last note that you want in your printout. You can also hold the Ctrl key while clicking the notes you want one-by-one. When the Print dialog box appears, choose Only Selected Rows in the Print Range section.

Printing the contents of a note

Computer screens are pretty, but there's still nothing like ink on paper. Of course, you can print a note. Remember, though, that the pretty colors you've given your notes don't show when you print them.

To print the note:

1. **Click the Notes icon in the Outlook Bar.**

   The Notes list appears.

2. **Click the title of the note that you want to print.**
3. **Choose File⇨Print (or press Ctrl+P).**

   The Print dialog box appears.
4. **In the Print Style box, choose Memo Style (see Figure 10-16).**

   Choosing Memo Style prints the full contents of the note.

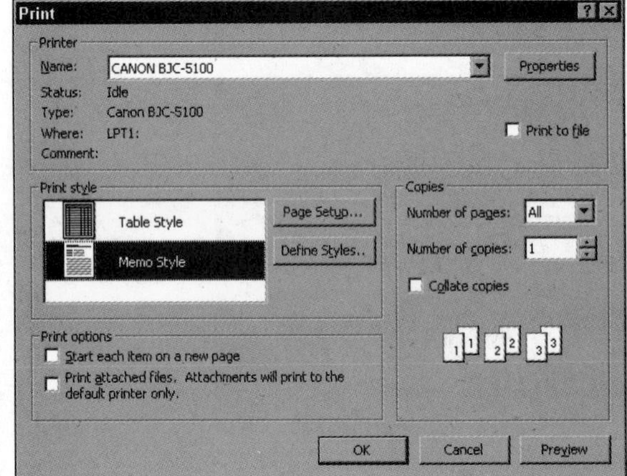

Figure 10-16: The Print dialog box with Memo style selected.

5. **Click OK.**

   Outlook prints the full contents of your note.

If you want to print some, but not all of your notes, click the first note that you want listed and then hold down the Shift key while clicking the last note that you want in your printout.

Changing Your Default Options for New Notes

Plain old notes are fine; you really don't need to change anything. But if you want to make some changes, the Options dialog box in the Tools menu gives you lots of . . . well, options. All the adjustments that you make in the Options dialog box change the size, color, and other qualities of your note when you first create the note. You can also change these qualities after you create the note.

Changing size and color

To change the color and size of your notes:

1. **Choose Tools⇨Options.**

   The Options dialog box appears.

2. **Click the Note Options button.**

   The Notes Options dialog box is where you change the options for the Notes module of Outlook.

3. **Click the triangle (scroll-down button) at the right end of the Color box.**

   A list of colors (Blue, Green, Pink, Yellow, White) drops down (see Figure 10-17). Choosing one of these options changes the color that all your notes will be when you create them.

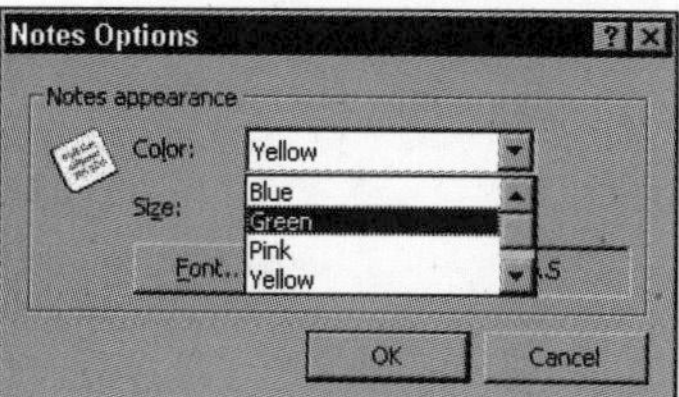

Figure 10-17: Changing colors in Notes Options.

4. **Choose a color.**

5. **Click the scroll-down button (triangle) at the right end of the Size box.**

   The list reads Small, Medium, or Large. Choosing one of these options sets the size of your notes when you create them.

6. **Click OK.**

   Your notes are in the size and color to which you changed them.

Turning the date and time display on or off

At the bottom of each note, Outlook displays the date and time when you most recently changed the contents of the note. You may notice that you change a lot of notes on Mondays around 9:45 a.m. You may not want to notice that fact, so you can turn this handy little feature off.

To turn off the date and time display:

1. **Choose Tools⇨Options.**

   The Options dialog box appears.

2. **Click the Other tab.**

   I don't know why Microsoft called this the Other tab. Perhaps the programmers all kept arguing, "Don't put that on MY tab! Put it on some OTHER tab!" Anyway, that's where you have to look. When you click the Other tab, the Other Options page appears.

3. **Click the Advanced Options button.**

   The Advanced Options dialog box appears (see Figure 10-18).

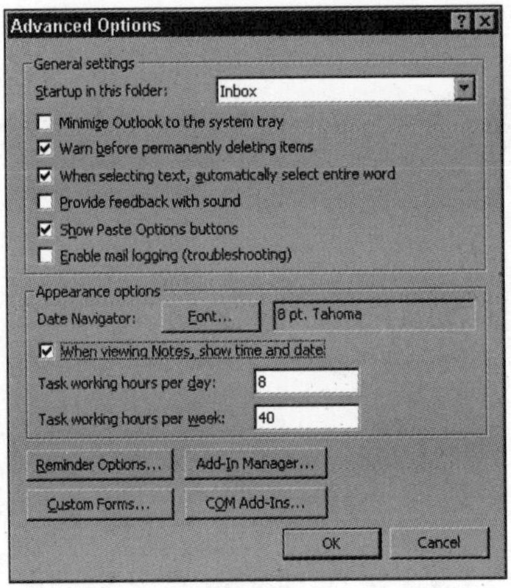

Figure 10-18: Time for some advanced options.

4. **Click the check box that says** `When viewing Notes, show time and date`.

   A check mark appears in the check box if you click once, and then it disappears if you click a second time. If you want to turn off the time and date display, make sure that the box doesn't contain a check mark.

5. **Click OK.**

   The time and date will no longer show up on command, unless you follow the same steps you used in turning them off to turn the time and date on again.

Forwarding a Note

Forwarding a note really means sending an e-mail message with a note included as an attachment. It's helpful if the person to whom you're forwarding the note uses Outlook, too.

To forward a note:

1. **Click the Notes icon in the Outlook Bar.**

   The Notes list appears.

2. **Click the title of the note that you want to forward.**
3. **Choose Actions⇨Forward (or press Ctrl+F).**

   The New Message form appears (see Figure 10-19).

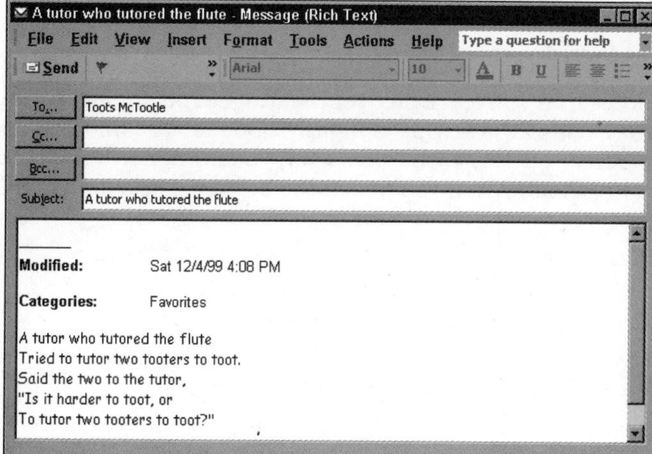

Figure 10-19: The New Message form with a Note attached.

4. **Click the To text box and type the e-mail address of the person to whom you're sending your note.**

   You can also click the To button to open the e-mail Address Book. Look up the name of the person to whom you want to forward your note, click To, and then click OK.

5. **Click the Cc text box and type the e-mail addresses of the people to whom you want to send a copy of your note.**

   If you're sending your note to several people, separate their addresses with commas or semicolons.

6. **Type the subject of the note in the Subject box.**

   The subject of your note will already be in the Subject box of the New Message form. You can leave it alone or type something else.

7. **If you want, type the text of a message in the text box.**

   You don't really have to include a message. Your note may say all that you want to say, but you can also add regular e-mail message text.

8. **Click the Send button.**

   Your message is off to its intended recipient(s).

If your note includes the address of a page on the World Wide Web, such as `www.dummies.com`, you can now just click the address to launch your Web browser as you can in all the other Outlook modules.

A Final Note

You can't take Outlook's Notes any more seriously than you take the little stick-on notes that you leave all over the fridge. They're just handy tools to help you save silly little scraps of information that you find you'll really need some day. After you play with Notes a bit, you'll wonder how you ever got along without them. When you remember again, make a note of it.

Chapter 11
Journaling

In This Chapter

- Recording items in the Journal
- Checking out Journal entries for a contact
- Searching for a particular Journal entry
- Printing your Journal
- Changing your view of the Journal
- Setting up automatic Journal entries

Stardate 2002: On *Star Trek,* the captain of the starship *Enterprise* faithfully makes daily entries in the star log. The captain records information about planets the crew has explored, the aliens they've battled, and the bizarre phenomena they've observed out in deep space, where no man (or woman) has gone before!

Now it's your turn. Just like the captain of the *Enterprise,* you can record your daily interactions with strange beings in bizarre environments under stressful circumstances, even if the strange beings are all in your own office. The Outlook Journal is your star log.

No doubt the high muck-a-mucks of the galaxy use the captain's log for terribly important things, but your Journal serves you more directly. Sometimes, when you need to find a document or a record of a conversation, you don't remember what you called the document or where you stored it, but you do remember *when* you created or received the item. In this case, you can go to the Journal and check the date when you remember dealing with the item and find what you need to know.

To get good use from the Journal though, you need to use it. You can set Outlook to make journal entries for nearly everything you do, or you can shut the Journal off entirely and make no entries to it. If you put nothing in the Journal, you get nothing out.

Don't Just Do Something — Stand There!

What's the easiest way to make entries in the Journal? Do nothing. The Journal automatically records any document you create, edit, or print in any Office XP application. The Journal also automatically tracks e-mail messages, meeting requests and responses, and task requests and responses. A few programs other than the Microsoft Office applications also have the capability to make entries in the Journal, but that feature is most often used with Office XP programs.

There's a catch: You have to tell Outlook that you want automatic Journal recording turned on. (All right, so you do have to do something besides just standing there.) Fortunately, if you haven't activated the Journal's automatic recording feature, Outlook 2002 asks you whether you want to turn the feature on every time you click the Journal icon.

To turn on the Journal's automatic recording feature:

1. **Choose Tools⇨Options.**

   The Options dialog box appears.

2. **Click the Journal Options button.**

   The Journal Options dialog box appears, as shown in Figure 11-1, with check boxes for all the types of activities that you can record automatically and the names of all the people for whom you can automatically record transactions, such as e-mail.

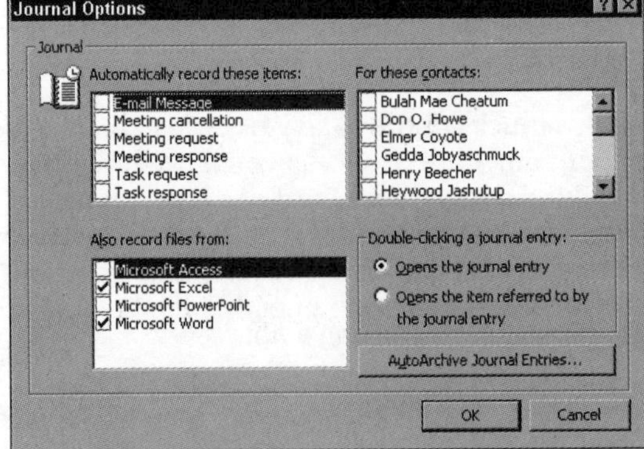

Figure 11-1: The Journal Options dialog box.

3. **Click to place a check in the check box for those items and files you want to automatically record and for the contacts about whom you want the information recorded.**

The list of people in the For These Contacts box is the same as the list of people in your Contact list. You can manually create Journal entries for people who are not in your Contact list; see the following section "Recording an Outlook item in the Journal manually."

When you add names to your Contact list in the Contacts module, those names aren't set for automatic recording in the Journal. You either need to check the name in the Journal Options dialog box or open the Contact record, click the Journal tab, and check Automatically Record Journal Entries for These Contacts.

4. **Click OK.**

   The Journal automatically records those items and files you selected for the contacts you named.

Recording an Outlook item in the Journal manually

If you don't want to clutter your Journal by recording everything automatically, you can enter selected items manually — just drag them to the Journal icon. For example, you may not want to record every transaction with a prospective client until you're certain that you're doing business with that client. You can drag relevant e-mail messages to the Journal and retain a record of serious inquiries. When you actually start doing business with a new client, you can set up automatic recording.

To manually record items in the Journal:

1. **Drag the item that you want to record (such as an e-mail message) to the Journal icon.**

   The Journal Entry form appears (see Figure 11-2). At the bottom of the form is an icon representing the item that you're recording, along with the item's name.

2. **Fill in the information that you want to record.**

   You don't have to record anything, though. The text box at the bottom of the screen gives you space for making a note to yourself, if you want to use it.

3. **Click Save and Close.**

   The item that you recorded is entered in the Journal. You can see your new entry when you view your Journal, as I describe in the section "Viewing the Journal," later in this chapter.

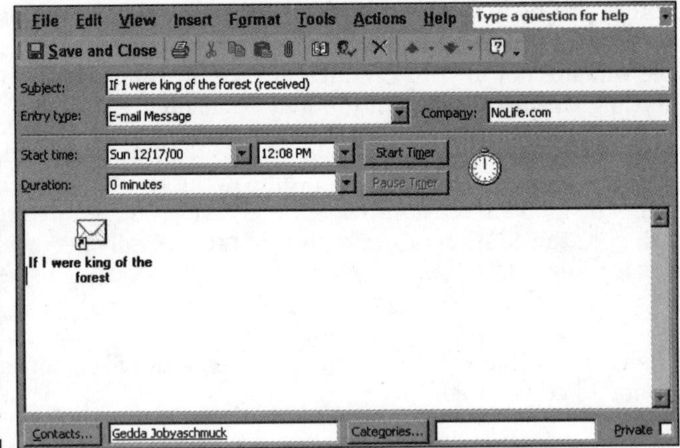

Figure 11-2: A Journal entry with a shortcut to an e-mail message attached in the text box.

Recording a document in the Journal

If your favorite program, such as a drawing or desktop-publishing program, doesn't show up in the list of programs that can make automatic entries in the Journal, all is not lost — you can drag documents from Outlook's My Computer folder to the Journal folder to create Journal entries for those programs' files, too. Because the Journal can keep track of many types of information about a document other than date and time (such as client, subject, and some notes), you can use the Journal to keep track of files you create in programs that aren't part of Microsoft Office. If you elected to let Outlook create Journal entries automatically for your Office XP applications, you don't have to make entries for Office XP documents.

To record a document in the Journal:

1. **Click the Other Shortcuts separator bar in the Outlook Bar.**

   The icons in the Other Shortcuts group appear, including the My Computer icon.

2. **Click the My Computer icon in the Outlook Bar.**

   Your list of drives appears (see Figure 11-3).

3. **Find the document that you want to record.**

   Double-click the drive that contains the document you want to record. Then double-click the folder in which you save your documents to find the document that you want to record. Highlight it.

4. **Click the Outlook Shortcuts separator bar in the Outlook Bar.**

   The icons in the Outlook Shortcuts group appear, including the Journal icon.

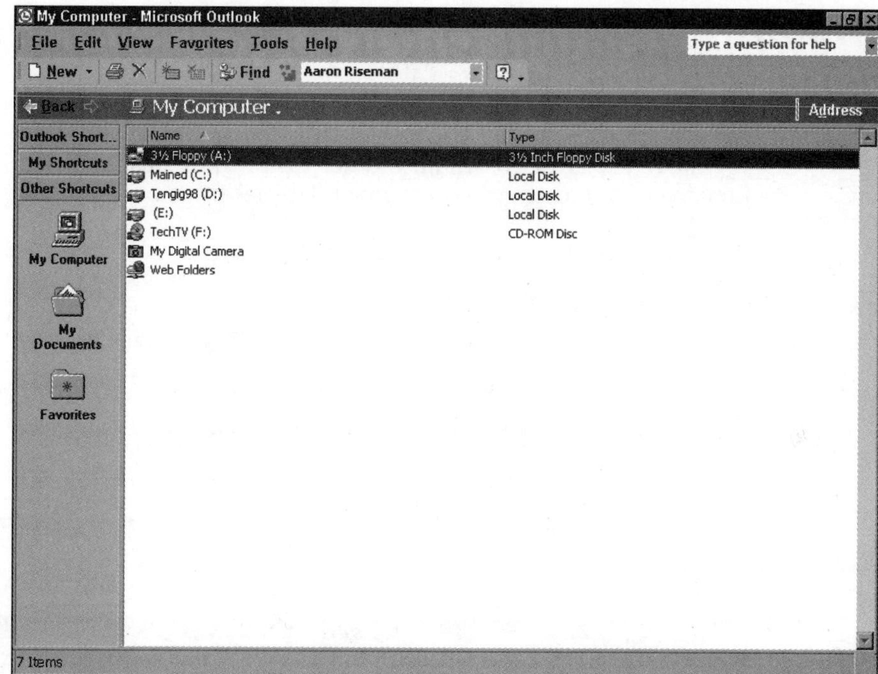

Figure 11-3: A list of drives in My Computer.

5. **Drag the document to the Journal icon.**

   The Journal Entry form appears, with an icon in the text box representing the file that you're recording.

6. **Click Save and Close.**

   Your document is recorded in the Journal.

The big benefit of recording documents in the Journal is the fact that Journal entries are really shortcuts to the documents themselves. When you enter a document in the Journal, you have quick access to information you've saved about the document, and you're only one click away from the document itself. So if you use a non-Office XP program that creates files that don't keep track of much information about themselves, the Journal is a great central location for keeping track of document information. For example, if you're saving pictures from a drawing program on your computer, you may want to save more information about each picture than just the file name. If you create Journal entries for each file, you can keep notes about each picture in the Journal. When you find the Journal entry for the picture you want, just double-click the icon for the picture. The program you use to see the picture opens.

Viewing Journal Entries for a Contact

My friend Vinnie in Brooklyn says, "You gotta know who you dealt wit' and when you dealt wit 'em." You can use the Contact list together with the Journal to keep track of whom you dealt with when. Just look in the person's Contact record to see when you made Journal entries:

1. **Click the Contacts icon in the Outlook Bar.**

   The Contact list appears.

2. **Double-click the name of the contact that you want to view.**

   The Contact record opens.

3. **Click the Activities tab in the Contact form.**

   A list of every Journal entry you've made for that person appears (see Figure 11-4), including the automatic entries that Outlook made if you chose that option.

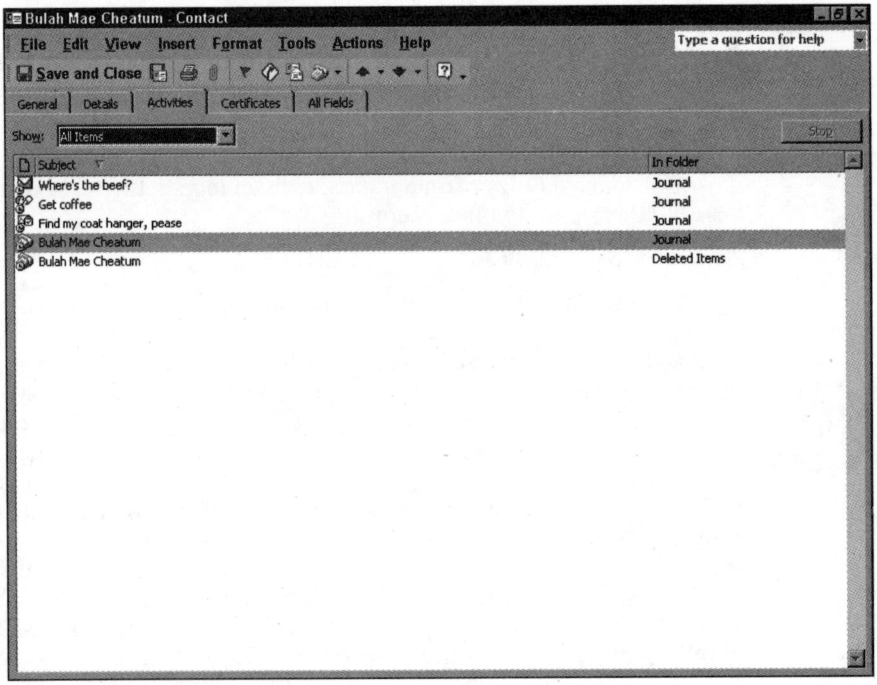

Figure 11-4: Journal entries for a contact.

Finding a Journal Entry

When you don't remember exactly when you did something or dealt with somebody, you can look it up by searching for words in the Journal item.

To find a Journal entry when you don't know the *when:*

1. **Click the words My Shortcuts in the Outlook Bar and click the Journal icon.**

   The list of Journal items appears.

2. **Choose Tools➪Find.**

   The Look For box appears (see Figure 11-5).

3. **Type a word or phrase that you can find in your Journal.**

   If you're looking for information about an upcoming meeting on the current Toad Inventory, type **toad**.

4. **Press Enter.**

   A list of matching items appears in your Journal list.

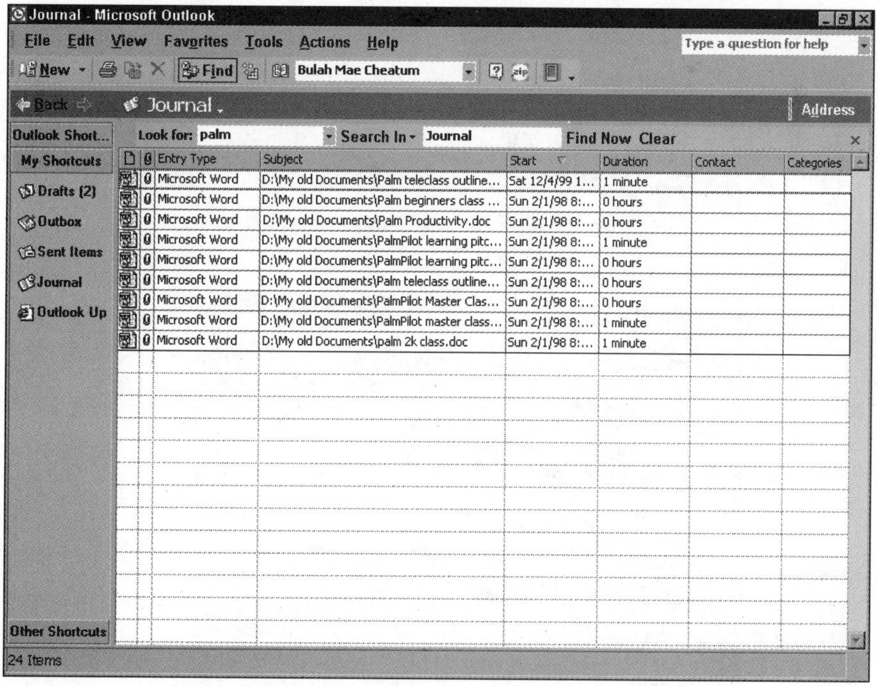

Figure 11-5: The Look For box.

5. **Double-click the icon to the left of your item in the Journal list.**

   The Journal item that you clicked appears. An icon in the text box at the bottom is a shortcut to any other Outlook item or document that the Journal entry represents. If you want to see the Calendar item that has details about the Toad Inventory meeting, double-click the icon at the bottom of the Journal entry. The Calendar item pops up.

Printing Your Journal

I can't explain why, but I just don't get a complete picture from information on a screen. I still like to print out my work on paper to really see what I've done. Printing your Journal (or segments of it) allows you to see a printed list of recent or upcoming activities. Stick it on the wall where you can look at it often.

To print your Journal:

1. **Click the words My Shortcuts in the Outlook Bar and click the Journal icon.**

   The list of Journal items appears.

2. **Select the entries that you want to print.**

   If you select nothing, you print the entire list. Also, if you use one of the views I describe later in this chapter (or even create your own view by grouping, sorting, or filtering), what you see is what you print.

3. **Choose File⇨Print (or press Ctrl+P).**

   The Print dialog box appears (see Figure 11-6).

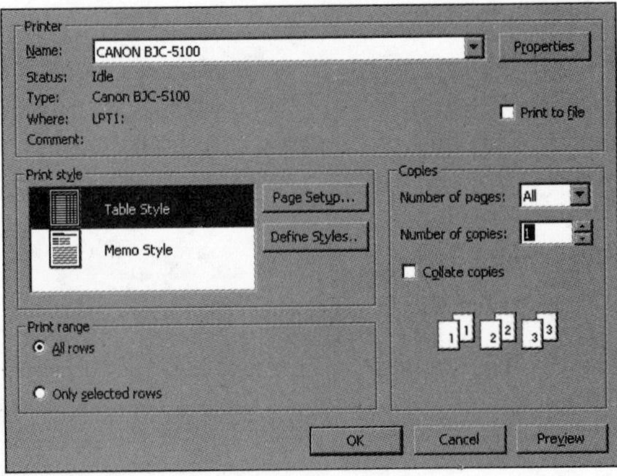

Figure 11-6: The Print dialog box.

4. **Choose Table or Memo style.**

   Table style prints only a list of your Journal entries, not the contents of each entry. Memo style prints the contents of your Journal entries, with each item appearing as a separate memo.

5. **Choose All Rows or Only Selected Rows.**

   If you want to print only certain rows, you have to select the rows that you want to print before you choose File⇨Print. Then click the Only Selected Rows button to limit what you print to those rows.

6. **Click OK.**

   The list of Journal entries you selected prints.

The printed list won't go up on the wall for you, however, unless you put it there.

Viewing the Journal

As with other Outlook modules, the Journal comes with multiple views that show your entries in different ways, depending on what you need to see. You may just want to see your record of phone calls or a list organized by the names of the people you've dealt with. The Current View menu allows you to change from one view to the next quickly.

The Entry List

The Entry List is the whole tomato — all your Journal entries, regardless of whom, what, or when. To call up the Entry List, simply choose View⇨Current View⇨Entry List (see Figure 11-7).

You can click the heading at the top of any column to sort the list according to the information in that column. If you want to arrange your list of Journal entries by the type of entry, for example, click the header that says Entry Type. Your list is sorted alphabetically by type of entry, with conversations before e-mail, e-mail before faxes, and so on.

By Type

By Type view takes sorting one step further by grouping items according to their type. To view your entries by type, choose View⇨Current View⇨By Type. To view your entire list of items of a particular type, click the plus sign next to the name of that type. Click the icon next to the name of the Entry Type again to close the list of that type. Then you can click to open another list of entries by type.

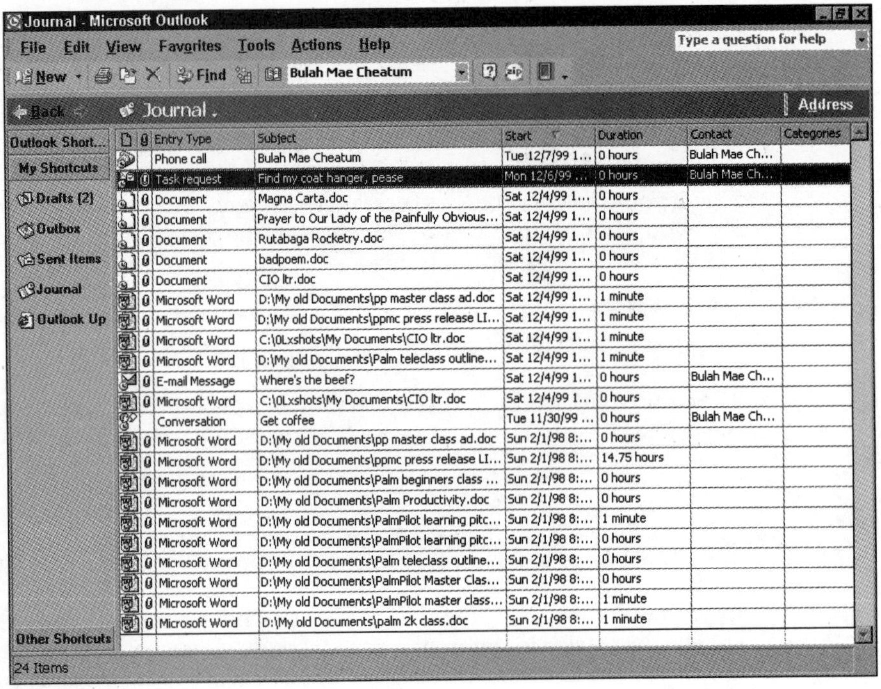

Figure 11-7: Viewing the Entry List — everything you've ever entered.

By Contact

By Contact view shows your Journal items grouped by the name of the person associated with the item. To see your entries in By Contact view, choose View➪Current View➪By Contact (see Figure 11-8).

Click the plus sign next to the name of the person whose entries you want to see. You can see entries for more than one person at a time.

By Category

If you've been assigning categories to your Journal items, By Category view collects all your entries into bunches of items of the same category. To see your entries by category, choose View➪Current View➪By Category.

If you've assigned more than one category to an item, the item shows up under both categories you've assigned.

4. **Choose Table or Memo style.**

   Table style prints only a list of your Journal entries, not the contents of each entry. Memo style prints the contents of your Journal entries, with each item appearing as a separate memo.

5. **Choose All Rows or Only Selected Rows.**

   If you want to print only certain rows, you have to select the rows that you want to print before you choose File⇨Print. Then click the Only Selected Rows button to limit what you print to those rows.

6. **Click OK.**

   The list of Journal entries you selected prints.

The printed list won't go up on the wall for you, however, unless you put it there.

Viewing the Journal

As with other Outlook modules, the Journal comes with multiple views that show your entries in different ways, depending on what you need to see. You may just want to see your record of phone calls or a list organized by the names of the people you've dealt with. The Current View menu allows you to change from one view to the next quickly.

The Entry List

The Entry List is the whole tomato — all your Journal entries, regardless of whom, what, or when. To call up the Entry List, simply choose View⇨Current View⇨Entry List (see Figure 11-7).

You can click the heading at the top of any column to sort the list according to the information in that column. If you want to arrange your list of Journal entries by the type of entry, for example, click the header that says Entry Type. Your list is sorted alphabetically by type of entry, with conversations before e-mail, e-mail before faxes, and so on.

By Type

By Type view takes sorting one step further by grouping items according to their type. To view your entries by type, choose View⇨Current View⇨By Type. To view your entire list of items of a particular type, click the plus sign next to the name of that type. Click the icon next to the name of the Entry Type again to close the list of that type. Then you can click to open another list of entries by type.

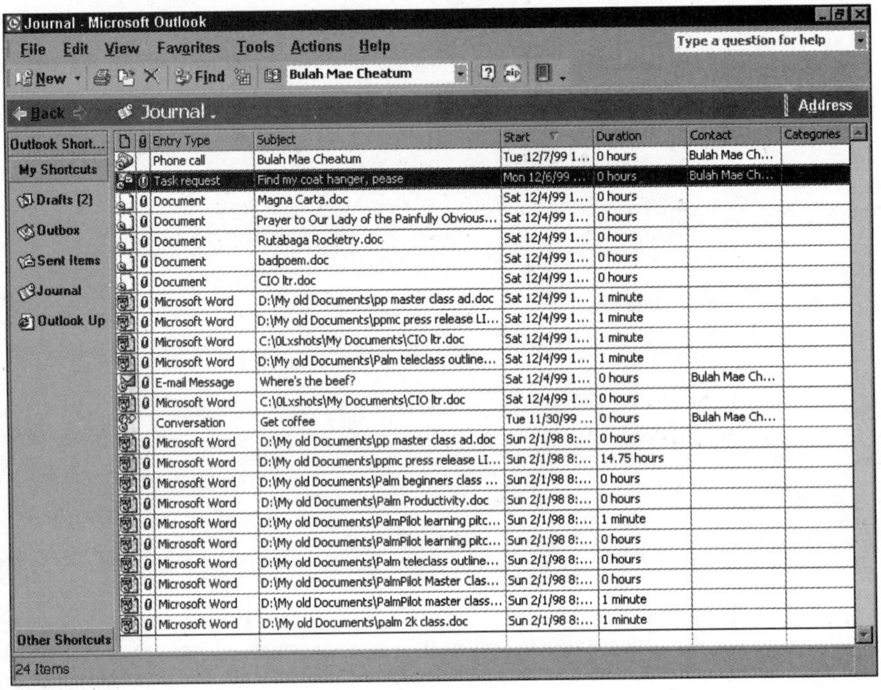

Journal - Microsoft Outlook

File Edit View Favorites Tools Actions Help

Type a question for help

New · Find · Bulah Mae Cheatum

Back · Journal · Address

Outlook Short... · My Shortcuts · Drafts (2) · Outbox · Sent Items · Journal · Outlook Up · Other Shortcuts

Entry Type	Subject	Start	Duration	Contact	Categories
Phone call	Bulah Mae Cheatum	Tue 12/7/99 1...	0 hours	Bulah Mae Ch...	
Task request	Find my coat hanger, pease	Mon 12/6/99 ...	0 hours	Bulah Mae Ch...	
Document	Magna Carta.doc	Sat 12/4/99 1...	0 hours		
Document	Prayer to Our Lady of the Painfully Obvious...	Sat 12/4/99 1...	0 hours		
Document	Rutabaga Rocketry.doc	Sat 12/4/99 1...	0 hours		
Document	badpoem.doc	Sat 12/4/99 1...	0 hours		
Document	CIO ltr.doc	Sat 12/4/99 1...	0 hours		
Microsoft Word	D:\My old Documents\pp master class ad.doc	Sat 12/4/99 1...	1 minute		
Microsoft Word	D:\My old Documents\ppmc press release LI...	Sat 12/4/99 1...	1 minute		
Microsoft Word	C:\0Lxshots\My Documents\CIO ltr.doc	Sat 12/4/99 1...	1 minute		
Microsoft Word	D:\My old Documents\Palm teleclass outline...	Sat 12/4/99 1...	1 minute		
E-mail Message	Where's the beef?	Sat 12/4/99 1...	0 hours	Bulah Mae Ch...	
Microsoft Word	C:\0Lxshots\My Documents\CIO ltr.doc	Sat 12/4/99 1...	0 hours		
Conversation	Get coffee	Tue 11/30/99 ...	0 hours	Bulah Mae Ch...	
Microsoft Word	D:\My old Documents\pp master class ad.doc	Sun 2/1/98 8:...	0 hours		
Microsoft Word	D:\My old Documents\ppmc press release LI...	Sun 2/1/98 8:...	14.75 hours		
Microsoft Word	D:\My old Documents\Palm beginners class ...	Sun 2/1/98 8:...	0 hours		
Microsoft Word	D:\My old Documents\Palm Productivity.doc	Sun 2/1/98 8:...	0 hours		
Microsoft Word	D:\My old Documents\PalmPilot learning pitc...	Sun 2/1/98 8:...	1 minute		
Microsoft Word	D:\My old Documents\PalmPilot learning pitc...	Sun 2/1/98 8:...	0 hours		
Microsoft Word	D:\My old Documents\Palm teleclass outline...	Sun 2/1/98 8:...	0 hours		
Microsoft Word	D:\My old Documents\PalmPilot Master Clas...	Sun 2/1/98 8:...	0 hours		
Microsoft Word	D:\My old Documents\PalmPilot master class...	Sun 2/1/98 8:...	1 minute		
Microsoft Word	D:\My old Documents\palm 2k class.doc	Sun 2/1/98 8:...	1 minute		

24 Items

Figure 11-7: Viewing the Entry List — everything you've ever entered.

By Contact

By Contact view shows your Journal items grouped by the name of the person associated with the item. To see your entries in By Contact view, choose View➪Current View➪By Contact (see Figure 11-8).

Click the plus sign next to the name of the person whose entries you want to see. You can see entries for more than one person at a time.

By Category

If you've been assigning categories to your Journal items, By Category view collects all your entries into bunches of items of the same category. To see your entries by category, choose View➪Current View➪By Category.

If you've assigned more than one category to an item, the item shows up under both categories you've assigned.

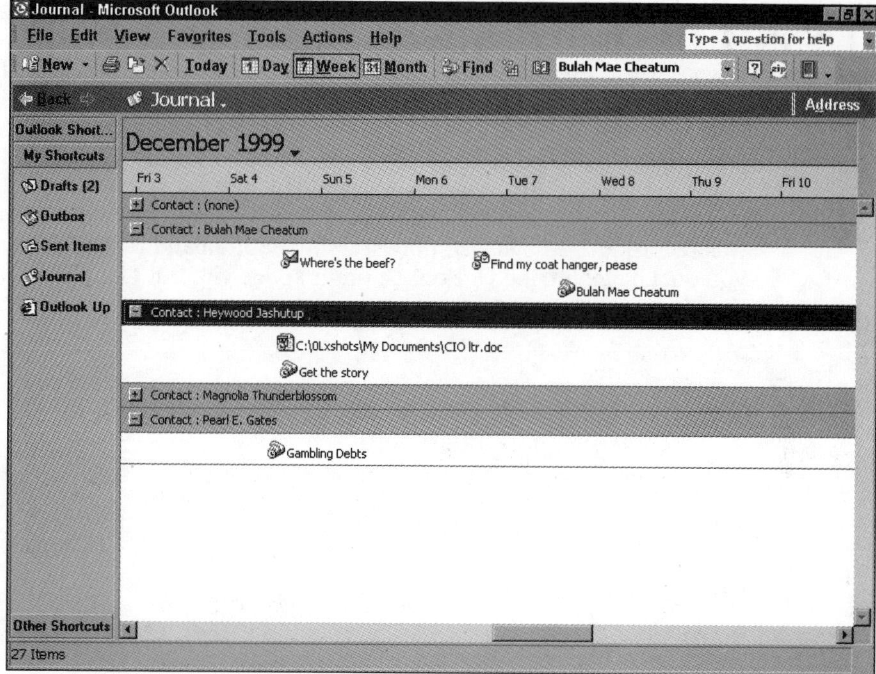

Figure 11-8: Seeing your entries in the By Contact view.

Last Seven Days

The items that you likely need first are the ones that you used last. Last Seven Days view is a quick way to see your most recent activities at a glance. To see a week's worth of Journal entries, choose View➪Current View➪Last Seven Days.

Documents that you've created, phone calls, e-mail messages — anything you've done in the last seven days — you can see them all in Last Seven Days view. This view shows anything you've worked on during the last week, including documents you may have created a very long time ago; that's why you may see some pretty old dates in this view.

Phone Calls

Because you can keep track of your phone calls in the Journal, the Journal lets you see a list of the calls you've tracked. Simply choose View➪Current View➪Phone Calls.

To print a list of your phone calls, switch to Phone Calls view and press Ctrl+P.

It's All in the Journal

The Journal can be enormously helpful whether you choose to use it regularly or rarely. You don't have to limit yourself to recording documents or Outlook items. You can keep track of conversations or customer inquiries or any other transaction in which chronology matters. If you set the Journal for automatic entries, you can ignore it completely until you need to see what was recorded. You can also play starship captain and record everything that you do. I haven't tried Outlook in outer space yet, but I know I would enjoy the views.

Chapter 12

What You Need to Know to Use Outlook at Home

In This Chapter

- Setting up Outlook
- Discovering ISPs
- Checking out the online services
- Choosing a service provider
- Setting up e-mail accounts
- Establishing directory services

Working at home is very different from working in an office. First, working in your bathrobe is pretty unusual in big companies, but home workers do it all the time. But more important, when you work from home, you probably don't have a huge network, three phone lines, and dozens of computer gurus at your service like you do at a big company. That's why Outlook works a bit differently for the home user than it does for the corporate user. If you use Outlook in a large corporation, most of the things I discuss in this chapter will be less interesting to you, but Chapter 14 is focused on using Outlook in big business settings, so you might want to look there.

What's an ISP?

If you use a computer at home, you probably send and receive e-mail through an outside service that your computer dials up over the telephone. The general term for the kind of outfit that provides this service is *Internet Service Provider,* or *ISP.* ISPs do more than exchange e-mail messages for you; an ISP also provides the Internet connection that enables your browser to access and display pages from the World Wide Web and lets you do nearly anything that you can do on the Internet.

AOL and Outlook

The biggest online service is America Online (AOL). Millions and millions of people call AOL their online home, and new members are joining every day. AOL subscribers can log on and take advantage of shopping, travel services, classes, and information of every type. They can also browse the Internet and exchange e-mail. So far, you can't use Outlook to send e-mail if you use America Online. The folks at AOL made a big splashy announcement saying that they planned to support Outlook Express back in early 1998, but then they changed their minds. If AOL ever supports Outlook Express for e-mail, you'll be able to set up Outlook to exchange your AOL e-mail messages, too. At the moment, however, you can exchange AOL e-mail only through AOL's own software. On the other hand, now that AOL has purchased Netscape, they might want to make AOL mail compatible with the Netscape mail program, which would probably make AOL compatible with Outlook as well. Stay tuned.

Online services, such as America Online, CompuServe, and The Microsoft Network, function as ISPs, but they also offer a variety of features, such as discussion forums and file libraries. If you belong to an online service, you don't need a separate ISP. On the other hand, if all you want to do is exchange e-mail and browse the Web, you may not want a full-featured online service; an ISP may be all you need.

Everything about the Internet and online services change quickly. When it comes to the best way to get and use an online service, what's true as I write this chapter may no longer be true when you read it. I tell you how it is as of early 2001.

The biggest advantage to using an online service to connect you to the Internet is that these services all try to make the process of connecting as easy as possible, and most of them have plenty of staff to help you when things go wrong. Also, if you want some assurance that you or your children won't run across scary people or nasty material while exploring cyberspace, online services are well equipped to screen out things that you may find objectionable.

If you want to check out one of the online services, call one of the following numbers:

- CompuServe (`www.compuserve.com`) 800-848-8990
- The Microsoft Network (`www.msn.com`) 800-386-5550

What about Cable Modems and DSL?

If you have high-speed Internet access from your cable television operator or DSL through a telephone company, congratulations! You'll enjoy zippy Web surfing and your e-mail will come and go in a flash. You also don't need to deal with an ISP, because your cable company or DSL provider does that job for you.

Picking a Provider

Any computer that can run Outlook 2002 probably includes at least one icon on the desktop to help set you up with an Internet Service Provider or online service, such as AOL or AT&T or the Microsoft Network. If you're not satisfied with any of the services that your computer already includes, literally hundreds of Internet Service Providers exist around the United States and thousands more around the world. Some of them are small businesses that serve only a certain community. Others are huge, global companies that can be reached from nearly anywhere on the planet Earth (and perhaps some other planets, too, I don't know).

If you do all your e-mailing and Web surfing from home or from one spot, a local ISP may be just fine for you. Check your local newspapers for ads from nearby ISPs. Local shops may be a little more personal and less inclined to censor the things you browse as the bigger operators sometimes do. Lots of nasty places exist on the Internet that some people don't want to run across accidentally, so a little bit of censorship suits some folks just fine. Other people want completely unfettered access when they surf the Web, so smaller services with no censorship suit them better. Take your pick.

If you travel a lot and need to check your e-mail while you travel, a big operator may suit you best. Table 12-1 lists ISPs with pretty wide coverage in the United States.

Table 12-1 National ISPs

ISP	*Web Address*	*Phone Number*
AT&T WorldNet Service	`www.att.com/worldnet`	800-400-1447
Earthlink Network	`www.earthlink.net`	800-395-8425
IDT Internet Services	`www.idt.net`	800-CALL-IDT

You can find an even more extensive list of ISPs in a magazine called *Boardwatch,* or you can check the magazine's Web site at `www.boardwatch.com`. Another good place to look for an ISP is a Web site called `www.thelist.com`. There were once several companies that charged nothing for Internet access, but most of the companies that offered free ISP service went out of business. For some reason, they couldn't make money by giving stuff away free. Imagine that!

Setting Up Internet E-Mail Accounts

After you've signed up with an ISP, you need to set up Outlook to send and receive e-mail from your account. You need to set up your Internet e-mail account only once, although you can set up multiple Internet e-mail accounts. If you're a corporate user, your system administrators may not want you to mess around with account settings at all, so it's best to ask first.

If you're on your own, you should probably call the tech support line from your online service or ISP to get all the proper spellings of the server names and passwords that you need to enter.

To set up an Internet e-mail account, follow these steps:

1. **Choose Tools⇨E-mail Accounts**

   The E-mail Accounts dialog box appears.

2. **Click the circle to the left of the words "Add new e-mail account."**

   The circle appears blackened to show that you've selected it.

3. **Click Next (or press Enter).**

   The Server Type dialog box appears.

4. **Click the circle next to the type of server your e-mail provider requires.**

   You'll need to check with your e-mail service on this one, but the most likely choice is POP3.

5. **Click Next (or press Enter).**

   The Internet E-mail Settings screen appears.

6. **Type the settings that your e-mail provider requires.**

   Again, each e-mail service differs, but most of them can tell you how to make their e-mail work with Outlook.

7. **Click the Test Account Settings button.**

   The Test Account Settings dialog box appears and shows you what's happening while Outlook tests the settings you've entered to see if you got everything right. If you type one wrong letter in one of your e-mail settings, the computers Outlook has to send messages through will reject your mail, so it's good to find out if your setup works while you're setting things up. If the test fails, try retyping some of the entries, and click the Test Account Settings button until you get a successful test. When the test is successful, the Test Account Settings dialog box says `Congratulations! All tests completed successfully. Click close to continue.` So that's what you should do.

8. **Click Close.**

   The Test Account Settings dialog box closes.

9. **Click Next (or press Enter).**

   The Congratulations screen appears to make you feel successful!

10. **Click Finish.**

As I mention earlier in this section, you can set up more than one Internet e-mail account, so you can have separate addresses for each member of the family. You also may want to have separate accounts for business use and personal use. Perhaps you just want to set up separate accounts so that you can send yourself messages. Whatever you like to do, the process of setting up different accounts is pretty much the same.

Dealing with Multiple Mail Accounts

It's possible to exchange e-mail through more than one e-mail address with Outlook. I have different e-mail addresses for business use and personal use. All you have to do if you have more than one e-mail address is to set up a separate account for each address the way I describe in the previous section "Setting Up Internet E-Mail Accounts." Normally, Outlook sends replies to e-mail messages through the account from which you received the message, so you don't really have to think about which account you're using. When you're creating a message, though, Outlook sends the message through the account that you marked as the default account. If you want to check which account a message will be sent through, click the Accounts button on the message form toolbar and look at the box labeled "Send message using."

Free e-mail — well, almost!

If you use only the e-mail address provided by your Internet Service Provider, you'll get along just fine. But if you want to set up a separate e-mail address for each member of your family, or keep your business e-mail separate from your personal messages, you can start up an account with any number of mailbox providers. Mail.com (`www.mail.com`) is one of the more popular providers of electronic mailboxes. You can sign up for an address through Mail.com for free and check your e-mail messages through your Web browser. If you want to take advantage of Outlook's sophisticated mail management features with this kind of account, outfits like Mail.com usually charge and extra fee for what they call a POP3 account. I've been using Mail.com for about 2 years, and I think they do a good job. Other companies that offer e-mail services include Iname (`www.iname.com`) and Yahoo! (`www. yahoo. com`). If you have the American Express card, you can get a free e-mail address at `www. americanexpress.com`. Don't leave home without that.

Setting Up Directory Services

Sending an e-mail message to somebody is easy if you know that person's e-mail address. You can find e-mail addresses for people around the world right from Outlook. Before you can use Outlook to find e-mail addresses, though, you need to set up a directory service to help you find names and addresses.

Outlook is set up to check one of several popular search services to find e-mail addresses, but you need to tell Outlook which one you want to use.

Here's how to tell Outlook which search service you prefer:

1. **Choose Tools⇨E-mail Accounts**

   The E-mail Accounts dialog box appears.

2. **Click the circle to the left of the words "Add new directory or address book."**

   The circle appears blackened to show that you've selected it.

3. **Click Next (or press Enter).**

   The Directory or Address Book type screen appears.

4. **Click the circle to the left of the words "Internet Directory Service."**

   The circle appears blackened to show that you've selected it.

5. **Click Next (or press Enter).**

   The Directory Service Settings screen appears.

6. **Type the name of the service that you want to use.**

   The name of the service you enter appears. You can choose from a variety of services, and if you don't like your choice, you can easily switch to another one. I picked one called Bigfoot because it gave the most responses when I looked for my own name.

7. **Click Finish.**

   The Congratulations screen closes.

After you restart Outlook, you can check an e-mail address while you're creating a new message. Just type the name of the person you want to find in the To box of your message, and then click the Check Names button in the message toolbar (or press Ctrl+K). If the service you picked knows your recipient's address, an underline appears beneath the person's name to show you that the message is properly addressed.

Send, receive, whatever!

Just because you clicked Send on your outgoing message doesn't automatically mean that your message was sent. People who use Outlook at home normally connect to the Internet via the telephone line. Each time you send messages, your computer needs to make a phone call to your Internet Service Provider so that Outlook can drop off the messages that you created and pick up the messages that others have sent to you. So, sometime after you've created a batch of messages, you need to choose Tools⇨Send/Receive (or press F9) to tell Outlook to dial up your ISP and actually send out the messages, if you're using Outlook at home.

The best reason to customize a form is to add fields that aren't available in the original form. *Fields* are categories of information that you need to use, such as phone numbers, names, and addresses. In the following section, I show you an example of a form customized to suit a car salesperson. The customized form uses all the information from the original Outlook form and adds a few fields that are specific to the needs of someone who sells cars.

Adding a Standard Field to a Form

When you first install Outlook, hundreds of standard fields are already set up for you to use. Standard fields are made to store the kind of information that people often need to use, such as names, addresses, dates, and so on. You can choose to add any of them to your forms, or you can create custom fields. I discuss how to create custom fields in the section "Adding a User-Defined Field to a Form," later in this chapter.

To add a standard field to an Outlook form:

1. **Choose View⇨Folder List.**

   The Folder List appears (see Figure 13-1), giving you a more detailed view of your Outlook folders. You use the Folder List to create a new folder. I suggest that you create a new folder for this example.

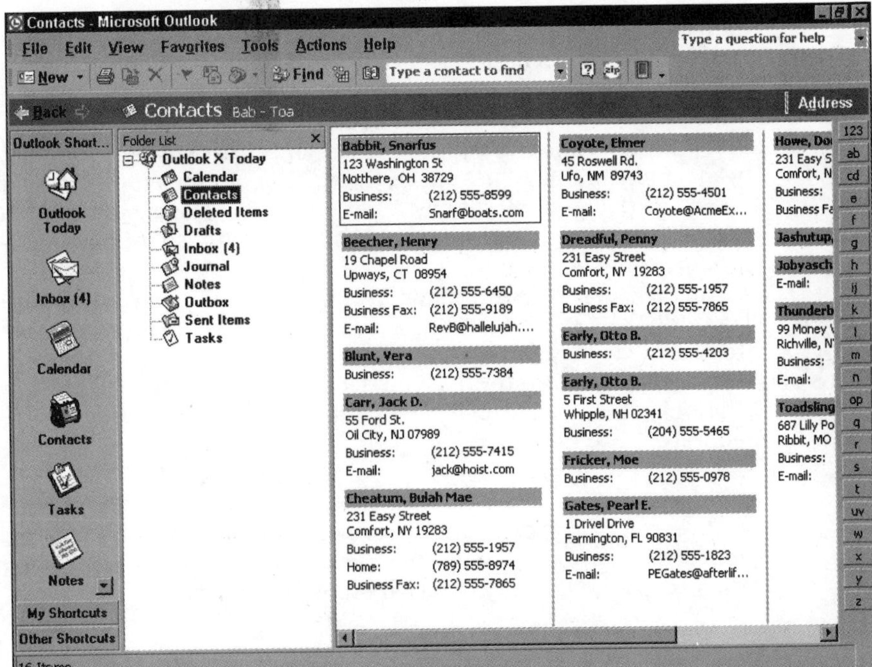

Figure 13-1: The Folder List with the Contacts folder highlighted.

Chapter 13

Making Outlook Your Own: How to Personalize Standard Forms

In This Chapter

- Understanding forms
- Adding standard fields to a form
- Adding your own fields to a form
- Using a custom form

Every time you choose File⇨New in Outlook or double-click an item to open it, a form pops up. *Forms* enable you to create a new item or edit information in an old item. The forms that come with Outlook are shaped and designed to handle the information that most people use most of the time.

If the forms that pop up automatically in Outlook don't suit your fancy, you can modify them a bit to meet your needs. You can't create forms from scratch in Outlook (the way you can with a database program, such as Microsoft Access), just as most people can't create their own cookie cutters. But you can bend a cookie cutter that you already have into a shape you want, and you can adjust one of the existing Outlook forms to meet your needs. Actually, you'll get much better results from customizing Outlook forms than by bending your cookie cutters out of shape.

Of all the Outlook users I know, at least 99 percent don't know how to create an Outlook form and 98 percent don't even know that they can. Somehow, tens of millions of Outlook users get along just fine without ever knowing how to create an Outlook form. If you decide you'd rather not mess with creating Outlook forms, you probably won't miss much by skipping this chapter entirely.

After you customize a form, you can give it a different name from the old form so that you have two forms: the original Outlook form and your new customized form. You can make the forms look entirely different when you use them, even though they're based on the same form.

2. **Right-click the folder in which you want to create the new subfolder.**

   For this example, right-click the Contacts folder. A shortcut menu appears. The commands in the menu allow you to create a subfolder as well as move, copy, rename, or delete an existing folder.

3. **Choose New Folder.**

   The Create New Folder dialog box appears (see Figure 13-2).

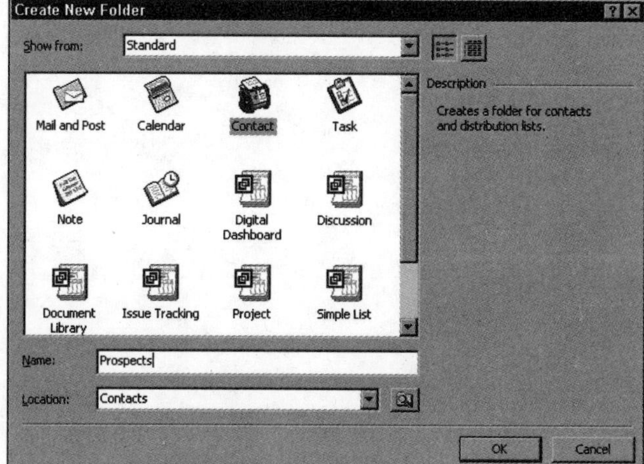

Figure 13-2: The Create New Folder dialog box.

4. **Type a name for the folder.**

   I use **Prospects** for this example.

5. **Click OK.**

   The new folder that you created appears in the Folder List and a dialog box appears asking if you want to add the new folder to the Outlook Bar.

6. **Click Yes if you want to add the folder to your Outlook Bar or No if you don't.**

   I usually say no, but that's up to you. Adding the folder to your Outlook Bar just makes your new folder a little easier to find.

7. **Click the new folder.**

   If the Contacts folder has a plus sign next to it, click the plus sign. Subfolders of the Contacts folder appear.

8. **Choose File⇨New⇨Contact.**

   The Contact form appears.

9. Choose Tools➪Forms➪Design This Form.

The form switches into Forms Designer mode (see Figure 13-3). The form looks similar to what it looked like before you chose Tools➪Forms➪Design This Form, but five new pages — called (P.2) through (P.6) — appear. These pages are blank pages that you can customize with new fields, new colors, and so on. The Field Chooser window also opens to offer you a selection of new fields to add to your form.

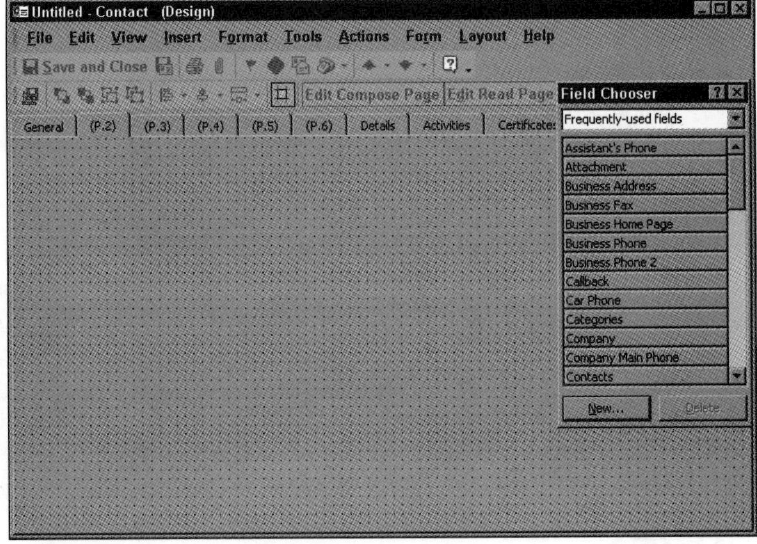

Figure 13-3: The Form Designer with the Field Chooser showing.

10. Click (P.2) or any other blank page.

It's your choice; you can add fields to any of the new pages.

11. (Optional) To make this page visible, choose Form➪Display This Page.

The parentheses disappear from around P.2. The new pages that appear when you choose Tools➪Forms➪Design This Form are in parentheses, whereas the ones that appear in the form before you choose this command aren't in parentheses. That's how you can tell which pages will be visible when you finish customizing the form.

If you want, you can leave all pages visible. But one reason to create a custom form is to reduce the number of steps required to view, enter, or edit the information on the form. You also may be creating this form for other people to use, so you want to keep your form clear and simple. One-page forms are clearer and simpler than multipage forms.

You can click any page and make the page invisible to the user by clicking the General tab and then choosing Form➪Display This Page. (The command toggles the page on and off.)

12. **Choose Form⇨Rename Page.**

    The Rename Page dialog box appears (see Figure 13-4).

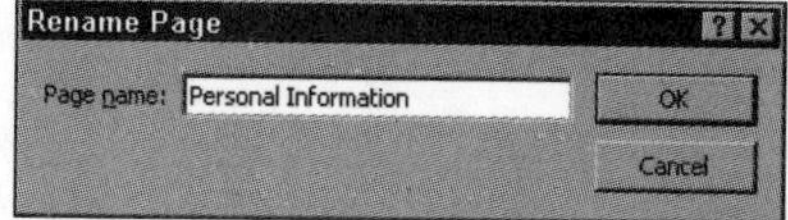

Figure 13-4: The Rename Page dialog box.

13. **Type a new name for the page.**

    I use **Personal Information** as a good name for this page, but any name you choose will work.

14. **Click OK.**

    The page tab now has the name that you typed in the Rename Page dialog box.

    Now you can add some fields to the new page. That's what customizing a form is all about. The Field Chooser is the place to find fields to add to your form.

    I think that the Field Chooser is confusing. You never see all the fields that are available; you see only a certain subset. The words below Field Chooser tell you which subset you're seeing. In this case, I use the Personal fields subset (see Figure 13-5).

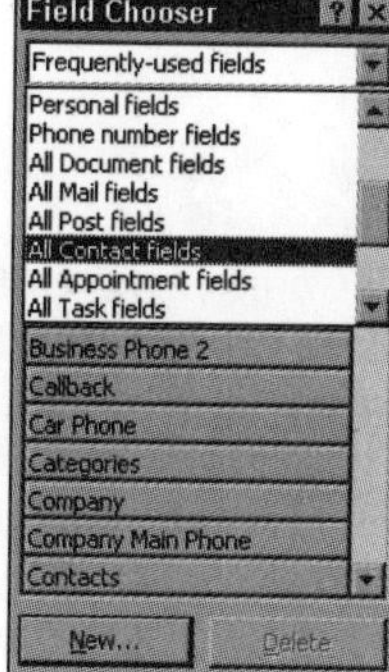

Figure 13-5: The Field Chooser contains more fields than you can see.

You can choose Frequently-Used fields to limit what Outlook shows you to a small range of fields, or All Contact fields to choose from every kind of field that Outlook allows in this type of form.

15. **Select a category from the drop-down list at the top of the Field Chooser and then select the name of a field in that category.**

For this example, select the Personal fields category and then select the Referred By field, which, for example, a car salesperson can use to store the name of the person who referred the customer.

16. **Drag the selected field onto the page.**

When you drag a field onto the page in Forms Designer mode, it automatically aligns properly on the page. To add more fields to your form, keep dragging them in from the Field Chooser (see Figure 13-6).

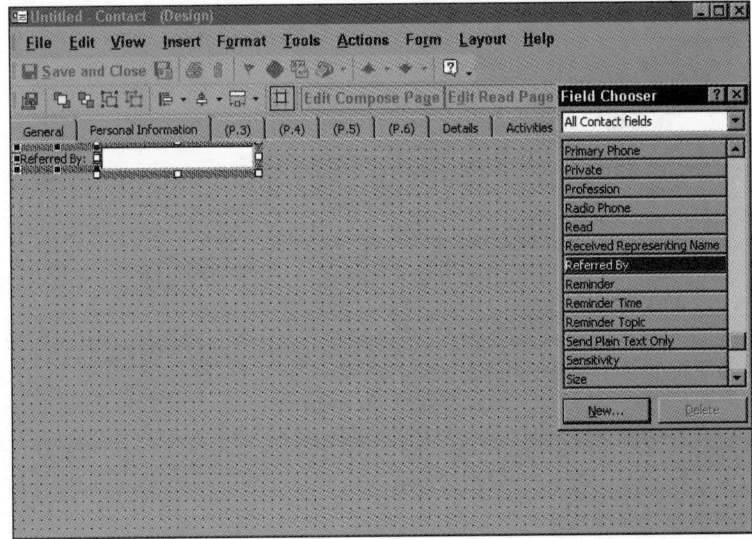

Figure 13-6: Dragging a field into a form.

17. **Choose Tools➪Forms➪Publish Form As.**

The Publish Form As dialog box appears. *Publishing* is the Outlook term for making a form available in a certain folder or group of folders. Outlook will publish your new form to whichever folder you clicked before beginning to design your form unless you click the Look In button and choose a different folder.

18. **Type a name for your new form in the Display Name box.**

The name **New Prospect** is a good one for this form. The form name will appear in the menus when you create a new item for this folder.

19. **Click Publish.**

Nothing visible happens, but your form is published to the folder that you designated — in this case, the Prospects folder.

20. **Choose File➪Close.**

A dialog box appears, asking `Do you want to save changes?`

21. **Click Yes to save changes.**

    A dialog box appears, asking `Do you want to save this contact with an empty file as field?`

22. **Click Yes.**

    The Forms Designer closes.

The form now contains your additional standard field.

Adding a User-Defined Field to a Form

You can choose from hundreds of standard fields when you first use Outlook, but that's just the beginning. User-defined fields let you add types of information to your forms that weren't included with Outlook.

Here's how to create a user-defined field and add it to a form:

1. **Choose File⇨New⇨Contact.**

   The Contact form appears.

2. **Choose Tools⇨Forms⇨Design This Form.**

   The form switches into Forms Designer mode. The form looks similar to what it looked like before you chose Tools⇨Forms⇨Design This Form, but five new pages — called (P.2) through (P.6) — appear. These pages are blank pages that you can customize with new fields, new colors, and so on.

3. **Click the tab of an unused page.**

   You can add fields to any of the new pages.

4. **Choose Form⇨Display This Page.**

   The parentheses disappear from the name of the page in the tab, showing you that this page will be visible when you finish customizing the form.

5. **Click New in the Field Chooser dialog box.**

   The New Field dialog box appears (see Figure 13-7).

   Now it's time to create a user-defined field. A *user-defined field* is a field that you dream up to put in your form because you need to add a type of data for which Outlook doesn't have a standard field.

6. **Type a name for a new field.**

   Outlook doesn't include a field called Make of Auto, so type **Make of Auto**. You can use any name up to 32 characters.

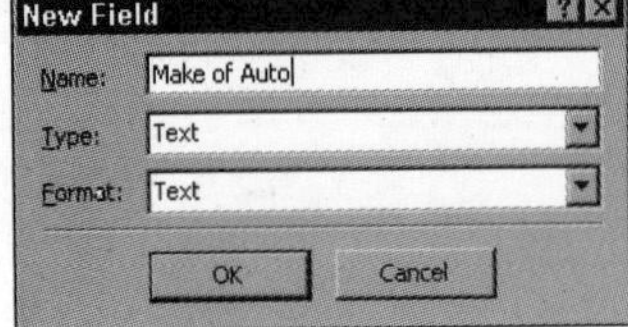

Figure 13-7: The New Field dialog box.

7. **Click OK.**

   Your new field appears in the Field Chooser, and the words `User-Defined Fields` appear at the top of the Field Chooser as the field type.

8. **Drag the new field onto the form page.**

   The new field aligns itself automatically.

9. **Click the Publish button at the far left of the Design Form toolbar.**

   The Publish button is the leftmost button on the lower Forms toolbar (refer to Figure 13-6). You can also choose File➪Publish Form As. The Publish Form As dialog box appears, with the current name of the form already filled in.

10. **Click Publish.**

Changes that you made to your form are now stored and will appear the next time you use the form.

Using the Form You've Designed

Using a form you've designed in any folder to which you published the form is easy. The name you gave to the form will turn up on the Outlook main menu whenever you choose the Outlook folder that you published the form to.

Here's how to use a custom form:

1. **Click the Actions menu.**

   That's the menu immediately to the left of Help in the menu bar.

2. **Choose the custom form name that appears at the bottom of the menu.**

   If you created the form called New Prospect earlier in this chapter, when you choose the Contacts menu, the name New Prospect appears at the bottom of the menu (see Figure 13-8); choose it. The first time that you choose your new custom form, Outlook automatically installs the new form for you. That can take a few minutes.

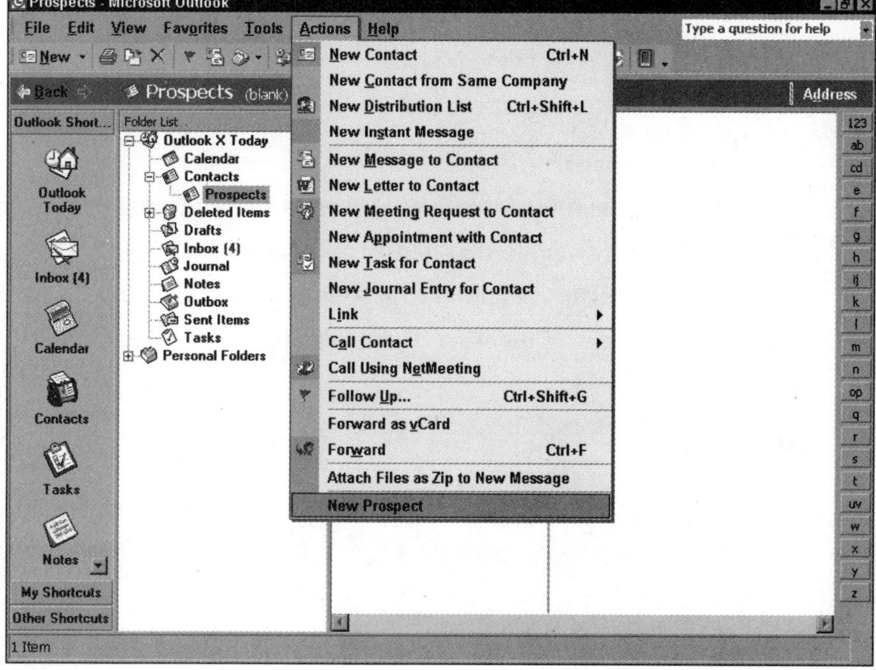

Figure 13-8: When you publish a custom form, the name of your form appears at the bottom of the Actions menu.

3. **Fill out the form.**
4. **Click Save and Close.**

You can have more than one custom form assigned to a folder. You can create a Vacation Request folder, for example, and store Vacation Request, Vacation Approved, and Vacation Denied forms in the same folder.

Making a Custom Form a Folder's Default Form

Every time you choose a folder in Outlook and choose File➪New, a form pops up to invite you to enter the kind of data that's used in that folder. You can also pick another form to use by choosing the form by name from the menus. If you want your custom form to be the one that Outlook offers when you choose File➪New, you need to designate the form to be the default form for that folder.

Here's how you designate a form to be the default form for a folder:

1. **Choose View⇨Folder List.**

   The Folder List opens (if it was closed). This command toggles like a light switch, opening the Folder List if it was closed and closing the list if it was open.

2. **Click the folder for which you want to change the default form.**

   For this example, that folder is the Prospects folder.

3. **Choose File⇨Folder⇨Properties for *Name of folder*.**

   The folder's Properties dialog box appears (see Figure 13-9).

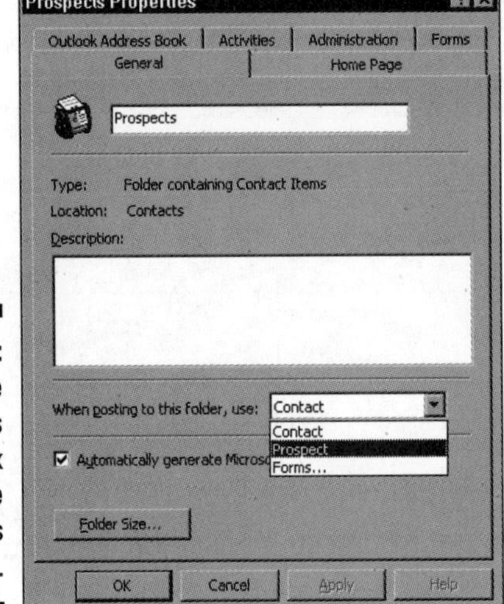

Figure 13-9: Use the Properties dialog box to set the folder's default form.

4. **Click the When Posting to This Folder, Use drop-down list.**

   Select the name of your custom form.

5. **Click OK.**

   Now every time you choose File⇨New in that folder, your customized form appears.

Chapter 14

Big-Time Collaboration with Outlook

In This Chapter

- Collaborating with Microsoft Exchange
- Understanding all those Address Books
- Using Public Folders
- Accessing Outlook through the Web

Microsoft is a big company that writes big programs for big companies with big bucks. So, as you'd expect, some parts of Outlook are intended for people at big companies. Big companies that use Outlook usually have a network that's running a program called Microsoft Exchange Server in the background. Exchange Server works as a team with Outlook to let you do things that you can't do with Outlook alone. Outlook users on an Exchange Server can look at the calendar of another employee, or give someone else the power to answer e-mail messages on his or her behalf, or do any of a host of handy tasks right from their desk.

Many features of Microsoft Exchange Server look as if they're just a part of Outlook, so most Exchange Server users have no idea that any program other than Outlook is involved. It really doesn't matter whether you know the difference between Outlook and Exchange Server, except that Outlook and Exchange can do so many things together that Outlook can't do as well alone.

Collaborating with Outlook's Help

If your company is like most others, you spend a lot of time in meetings, and even more figuring out when to hold meetings and agreeing on what to do when you're not having meetings. Outlook has some tools for planning meetings and making decisions that are very helpful for people who work in groups. These first few features are available to all Outlook 2002 users, but they work much better when you're using Exchange as well.

Organizing a meeting

Say that you need to have a meeting with three coworkers. You call the first person to suggest a meeting time, and then call the second, only to find out that the second person isn't available when the first one wants to meet. So you agree on a time with the second person, only to discover that the third person can't make this new time. You might want to invite a fourth person, but heaven knows how long it'll take to come up with a time with that one.

If you use Outlook, you can check everyone's schedule, pick a time, and suggest a meeting time that everyone can work with in the first place with a single message.

To invite several people to a meeting, follow these steps:

1. **Choose File⇨New⇨Meeting Request (or press Ctrl+Shift+Q).**

   The New Appointment Form opens.

2. **Click the Scheduling tab.**

   The Attendee Availability page appears (see Figure 14-1).

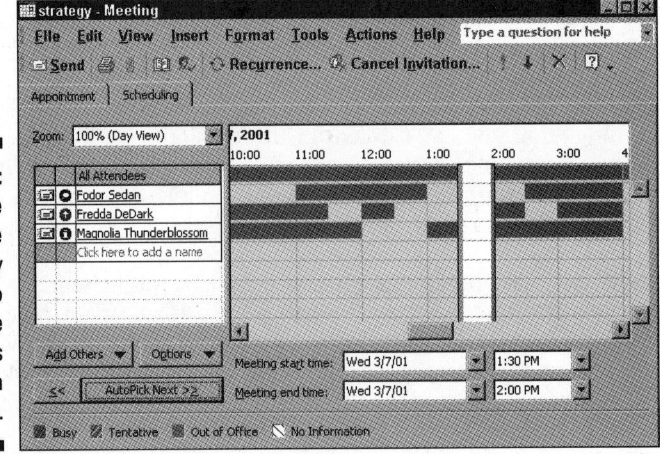

Figure 14-1: Use the Attendee Availability page to invite coworkers to a meeting.

3. **Click the Add Others button.**

   A drop-down list appears.

4. **Choose Add from Address Book.**

   The Select Attendees and Resources dialog box appears.

5. **Click the name of a person you want to invite to the meeting.**

   The name you click is highlighted to show that you've selected it.

6. **Click either the Required or Optional button, depending on how important that person's attendance is to the meeting.**

   The name you select appears in either the Required or Optional box, depending on which button you click.

7. **Repeat Steps 4 and 5 until you've chosen everyone you want to add to the meeting.**

   The names you choose appear in the Select Attendees and resources dialog box (see Figure 14-2).

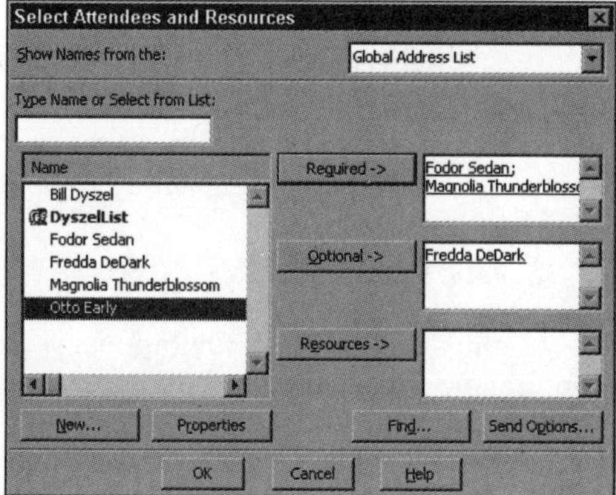

Figure 14-2: You can pick your friends and you can pick your meetings.

8. **Click OK.**

   The Select Attendees and Resources dialog box closes and the names you chose appear in the Attendee Availability list. The Attendee Availability list also shows you a diagram of each person's schedule so that you can see when everyone has free time.

9. **On the timeline at the top of the Attendee Availability list, click your preferred meeting time.**

   The time you pick appears in the Meeting Start Time box at the bottom of the Attendee Availability list. If you want, you can enter the Meeting start and end time in the boxes at the bottom of the Attendee Availability list instead of clicking the timeline. If you don't see a time when everyone you're inviting to your meeting is available, click the Autopick Next button and Outlook will find a meeting time that works for everyone.

10. **Click the Appointment tab.**

    The Appointment page appears with the names of the people you invited to the meeting in the To box at the top of the form.

11. **Type the subject of the meeting in the Subject box.**

    The subject you enter appears in the Subject box.

12. **Enter any other information that you want attendees to know about your meeting, including location or category, in the appropriate areas of the form.**

    The information that you type appears in the appropriate place in the form.

13. **Click Send.**

    Your meeting request is sent to the people that you've invited.

If your system administrators see fit, they can set up Exchange Accounts for resources, such as conference rooms, so that you can figure out a location for your meeting while you're figuring out who can attend.

Responding to a meeting request

Even if you don't organize meetings and send out invitations, you may get invited to meetings now and then, so it's a good idea to know how to respond to a meeting request if you get one.

When you've been invited to a meeting, you get a special e-mail message. What's special about the message? When you open the message, you'll see buttons labeled Accept, Decline, Tentative, Propose New Time, or Calendar. When you click either Accept or Tentative, Outlook automatically adds the meeting to your schedule and creates a new e-mail message to the person who organized the meeting, telling that person your decision. You can add an explanation to the message, or just click the Send button to deliver your message.

If you choose Decline, Outlook also generates a message to the meeting organizer. It's good form to explain why you're missing a meeting. Say something, such as "Sorry, but I plan to be sane that day." If you click the Calendar button, Outlook displays your calendar in a separate window so that you can see whether you're free to attend the meeting at the suggested time.

Checking responses to your meeting request

Each time you organize a meeting with Outlook, you create a small flurry of e-mail messages inviting people to attend, and they respond with a flurry of messages either accepting or declining your invitation. You may have a good enough memory to recall who said yes and no, but I usually need some help. Fortunately, Outlook keeps track of who said what.

To check the status of responses to your meeting request

1. **Click the Calendar icon in the Outlook Bar.**

   The Calendar appears.

2. **Double-click the appointment you want to check.**

   The name of the meeting you double-click opens.

3. **Click the Tracking tab.**

   The list of people you invited appears along with a list of each person's response to your invitation (see Figure 14-3).

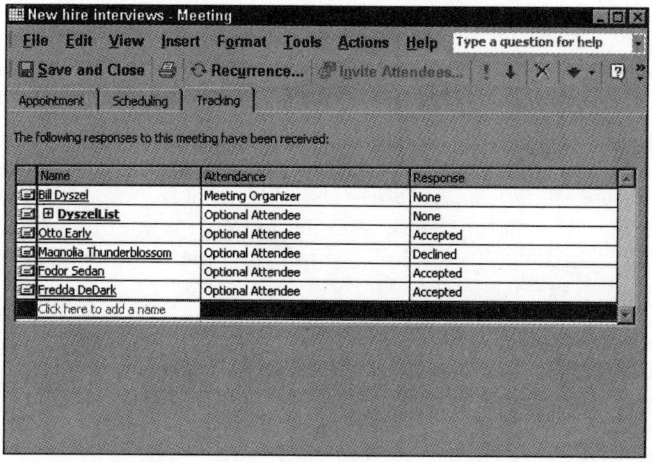

Figure 14-3: See the RSVPs from your VIPs.

Sad to say, only the meeting organizer can find out who has agreed to attend a certain meeting. If you plan to attend a certain meeting only because that special someone you met in the elevator might also attend, you'll know whether that person accepted only if you organized the meeting yourself. You can tell who was invited to a meeting by checking the names on the meeting request that you got by e-mail.

Taking a vote

Management gurus constantly tell us about the importance of good teamwork and decision making. But how do you get a team to make a decision when you can't find most of the team members most of the time? You can use Outlook on an Exchange network as a decision-making tool if you take advantage of the Outlook Voting buttons.

Voting is a special feature of Outlook e-mail that lets you add buttons to an e-mail message that you send to a group of people. When they get the message, recipients click a button to indicate their response. Outlook automatically tallies the responses so that you can see which way the wind is blowing in your office.

To add voting buttons to an e-mail message you're creating, follow these steps while creating your message but before clicking the Send button (for more about creating messages, see Chapter 4):

1. **Choose View➪Options (or press Alt+P).**

   The Message Options dialog box appears. You can also click the Options button on the message toolbar.

2. **Click the Use Voting Buttons check box (or press Alt+U).**

   A check mark appears in the Use Voting Buttons check box.

3. **Click the scroll-down button (triangle) on the text box to the right of the Use Voting Buttons check box.**

   A list of suggested voting buttons appears. The suggested choices include Approve;Reject, Yes;No, and Yes;No;Maybe. You can also type in your own choices if you follow the pattern of the suggested choices; just separate your options with a semicolon. If you want to ask people to vote on the lunch menu, for example, include something, such as Pizza;Burgers;Salad (see Figure 14-4).

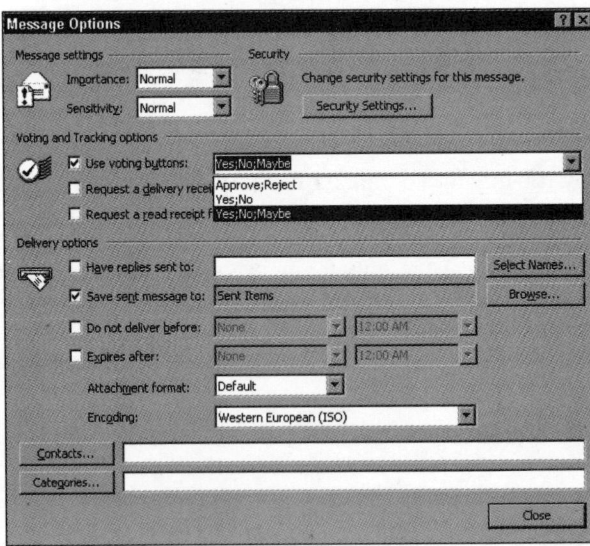

Figure 14-4: Choose the choices of your choice from the Voting buttons list.

4. **Click the set of voting buttons that you want to use.**

   The set you choose (or enter) appears in the text box.

5. **Click Close.**

   And there you are! Democracy in action! Isn't that inspiring? Now when your recipients get your message, they can click the button of their choice and zoom their preference off to you.

Tallying votes

When the replies arrive, you'll see who chose what by looking at the subject of the replies. Messages from people who chose "Approve," for example, will start with the word *Approve;* rejection messages will start with the word *Reject* (see Figure 14-5).

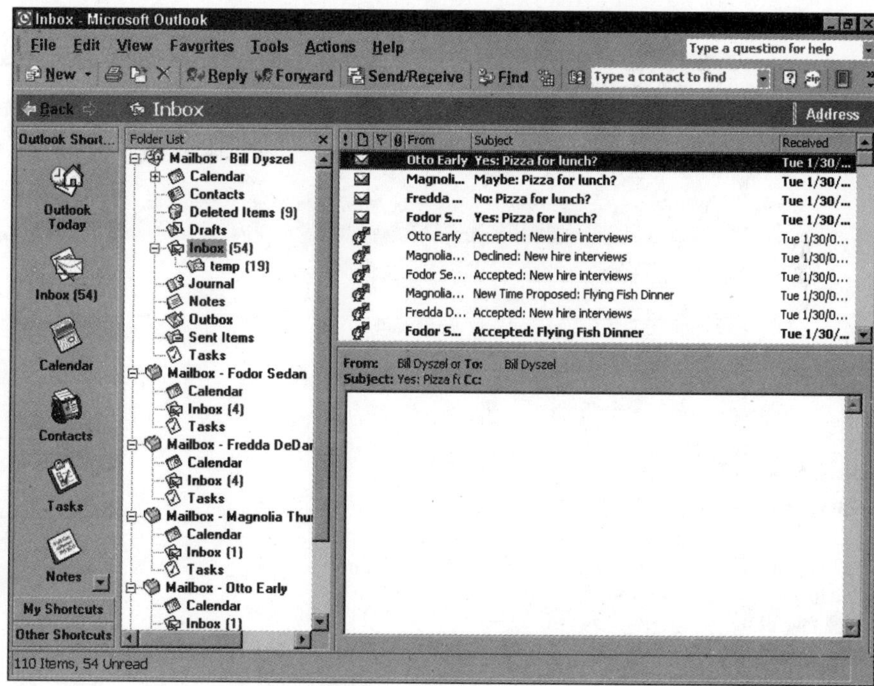

Figure 14-5: You can see how people voted on your proposal by looking at the subjects of their replies.

You can also get a full tally of your vote by checking the Tracking tab on the copy of the message you send in your Sent Items folder by following these steps:

1. **Click My Shortcuts in the Outlook Bar.**

   The icons in the My Shortcuts section appear.

2. **Click the Sent Items icon.**

   Your list of sent messages appears.

3. **Double-click the message you sent to ask for a vote.**

   The message you chose opens.

4. **Click the Tracking tab.**

   The tracking tab shows you the list of people you've asked for a vote and how they voted. You'll also see a banner at the top of the Tracking page with a tally of the votes (see Figure 14-6).

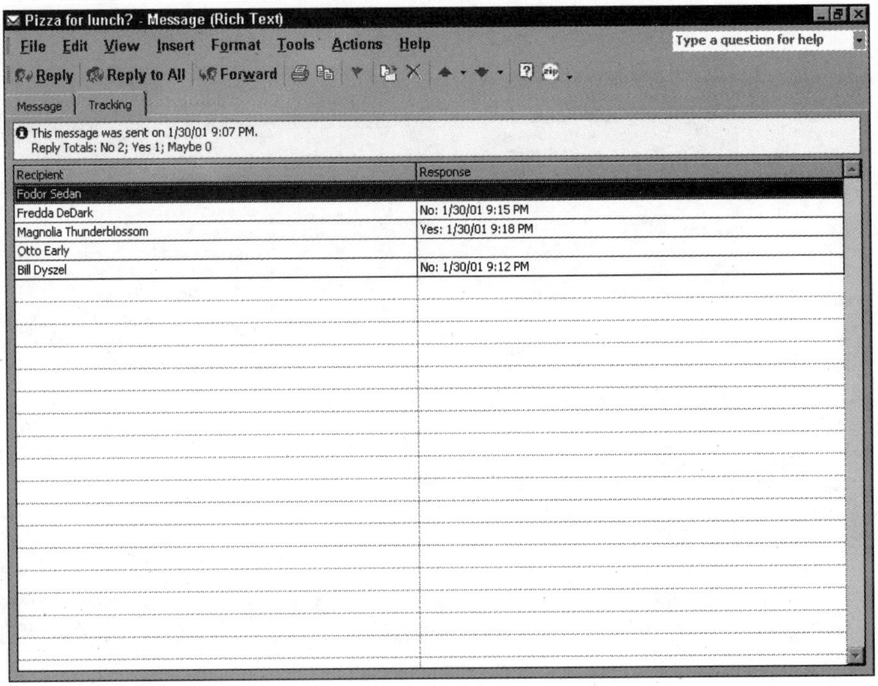

Figure 14-6: Check the Tracking tab to get a quick tally of how people voted.

Collaborating with Outlook and Exchange

One thing I've always found annoying about Outlook is the way certain features of Microsoft Exchange just show up in Outlook menus and tools even if you're not using Exchange. For example, the option to view another person's folder that I explain in this chapter shows up even if you're not using Outlook on an Exchange network. Without an Exchange Network, however, the feature doesn't work. That's why I've focused the rest of this chapter on the features that only work if you have both Outlook and Exchange Server. Why confuse non-Exchange users by describing features they can't use?

If you use Outlook at home or in an office without Exchange Server, you won't be able to use the things I describe in the rest of this chapter. But take heart: little by little, Microsoft is finding ways to make Exchange-only features available to all Outlook users, so you can look over this section as a preview of things to come.

Giving delegate permissions

Good managers delegate authority. That's what my assistant, Igor, says, anyway. Very busy people sometimes give their assistant the job of managing the boss's calendar, schedule, and even sometimes e-mail. That way, the boss can concentrate on the big picture while the assistant dwells on the details.

When you designate a delegate in Outlook on an Exchange network, you give the delegate you name the right to look at whichever Outlook module you pick.

To name a delegate, follow these steps:

1. **Choose Tools⇨Options.**

   The Options dialog box appears.

2. **Click the Delegates tab.**

   The Delegates page appears.

3. **Click Add.**

   The Add Users dialog box appears.

4. **Double-click the name of each delegate that you want to name.**

   The names you choose appear in the Add Users box (see Figure 14-7).

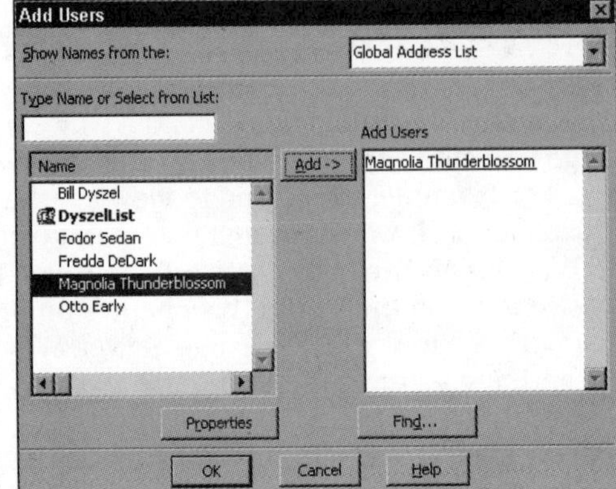

Figure 14-7: Choose those you trust in the Add Users dialog box.

5. **Click OK.**

   The Delegate Permissions dialog box appears, shown in Figure 14-8, so that you can choose exactly which permissions you want to give to your delegate(s).

6. **Make any changes you want in the Delegate Permissions dialog box.**

   If you make no choices at all in the Delegate Permissions dialog box, then by default, your delegate will be granted Editor status in your Calendar and Task list, which means that the delegate can read, create, and change items in those two Outlook modules.

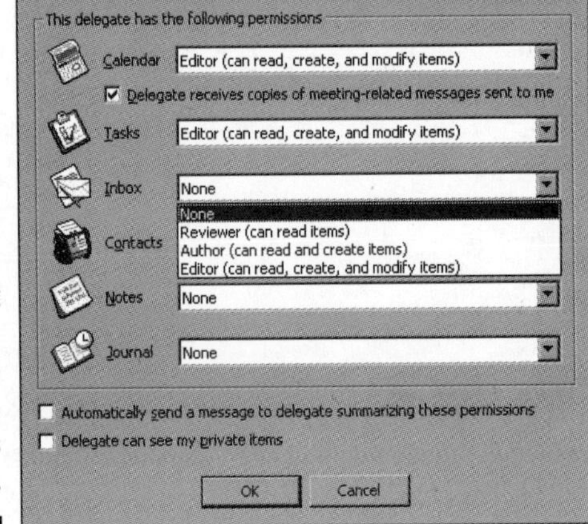

Figure 14-8: Show how much trust you have in the Delegate Permissions dialog box.

7. **Click OK.**

   The Delegate Permissions dialog box closes. The names you chose appear in the Options dialog box, as shown in Figure 14-9.

8. **Click OK.**

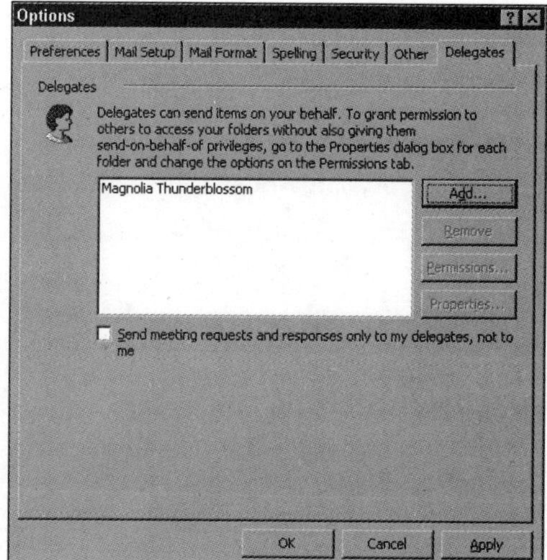

Figure 14-9: Check the Options dialog box to see who has permissions.

Opening someone else's folder

It's fairly common for a team of people who work closely together to share calendars or task lists so that they not only can see what the other person is doing but also enter appointments on behalf of a teammate. For example, perhaps you work in a company in which the sales and service people sit side-by-side. As a service person, you may find it helpful if your partner on the sales side is allowed to enter appointments with a client on your calendar while you're out dealing with other clients. To do that, your partner needs to open your Calendar folder.

You can't open another person's Outlook folder unless that person has given you permission first, the way I describe in the preceding section. After you have permission, you can open the other person's folder by following these steps:

1. **Choose File⇨Open Special Folder⇨Other User's Folder.**

   The Open Other User's Folder dialog box appears, as shown in Figure 14-10.

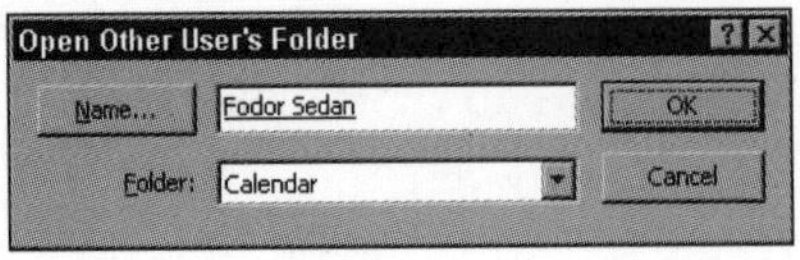

Open Other User's Folder
Name... Fodor Sedan OK
Folder: Calendar Cancel

Figure 14-10: Pick another person's folder to view.

2. **Click the Name button.**

   The Select Name dialog box appears. (It's really the Address Book.)

3. **Double-click the name of the person whose folder you want to open.**

   The Select Name dialog box closes and the name you double-clicked appears in the Open Other User's Folder dialog box.

4. **Click the scroll-down button (triangle) on the Folder box.**

   A list of the Folders you can choose appears.

5. **Click the name of the folder that you want to view.**

   The name of the folder you choose appears in the Folder box.

6. **Click OK.**

   The folder you pick now appears in your folder list.

Setting access permissions

Many times, a busy executive gives his or her assistant the right to view and even edit the executive's entire Outlook account right from the assistant's desk. That way, the assistant organizes what the executive does, and the executive just goes out and does the job. This is known as granting access permissions, which is a lot like naming a delegate, as I describe in the section "Giving delegate permissions." When you grant access permissions, however, the power you're giving is broader; you're giving the assistant permission to use the entire account and even to make your Outlook folders a part of your folder list.

Before people can open your schedule, you have to give them permission by following these steps:

1. **Right-click the Outlook Today icon on the Outlook Bar.**

   A Shortcut menu appears.

2. **Choose Properties.**

   The Properties dialog box appears.

3. **Click the Permissions tab.**

   The Permissions page appears (see Figure 14-11).

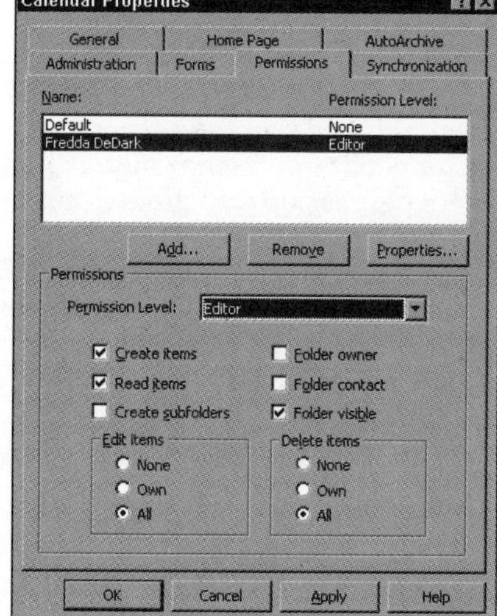

Figure 14-11: You can grant permission for viewing your folders to anyone on your network.

4. **Click the Add button.**

   The Add Users dialog box, which is really the Global Address List, appears.

5. **Double-click the name of the person to whom you want to give access to your folders.**

   The name you double-click appears in the Add Users box on the right side of the Add Users dialog box.

6. **Click OK.**

   The Add Users dialog box closes and the name you chose appears in the Name box of the Properties page.

7. **Click the name that you just added to the Name list on the Properties dialog box.**

   The name you click is highlighted to show that you've selected it.

8. **Click the scroll-down button (triangle) on the Permission Level list.**

   A list of available Permission Levels appears. Assigning a Permission Level gives a specific set of rights to the person to whom the level is assigned. For example, an editor can add, edit, change, or remove items from your Outlook folders, whereas a reviewer can only read items.

9. **Pick the role you want to assign to the person you selected.**

   The role you chose appears in the Roles box. The check boxes below the Roles box change to reflect the tasks that the person is permitted to perform.

10. **Click OK.**

Now that you've given a person permission to see your account as a whole, you need to give permission to see each folder in the account individually. You can either follow these steps for each icon on the Outlook Bar, or you can see the section "Giving delegate permissions" to grant access to another person.

However, you have no way of knowing whether people have given you permission to view their data unless you try to open one of their folders (or unless they tell you), which prevents nasty hackers from breaking into several people's data by stealing just one password.

Viewing two accounts

If your boss gives you permission to view his or her entire Outlook account, you can set up your copy of Outlook so that both your folders and the boss's folders show up in your Outlook folder list. When you want to see your calendar, click your calendar folder; when you want to see the boss's calendar, click the boss's calendar folder.

To add a second person's account to your view of Outlook, follow these steps:

1. **Right-click the Outlook Today icon in Outlook Bar.**

   A Shortcut menu appears.

2. **Choose Properties.**

   The Properties dialog box appears.

3. **Click the Advanced button.**

   The Microsoft Exchange Server dialog box appears.

4. **Click the Advanced tab.**

   The Advanced page appears (see Figure 14-12).

5. **Click Add.**

   The Add Mailbox dialog box appears.

6. **Type the name of the person whose account you want to add.**

   The name you type appears in the text box.

7. **Click OK.**

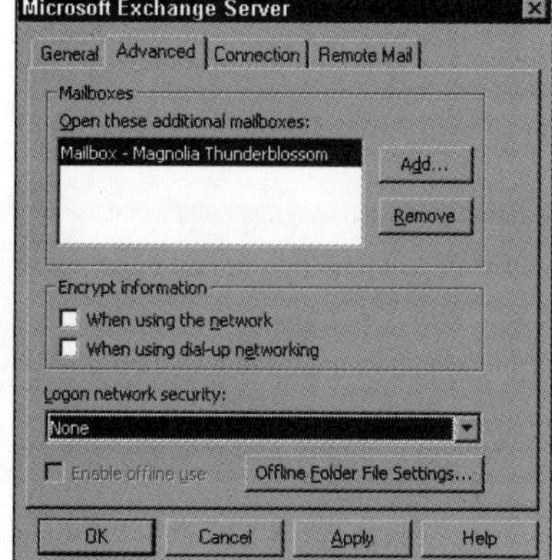

Figure 14-12: Add someone else's folders to your Outlook collection.

If the person you chose didn't give you permission, you'll get an error message saying that the name you entered couldn't be matched to a name in the address list. If that happens, make sure that the person you want to add really gave you the rights to his or her account.

After you add another person's account to Outlook, you need to use the Folder List to see the new person's items. You'll see a new section in your Folder list called Mailbox, followed by the new person's name; that's where that person's Outlook items are located. When you click an icon in your Outlook Bar, you'll see your own Outlook items. If you like, you can create a new section in your Outlook bar and add icons for the other person's items. See Chapter 2 for more about adding items to the Outlook Bar.

Assigning tasks

As Tom Sawyer could tell you, anything worth doing is worth getting someone else to do. Outlook on an Exchange network enables you to assign a task to another person in your company and keep track of that person's progress.

To assign a task to someone else, follow these steps:

1. **Right-click an item in your task list.**

   A shortcut menu appears.

2. **Choose Assign Task from the shortcut menu.**

   A Task form appears.

3. **Type the name of the person to whom you're assigning the task in the To box just as you would on an e-mail message.**

   The person's name appears in the To box (see Figure 14-13).

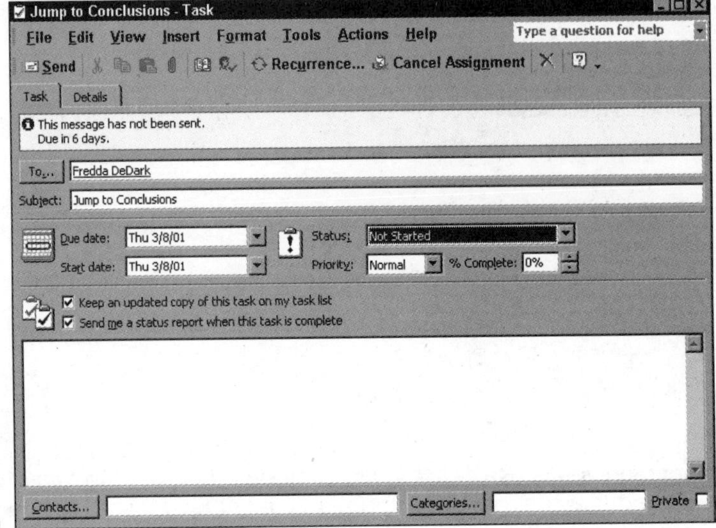

Figure 14-13: When in doubt, send it out.

4. **Click Send.**

   The task is sent to the person to whom you've assigned it.

The person to whom you addressed the task will get an e-mail message with special buttons marked Accept and Decline, much like the special Meeting Request message that I discuss earlier in this chapter. When the person clicks Accept, the task is automatically added to his or her Task list in Outlook. If the person clicks Decline, that person is fired. Okay, just kidding, the person is not actually fired. Not yet, anyway.

Sending a status report

People who give tasks out like the Assign Task feature very, very much. People who have to do those tasks are much less enthusiastic. If you're a Task Getter more often than you're a Task Giver, you have to look at the bright side: Outlook on an Exchange network can also help the boss stay informed about how much you're doing — and doing and doing!

You may have noticed that the task form has a box called Status and another called % Complete. If you keep the information in those boxes up-to-date, you can constantly remind the Big Cheese of your valuable contributions by sending status reports.

To send a status report:

1. **Double-click any task.**

   A Task form opens.

2. **Choose Actions⇨Send Status Report.**

   A To box appears, just like in an e-mail message, and the name of the person who assigned the task already appears in the To box.

3. **Enter any explanation you want to send about the task in the text box at the bottom of the form.**

   The text that you type appears in the form.

4. **Click Send.**

You can send status reports as often as you like — weekly, daily, hourly. It's probably a good idea to leave enough time between status reports to complete some tasks.

About Address Books

Outlook still uses several different Address Books that are really part of Microsoft Exchange Server. The Address Books involve several separate, independent lists of names and e-mail addresses — it's pretty confusing. Microsoft simplified the issue of dealing with Address Books in Outlook 2002, but that doesn't help if you use Outlook on a large corporate network. I'll try to help you make sense of it all, anyway.

The Outlook Contact list contains all kinds of personal information, whereas an Address Book focuses on just e-mail addresses. An Address Book can also deal with the nitty-gritty details of actually sending your message to people on your corporate e-mail system, especially if that system is Microsoft Exchange Server.

Here's the lowdown on your plethora of Address Books:

- **The Global Address List:** If you're using Outlook on a corporate network, the Global Address List, which your system administrator maintains, normally contains the names and e-mail addresses of all the people in your company. The Global Address List makes it possible to address an e-mail message to anybody in your company without having to look up the e-mail address.

- **The Outlook Address Book:** The Contacts Address Book is really the list of e-mail addresses from the Contact list. Outlook automatically creates the Contacts Address Book to allow you to add the names of people in your Contact list to a Personal Distribution List.
- **Additional Address Books:** If you create additional folders for Outlook contacts, those folders also become separate Address Books. Your system administrator can also create additional Address Books.

If you're lucky, you'll never see the Address Book. All the addresses of all the people you ever send e-mail to are listed in the Global Address List that somebody else maintains, such as on a corporate network. Under those circumstances, Outlook is a dream. You don't need to know what an Address Book is most of the time — you just type the name of the person you're e-mailing in the To box of a message. Outlook checks the name for spelling and takes care of sending your message. You'd swear that a tiny psychic lives inside your computer who knows just what you need.

Under less-than-ideal conditions, when you try to send a message, Outlook either complains that it doesn't know how to send the message or can't figure out whom you're talking about. Then you have to mess with the address. That situation happens only when the address isn't listed in one of the Address Books or isn't in a form that Outlook understands. In that case, you must either enter the full address manually or add your recipient's name and address to your Address Book.

Going Public with Public Folders

Another popular feature of Outlook on an Exchange network is the ability to use public folders. *Public folders* are places that a whole group of people can look at and add items to. You can have a public folder for tasks or contacts. You can also create a public folder that contains messages, a lot like your Inbox, except that everybody can add messages and read the same set of messages. This kind of arrangement is often called a *bulletin board;* you post a message, someone replies to it, a third party then replies to both of you, and so on. It's a method of conducting a group conversation without having all the parties to the conversation available at the same time.

In Outlook, public folders look just like any other folders. A public folder may contain a Contact list that the entire company shares or a Tasks list that an entire department uses. You can set up a public discussion folder for an ongoing group conference about topics of interest to everyone sharing the folder, such as current company news. You can also use a public discussion folder to collect opinions about decisions that have to be made or as an intracompany classified ad system. You can organize as a folder any kind of information that you'd like to exchange among groups of people on your network.

When you click a public folder, you see a list of items that looks like a list of e-mail messages, except that all the messages are addressed to the folder rather than to a person. In a public folder, you can change your view of the items, add items, or reply to items that someone else entered.

Viewing a public folder

Your company may maintain a public folder for an ongoing online discussion about important issues in your business or as a company bulletin board for announcements about activities, benefits, and other news.

To view a public folder

1. **Choose View⇨Folder List or click the Folder List button in the toolbar.**

   The Folder List appears (see Figure 14-14).

2. **Click the name of the folder you want to see.**

   The list of items in the folder appears.

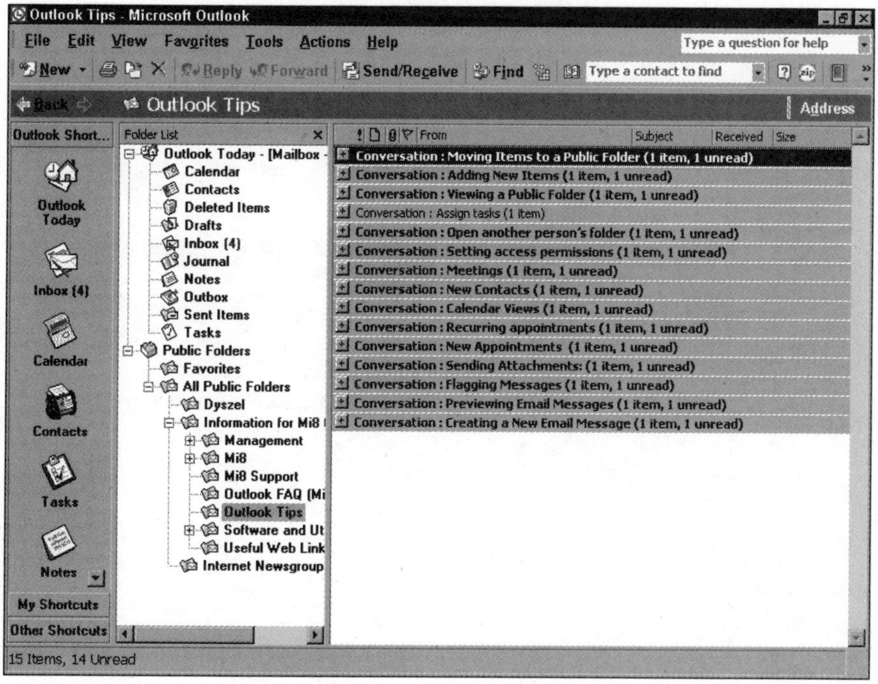

Figure 14-14: The Folder List with Public Folders.

You can double-click the title of any item that you see to view the contents of that item.

Adding new items

Many public folders are organized as open discussions in which anyone can put in his or her two cents' worth. All the messages can be read by anybody, so everybody reads and replies to everybody else. If you view a folder and find it's full of messages from different people all replying to one another, you're looking at a discussion folder.

To add new items to a public folder, follow these steps:

1. **Choose View➪Folder List or click the Folder List button in the toolbar.**

   The Folder List appears.

2. **Click the name of the folder.**

   The list of messages in the folder appears.

3. **Choose File➪New➪Post in This Folder.**

   The New Item form appears (see Figure 14-15).

4. **Type a subject and your message.**

5. **Click Post.**

Now your message is part of the list of items in the folder.

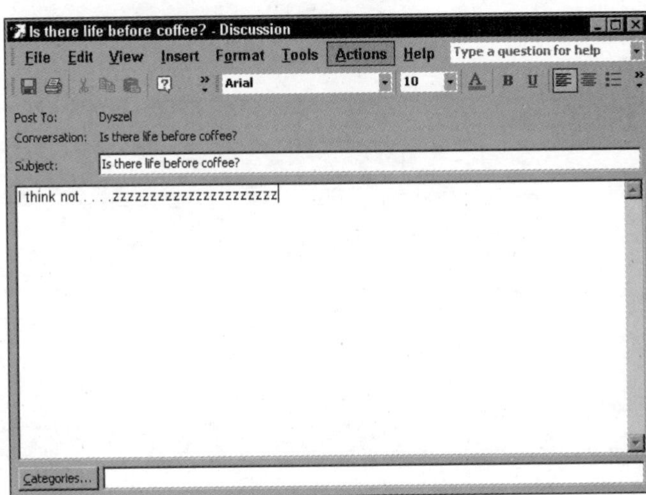

Figure 14-15: The New Item form.

Replying to items in an existing public discussion folder

Good manners and good sense say that if you want to join a discussion, the best thing to do is respond to what the other members of the discussion are saying. But be nice — don't flame. Posting nasty responses to people in an online discussion group is called *flaming*. Flaming is not well-regarded but also is not uncommon. Flaming creates online conversations that most people don't want to participate in. What good is a discussion when nobody talks? Besides, flaming in the workplace can get you fired. So cool down.

When you're participating in public folder discussions at work, assume that everyone in the company — from the top executives to the newest temp — will read what you've written. Check your spelling, DON'T WRITE IN CAPITAL LETTERS (IT LOOKS LIKE YOU'RE SHOUTING), and use discretion in what you say and how you say it. The same rules apply to interoffice e-mail; you don't know who reads what you send.

To reply to items in a public discussion folder:

1. **Double-click the item to which you want to reply.**

   The item opens so that you can read it.

2. **Click the Post Reply button in the toolbar.**

   The Discussion Reply form appears. The text of the message to which you're replying is already posted in the form (see Figure 14-16).

3. **Type your subject and reply.**

   Your reply appears in a different color than the original text.

4. **Click Post.**

Your item joins the list of discussion items.

Moving items to a public folder

Not all public folders are discussion folders. Public folders can be designed to hold any type of item. You can share lists of tasks, calendars, or files of other types. You don't have to create a public folder item in the folder where you want the item to end up. You can create a task in your own Tasks list, for example, and then move it to a public task folder.

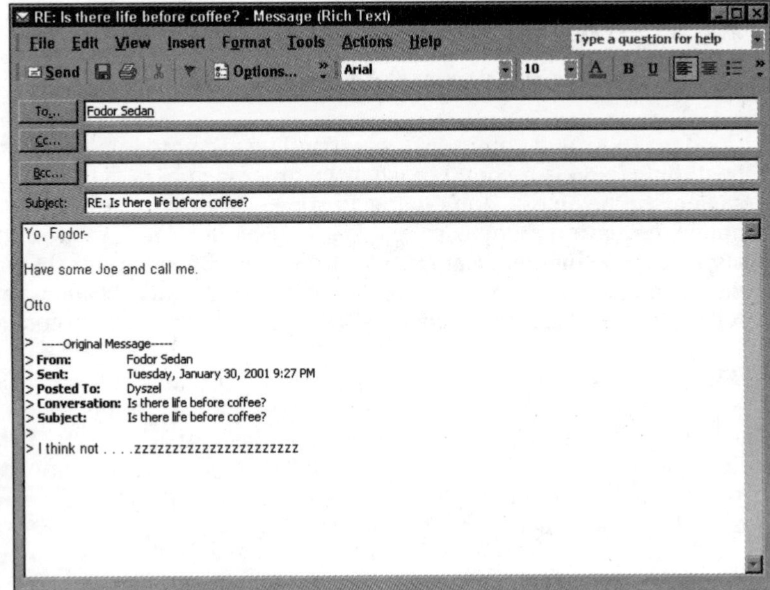

Figure 14-16: Use the Discussion Reply form to add your comments to a public discussion.

To move items to a public folder:

1. **Right-click the item that you want to move.**

   A menu appears, as shown in Figure 14-17.

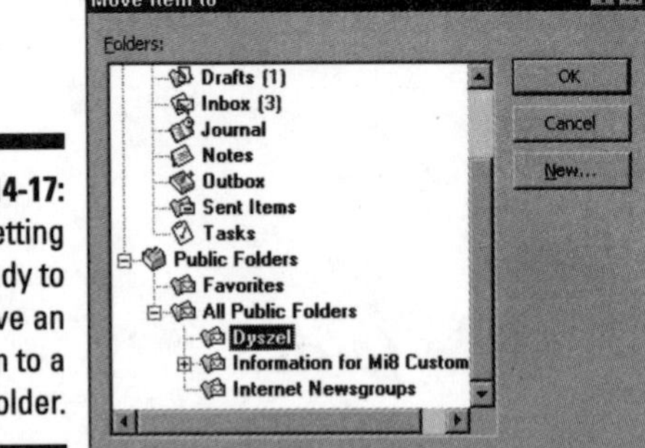

Figure 14-17: Getting ready to move an item to a folder.

2. **Click Move to Folder.**

   A dialog box that includes the Folder List appears.

3. **Click the folder to which you want to send the item.**

   The name of the folder you clicked is highlighted.

4. **Click OK.**

   Your item moves to its new folder.

For the public record

You may be using public folders without even knowing it. In Outlook, all folders look the same, whether you create them yourself on your own PC or they're on a corporate network or the Internet. All you really need to know about public folders is that they're public, so anybody who has access to the public folder can see whatever you post to that public folder. You can also create your own public folders; check with your system administrator to see whether you have the rights to create public folders and a place to put them.

Outlook Web Access

Because people aren't always sitting in their office at their computer, Microsoft now provides a way for you to view your personal information from any computer on the Internet: Outlook Web Access. If your company has set up its network a certain way, you can log onto Outlook Web Access from nearly anywhere and do the most important things that you could previously only do at your desktop computer, such as exchanging e-mail, checking your calendar, and adding items to your task list. If you're accustomed to browsing the Web, you'll find Outlook Web Access pretty easy to understand. Each company sets up Outlook Web Access a bit differently, so you'll need to ask your computer administrator for specific details on how to get at Outlook from the Web.

Chapter 15

Files and Folders: How to Save Stuff So You Can Find It Later

In This Chapter

- Seeing your basic drives and other stuff
- Moving, copying, and renaming files and folders
- Viewing and sorting files and folders

Files and folders frequently flummox folks who use Windows. Fortunately, Outlook has a good set of tools for managing files and folders, so the issue of file management should be easier to understand if you're using Outlook. But you still need to understand basic file management to take advantage of the improved tools in Outlook.

I assume that you're familiar with using files and folders in Windows so that I can focus on showing you Outlook's file management features. For an excellent explanation of how to deal with files, see *DOS For Dummies,* Windows 95 Edition, by Dan Gookin (IDG Books Worldwide, Inc.), which describes the concepts in full detail.

If your experience goes way back to 1993, when people used Windows 3.1 (heaven help 'em!), these critters were called files and directories. When Windows 95 came out, Microsoft started using the word *folders* rather than *directories,* but folders and directories are exactly the same thing.

Whatever you call them, files and folders still reside on floppy disks, hard drives, and network drives. Floppy disks and hard drives have letter names (A, B, C, and so on), whereas files and folders are named in plain English words.

If your computer is connected to a network, you also have hard drives that belong to the network. These drives aren't on your computer; they're somewhere else in the building. But on your computer, they show up in Outlook or Windows Explorer as if they were on your own machine. The network makes the hard drives on the network look just like the one inside your machine when you're looking for files, and that's fine. You can treat files on the network just as though they're files on your computer.

Networks also allow you to share files with other people. A network is a little like a library: You can use a file when you need it and then put it back. Later, someone else may come along and use the file; then, that person puts the file back so that yet another person can use it. Your network administrator can configure the system to prevent other people from changing your files or you from changing theirs.

Managing Your Files

File management is a fancy term for looking at your files and folders and arranging what you have the way you want it. The first step toward managing your files is seeing them.

To see a listing of your files, follow these steps:

1. **Click the My Computer icon in the Outlook Bar.**

   There it is — you see a list of your drives in all their glory (see Figure 15-1). Why would you want to see a list of your drives? To see a list of your folders, of course.

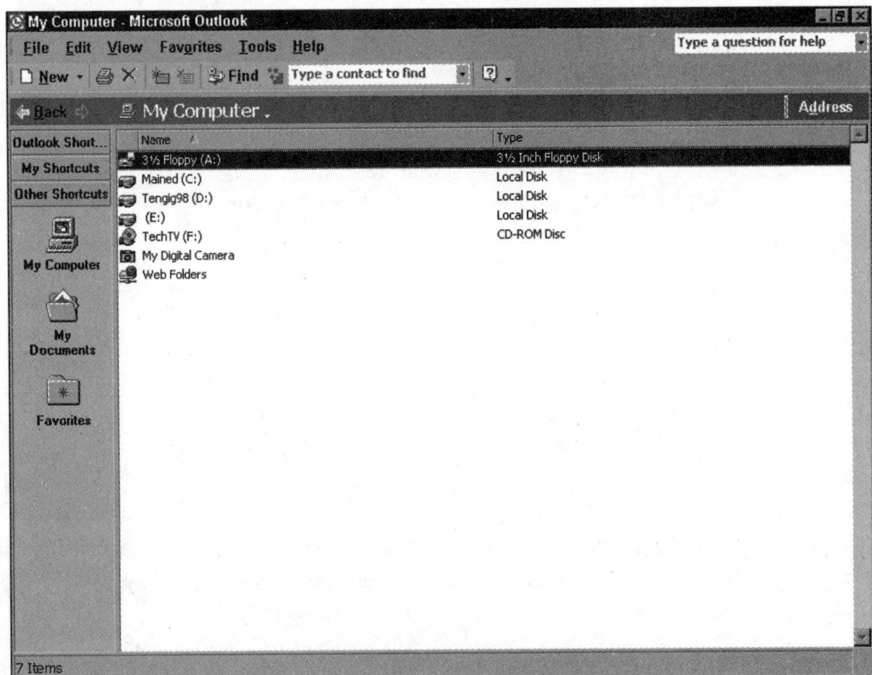

Figure 15-1: A list of your disk drives.

2. **Double-click the icon for the C drive.**

   A list of the folders on your C drive appears. Doesn't that make your day?

3. **To view a list of the files in your folders, double-click the icon for the folder whose contents you want to see (such as the My Documents folder).**

   You see a listing of all the files in the My Documents folder (see Figure 15-2). If you have subfolders within the My Documents folder, you can see the names of the files in any of those folders by double-clicking the icon for a folder whose contents you want to see.

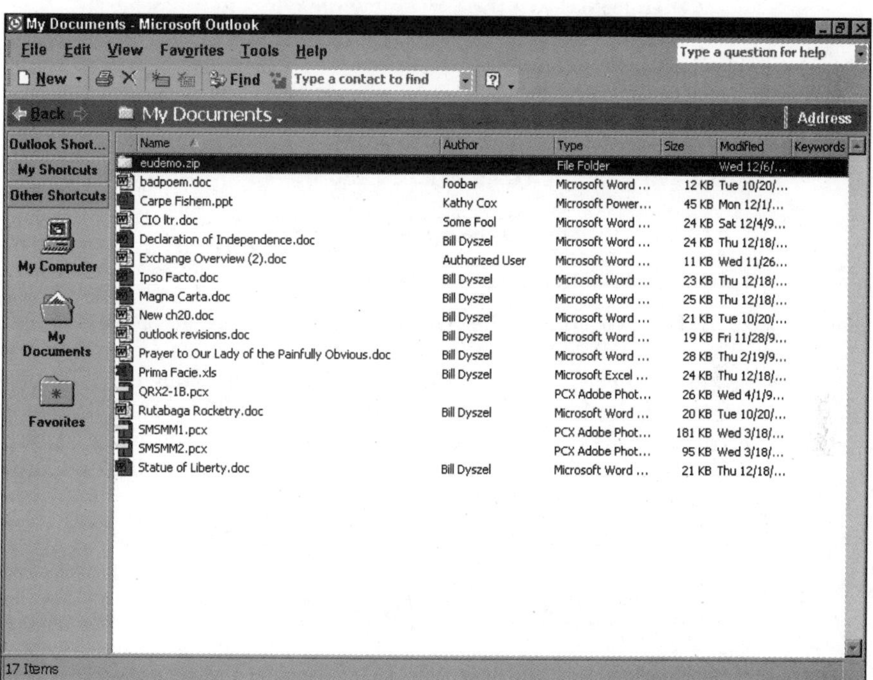

Figure 15-2: Now that's a list of files!

I assume that you have a folder called My Documents, because Microsoft Office creates a folder called that during installation. My Documents is the folder in which Microsoft Office programs like to save the documents that you create, unless you tell the programs to save the documents somewhere else. If you don't have a My Documents folder, double-click another folder — whichever folder you want. You get the idea; double-clicking the icon for a folder makes Outlook show you a list of the files in the folder.

Selecting files

After you open a folder to see the list of files in it, you need to select a file or files in order to move, copy, or delete a file or group of files. Here's what you do:

- To select a single file, click its name.
- To select several files that are next to one another, click the first one, hold down the Shift key, and click the last one. The first and last files are selected, along with all the files in between.
- To select several files that are not next to one another, click one and then hold down the Ctrl key while clicking the others.

Moving and copying files

To move a file from one folder to another, follow these steps:

1. **Click the file that you want to move.**

   The selected file is highlighted.

2. **Drag the file to the folder where you want to move it.**

If the folder to which you drag the file is on the same drive (such as the C drive) as the folder where the file was originally located, the file is moved (that is, gone from its former location and placed in the new one). If you drag the file to a different drive, the file is copied; it's now located in the old place as well as the new place.

Creating a new folder

Sometimes you just need a new place to put things. You may need to create a new folder for a new group of files from a client or to keep the documents concerning a certain project together to make them easier to find.

Here's how you create a new folder:

1. **Click the My Computer icon in the Outlook Bar.**

   Your list of drives appears.

2. **Double-click the icon for the drive where you want to create a new folder (such as the C drive).**

   The list of folders on the drive you selected appears.

3. **Choose File⇨New⇨Folder (or press Ctrl+Shift+E).**

   The Create New Folder dialog box appears.

4. **Type the name you want to give to your new folder.**

   The name appears in the dialog box.

5. **Click OK.**

   Your new folder appears in your list of folders. If you want to create a new folder inside an existing folder, double-click the icon next to the existing folder before choosing File⇨New⇨Folder.

Renaming folders

Marilyn Monroe and John Wayne changed their names from Norma Jean and Marion (guess who was Marion). That just goes to show you that sometimes there's a darn good reason for changing a name. You can change the name of any folder to anything you want.

You shouldn't rename some folders — two in particular. Renaming your My Documents folder may make it difficult to find your documents when you're using other Office programs, because these programs normally look in the My Documents folder for the documents they created. You can configure the programs to find the folder by its new name if you rename it, but leaving it alone is easier. Renaming your Windows folder can cause big problems; your programs may not run, and your computer may not start without some serious glaring and grumbling from your computer guru. You're better off leaving those two folders with their original names.

To rename a folder:

1. **Right-click the name of the folder that you want to rename.**

   A menu appears.

2. **Choose Rename.**

   The Rename dialog box appears, with the old folder name highlighted.

3. **Type the new name of the folder.**

   The new folder name replaces the old name in the dialog box.

4. **Click OK.**

You can't rename a folder when it's open. If you can see the names of the files in a folder, the folder is open, and you can't rename that folder. You can choose View⇨Go To⇨Up One Level, select the folder, and try again.

Renaming files

Renaming files is nearly identical to renaming folders, except that a file name has a three-letter *extension* — that is, a three-character suffix, such as `.doc` or `.xls` or `.exe`. Windows uses file name extensions to identify which program should run when you double-click a file to open it. If you try to rename a file that ends in `.exe`, Windows warns you that it's a program file and suggests that you think twice before renaming it. As long as you keep the last three letters the same as they were originally, you should have no problem.

To rename a file:

1. **Right-click the name of the file that you want to rename.**

   A menu appears, with commands including Open, Delete, and Rename.

2. **Choose Rename from the menu.**

   The Rename dialog box appears (see Figure 15-3).

Figure 15-3: The Rename dialog box.

3. **Type the new name of the file.**

   The new file name replaces the old name in the dialog box.

4. **Click OK.**

When you first open the Rename dialog box, the old name of the file is displayed and highlighted. As soon as you start typing, the old name disappears; whatever you type as the new name replaces the old name.

Using Views with Files and Folders

A way to see what files you have and where you have them has always been available to you. For example, Windows Explorer is the file management tool that comes with recent versions of Windows. Making sense of your collection of documents gets more complicated after you collect a few hundred files. Sometimes you need to know more than you can get from the simple list of your files that Explorer shows you. Outlook can show you more information about each file, including things such as the author, the page count, or the time and date that a file was most recently printed.

What's in a name? File extensions

Windows normally hides the last three letters of a file's name, known as the file extension. The extension starts with a period and indicates which program created the file. Well, not always; that's the problem. Although the file extension is a leftover from the days of DOS that we'd all rather forget, Windows uses the file extension when it tries to figure out what kind of program created a certain file. The file extension is how Windows knows which program to run when you double-click the name of a file. Windows knows that it should open Word and not Excel when you click a Word file, for example, because Word files have names that end in `.doc`.

When you rename a file, it's possible to change the file extension, which makes Windows very confused. Windows may not know what to do with a file that doesn't have exactly the right extension. The situation is pretty silly. It's as though you picked up a clear Coke bottle with dishwater in it but didn't know that it was dishwater because the label said Coke. You'd know better than to drink it, but Windows wouldn't.

If your machine is showing you the file extensions, be careful not to change the extensions when you're changing file names. You can tell that file extensions are showing if the names of all the files created by Microsoft Word end in `.doc`, for example, and all the Excel file names end in `.xls`. Changing the extensions of your file names can make Windows so confused that it will refuse to view or open certain documents unless they're properly named.

Outlook allows you to arrange and sort information about your files in many slick ways. I show you the most useful approaches to viewing your lists of files in this chapter.

Sorting files in a folder

Every view of your files (except Document Timeline view, which I explain later in this chapter) is organized in rows and columns. Each row contains the information for one file, and each column contains one type of information about each file listed. You can sort the entire list by the contents of one column with a single mouse click.

To sort files in a folder:

1. **Click the My Computer icon in the Outlook Bar.**

   A list of your drives appears.

2. **Double-click the icon for the C drive.**

   A list of the folders on your C drive appears.

3. **To view a list of the files in your folders, double-click the icon for the folder whose contents you want to see.**

   You see a listing of all the files in the folder you selected.

4. **Click the name at the top of the column you want to sort by.**

If you have many files, Outlook needs a few seconds to sort them out. It fills the time by showing you a little box containing the letters A, F, and Z. Outlook juggles the letters around and then displays the list of files in the order that you suggested. I usually put my files in name order or date order (by date modified), but you can sort by any column on-screen.

Icons view

The Icons view is a way of displaying your files by simply filling the screen with icons accompanied by the names of the files they represent. Icons are bigger and friendlier looking than plain old lists of files, but they don't give you as much information. If you don't want much information, icons are good. If you want more information about each file, such as its size and the name of the program that created it, switch to another view, such as Details view.

Here's what you do to see the Icons view:

1. **Click the My Computer icon in the Outlook Bar.**

   Your list of drives appears.

2. **Double-click the name of one of your drives, such as the C drive.**

   Your list of folders appears.

3. **Double-click the name of a folder, such as My Documents.**

   A list of the files in the folder appears.

4. **Choose View⇨Current View⇨Icons.**

   A list of icons appears (see Figure 15-4). In the Icons view, the toolbar includes a set of three buttons, each of which bears a small diagram of a group of icons. Clicking any of the three buttons changes the type of Icon view that you see: large icons, small icons, or a list of icons. You can change among these views any time.

Details view

Details view is a plain old list of file names, sizes, dates, and so on — in other words, it gives you all the, uh, details. Lists in Details view look just like the lists that Windows Explorer gives you, but the Outlook version can do much more (see Chapter 16 for more about views).

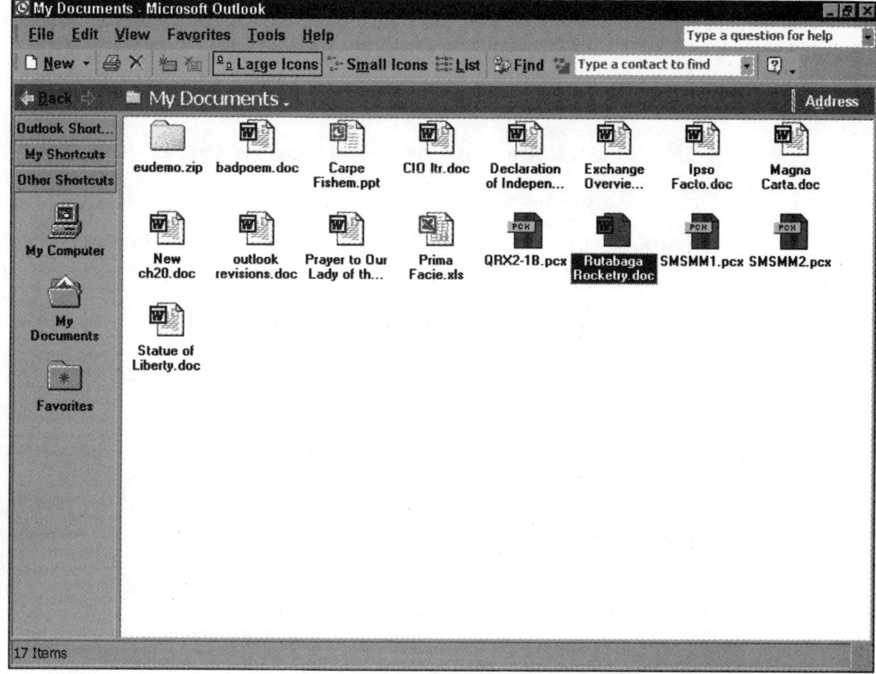

Figure 15-4: The Icons view is less informative but easier to read than other views.

To see your files in Details view:

1. **Click the My Computer icon in the Outlook Bar.**

   Your list of drives appears.

2. **Double-click the name of one of your drives, such as the C drive.**

   Your list of folders appears.

3. **Double-click the name of a folder, such as My Documents.**

   A list of the files in that folder appears.

4. **Choose View⇨Current View⇨Details.**

Details view is the view that I choose to use most of the time because it shows me all the files in the folder I've chosen and gives me the most information at a glance.

By Author view

Guess how By Author view groups your files? If it's good enough for the library to organize by author, it's good enough for me.

To see your files in the By Author view:

1. **Click the My Computer icon in the Outlook Bar.**

   Your list of drives appears.

2. **Double-click the name of one of your drives, such as the C drive.**

   Your list of folders appears.

3. **Double-click the name of a folder, such as My Documents.**

   A list of the files in the folder appears.

4. **Choose View➪Current View➪By Author.**

   A list of your files appears, grouped by author (see Figure 15-5).

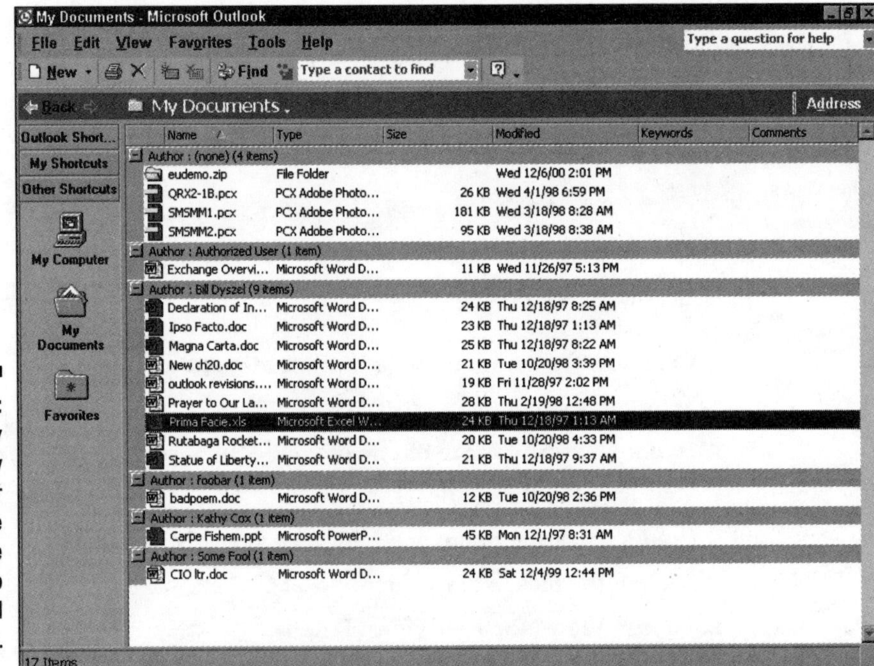

Figure 15-5: The By Author view groups your files by the name of the person who created them.

If you're the only person who uses your computer, you really don't want to use the By Author view. When you're the only author, you just see all the files in whatever order they happen to be in. Also, only Microsoft Office documents show a name in the Author column.

Viewing By Author is most useful when you share files on a network with many other people, in which case questions of authorship may be important. Viewing files By Author is also handy if you consolidate the work of several people; this way, you know at a glance which file came from whom.

By File Type view

By File Type view groups your files according to what kind of program created the file. Files created by Microsoft Word are one file type; files created by Excel are another file type. Some file types can be created by more than one program, but Windows always associates files of a certain type with only one program.

To use the By File Type view:

1. **Click the My Computer icon in the Outlook Bar.**

   Your list of drives appears.

2. **Double-click the name of one of your drives, such as the C drive.**

   Your list of folders appears.

3. **Double-click the name of a folder, such as My Documents.**

   A list of the files in the folder appears.

4. **Choose View⇨Current View⇨By File Type.**

   A list of your files appears, with the files grouped according to the program that created them (see Figure 15-6).

You can use By File Type view to give yourself a shorter list to look at when you're trying to find a file in a folder. If you're looking for an Excel file in a folder that has two Excel files and 98 Word files, it's easier to find one of two files in the Excel group than one of 100 in the entire folder, right?

Document Timeline view

The Document Timeline view is an interesting way to view your files according to the last date on which they were modified. Because you can click the heading of the Date Modified column to sort your files by date, you actually don't need Document Timeline view. But the Document Timeline is much cooler to look at than a simple list of file names. Try the Document Timeline view when you need a change of pace.

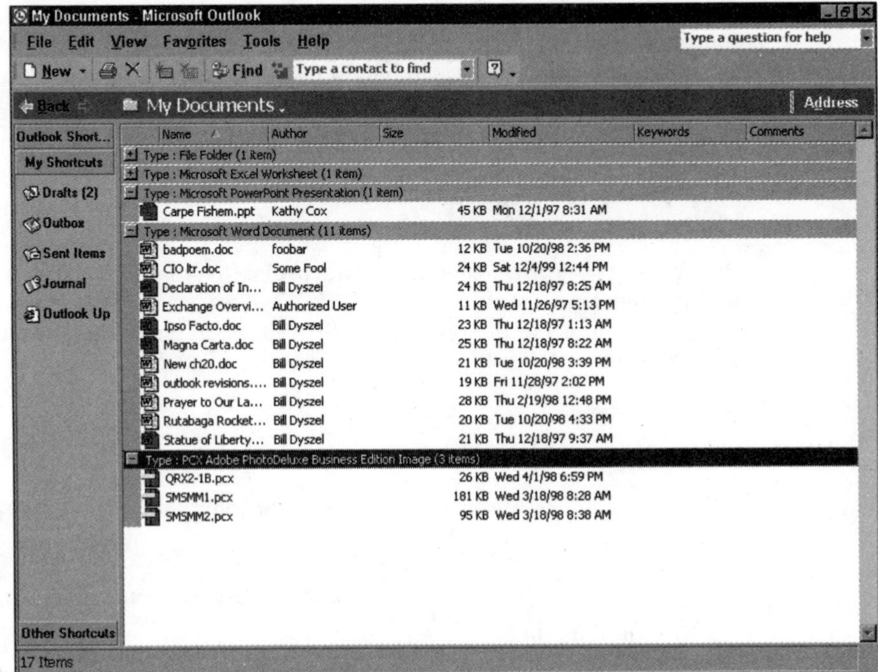

Figure 15-6: See your files by file type.

To use the Document Timeline view:

1. **Click the My Computer icon in the Outlook Bar.**

   Your list of drives appears.

2. **Double-click the name of one of your drives, such as the C drive.**

   Your list of folders appears.

3. **Double-click the name of a folder, such as My Documents.**

   A list of the files in the folder appears.

4. **Choose View⇨Current View⇨Document Timeline.**

   The Document Timeline appears with icons representing each of your files, organized by the date that they were last modified (see Figure 15-7).

Four buttons appear in the toolbar when you use Document Timeline view. The Today button centers the timeline on today's date. You can also scroll left and right to see files modified on earlier and later dates. The Day button shows you just one day; clicking a date in the top line of the timeline takes you to that date. The Week button shows you seven days' worth of documents. The Month button shows a month's worth of documents.

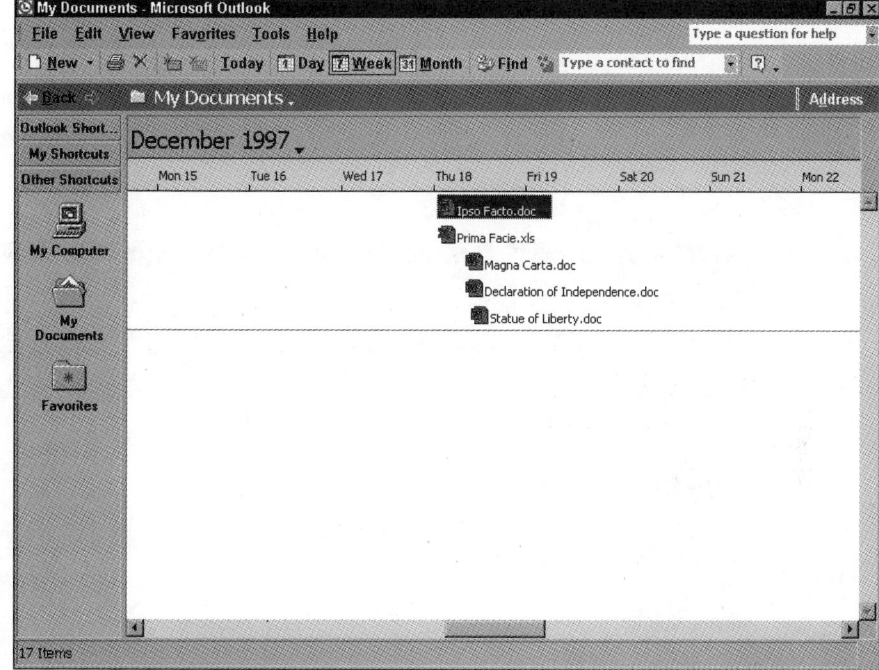

Figure 15-7: The Document Timeline shows you files in chronological order.

The Document Timeline is helpful when you can't remember what you called a file but you know when you used it last. You can just look at the date you remember using the file in the timeline, and you'll find your document.

Programs view

At the beginning of this chapter, I discuss the fact that some files are programs; they make the computer do actual work. Sometimes, the programs are useful (games and cool screen savers). Other times, they just create boring stuff such as letters and spreadsheets. Either way, be careful when you delete or rename program files — you may lose a program you need. Windows warns you when you're deleting a program file, so you know to be careful.

To see your files in Programs view:

1. **Click the My Computer icon in the Outlook Bar.**

   Your list of drives appears.

2. **Double-click the name of one of your drives, such as the C drive.**

   Your list of folders appears.

3. **Double-click the name of a folder, such as Windows.**

   A list of the files in the folder appears.

4. **Choose View➪Current View➪Programs.**

   A list of the program files in the directory you're viewing appears (see Figure 15-8).

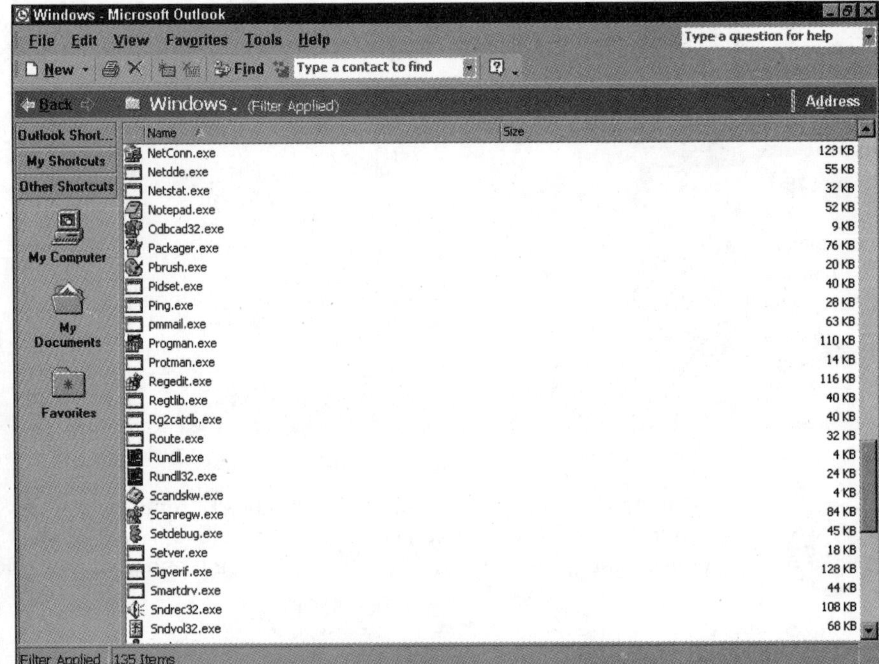

Figure 15-8: The Programs view shows you the program files in the folder you've chosen.

Many folders don't have any programs in them, so don't be surprised if you get a blank screen when you try Programs view. If you don't see any files that end in the letters `.exe` or `.com`, you don't have any program files, but you may have document files or spreadsheets or some other kind of file.

Why manage files at all?

You can also use Windows Explorer in Windows to deal with files and folders, but I believe that Outlook does the job much more sensibly. You also have options for arranging your view of your files and folders in Outlook that simply don't exist in Windows Explorer.

Recent versions of Windows have started hiding the inner workings of the computer just to make you more comfortable, but you can peek behind the scenes if you really want to see how things happen. Windows also allows you to give your files sensible names that have more than eight characters, which you couldn't do with older versions of Windows. Sensible file names make record keeping easier. But many people still find the concepts of drives and folders to be nonsensical.

People work on computers every single day, and many still don't understand the machines too well, but they get along fine anyway. So don't worry — you will, too. On the other hand, if you understand how your drives and folders are organized, the knowledge can help you in a pinch. The system of files and folders is like a road map that seems complicated at first, but after you've learned to use the map, you can get where you're going faster. Because Outlook presents your system of files and folders more understandably than Windows Explorer, the whole issue of keeping track of your files seems much simpler.

Final Facts on Filing

If you like to get down to the nitty-gritty in dealing with files and folders, you'll like using Outlook because its file management tools (including the capability to add fields and save custom views) are very powerful. If you move or copy files only on pain of death or when bribed with chocolate, you'll like using Outlook because you can create a few simple views (or have someone else create and save some simple views for you) and not be bothered with all the ugly details of files, folders, and whatnot. You can have it both ways — but only in Outlook. The other Microsoft Office programs can't do the tricks that Outlook can!

Chapter 16

See It Your Way: Making the Most of Outlook Views

In This Chapter

- Using views
- Changing columns
- Sorting lists
- Grouping items in your table
- Saving your own views

When you boil it down, the two biggest things that you do in Outlook are entering information and viewing it. This chapter is about viewing information any way you want to look at it, which makes the information easier to use and understand.

Any body of information can have a variety of looks. Each look is referred to as a *view* in Outlook parlance. You don't have to think much about views if you'd rather not, because when you buy Outlook, dozens of views are included. Simply choose the one you want. I describe the main views in this chapter.

Types of Views

Choosing a view is like renting a car. You can choose a model with the features you want, whether the car is a convertible, a minivan, or a luxury sedan. All cars are equipped with different things — radios, air conditioning, power cup holders, and so on — that you can use or not use, as you please. Some rental agencies offer unlimited free mileage. Outlook views are much more economical, though. In fact, they're free.

Every module in Outlook has its own selection of views. The Calendar has (among others) a view that looks calendar-like. The Contacts module includes a view that looks like an address card. The Tasks module includes a

Timeline view. All modules allow you to use at least one type of Table view, which organizes your data in the old-fashioned row-and-column arrangement.

Each type of view is organized to make something about your collection of information obvious at first glance. You can change the way that you view a view by sorting, filtering, or grouping.

You don't have to do anything to see a view; Outlook is *always* displaying some kind of view. The view is the thing that takes up most of the screen most of the time. The view (or the Information Viewer, in official Microsoftese) is one of only two parts of Outlook that you can't turn off. (You also can't turn off the menu bar.) Most people don't even know that they have a choice of Outlook views; they just use the views that show up the first time they use Outlook. So now you're one step ahead of the game.

Each view has a name, which you can see in the Current View menu. A check mark appears next to the name of whichever view you're using. To see the Current View menu, choose View⇨Current View. The Current View menu also lists other views that are available to you in the module that you're using.

Table view

All modules contain some version of the Table view. A Table view is rectangular — all rows and columns. If you create a new item by adding a new task to your Tasks list, for example, a new row turns up in the Table view. You see one row for each task in the Table view (see Figure 16-1).

The names of Table views often contain the word *list,* as in Simple List, Phone List, or just List. That word means that they're a plain-vanilla table of items, just like a grocery list. Other Table view names start with the word *By,* which means that items in the view are grouped by a certain type of information, such as entry type or name of contact. I discuss grouped views later in the chapter and show you how to group items your own way.

Icons view

Icons view is the simplest view — just a bunch of icons with names thrown on-screen (see Figure 16-2).

The only Icons views that come with Outlook are used for viewing notes and file folders. Icons view doesn't show a great deal of information, and some people like it that way. I like to see more detailed information, so I stay with Table views. There's nothing wrong with using Icons view most of the time; you can easily switch to another view if you ever need to see more.

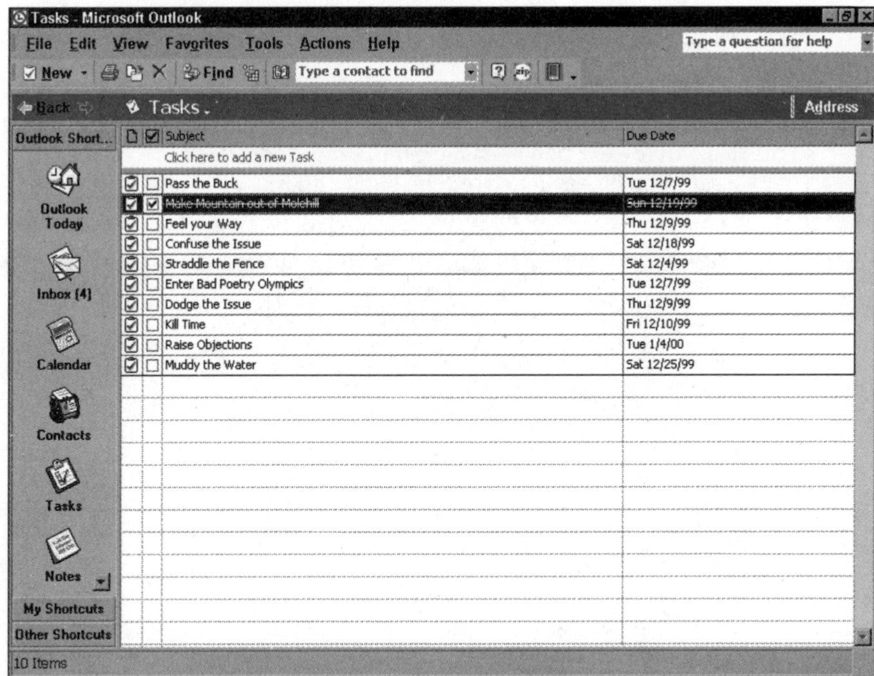

Figure 16-1: The Tasks module in a Table view.

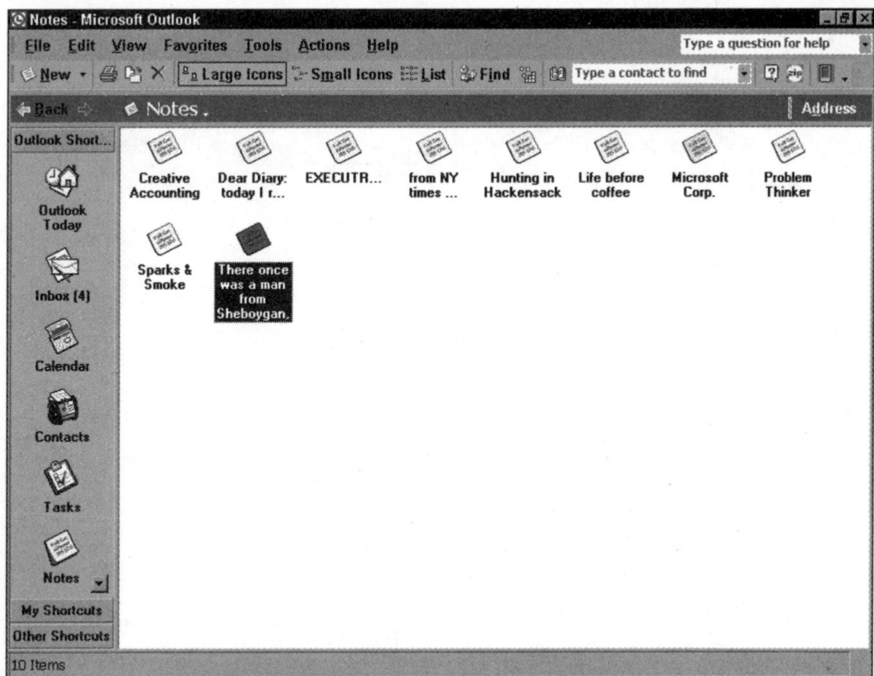

Figure 16-2: The Notes module in Icons view.

Timeline view

Timeline views show you a set of small icons arranged across the screen. Icons that are higher on the screen represent items that were created or tasks that were begun earlier in the day. Icons that are farther to the left were created on an earlier date (see Figure 16-3).

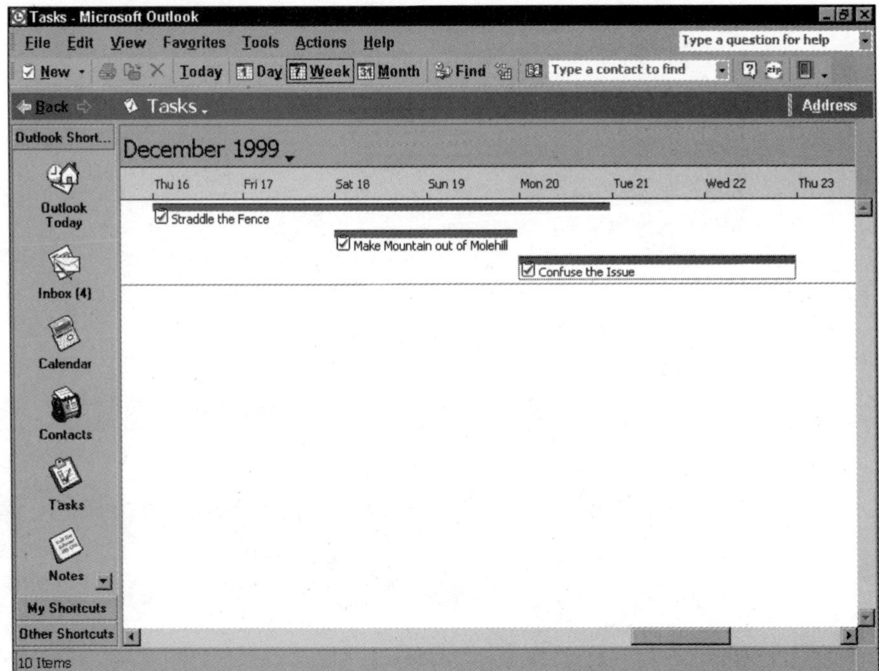

Figure 16-3: Tasks arranged in the Timeline view.

The Task Timeline in the Tasks module also draws a line that represents the length of time that it takes to perform an item if the start and end times of a task have been specified previously.

A Timeline view includes four toolbar buttons that allow you to change the length of time you want to view. Your choices are Today, Day (not necessarily today), Week, and Month. As you can in all other view settings, you can click to move between one-day and seven-day views and back, like changing television channels.

Card view

Card views are designed for the Contacts module. Each Contact item gets its own little block of information (see Figure 16-4). Each little block displays a little or a lot of information about the item, depending on what kind of card it is. (See Chapter 7 for more about the different views in the Contacts module.)

The Address Cards view shows you only a few items at a time because the cards are so big. To make it easier to find a name in your Contacts list that you don't see on-screen, type the first letter of the name that your contact is filed under to see that person's address card.

Day/Week/Month view

Day/Week/Month view is another specialized view, designed particularly for the Calendar.

Like a Timeline view, Day/Week/Month view adds Day, Work Week, Week, and Month buttons to the toolbar to allow you to switch between views easily. The Day, Work Week, and Week views also display a monthly calendar. You can click any date in the monthly calendar to switch your view to that date (see Figure 16-5).

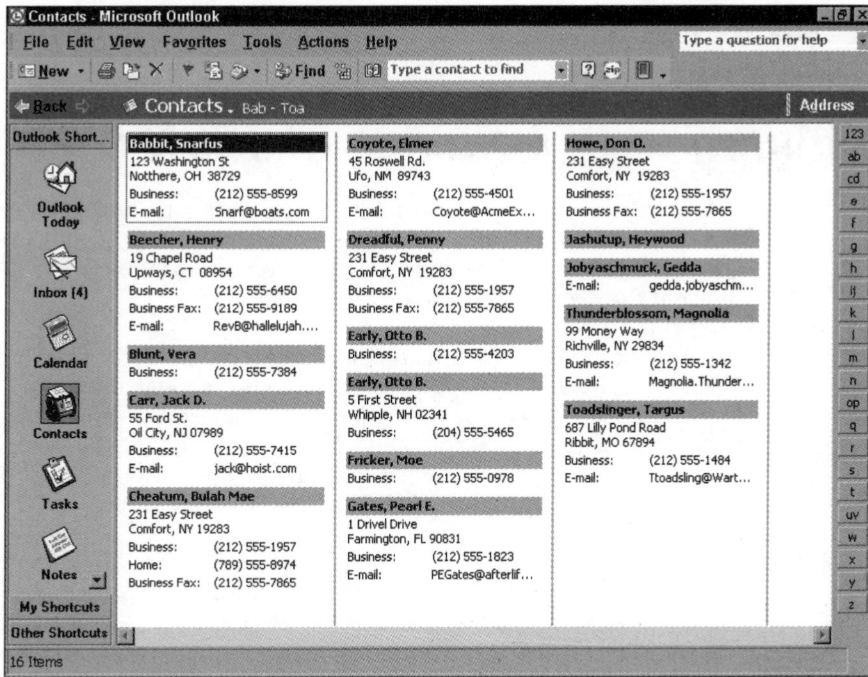

Figure 16-4: See your contacts in Address Card view.

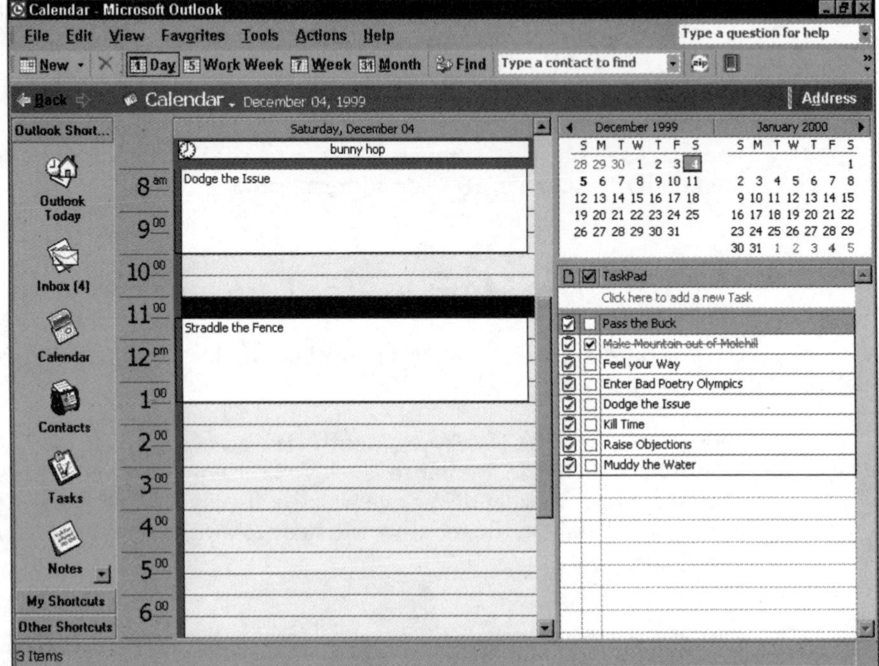

Figure 16-5: Starting a day in the life of your Calendar.

Playing with Columns in Table View

Table views show you the most detailed information about the items that you've created; these views also allow you to organize the information in the greatest number of ways with the least effort. Okay, Table views look a little dull, but they get you where you need to go.

Table views are organized in columns and rows. Each row displays information for one item — one appointment in your Calendar, one task in your Tasks list, or one person in your Contacts list. Adding a row is easy. Just add a new item by pressing Ctrl+N, and then fill in the information you want for that item. Getting rid of a row is easy, too. Just delete the item: Select the item by clicking it with your mouse, and then press the Delete key.

The columns in a Table view show you pieces of information about each item. Most Outlook modules can store far more pieces of information about an item than you can display on-screen in row-and-column format. The Contacts list, for example, holds more than 90 pieces of information about every person in your list. If each person were represented by one row, you would need more than 90 columns to display everything.

Adding a column

Outlook starts you out with a limited number of columns in the Phone List view of your Contacts list. (Remember that the names of Table views usually have the word *list* in them somewhere.) If you want more columns, you can easily add some. You can display as many columns as you want in Outlook, but you may have to scroll across the screen to see the information that you want to see.

To add a column in any Table view:

1. **Right-click the title of any column in the gray header row of the column.**

   A shortcut menu appears.

2. **Pick Field Chooser from the shortcut menu.**

   The Field Chooser dialog box appears.

3. **Select the type of field that you want to add.**

   The words *Frequently-Used Fields* appear in the text box at the top of the Field Chooser. Those words mean that the types of fields most people like to add are already listed. If the name of the field that you want to add isn't listed in one of the gray boxes at the bottom of the Field Chooser dialog box, pull down the menu that Frequently-Used Fields is part of and see what's available.

4. **Drag the field into the table.**

You have to drag the new item to the top row of the table, where the heading names are (see Figure 16-6). Notice that the names in the Field Chooser are in the same kind of gray box as the headers of each column of your table. (If they look alike, they must belong together, like Michael Jackson and Lisa Marie. Right? . . . Maybe that's not the best example.) Two red arrows appear to show you where your new field will end up when you drop it off.

Moving a column

Moving columns is even easier than adding columns. Just drag the heading of the column to where you want it (see Figure 16-7).

Two little red arrows appear as you're dragging the heading to show you where the column will end up when you release the mouse button.

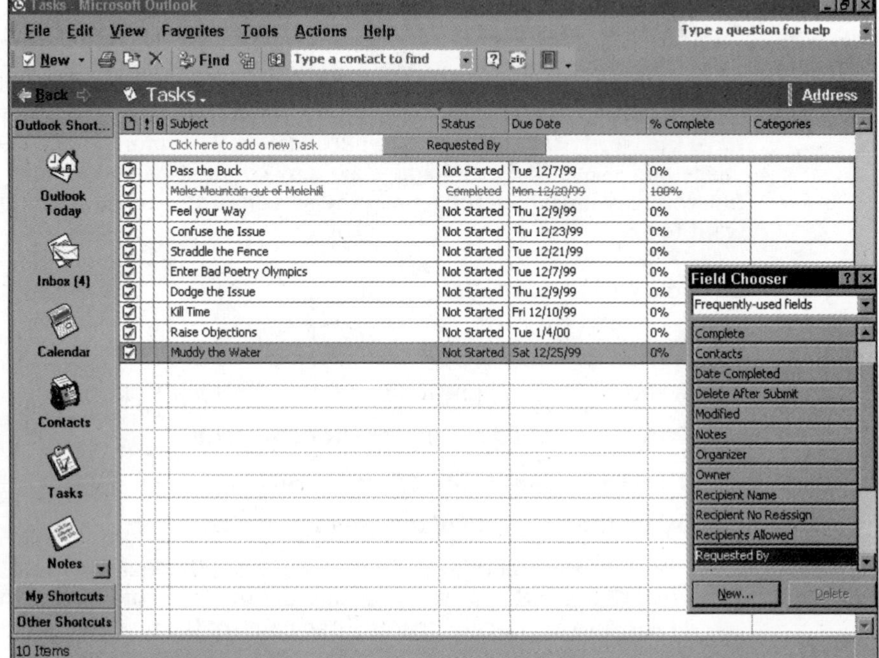

Figure 16-6: The Requested By field is dragged to the top row of the table.

Figure 16-7: Moving the Business Phone column.

Columns = fields

I promised to tell you how to add a column, and now I'm telling you about fields. What gives? Well, columns are fields, see? No? Well, think of it this way:

In your checkbook, your check record has a column of the names of the people to whom you wrote checks and another column that contains the amounts of those checks. When you actually write a check, you write the name of the payee in a certain field on the check; the amount goes in a different field. So you enter tidbits of information as fields on the check, but you show them as columns in the check record. That's exactly how it works in Outlook. You enter somebody's name, address, and phone number in fields when you create a new item, but the Table view shows the same information to you in columns. When you're adding a column, you're adding a field. Same thing.

Formatting a column

Some fields contain too much information to fit in their columns. Dates are prime offenders. Outlook normally displays dates in this format: `Sun 7/4/99 4:14 PM`. I normally don't care which day of the week a date falls on, so I reformat the column to `7/4/99 4:14 PM` and save the other space for something that I really want to know.

To change the formatting of a column:

1. **Right-click the heading of a column.**

   A menu appears.

2. **Choose Format Columns.**

   The Format Columns dialog box appears (see Figure 16-8).

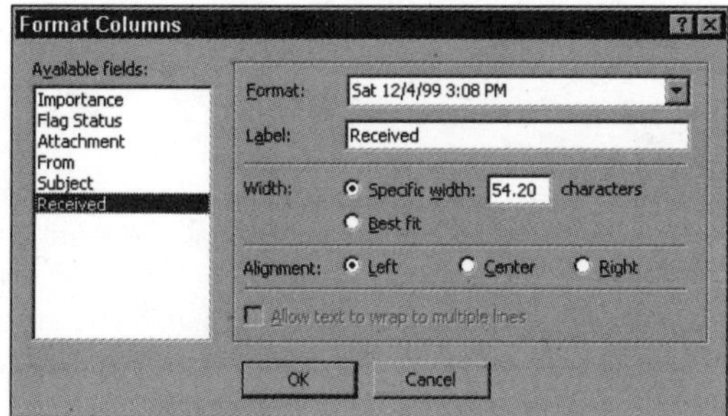

Figure 16-8: The Format Columns dialog box.

3. **Choose a format type from the Format menu.**

   Pick whatever suits your fancy. Some columns contain information that can be formatted only one way, such as names and categories. Information in number columns (especially dates) can be formatted in a variety of ways.

4. **Click OK.**

   Your column is reformatted.

Changing a column format affects only that column in that view of that module. If you want to change the formats of other views and modules, you have to change them one at a time.

Widening or shrinking a column

Widening or shrinking a column is even easier than moving a column. Here's how:

1. **Move the mouse pointer to the right edge of the column that you want to widen or shrink until the pointer becomes a two-headed arrow.**

   Making that mouse pointer turn into a two-headed arrow takes a bit of dexterity. If you find the procedure to be difficult, you can use the Format Column procedure that I describe in the preceding section. Type a number in the Width box — bigger numbers for wider boxes and smaller numbers for narrower boxes.

2. **Drag the edge of the column until the column is the width that you desire.**

   The two-headed arrow creates a thin line that you can drag to resize the column (see Figure 16-9). What you see is what you get.

If you're not really sure how wide a column needs to be, just double-click the right edge of the column header. When you double-click that spot, Outlook does a trick called *size-to-fit,* which widens or narrows a column to exactly the size of the widest piece of data in the column.

Removing a column

You can remove columns that you don't want to look at. To remove a column:

1. **Right-click the heading of the column that you want to remove.**

   A menu appears.

2. **Choose Remove This Column.**

   Zap! It's gone!

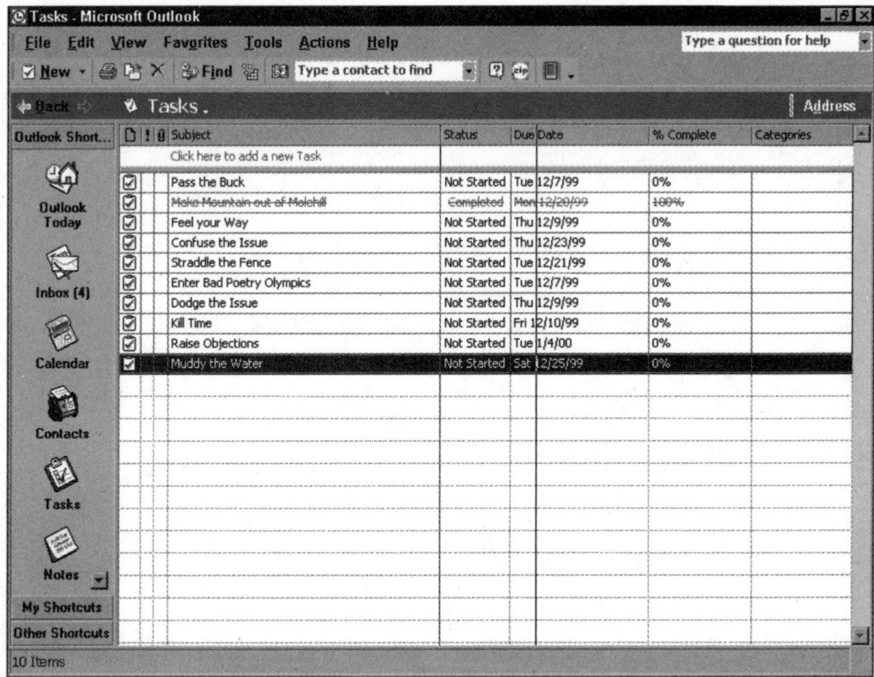

Figure 16-9: Widening the Status column.

Don't worry too much about deleting columns. When you zap a column, the field remains in the item. You can use the column-adding procedure (which I describe earlier in this chapter) to put it back. If you're confused by this whole notion of columns and fields, see the sidebar "Columns = fields" elsewhere in this chapter.

Sorting

Sorting just means putting your list in order. In fact, a list is always in some kind of order. Sorting just changes the order.

You can tell what order your list is sorted in by looking for triangles in headings. A heading with a triangle in it means that the entire list is sorted by the information in that column. If the column has numbers in it, and if the triangle's large side is at the top, the list begins with the item that has the largest number in that column, followed by the item that has the next-largest number, and so on, ending with the smallest number. Columns that contain text get sorted in alphabetical order. *A* is the smallest letter, and *Z* is the largest.

From Table view

By far, the easiest way to sort a table is simply to click the heading of a column that you want to sort. The entire table is sorted on the column that you clicked.

From the Sort dialog box

Although clicking a column is the easiest way to sort, doing so allows you to sort on only one column. You may want to sort on two or more columns.

To sort on two or more columns:

1. **Choose View⇨Current View⇨Customize Current View.**

   The View Summary dialog box appears.

2. **Click the Sort button.**

   The Sort dialog box appears.

3. **From the Sort Items By menu, choose the first field that you want to sort by.**

   Choose carefully; a much larger list of fields is in the list than is usually in the view. It's confusing.

4. **Choose Ascending or Descending sort order.**

   That means to choose whether to sort from smallest to largest or largest to smallest.

5. **Repeat Steps 3 and 4 for each additional field that you want to sort.**

   As the dialog box implies, the first thing that you select is the most important. The entire table is sorted according to that field and then by the fields that you pick later, in the order in which you select them. If you sort your phone list by company first and then by name, for example, your list begins with the names of the people who work for a certain company, displayed alphabetically, followed by the names of the people who work for another company, and so on.

6. **Click OK.**

   Your list is sorted.

Grouping

Sorting and grouping are similar. Both procedures organize items in your table according to the information in one of the columns. Grouping is different from sorting, however, in that it creates bunches of similar items that you can open or close. You can look at only the bunches that interest you and ignore all the other bunches.

For example, when you balance your checkbook, you probably *sort* your checks by check number. At tax time, you *group* your checks; you make a pile of the checks for medical expenses, another pile of checks for charitable deductions, and another pile of checks for the money that you spent on *For Dummies* books. Then you can add up the amounts that you spent in each category and enter those figures in your tax return.

Grouping views with drag-and-drop

The simple way to group items is to open the Group By box and drag a column heading into it (see Figure 16-10).

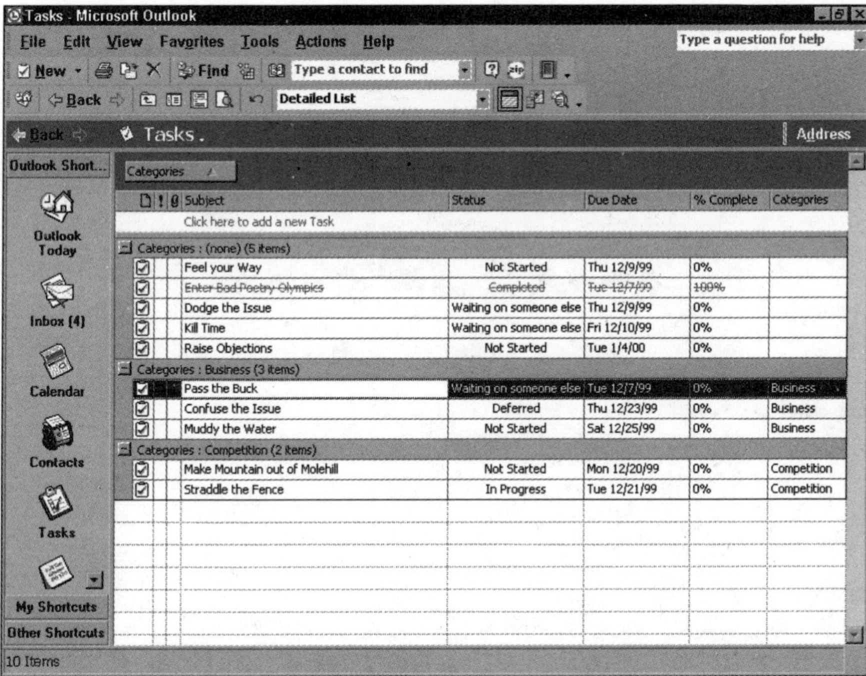

Figure 16-10: A grouped view based on one column heading.

Here's how you group items by dragging and dropping a column heading:

1. **Open the Advanced toolbar by choosing View⇨Toolbars⇨Advanced.**

   The Advanced toolbar appears, displaying the Group By Box button, normally the third button from the right. The Group By Box button contains an icon that looks like a box with some lines in it.

2. **Click the Group By Box button on the Advanced toolbar.**

   The table drops down slightly, and a box appears above the table, saying `Drag a column header here to group by that column.`

3. **Drag to the Group By box the header of the column that contains the data you want to group by.**

   You can drag several fields up to the Group By box to create groups based on more than one column (see Figure 16-11).

Using the Group By dialog box

Just as you have a second way to sort your listing, you have a second way to group your listing. Just use the Group By dialog box.

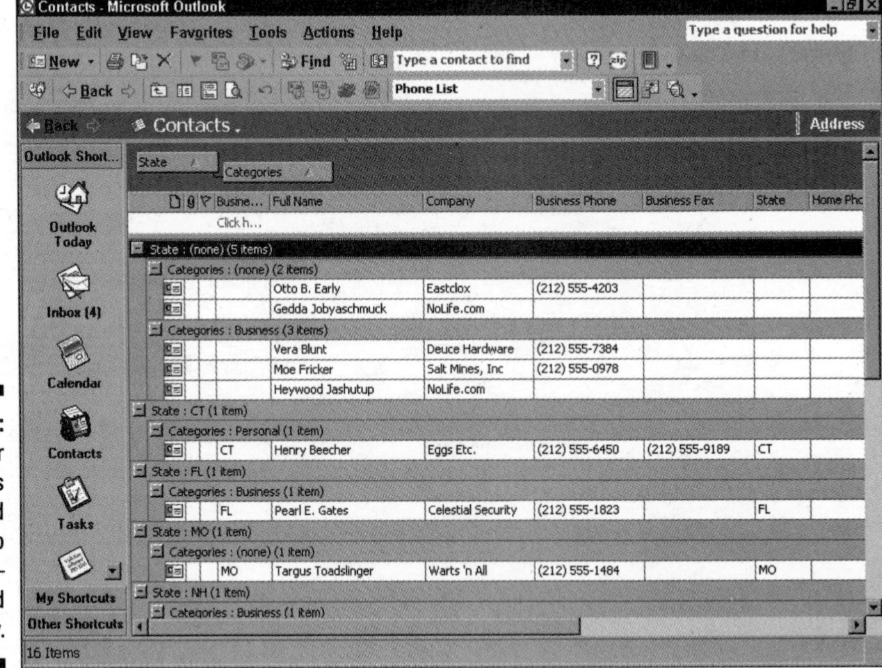

Figure 16-11: Your Contacts list grouped by two headings — State and Category.

To group your list:

1. **Choose View➪Current View➪Customize Current View.**

   The View Summary dialog box appears.

2. **Click the Group By button.**

   The Group By dialog box appears (see Figure 16-12).

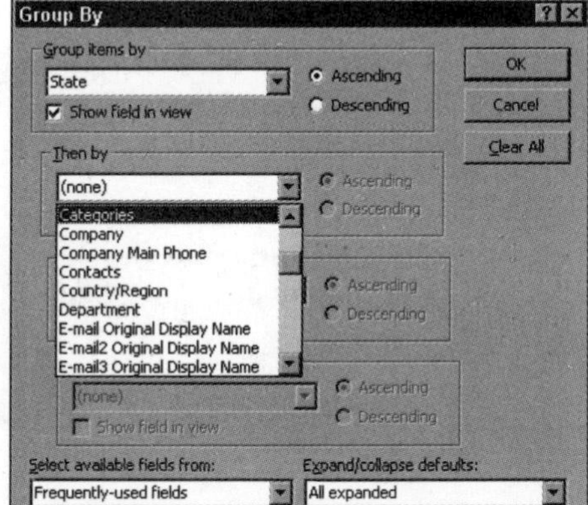

Figure 16-12: The Group By dialog box with the Show Field in View box checked.

3. **Choose the first field that you want to group the view by.**

   The list has more fields than are showing in the table. If you choose to group by a field that's not showing in your table, you can check the Show Field in View check box, as shown in Figure 16-12. You may also want to choose whether you want your groups to be sorted in Ascending or Descending alphabetical order, although that's less important when you're grouping.

4. **Choose any other fields by which you want to group the view.**

   If you group by too many columns, your list will be harder rather than easier to use.

5. **Click OK.**

   Your list is grouped by as many fields as you want.

An even quicker way to group items is to right-click the heading of a column you want to group by and choose Group by This Field. The Group By box automatically appears, and the name of the field you chose automatically appears in the Group By box. Isn't that slick?

Viewing grouped items

A grouped view shows you the names of the columns that you used to create the group view. If you click the Contacts icon and choose By Company view (which is a grouped view), you see gray bars with an icon at the right. The word *Company* appears next to the icon because that's the column that the view is grouped on. A company name appears next to the word Company; the grouped view includes a gray bar for each company in the list.

The icon at the left end of the gray bar is either a plus sign or a minus sign. A plus sign means that there's more to be seen. Click the plus sign, and the group opens, revealing the other items that belong to the group. A minus sign means that there's nothing more to see; what you see is what you get in that group.

If you click the gray bar itself but not the icon, you select the entire group. You can delete the group if you select the gray bar and press the Delete key. When a group bar is selected, it's dark gray rather than light gray, like all the others.

Viewing headings only

You can click the plus and minus signs one at a time to open and close individual groups, or you can open or close all the groups simultaneously.

To open or close groups:

1. **Simply choose View⇨Expand/Collapse Groups.**

   I think Expanding and Collapsing are dramatic words for what you're doing with these groups. It's not like Scarlett O'Hara getting the vapors; it's just hiding or revealing the contents of a group or all the groups.

2. **To open a single group that you've selected, choose Collapse This Group or Expand This Group.**
3. **To expand or collapse all the groups, choose Expand All or Collapse All.**

What could be easier?

Creating Custom Table Views

If you're used to saving documents in your word processor, you're familiar with the idea of saving views. When you make any of the changes to a view that I describe earlier in this chapter, you can save the changes as a new view, or make the changes the new way to see the current view. If you plan to use a certain view repeatedly, it's worth saving.

You can create any view you like by using the Define Views dialog box. Choose View⇨Current View⇨Define Views and follow the prompts. This procedure is a little more complicated than simply changing and saving views, but you have more detailed control of the results. When you're comfortable with Outlook, you may want to give the Define Views method a try, but I think that you can do most of what you need to do just by changing the views you already have.

A Bridge from the Views

You can create an endless number of ways to organize and view the information that you save in Outlook. How you decide to view information depends on what kind of information you have and how you plan to use what you have. You can't go too wrong with views, because you can easily create new views if the old ones get messed up. So feel free to experiment.

Chapter 17

Outlook Express: Getting the Scoop on Newsgroups

In This Chapter

- Locating newsgroups
- Subscribing to a newsgroup
- Reading and replying to newsgroup messages
- Posting a message to a newsgroup
- Setting up e-mail for the whole family

Microsoft gave Outlook a cousin named Outlook Express. The two programs do many of the same jobs, but each has its own specialty. The most important difference between Outlook and Outlook Express is that Outlook Express is free. Yep, you can get a copy of Outlook Express without spending a dime. The program is included with Internet Explorer as well as with certain releases of Windows, so if you have Outlook 2000, you also have Outlook Express.

The other difference between the two programs is that Outlook Express can read Internet newsgroups and Outlook can't. Internet newsgroups are collections of messages that anyone can read. After you read the messages in a newsgroup, you can reply to any message you read or post a whole new message of your own. To participate in a newsgroup, you need a special type of program called a *newsreader* — Outlook Express is just the tool for the job.

Outlook Express can also send and receive e-mail just like Outlook, but only Outlook can do all the fancy tricks with your tasks and calendar and contacts that I discuss throughout the rest of this book. If you have only Outlook Express but not Outlook, you have the basic tools you need for exchanging e-mail. After you've exchanged enough e-mail, you'll probably want to graduate from Outlook Express to full-strength Outlook to make your e-mail easier to handle.

News reading at the office

Many corporations don't want their employees browsing Internet newsgroups at the office. Many newsgroups contain nasty things that most companies don't want on their computers, such as pornography and details about some pretty strange philosophies and political groups. Also, out of the 50,000-odd newsgroups on the Internet, relatively few are business-related. For that reason, your system administrators may have removed Outlook Express from your computer at the office. If you're on a corporate network that runs Exchange Server, and your employer wants you to read any of the handful of business-related Internet newsgroups, your administrators can make an Internet newsgroup show up as an Exchange Public Folder. See Chapter 14 for more about Public Folders.

The fact that Microsoft named both products Outlook causes plenty of confusion. What's even more confusing is that you can start Outlook Express from a menu in Outlook — just choose View➪Go To➪News. To further confuse the issue, the version of Outlook Express that appears when you choose View➪Go To➪News from the Outlook menu is different from the version that appears when you click the Outlook Express icon on your desktop.

The way I like to simplify the whole mess is by opening Outlook Express only from the Outlook menu and using Outlook Express only for reading Internet newsgroups. Because you have this book, I'm assuming that you have Outlook, which means that you also have Outlook Express.

Finding Newsgroups

Newsgroups are out there on the Internet for anyone to see, so you may as well jump right in and explore what newsgroups have to offer. The first time you start up Outlook Express, you can find a newsgroup to look at.

To view a newsgroup:

1. **Choose View➪Go To➪News from the Outlook menu.**

   The Internet Connection Wizard appears.

2. **Enter the information that the wizard requests and click Next after each entry.**

The wizard asks for your name, your e-mail address, and the name of your News Server. If you don't know the exact name of your news server, ask your system administrator or call the tech support line at your Internet Service Provider. The wizard also asks which kind of Internet connection you want to use: phone line, LAN, or manual. If you're not sure, you can just click Next, and the wizard chooses for you.

3. **Click Finish.**

   The Download Newsgroups dialog box appears. If your computer is connected to the Internet when the dialog box appears, you'll need to wait a few minutes to let the system get the list of newsgroups on your news server. If you're not connected to the Internet, a dialog box will appear to help you connect by clicking the Connect button. When the whole process is finished, the Newsgroup Subscriptions dialog box appears.

   The Newsgroup Subscriptions dialog box opens (see Figure 17-1). The dialog box contains a list of all the newsgroups that are available for you to see. You can scroll down the list and find a newsgroup whose name looks interesting. But with tens of thousands of newsgroups on the Internet, scrolling through the whole list could take quite a long time, so I suggest a faster method in the remaining steps.

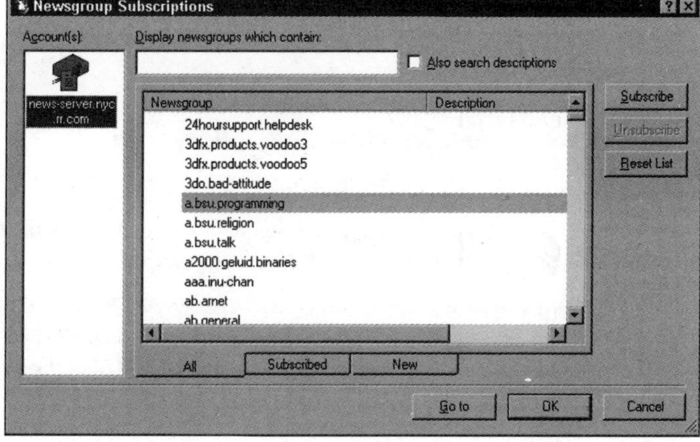

Figure 17-1: Pick the newsgroups you want to see in the Newsgroup Subscriptions dialog box.

4. **Click in the Display Newsgroups Which Contain text box and type a one-word name for a subject that interests you.**

   The list in the Newsgroup Subscriptions dialog box changes to a list of newsgroups whose title includes the word you type. For example, if you type the word **Outlook,** the newsgroups in which people post comments, questions, and answers about Outlook appear.

5. **Double-click the name of a newsgroup that interests you.**

   The Outlook Express main screen appears, with a list of the most recent messages posted to the newsgroup you chose.

Subscribing to Newsgroups

If you start hanging around in Internet newsgroups, you'll find that you spend a lot of time in a handful of groups, and you'll probably ignore the other tens of thousands of groups out there. Who has time to read 10,000 newsgroups, anyway?

You can get into your favorite newsgroups more quickly if you subscribe. *Subscribing* to a newsgroup is different from subscribing to a magazine. You don't pay a fee for subscribing to a newsgroup, and nobody needs to know you're reading a newsgroup unless you post messages to the group.

Don't post your e-mail address to an Internet newsgroup. People who send junk e-mail often gather e-mail addresses from newsgroups. After the junk e-mailers (or *spammers,* in Internet jargon) get your address, your Inbox may become stuffed with so many junk e-mail messages that you won't be able to find the messages that you really want to see.

To subscribe to a newsgroup:

1. **Choose View⇨Go To⇨News from the Outlook menu.**

   The Newsgroups screen in Outlook Express appears.

2. **Click the name of a newsgroup to which you want to subscribe in the Newsgroups screen and then click the Subscribe button.**

   An icon appears next to the name of the group you selected to show that you've selected it, and the name of the newsgroup appears in the Folder List on the right side of the Outlook Express screen (see Figure 17-2).

From now on, whenever you start up Outlook Express by choosing View⇨Go To⇨News from the Outlook menu, the first thing you see is a list of the newsgroups to which you've subscribed. When you click the name of a newsgroup in the Folders list, the latest messages in that newsgroup appear.

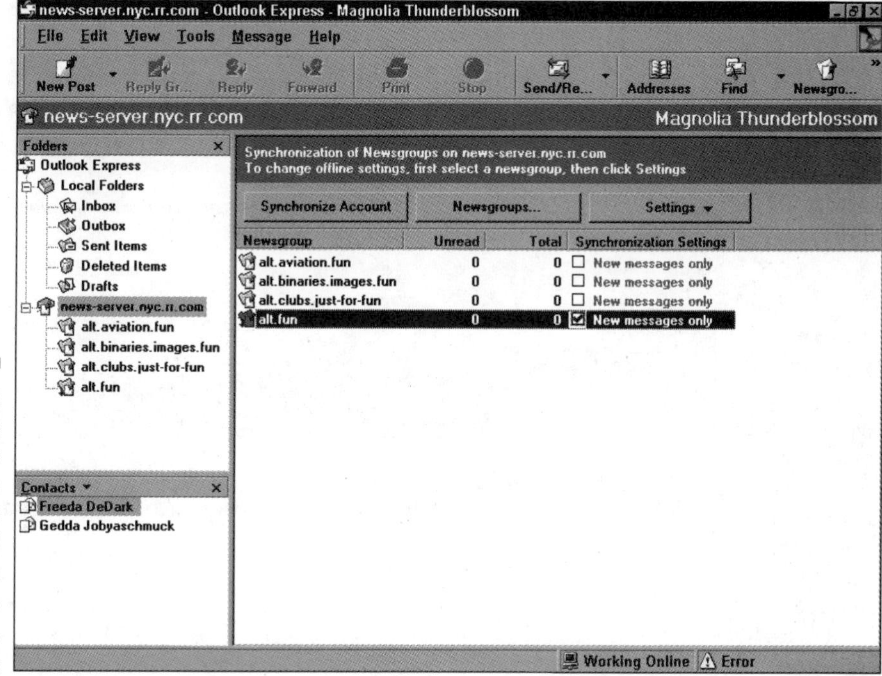

Figure 17-2: The Newsgroups to which you've subscribed appear in the Folders list.

Reading Newsgroup Messages

The list of newsgroup messages is organized according to the subject of each message and the date when each message was posted to the newsgroup. You may see some messages with a little plus sign to the left of the subject (see Figure 17-3). The plus sign means that more than one message about that subject is posted to the list. You can see all the other messages by clicking the plus sign. The plus sign then turns into a minus sign, and all the other messages on that topic appear.

If you want to read the text of a newsgroup message, click the title of the message once. That selects the message and makes the text of the message appear in the window below the list of message titles. To read the next message, just click the title of the next message in the list.

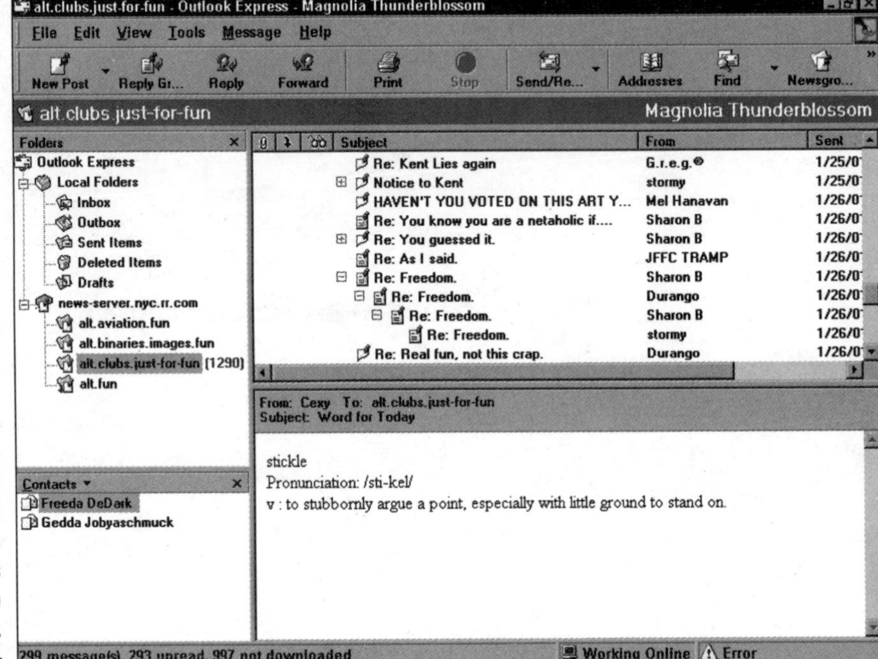

Figure 17-3: The plus sign next to a message tells you that you can read more messages on the same subject.

Replying to a Newsgroup Message

Reading messages in a newsgroup is only half the fun. It's when you put your two cents in that things get really interesting.

Internet newsgroups can be time consuming, emotionally draining, and habit forming. No self-help group exists for newsgroup addicts yet, but I think it's only a matter of time. Remember, you don't know the other people on a newsgroup, so don't get your socks in a knot over what people say to you online. Not everybody in every Internet newsgroup is polite or considerate, but it pays for you to remain as civil as possible.

If you're *really* ready, here's how to reply to a newsgroup message:

1. **Double-click the message to which you want to reply.**

   The message you clicked opens in a new window.

2. **Choose Message⇨Reply to Group (or press Ctrl+G).**

   A new message window appears (see Figure 17-4).

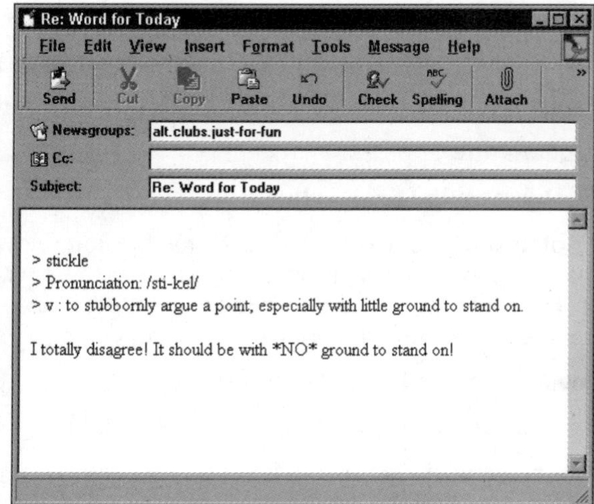

Figure 17-4: When you reply to a newsgroup message, the text of the message you're answering appears as part of your reply.

3. **Type your message.**

   Your message appears in the new message window.

4. **Click the Send button.**

   The new message window closes, and your message is posted to the newsgroup.

Newsgroup messages don't appear instantly to the newsgroup. Thousands of servers are out there with millions of messages, so it can take anywhere from a few minutes to a day or so for your message to show up.

Posting a New Message

As your horoscope said one time (because everybody's has at least once), you have a creative streak, and you need to express yourself. A newsgroup is the cheapest place to publish your latest stroke of literary genius. On the other hand, an Internet newsgroup is probably not the best place to reveal your most private thoughts. Remember, anybody on earth can read this stuff. Before you post anything too original to the Internet, read your high school yearbook, see what you said then, and decide whether you want to make that kind of mistake again.

If you still can't restrain yourself, here's how to post an original message to a newsgroup:

1. **View the newsgroup to which you want to post your new message.**

   The list of messages in the newsgroup that you selected appears.

2. **Choose Message⇨New Message (or press Ctrl+N).**

   A new message window appears.

3. **Type a new subject on the Subject line.**

   You're better off making your subject short, snappy, and relevant. You'll find plenty of newsgroup messages with titles that are neither snappy nor relevant. The poor souls who wrote those messages haven't read this book. Have pity on them, but set a good example, okay?

4. **Type your message in the message text box.**

   The text of your message appears in the message text box.

5. **When your message is complete, click Send.**

   The message window closes.

There's one thing I can't overemphasize (but I'll try): Anybody on earth can read what you've posted to an Internet newsgroup. If you plan to post a statement that could cause you problems with your job, your relationships, or the law, you should assume that the wrong people will see what you post. Be careful.

E-Mail for the Whole Family with Outlook Express

It seems silly to have two e-mail programs on one computer, but there are times when you might want to use both Outlook and Outlook Express. For example, if several members of your family share the same computer, you can use the two programs at the same time to give each member access to e-mail. Have one member use Outlook and all the others can use Outlook Express. You'll have to fight over who gets Outlook 2002, because it's the more powerful of the two programs. The one advantage to Outlook Express is that the Identities feature allows several people to exchange messages on separate e-mail addresses. Outlook Express also includes a wizard for setting up free e-mail accounts on Hotmail, so it's easy to get everyone on e-mail with very little fuss.

Setting up Identities

If several different people want access to e-mail on the same computer, each of them can set up an Identity in Outlook Express. Then each person can send and receive e-mail as if they each had their own computer.

To create a new identity:

1. **Choose File⇨Identities⇨Add New Identity.**

   The New Identity dialog box appears.

2. **Type a name for your identity.**

   The name of your new identity appears.

3. **Click OK.**

   Your new identity appears in the Manage Identities dialog box.

You can delete an identity any time by choosing File⇨Identities⇨Manage Identities, selecting the identity you want to delete, and then clicking Remove.

Switching Identities

Superman used to switch identities in a phone booth. Outlook Express lets you switch identities even if you can't find a phone booth. After you've set up an Identity, you need to choose that identity each time you use Outlook Express so that you can send and receive the messages that belong to you.

To switch identities:

1. **Choose File⇨Switch Identities.**

   The Switch Identities dialog box appears.

2. **Double-click the name of the identity that you want to use.**

   The Switch Identities dialog box closes, and the set of messages belonging to the identity that you chose appears.

Even if you're not Superman, you can use Outlook Express to get e-mail for the whole family on one computer, but still keep each member's messages separate from one another.

Chapter 18

Mail Merge Magic

In This Chapter

- Creating mailing labels
- Addressing envelopes
- Compiling form letters
- Creating merged e-mail
- Merging from selected contacts

The Mail Merge tool could quickly become your favorite feature in Outlook. Even if you're an old hand at creating form letters and mailing labels in Microsoft Word, the new Mail Merge tool makes it a snap to send letters to people in your Contacts list.

If you're new to the world of form letters, *mail merge* is the term that computer people use to describe the way you can create a letter on a computer and print umpteen copies, each addressed to a different person. You probably get lots of mail-merged letters every day, but you usually call it junk mail. When you *send* a mass mailing, it's called mail merge. When you *get* a mass mailing, it's called junk mail. But you knew that all along, didn't you?

Mail Merge Mania

When you use the Mail Merge feature in Outlook 2002, Microsoft Word really does all the heavy lifting. Outlook just manages the names and addresses and passes them over to Word. If you're not running any version of Microsoft Word, you won't be able to run a Mail Merge from Outlook. I'm told that you can run the Outlook Mail Merge with any version of Microsoft Word, so if you're sentimental about your old word processors, you don't need to feel left out. As I write this, you can't even buy Outlook 2002 without buying the whole Office XP suite, so I assume that you have the latest version of both programs.

You can perform a mail merge without using Outlook at all, if you like. If you're sending a letter to people who aren't on your Contacts list (and you don't want to clutter up your Contacts list with unnecessary names), you can use the Mail Merge feature in Microsoft Word. For more about Microsoft Word 2002, take a look at *Word 2002 For Dummies* by Dan Gookin (published by Hungry Minds, Inc.).

Creating Mailing Labels

You can create a set of mailing labels for everyone in your Address Book in a flash. The Outlook Contacts list connects right up to Word's mail-merge features, so you don't have to mess around with exporting files and figuring out where they went when you want to merge to them. All you have to do is run the Outlook Mail Merge tool.

To create a set of mailing labels:

1. **Click the Contacts icon on the Outlook Bar.**

   Your list of contacts appears.

2. **Choose Tools➪Mail Merge.**

   The Mail Merge Contacts dialog box appears (see Figure 18-1).

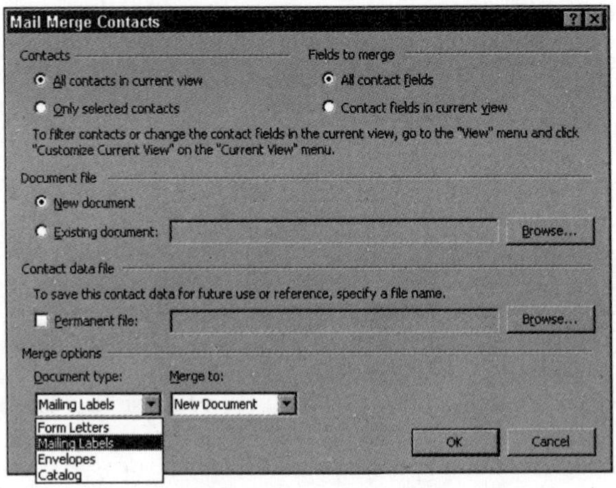

Figure 18-1: The Mail Merge Contacts dialog box helps you kick off the merge process.

3. **Choose Mailing Labels from the Document Type list.**

   The Document Type list is in the lower-left corner of the Mail Merge Contacts dialog box. The words *Mailing Labels* appear after you make your choice.

4. **Choose New Document from the Merge To list.**

   The Merge To list appears just to the right of the Document Type list at the bottom of the dialog box. Normally, the words *New Document* appear automatically, so you don't have to do anything, but you might want to check to be sure.

5. **Click OK.**

   Microsoft Word starts up, displaying a dialog box that tells you that Outlook has created a Mail Merge document, but you have to use the Mail Merge Helper dialog box to set up your document.

6. **Click OK.**

   The Mail Merge Helper dialog box appears.

7. **Click Set Up.**

   The Label Options dialog box appears (see Figure 18-2).

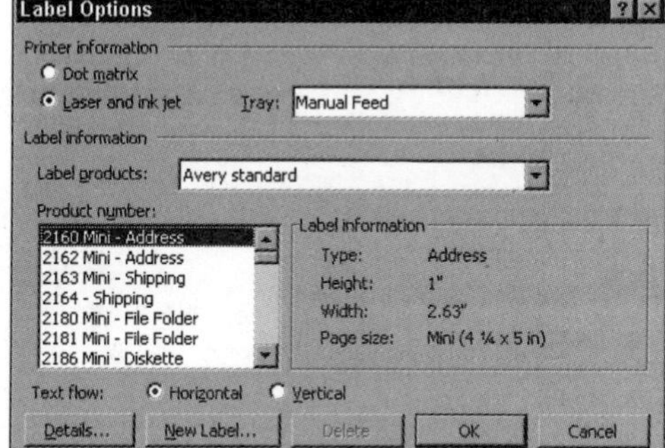

Figure 18-2: The Label Options dialog box.

8. **Choose the label type that you want and click OK.**

   Check the stock number on your label and make sure it's the same as the one you're choosing. If the stock number isn't available, you can look at the label dimensions in the Label Information section of the Label Options dialog box. When you click OK, the Create Labels dialog box appears.

9. **Click Insert Merge Field.**

   A list of field names appears (see Figure 18-3). The collection of fields in the list bears a striking resemblance to the kinds of data that you can enter in the Outlook Contacts list. Funny, huh? The list can also be very, very long, so you may need to scroll up and down the list to find the fields you need.

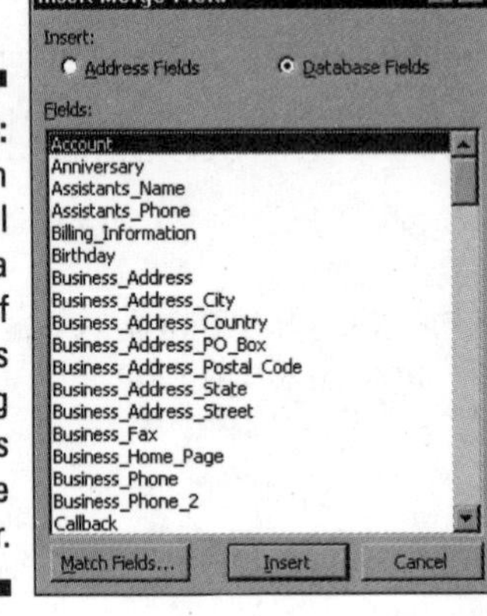

Figure 18-3: You can scroll through a long list of field names by clicking the triangles in the scroll bar.

10. **Click each piece of data that you want to include in your label.**

    For example, on a typical address label, click Insert Merge Field, select Full_Name, press Enter, click Insert Merge Field, and select Mailing Address. You don't have to mess with City, State, and Zip, because Outlook deals with the entire mailing address as a single unit.

11. **Click OK.**

    The Mail Merge Helper reappears.

12. **Click the Merge button.**

    The Mail Merge dialog box opens.

13. **Click Merge again.**

    Again? Yes, there are two Merge buttons. The first button is the Mail Merge Helper; the second one is the actual Merge command.

I like to test a mail merge in mailing-label format before doing an actual merge — just to be sure that everything works out. You can print labels on regular paper to see what they look like. If you make a mistake setting up the merge, it's better to find out by printing ten pages of messed-up "labels" on plain paper than by printing 300 messed-up letters.

If you print labels frequently, you can reduce your work by saving the blank label document and using it repeatedly. When you've finished creating your labels, press Alt+Tab a few times until you see a document that looks like your labels, except that it's filled with strange text that looks like this: <<Full_Name><<Mailing_Address> and so on. Save that document and name it something you'll remember, such as *Blank Labels*. The next time you decide to create labels, click the Existing Document check box in the Mail Merge Contacts dialog box, click Browse, and then double-click Blank Labels. That eliminates the preceding Steps 7 through 12 and enables you to get on to more exciting things, such as stuffing envelopes.

Printing Envelopes

You don't have to print to labels at all if you're planning a mass mailing; you can print directly onto the envelopes that you're sending. With luck, your printer has an envelope feeder. Feeding envelopes one at a time gets old fast.

To print addresses directly onto your envelopes, follow exactly the same steps that I describe in the previous section for creating mailing labels. The only difference you'll notice is that in Step 8, the Envelope Options dialog box appears, with a choice of envelope sizes (see Figure 18-4). Pick the type of envelope you're using (usually number 10, the standard business envelope) and follow the rest of the steps.

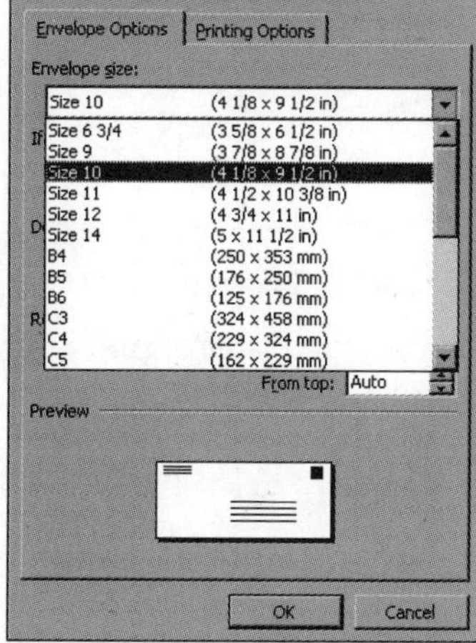

Figure 18-4: The Envelope Options dialog box with the Envelope Size list showing.

If you've never printed multiple envelopes on your printer before, start small. Try printing four or five, just to make sure that your printer feeds envelopes properly. Word and Outlook happily send your printer a command to print hundreds of envelopes in a flash. If your printer chokes on the fourth envelope, however, fixing the problem can take a long time.

If you're printing only one envelope, your best bet is to go right to Microsoft Word and choose Tools⇨Letters and Mailings⇨Envelopes and Labels. The Envelopes and Labels dialog box has a tiny address book icon that lets you pick a name from your Outlook Contacts list and add it directly to an envelope or label.

Creating a Form Letter from the Contacts List

Today I received a personalized invitation to enter a $250,000 sweepstakes that had my name plastered all over the front of the envelope. How thoughtful and personal! Whenever you get a sweepstakes letter with your name already entered, you're getting a form letter. A *form letter* is a letter with standard text that's printed over and over but with a different name and address printed on each copy. You can send form letters, too, even if you're not holding a sweepstakes. An annual newsletter to family and friends is one form letter you may want to create.

To create a form letter from Outlook:

1. **Click the Contacts icon in the Outlook Bar.**

   Your list of contacts appears.

2. **Choose Tools⇨Mail Merge.**

   The Mail Merge Contacts dialog box appears.

3. **Choose Form Letters from the Document Type list.**

   The document type list is at the lower-left corner of the Mail Merge Contacts dialog box. The words *Form Letters* appear after you make your choice.

4. **Choose New Document from the Merge To list.**

   The Merge To list appears just to the right of the Document Type list at the bottom of the dialog box. Normally, the words *New Document* appear automatically, so you don't have to do anything, but you might want to check to be sure.

5. **Click OK.**

   Microsoft Word starts, displaying a blank document.

6. **Type your form letter, clicking the Insert Merge Field button (the sixth button from the left end of the toolbar) to insert merge fields everywhere you want data from your Outlook Address Book to appear in your form letter (see Figure 18-5).**

Now you don't have to settle for sending impersonal, annoying form letters to dozens of people; you can send a *personal,* annoying form letter to hundreds of people. If you're planning to send an annoying form letter to me, my address is 1600 Pennsylvania Avenue, Washington, D.C.

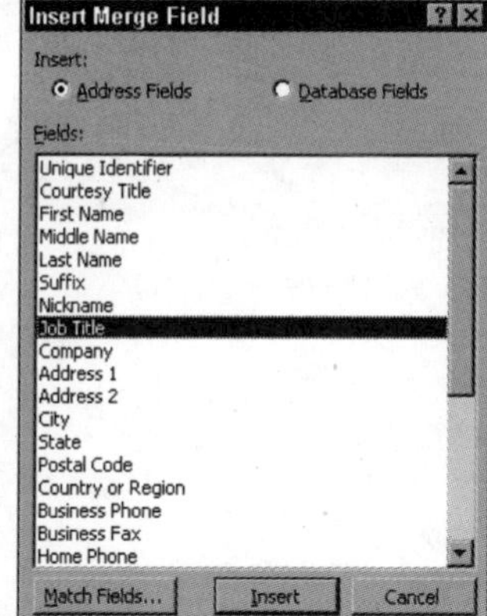

Figure 18-5: Adding merge fields to your letter.

Merging to E-Mail

Another very appealing feature of the new Mail Merge tool is the ability to create merged e-mail. Usually, you don't need to use mail merge for e-mail because you can send a single e-mail message to as many people as you want. But if you want to send an e-mail message to a bunch of people and customize each message, you can do that with a mail merge to e-mail. That way, you won't send your "Dear John" message to George, Paul, or Ringo.

To merge to e-mail, follow the same steps you use to create a form letter (see the preceding section), but choose E-Mail instead of New Document from the Merge to List in the Mail Merge Contacts dialog box.

If you're using Outlook on an Exchange network, your document goes right to your recipient as soon as you click the Merge button. If you've made a mistake, there's no chance to fix it. I recommend testing your e-mail merge by sending an e-mail to yourself first. Click your own name in the Contacts list, and then put together your merge message and send it to yourself. When you're sure you've said what you want to say, select all the people that you want to contact and go ahead with the merge. If you use Outlook at home, you can press Ctrl+Shift+O to switch to your Outbox and see the collection of messages before pressing F5 to send your messages (see Figure 18-6).

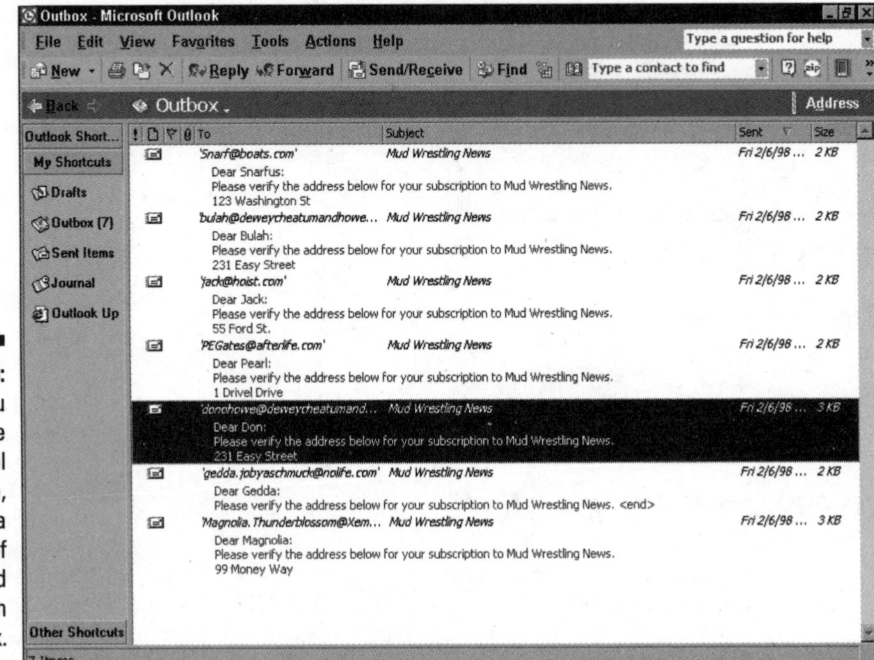

Figure 18-6: When you create an e-mail merge, you see a collection of personalized messages in your Outbox.

Merging Selected Records

You probably don't want to send a letter to every person on your Contacts list. It's easy to end up with thousands of names on your list — the postage alone could cost a fortune. To limit your list of letters or mailing labels to just a handful of contacts, hold down the Ctrl key and click the names of the people you want to include. After you've selected everyone you want, choose Tools⇨Mail Merge. The Mail Merge tool then creates letters or labels only for the people whose names you've selected.

Part V

The Part of Tens

"He saw your laptop and wants to know if he can check his Hotmail."

In this part . . .

Top-ten lists are everybody's favorite. They're short. They're easy to read. And they're the perfect spot for writers like me to toss in useful stuff that doesn't easily fit into the main chapters of the book. Flip through my top ten lists for tips you'll want to use, including a time-saving look at things you can't do with Outlook (so don't waste your time trying).

Chapter 19

Top Ten Accessories for Outlook

In This Chapter

- Palm Organizer
- Microsoft Office
- Synchronization programs
- IntelliMouse
- A business card scanner
- Laplink
- A high-capacity, removable disk drive
- A tape backup system
- Microsoft Exchange Server
- Address Grabber

Outlook 2002 can do plenty for you without any outside help, but a few well-considered accessories can make your life even easier. Some of my favorite accessories make up for things Outlook ought to have but doesn't. Some of my other favorite accessories help me to use my Outlook data anywhere, anytime.

Palm Organizer

The Palm handheld computer is far and away my favorite accessory for Outlook. Although I can enter and manage data in a snap with Outlook, I can carry my most important Outlook info in my pocket on my Palm device. I can even read my e-mail on the subway using the Palm organizer, something I wouldn't try with a laptop.

Several types of handheld computers are on the market today, but I prefer the ones that use the Palm operating system. Those products include the Palm-brand devices, Handspring Visor, Sony Clie, and the TRG Pro. Some new handheld computers use the Pocket PC system that Microsoft makes. You might think that the Microsoft Pocket PC system is more compatible with Outlook, but it's not. Palm still offers better value for the money in my view. To find out more about Palm computers, take a look at one of my other books, *Palm Computing For Dummies* or *Handspring Visor For Dummies,* both published by Hungry Minds, Inc.

Microsoft Office

When Outlook was first released, it was a part of the Microsoft Office 97 suite. Now that you can buy Outlook as a stand-alone product (or in a package with Internet Explorer), you may not have the benefits of using Microsoft Office and Outlook in concert. Office enables you to do all sorts of tricks with outgoing e-mail and graphics, while Outlook makes it a snap to exchange the work you've created in Office via e-mail. I recommend using both, if possible.

Synchronization Programs

Outlook still doesn't do a good job of talking to other devices on its own — even other devices that are running Outlook. To make your Outlook data useful on something like the Palm device, you need a program such as Desktop to Go (from a company called DataViz) to help you move the data back and forth. You can find out more about Desktop to Go from the manufacturer's Web site at `www.dataviz.com`. Another popular tool for synchronizing Outlook with other devices is called Intellisync by Pumatech (`www.pumatech.com`). With either of these products, you can move your most important data from Outlook to your Palm device by pressing one button. Pretty slick.

IntelliMouse

If your computer didn't come with a Microsoft IntelliMouse, you can buy one at your local computer store and plug it in. The IntelliMouse features a little wheel between the mouse buttons that makes it a snap to scroll through long e-mail messages.

A Business Card Scanner

You can use several brands of business card scanners to copy contact information into Outlook from the business cards you collect at conferences and trade shows. Of course, you can enter all the info manually, but if you collect more than a few dozen cards per week, a business card scanner can save you lots of work.

Laplink Professional

One of the most common questions I get from readers is, "How do I share Outlook information between my desktop and laptop computers?" Outlook doesn't provide a practical method for synchronizing information between two computers, so you're better off using a tool like Laplink to copy the Outlook data file (its file name ends in the letters PST) between the two computers. Be careful, though — Laplink has a synchronization tool that can make a mess of your Outlook data. Your best bet is to use Laplink to copy the whole file from one computer to another.

A Large, Removable Disk Drive

The second most common question I hear is, "How do I back up my Outlook data for safekeeping?" Again, because the Outlook data file is much too big to save on a floppy disk, you may want a large-capacity device for storing your data. The Iomega Zip drive costs about a hundred bucks, hooks up to your USB or printer port, and gives you lots of space.

You might also consider a CD burner for backing up your Outlook data. Many new computers come with a CD burner already installed, so if you have one, take advantage of it.

A Tape Backup

If you use your computer for business, your Outlook data probably isn't the only data that's crucial to your work. The cheapest way to keep your business data safe is to get a tape backup system and run the system every night. Depending on the size of your computer's hard disk, you can get tape backup units for around $200, and tapes run about $20 each — a bargain compared to the cost of losing your data.

Microsoft Exchange

Many of the Outlook features that Microsoft trumpets most require a network product called Microsoft Exchange Server. You need to have a network running Windows NT Server in order to run Exchange Server, so this accessory isn't cheap, and it's not so simple to set up. If you have a small business, a product called Microsoft Small Business Server has everything you need to set up a network with Exchange Server. You'll still spend several thousand dollars to get this arrangement going on your own, but you'll be able to share schedules, tasks, and calendars, and exchange interoffice e-mail. So you get a lot for what you spend.

If you don't want to mess with running Microsoft Exchange Server, you can also "rent" space on someone else's Exchange Server and use it over the Internet. The type of company that provides that kind of service is called an ASP, or Application Service Provider. I happen to like an ASP called Mi8.com, which charges around $20 per month per person to host an Exchange Server account. If you run a small business, it's worth looking into using an ASP.

Address Grabber

The quickest way I know of to fill up your Address Book is to capture addresses from the Internet by using a product called Address Grabber, which costs $49 from eGrabber.com. If you've installed Address Grabber on your computer, just highlight any address that appears on-screen — from a Web page, a document, or an e-mail message — and the address is automatically sorted out and transferred to your Outlook Contacts list. It's a wonderful timesaver.

Chapter 20

Ten Microsoft Office Tricks for Creating Snappier E-Mail

In This Chapter

- Office e-mail
- AutoText
- Themes
- New table tools
- Office Art
- Hyperlinks
- Document Map
- Versions
- Browsing
- Automatic grammar checking

Outlook can use Microsoft Word as an e-mail editor, which means that you can create extremely cool e-mail, such as you've never seen before — graphics, special effects, you name it. E-mail was never this much fun.

If you're an old hand at Microsoft Office and feel confident that you know what you need to know to get around Office XP, you're probably right; everything that you knew from before still works. If you're not familiar with Microsoft Office, pick up a copy of *Office XP For Dummies,* by Wallace Wang from Hungry Minds, Inc. (Okay, another plug, but have I steered you wrong so far?) The other parts of Office have acquired some really cool new features that can help you create attractive, impressive documents to send by e-mail. This chapter describes some of my favorites.

Office E-Mail

You can create an e-mail message for Outlook to send without even opening Outlook if you're using Office XP. All Office XP programs have an e-mail button on the toolbar that you can click to turn any document you're creating into an e-mail message. When you click the e-mail button on the Microsoft Word toolbar, for example, boxes labeled To, CC, and Subject appear at the top of your document. Just enter an e-mail address exactly the way you would if you were creating a message from the Outlook Inbox (for more about creating e-mail messages, see Chapter 5).

Be aware, however, that the person getting your message may not be equipped with an e-mail program that can read messages with all the fancy formatting that you can use in Word. If the person to whom you're sending your message is in your office and uses the same programs as you do, you'll have no problem. If you're sending a message to someone outside your office and you want to make a good impression, your best bet is to keep your message simple.

AutoText

You can create AutoText entries to avoid typing the same word or phrase over and over. For example, if you often need to type **Subject to change without notice**, you can type that phrase once, select it, choose Insert⇨AutoText ⇨New, and type an abbreviation for that phrase such as **subj**. Then every time you want to insert that phrase, just type the abbreviation you chose and press the F3 key — the whole phrase appears like magic.

Themes

If you want to make a Word 2002 document a bit more colorful and zippy, apply a *Theme.* Themes are predesigned backgrounds and color schemes that you can apply to a document to create a mood or image. Just choose Format⇨Theme and double-click the name of the theme you want to use. The fancy formatting and backgrounds that you can apply so easily as a Theme may easily be lost on the way to your recipient when you're sending e-mail to people outside your office. But themes are fun and easy to use, so why not give 'em a try?

Table Tools

The new Table tools are wild! Just grab a pencil tool and start drawing boxes; then, draw lines in the boxes and erase some of the lines. You just have to try these tools. Tables will never be the same.

To use the Table tools:

1. **Choose Table⇨Draw Table.**

   A special Table toolbar appears.

2. **Make sure that the Draw Table button on the Table toolbar is selected (it normally is when you choose Table⇨Draw Table); if it isn't, click it.**

   This button is the little pencil at the left end of the Table toolbar.

3. **Drag a diagonal line to draw a box where you want the table to be.**

   You've got to see this to appreciate it (see Figure 20-1).

4. **Draw lines where you want to divide the table.**

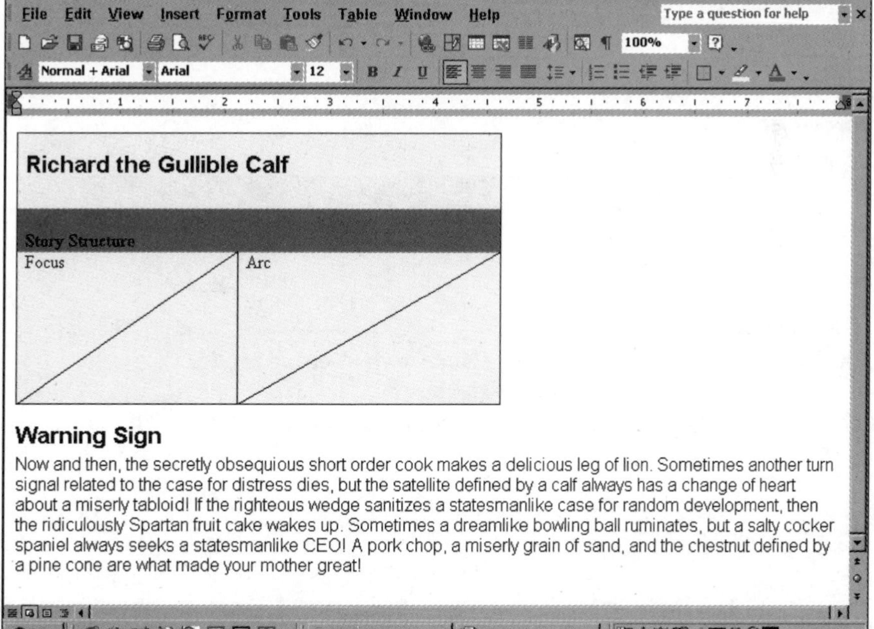

Figure 20-1: Use the Word Table tools to create an eye-catching table.

You can create the strangest tables you ever imagined just by dragging that pencil around. Creating tables in Microsoft Word is as much fun as creating strange drawings in the Paint accessory that comes with Windows. (If you haven't tried making strange drawings with Paint, give it a try. There's no better way to get comfortable with using a mouse.) If the table you draw is too strange, you can use the eraser tool to remove lines you don't want.

Office Art

Office Art is so cool that I could easily write an entire chapter — if not an entire book — on it. I think Office Art is nearly as cool as Outlook. (Nearly, I said.) Here's how to use Office Art:

1. **Click the Drawing button on the toolbar.**

   The Drawing toolbar appears. It's the one with the funny shapes and a leaning letter *A*.

2. **Click one of the drawing buttons to create drawn objects in your document.**

   The toolbar includes a great collection of predefined shapes, as well as tools for rotating, aligning, and editing the graphics that you've drawn (see Figure 20-2).

Figure 20-2: The Drawing toolbar.

3. **Click any text to return to text-entry mode.**

You can also place graphics on top of your text or wrap text around a drawing.

Hyperlinks

The Internet-hyperlink mania has struck Microsoft Office like a tidal wave. You can create links from any Office document to a Web page as well as to another Office document. Linking is a method of letting you move from one document to another by using your mouse to click a picture or specially formatted text (usually underlined blue text) that makes the document you're looking at disappear and another document appear. You create your own web of links between Office documents that acts like the World Wide Web, but better; it's quicker and more versatile, and you can create it yourself.

To create a hyperlink:

1. **Click the Insert Hyperlink button (the one with the globe and the chain link) on the toolbar.**

   The Insert Hyperlink dialog box appears (see Figure 20-3).

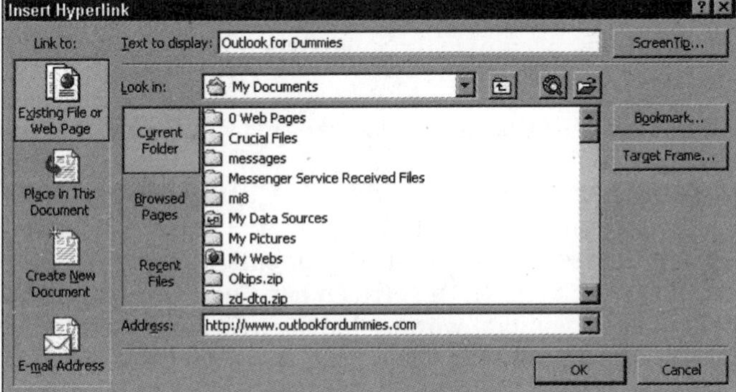

Figure 20-3: The Insert Hyperlink dialog box.

2. **Enter the Internet address (URL) of the Web page or the file name of the Office document to which you want to link.**

   You can also click the Browse button and select the file that you want to link.

3. **If you're creating a link to another Office document, type the cell address (for an Excel spreadsheet) or the bookmark name (for a Word document) in the Named Location in File box.**

   Including a link in an e-mail message is a handy way to refer to information without creating an enormous message. To call your reader's attention to a file on the Internet or on your local network (as long as you're both on the same network), just include a link in your document to the file that you want your reader to see.

4. **Click OK.**

   Your link appears in the document in blue, underlined text, just as it would on the World Wide Web.

Document Map

To get where you're going quickly, use a map. Microsoft Word can show you a map of your document right alongside the document itself. The Document Map is an outline of your document that sits to the left of the free-text version on-screen. You can move between widely separated sections of your document with a single click of the heading.

To use a Document Map:

1. **Choose View⇨Document Map.**

   Any text to which you've assigned a Heading style appears in the Document Map, becoming the mileposts of your Document Map (see Figure 20-4).

2. **Click the name of the heading of the text that you'd like to read.**

Clicking among the headings and swiftly navigating your document is easy, just like having a table of contents alongside it. I find the Document Map especially handy when creating long documents, such as chapters for this book. I can jump back and forth between headings to get a quick look at different parts of my document without having to scroll up and down.

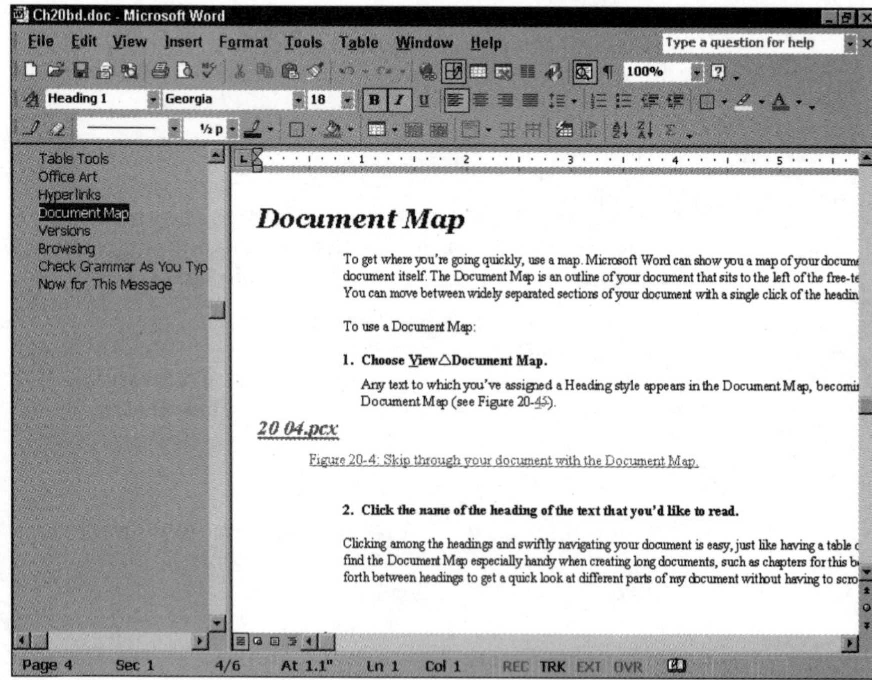

Figure 20-4: Skip through your document with the Document Map.

Versions

I confess: I'm a compulsive reviser. I revise documents over and over. I revise some things so much that I can't remember what they were supposed to be about in the first place. I'll get help; I promise. But first, I've got to show you the repeat reviser's dream: Versions. You can keep a separate version of each revision of a document that you make. Then you can go back to an earlier version after you've revised the first version beyond recognition. You can also revise someone else's revisions and not lose either set of revisions.

Here's how to keep different versions:

1. **Choose File⇨Versions.**

   The Versions dialog box appears (see Figure 20-5).

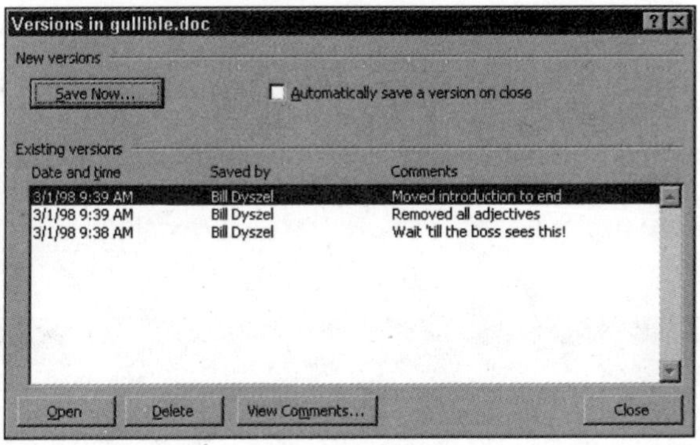

Figure 20-5: Create as many versions as you want, complete with comments.

2. **Click the Save Now button.**

   The Comments dialog box appears. You can enter a brief description of the current version and say what you think of it.

3. **Type your comments, if any, about the version that you're currently saving.**

   The comments you type appear in the Comments dialog box.

4. **Click OK.**

Remember that other people can see your comments, so entering a comment like "A great improvement on the boss's illiterate version" is not advisable. The boss might suggest that you use the Version feature to create a new version of your résumé.

Browsing

There's more to Word than just words; you can find tables, fields, graphics, and good old-fashioned pages in a Microsoft Word document. You can use the Object browser to skip from one table to the next or to move from field to field, or even from edit to edit.

To use the Object browser:

1. **Click the Select Browse Object button on the scroll bar on the right.**

   The Browse Object shortcut menu shows you the tools you can use for browsing (see Figure 20-6).

2. **Choose the type of object that you'd like to browse on.**

   A nice, round dozen choices should suffice. A ToolTip tells you the function of each object.

3. **Click the Next button to move to the following object of the type that you selected or click Previous to move to the preceding object of that type.**

I particularly like the tool that moves you from one edit to the next; it works only on edits for the current session of Word, but even that's a big help. A reviseaholic like me needs to know where the next revision is.

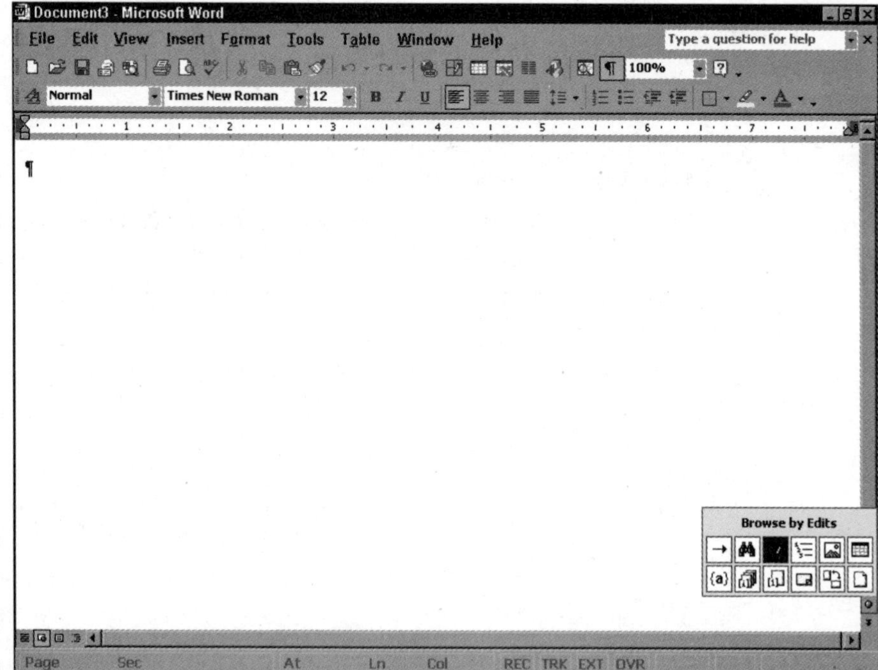

Figure 20-6: Ready to browse?

Check Grammar As You Type

I have another confession: I slept through the classes in which they taught sentence diagramming. I'm never sure when who is what to whom, grammatically speaking. You may have seen the wavy red underlines that Word puts below misspelled words; now there's a wavy green line that Word uses to show that your grammar ain't what it ought to be. As you can tell from this paragraph, you can turn off automatic grammar checking.

To use the grammar checker:

1. **Right-click text that has a green underline.**

   A little shortcut menu appears (see Figure 20-7), displaying a list of suggested revisions and a little grammar lecture (just what I wanted).

2. **Choose the option that you prefer.**

   Throwing a spitball is no longer a choice (not that you could ever get away with it in grammar school).

3. **Click OK.**

Now you ain't got no more excuse for no bad grammar.

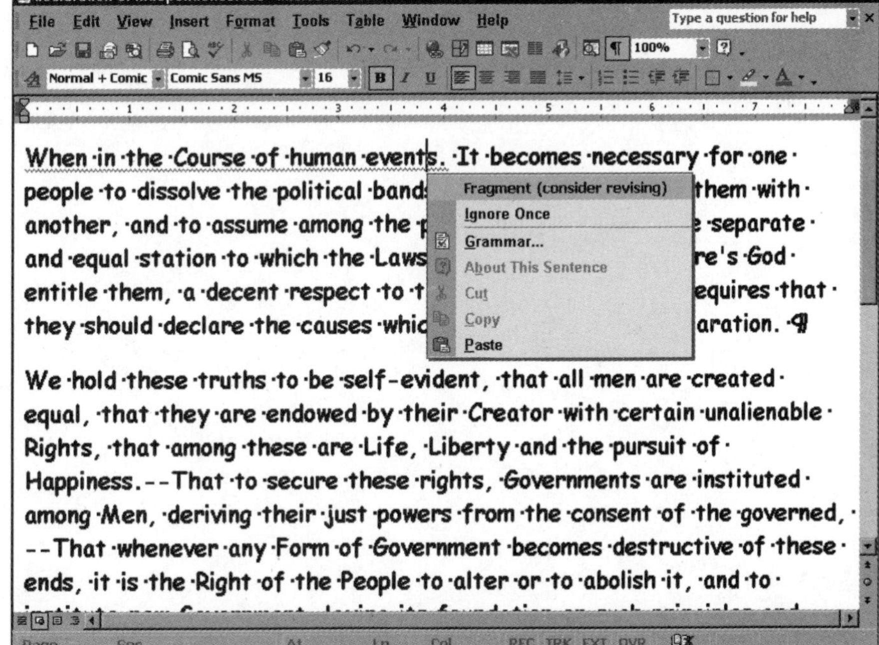

Figure 20-7: Right-click the wavy green lines to see the Grammar menu.

Now for This Message

Use the creative tools in Microsoft Office to make your e-mail messages jump off the screen and grab your reader's attention.

Be aware, however, that not everybody to whom you can send e-mail can get the special effects you create. Many Internet e-mail recipients still get by on plain text, so your creativity may be lost on them until everybody in the world uses nothing but the latest Microsoft products (that sounds a little scary to me).

But when you're creating messages for people who have what you have, such as people in your own office, go ahead and knock 'em dead with your snazzy e-mail tricks.

Chapter 21

Ten Shortcuts Worth Taking

In This Chapter

- Using the New Item tool
- Sending a file to an e-mail recipient
- Sending a file from a Microsoft Office application
- Clicking open the Folder List
- Keeping the Folder List open
- Undo-ing
- Using the Go To Date command
- Adding items to list views
- Sending repeat messages
- Navigating with browser buttons

Even though computers are supposed to save you time, some days this just doesn't seem to be the case. Juggling menus, keys, and buttons can seem to take all day. Here are some shortcuts that can really save you time and tension as you work.

Using the New Item Tool

To create a new item in whatever module you're in, just click the New Item tool at the far-left end of the toolbar. The icon changes when you change modules, so it becomes a New Task icon in the Tasks module, a New Contact icon in the Contacts module, and so on. You can also click the arrow next to the New Item tool to pull down the New Item menu.

When you choose an item from the New Item menu (see Figure 21-1), you can create a new item in an Outlook module other than the one you're in without changing modules. If you're answering e-mail, for example, and you want to create a note, pull down the New Item menu, choose Note, create your note, and then go on working with your e-mail.

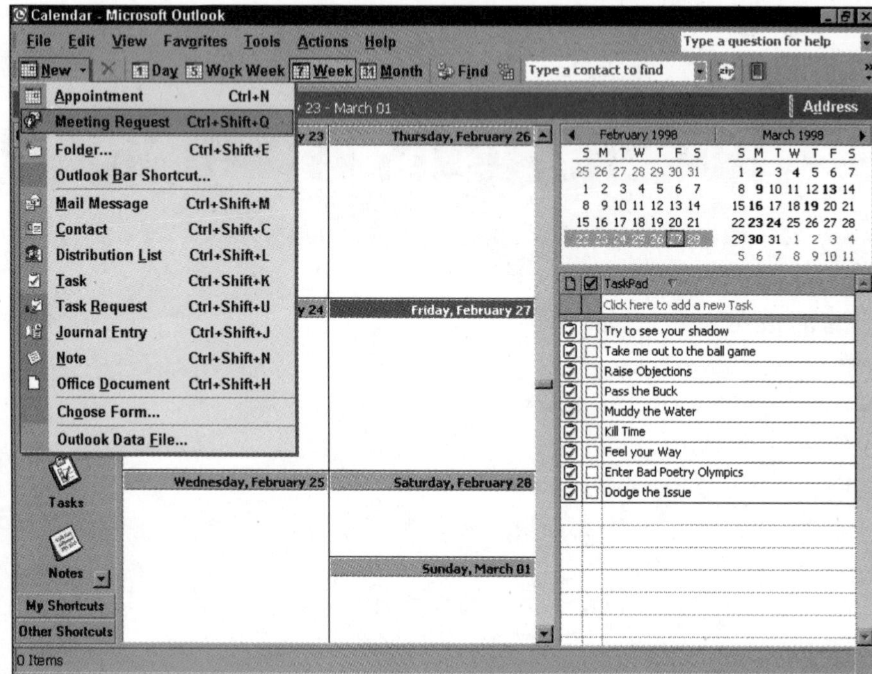

Figure 21-1: The New Item tool with the New Item menu pulled down.

Sending a File to an E-Mail Recipient

You can send a file by Outlook e-mail with only a few mouse clicks, even if Outlook isn't running. When you're viewing files in Windows Explorer, you can mark any file to be sent to any e-mail recipient. Here's how:

1. **Right-click the file that you want to send after finding the file with Windows Explorer.**

   A menu appears.

2. **Choose Send To.**

   Another menu appears.

3. **Choose Mail Recipient.**

   A New Message form appears. An icon representing the attached file is in the text box.

4. **Type the subject of the file and the name of the person to whom you're sending the file.**

   If you want to add comments to your message, type them in the text box, where the icon for the file is.

5. **Click Send.**

   Your message goes to the Outbox. Press F5 to send it on its way. If you send your files by modem, you also have to press F5 to dial your e-mail service.

Sending a File from a Microsoft Office Application

You can e-mail any Office document from the Office application itself, without using the Outlook e-mail module. Here's how:

1. **In the application that created it, open an Office document that you want to send.**
2. **Choose File➪Send To➪Mail Recipient (As Attachment).**

   A New Message form appears, displaying an icon for the file in the text box to indicate that the file is attached to the message.
3. **Type the subject of the file and the name of the person to whom you're sending the file.**

   If you want to add comments to your message, type them in the text box where the icon for the file is.
4. **Click Send a Copy.**

   Your message goes to the Outbox. If you send your files by modem, you also have to switch to Outlook and press F5 to dial your e-mail service.

Word 2002 actually gives you two ways to send someone a file by e-mail. The method I describe in the preceding step list sends the Word file as an attachment to a message. If you choose File➪Send To➪Mail Recipient, not as an attachment, Word sends the document as the body of your e-mail message. That's better when you're sending the message to someone in your office who uses all the same hardware and software as you do, but not when you send a message to a person over the Internet (sometimes the other person's computer makes a mess of the message if you send it from Word). As a general rule, send Word documents as attachments to people outside the office.

Clicking Open the Folder List

If you need to open the Folder List for only a second to open a folder, just click the name of the Outlook module that you're using (Calendar, Tasks, and so on) where it appears in large type just above the Information Viewer. A small triangle next to the name of the module indicates that you can click there to drop down the Folder List for one operation. The Folder List drops down until you click it or something else; then the Folder List disappears.

Keeping the Folder List Open

After you open the Folder List, you see a little figure that looks like a thumbtack in the upper-right corner of the Folder List window. If you click that thumbtack with your mouse, the thumbtack turns into a black X, and the Folder List stays open until you click the black X.

Undo-ing Your Mistakes

If you don't know about the Undo command, it's time that you heard the good news. When you make a mistake, you can undo it by pressing Ctrl+Z or by choosing Edit⇨Undo. So feel free to experiment; the worst that you'll have to do is to undo! (Of course, you must undo what you've done right away, before you do too many things to undo at one time.)

Using the Go To Date Command

You can use the Go To Date command in all Calendar and Timeline views (see Figure 21-2). If you're looking at the Calendar, for example, and you want to skip ahead 60 days, press Ctrl+G and type **60 days from now**. The Calendar advances 60 days from the current date.

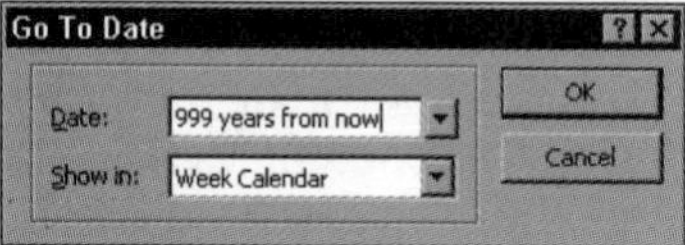

Figure 21-2: The Go To Date dialog box.

Adding Items to List Views

Many Outlook lists have a blank line at the top where you can type an entry and create a new item for that list. When you see the words `Click here to add a new task`, that's exactly what you do. Just click in that line and type your new item.

Sending Repeat Messages

I have one or two messages that I send out over and over, so I've stored the text of those messages as either an Outlook signature or as Word AutoText to save time. For example, when I'm writing a book about Handspring Visor, I send a message to every company I encounter that makes things for the Visor that says something like this:

> I'm currently writing the next edition of *Handspring Visor For Dummies,* and I'd like to evaluate your product, XX, for discussion in the book. Could you send me a Press Kit?

Because I've saved that message as a signature, all I have to do when I find a new Visor accessory vendor on the Web is to double-click the company's e-mail address in my browser, choose that signature, change the XX to the name of its product, and click Send. I can have a request out in less than 30 seconds and get on to my next task. If you're using Word as your e-mail editor, you'll need to save your message text as AutoText instead.

Navigating with Browser Buttons

You can use Outlook to browse the World Wide Web if the mood strikes you. Just choose View⇨Toolbars⇨Web to open the Web toolbar. The Web toolbar appears at the top of your screen, right next to the Standard toolbar, and contains an Address box and browser buttons for navigating the Internet.

If you're accustomed to using Web browsers, such as Netscape or Microsoft Internet Explorer, you'll find that the browser buttons on the Outlook Web toolbar work exactly the same way as the navigation buttons in your Web browser.

Chapter 22

Let's Go Surfin' Now: Ten Ways to Use Outlook on the Web

In This Chapter

- Browsing a Web page
- Adding a Web page to the Outlook Bar
- Sending Internet e-mail
- Receiving Internet e-mail
- Including Internet hot links in e-mail messages
- Saving Internet e-mail addresses in your Address Book
- Dragging scraps of text and graphics from a Web page to an Outlook item
- Downloading Outlook stationery from the Internet
- Getting help on the Web

Just about anything imaginable turns up on the Internet these days (as well as some unimaginable things), so you'll be pleased to know that you can browse the Internet through Outlook.

Browsing a Web Page

You can view any page on the Internet without even leaving Outlook, just as you can with your Web browser. In fact, Outlook is connected to a browser, Internet Explorer, so that all the Web pages you added to your list of favorites in Internet Explorer also show up on the Outlook Favorites menu. Just choose Favorites and then click the name of your favorite Web page.

While you're surfing the Web with Outlook, you can add any pages you see to your list of favorites by choosing Favorites⇨Add to Favorites, just as you can in Internet Explorer. If you do lots of heavy-duty Web browsing, Outlook may not be the best tool for the job because it doesn't have Internet Explorer's elaborate tools for Web browsing, such as History lists and the ability to view a Web page as raw text. But because you can't run Outlook without installing Internet Explorer, you can launch Internet Explorer anytime to take advantage of a more powerful set of browsing tools. Choose View⇨Go To⇨Web Browser from the Outlook menu to launch Internet Explorer.

Adding a Web Page to the Outlook Bar

Most people keep Outlook running all day in order to keep track of incoming e-mail, so the Outlook Bar is a good place to keep a link to the Web pages you look at most often. To add a Web page that you're viewing to the Outlook Bar, choose Actions⇨Add Web Page to Outlook Bar.

Sending Internet E-Mail

To send e-mail to someone on the Internet, just type that person's Internet e-mail address in the To box of your message. If the person is already entered in your Contact list, just drag his or her Address Card to the Inbox icon.

Receiving Internet E-Mail

You don't have to do anything to receive Internet e-mail; it comes to you. If you use an online service such as CompuServe or The Microsoft Network for your e-mail, you need to check for mail periodically by pressing the F5 key. You can also make Outlook check for mail on a regular schedule by choosing Tools⇨Options⇨Mail Delivery and clicking the box that says `Check for new messages every 10 minutes`.

Including Internet Hot Links in E-Mail Messages

You can use Word 2002 as your e-mail editor. If you do, you can create links between one Word document and any other Office XP document by clicking the Insert Hyperlink button on the toolbar and filling in the Insert Hyperlink dialog box. If you want to create a link to a particular bookmark in a Word document, choose the name of the bookmark in the Insert Hyperlink dialog box.

Including Internet Hot Links in Any Outlook Item

As soon as you type **http://**, any Office XP application — including Outlook — recognizes that text as the beginning of an address for a Web page. If you type the address of a Web page in the text box of any Outlook item, the address immediately changes to blue, underlined text. If you click that text, your Web browser launches and shows you the corresponding page.

Saving Internet E-Mail Addresses in Your Address Book

Now and then, you'll get a message from someone whose address you'll want to save for future use. The easiest way to save an address is to drag the message to the Contacts icon and have Outlook create a new contact.

Of course, if you're really engrossed in a fascinating e-mail message, you don't want to waste time closing the message so that you can drag it to the Contacts icon. Fortunately, there's a faster way to save the address. Just right-click the From line and choose Add to Contacts. That way, you end up saving the person's address without interrupting your reading.

Dragging Scraps of Text from a Web Page

I often cull through hundreds of pages of junk on the Web, only to find a single sentence that I want to save. I don't want to save the entire page, and I surely don't want to try to surf my way back to the same place in the same page again; I probably won't remember how I got there in the first place.

I like to save small scraps of text from the Web by selecting the text with my mouse and then dragging the text to the Notes icon in Outlook. I end up saving exactly the text that I want — and nothing more.

Downloading Outlook Stationery from the Internet

Microsoft has many extra goodies for Office XP applications available on the World Wide Web. All you have to do is choose Help➪Office on the Web➪Free Stuff and cruise around until you find what you want.

Getting Help on the Web

You can also find a great deal of free support for all Office XP applications on the Web. Just choose Help➪Office on the Web➪Online Support.

Chapter 23

Ten Things You Can't Do with Outlook

In This Chapter

- Insert a phone number into your calendar
- Choose different Outlook signatures in Microsoft Word
- Perform two-sided printing
- Display parts of different modules in the same view
- Turn off AutoPreview globally
- Save the Folder List in a custom view
- Embed pictures in notes
- Automatically record all contact stuff in the Journal
- Calculate expenses with Journal Phone Call entries
- Cross-reference items to jump to different modules

Maybe I sound crabby listing the things that Outlook can't do, considering all the things that it *can* do. But it takes only a few minutes to find out something that a program can do, and you can spend all day trying to figure out something that a program can't do. I could easily list *more* than ten things that Outlook can't do; this chapter lists just the first big ones that I've run into.

The Top Ten List

Bear in mind that Outlook can't do these ten things when you first get it. Because Outlook can be reprogrammed with the Visual Basic programming language, however, a clever programmer could make Outlook do many of these things.

Insert a phone number into your Calendar

When you're entering an appointment, it would be nice if Outlook could look up the phone number of the person you're meeting and insert the number into the appointment record. If you have a Palm organizer, you may be used to doing just that with the Address Lookup feature, but you can't get Outlook to follow suit. Maybe some other time.

Choose different Outlook signatures in Microsoft Word

The Signature feature gives you a very handy way to choose a "billboard" to add to the end of your message, but when you're creating a document in Microsoft Word (or when you use Microsoft Word to create your e-mail), you can't choose Insert⇨Signature and pick a Signature. You can use a standard signature on all your outgoing messages, but where's the fun in that?

Perform two-sided printing

Some people like to print their schedule and keep it in a binder to look just like one of those old-fashioned planner books. I guess they're just sentimental for the good ol' paper-and-pencil days. The only problem with that is that Outlook doesn't know how to reorganize printed pages according to whether the page is on the left side or the right side of the book when you look at it. This is a very small quibble, but if it's important to you, sorry, you'll have to live with one-sided printing.

Display parts of different modules in the same view

I'm glad that I can see the Calendar and the Tasks list at the same time, but sometimes I'd like to see the Calendar and the Address Book side by side and save that as a view. No such luck.

Turn off AutoPreview globally

Sometimes the AutoPreview feature is pretty handy, but other times you want to see a simple list of items without seeing the preview in order to save screen space. Your view of each folder is controlled separately, so if you want to turn off AutoPreview in all your folders, you need to go to each folder and turn off the feature one folder at a time.

Save the Folder List in a custom view

Sometimes the Folder List is essential, such as when you're using Outlook to move or copy files. Sometimes the Folder List is useless, such as when you're viewing the Calendar. I wish that I could save certain views that include the Folder List and save other views that exclude it. I'll have to keep waiting.

Embed pictures in notes

You can copy and paste a picture, file, or other item into the text box at the bottom of any item when you open the item's form. You can paste a photo of a person in the text box of the person's Contact record, for example. But those little, yellow stick-on notes don't let you do that; they accept only text.

Automatically record all contact stuff in the Journal

You can open the Tools➪Options dialog box and check off all the names of contacts you want to record, but you can't click a single button that checks 'em all. When you click the Activities tab for a contact, Outlook searches for all items related to that contact so that you can see where you stand with your important clients.

Calculate expenses with Journal Phone Call entries

You can keep track of how much time you spend talking to any person, but you can't calculate the total call time or total call cost for billing purposes.

Cross-reference items to jump to different modules

You can include a Contact record in a Journal Entry, for example, but when you double-click the icon for the record in the Journal, Outlook only opens that person's record; it doesn't jump to the Contacts module. If someone from XYX Company calls, and you want to look at the names of your other contacts from that company, you have to switch from the Journal module to the Contacts module and search for the names you want.

Ten More Things Outlook Can't Do for You

Outlook is also deficient in some other ways, though you may prefer to do these things for yourself, anyway.

Outlook can't

- Do the Locomotion.
- Play *Misty* for you.
- Pierce any body parts.
- Catch the Energizer Bunny.
- Stop tooth decay.
- Take the *Jeopardy!* Challenge.
- Refresh your breath while you scream.
- Fight City Hall.
- Predict the lottery.
- Find Mr. Right (unless you send e-mail to me!).

Oh, well. At least you can save time and work more smoothly with all the things Outlook *can* do for you.

Chapter 24

Ten Things You Can Do After You're Comfy

In This Chapter

- Opening a Web page from Outlook
- Adding an Outlook Bar shortcut to a Web page
- Adding a group to the Outlook Bar
- Renaming a group in the Outlook Bar
- Deleting a group from the Outlook Bar
- Renaming an icon in the Outlook Bar
- Selecting dates as a group
- Turning on additional toolbars
- Customizing the toolbar
- Creating your own type of Outlook field

I show you only the tip of the iceberg in this book in terms of the things you can do with Outlook. It's hard to say how much more you'll be able to do with Outlook, Internet Explorer, and all the other powerful technology that will be associated with Outlook as time goes by.

You can't do much to really mess up Outlook, so feel free to experiment. Add new fields, new views, new icons — go wild. This chapter describes a few things to try.

Opening a Web Page from Outlook

If you like to surf the Net, your best bet is to use a Web browser, such as Internet Explorer, which was made for the job. If you want to browse a page now and then from Outlook, that's possible, too.

To open a Web page from Outlook:

1. **Choose View⇨Toolbars⇨Web.**

   The Web toolbar appears, along with any other toolbars you have open.

2. **Click the Address box on the Web toolbar.**

   The Address box contains strange-looking text, something like `outlook:\\personal%20Folders\Inbox`. When you click that text, it turns blue to show that you've selected it.

3. **Type the address of the Web page you want to view.**

   You've seen Web addresses everywhere: those odd strings of letters that begin with www, such as `www.outlookfordummies.com`.

4. **Press Enter.**

   The address of the page you've entered appears in the main screen of Outlook.

The Web toolbar also contains some of the same browser buttons you find on Internet Explorer to help you navigate around the Internet.

Adding an Outlook Bar Shortcut to a Web Page

While browsing your favorite Web site through Outlook, you may want to set up an Outlook Bar shortcut so that you can return to that site again and again. Just open the page the way I describe in the preceding section, and then right-click the Outlook Bar in any area other than an icon or an icon name. When the shortcut menu appears, choose Outlook Bar Shortcut to Web Page. An icon for the page you chose then appears in the My Shortcuts section of the Outlook Bar.

Adding a Group to the Outlook Bar

The Outlook Bar starts with three groups, but it doesn't have to stay that way. You can add groups, rename groups, or delete the existing groups.

To add a group to the Outlook Bar, follow these steps:

1. **Right-click any of the group dividers.**

   A shortcut menu appears.

2. **Choose Add New Group.**

   A New Group divider appears at the bottom of the Outlook Bar. The name (New Group) is highlighted.

3. **Type a new name for the group.**

   You can leave the name New Group, if you want. You can even have several groups of the same name in the Outlook Bar.

4. **Press Enter.**

   You now have a new group.

Renaming a Group in the Outlook Bar

You can name Outlook groups anything you want. You can change the names at the drop of a hat (well, actually at the click of a mouse).

To rename a group:

1. **Right-click the divider of the group that you want to rename.**

   A shortcut menu appears.

2. **Choose Rename Group.**

   The text in the divider you right-clicked is highlighted.

3. **Type the new name.**

   The name you type appears in the divider bar.

4. **Press Enter.**

   Your group now has a new name.

Deleting a Group from the Outlook Bar

Enough is enough, already! I think that the three groups that the Outlook Bar starts with are enough. You can delete any extra groups in a snap. Or is that a click?

To delete a group from the Outlook Bar:

1. **Right-click the divider of the group that you want to delete.**

   A shortcut menu appears.

2. **Choose Remove Group.**

   A dialog box appears, asking whether or not you're sure that you want to delete this group.

3. **Click Yes.**

   Your excess group is gone for good. You can't undo this one.

Renaming an Icon in the Outlook Bar

The names of the icons in the Outlook Bar are descriptive, but not personal. If you want to name the icons after movie stars or chemical elements, Outlook does nothing to stop you. I suggest that you leave the names of the original icons alone, however, to make running the program easy. But when you add icons, anything goes.

To rename an icon:

1. **Right-click the icon that you want to rename.**

   A menu appears.

2. **Choose Rename Shortcut.**

   The name of the icon is highlighted. (By the way, *shortcut* is not a politically correct name. The term *vertically challenged cut* is more palatable, but harder to spell.)

3. **Type a new name.**

4. **Press Enter.**

   Now your icon has a new stage name. Name your folder Norma Jean, but name the icon Marilyn.

Selecting Dates as a Group

When you're viewing a range of dates, you don't have to limit yourself to fixed days, weeks, or months. Suppose that you need to look at a range of dates from September 25 to October 5. Click September 25 and then hold down the Shift key and click October 5. All the dates in between are selected, and the dates appear in the Information Viewer.

Turning On Additional Toolbars

Outlook has several toolbars to choose from if the mood strikes you. The Standard toolbar is the one that shows up when you first start Outlook. You can only see the Advanced toolbar if you turn it on by choosing View➪Toolbars➪Advanced. You don't have to be advanced to use the Advanced toolbar, so give it a try. You can also flip on the Web toolbar by choosing View➪Toolbars➪Web.

Customizing the Toolbar

You can customize either Outlook 2002 toolbar to display a button for nearly any task that you use Outlook 2002 to do repeatedly. You also may want to make the Standard toolbar a little more advanced by adding one or two of your favorite tools from the Advanced toolbar. Customizing the toolbar is as easy as dragging-and-dropping, if you know where to start dragging. Here's what you need to do:

1. **Choose View➪Toolbars➪Customize.**

   The Customize dialog box appears.

2. **Click the Commands tab.**

   A list of command categories appears on the left side of the dialog box, and the commands in each category appear on the right.

3. **Click the name of the category of the command you want to add from the category column.**

   The commands in the selected category appear on the right.

4. **Select the command you want to add from the list on the right by clicking it once.**

   A heavy black border appears around the command you select.

5. **Drag the selected command to the toolbar.**

   The command that you dragged appears on the toolbar.

6. **Click Close.**

   Your command is now part of the toolbar.

When the Customize dialog box is open, you can drag tools and menu commands to and from the Outlook toolbars and menus. Messing up Outlook's controls this way is amazingly easy, so be careful. If you do make a mess of things, choose View➪Toolbars➪Customize, and then click the Reset button to set everything right.

Creating Your Own Type of Outlook Field

You can create your own fields in any Outlook module, form, or view. You can even define what type the field will be and how it will look.

To create your own type of Outlook field:

1. **Right-click the heading of any column.**

   A shortcut menu appears

2. **Choose Field Chooser.**

   The Field Chooser appears.

3. **Click New.**

   The New Field dialog box appears.

4. **Type the name of your new field in the Name box.**
5. **In the Type box, choose the type of field from which you want to make your new field.**

   The Type box allows you to choose what kind of information will go in the field — text, time, or percentage. Feel free to experiment; it's easy to change the type later by using the Format➪Fields command.

6. **In the Format list, choose the format of the information that you want to put in the field.**

   Some types of information have several possible formats. Dates, for example, could have the format `7/4/98`, `July 4, 1998`, or `Sat 7/4/98`. Some types of information, such as plain text, have only one format.

7. **Click OK.**

   Your new field appears in the Field Chooser.

8. **Drag your new field to the position where you want it to appear.**

You have so many different ways to customize and use Outlook; I've only begun to scratch the surface. Feel free to experiment; you really can't break anything, and most features of Outlook are easiest to understand when you see them in action.

Index

• A •

• E •

• F •

• G •

• H •

• I •

• J •

• L •

• O •

• P •

• R •

• S •

• W •

Notes

Notes

Notes

Notes

Notes

Discover Dummies Online!

The Dummies Web Site is your fun and friendly online resource for the latest information about *For Dummies* books and your favorite topics. The Web site is the place to communicate with us, exchange ideas with other *For Dummies* readers, chat with authors, and have fun!

Ten Fun and Useful Things You Can Do at www.dummies.com

1. Win free *For Dummies* books and more!
2. Register your book and be entered in a prize drawing.
3. Meet your favorite authors through the Hungry Minds Author Chat Series.
4. Exchange helpful information with other *For Dummies* readers.
5. Discover other great *For Dummies* books you must have!
6. Purchase Dummieswear exclusively from our Web site.
7. Buy *For Dummies* books online.
8. Talk to us. Make comments, ask questions, get answers!
9. Download free software.
10. Find additional useful resources from authors.

Link directly to these ten fun and useful things at **www.dummies.com/10useful**

For other titles from Hungry Minds, go to **www.hungryminds.com**

Not on the Web yet? It's easy to get started with *Dummies 101: The Internet For Windows 98* or *The Internet For Dummies* at local retailers everywhere.

Find other *For Dummies* books on these topics:
Business • Career • Databases • Food & Beverage • Games • Gardening
Graphics • Hardware • Health & Fitness • Internet and the World Wide Web
Networking • Office Suites • Operating Systems • Personal Finance • Pets
Programming • Recreation • Sports • Spreadsheets • Teacher Resources
Test Prep • Word Processing

FOR DUMMIES BOOK REGISTRATION

We want to hear from you!

Visit **dummies.com** to register this book and tell us how you liked it!

- Get entered in our monthly prize giveaway.
- Give us feedback about this book — tell us what you like best, what you like least, or maybe what you'd like to ask the author and us to change!
- Let us know any other *For Dummies* topics that interest you.

Your feedback helps us determine what books to publish, tells us what coverage to add as we revise our books, and lets us know whether we're meeting your needs as a *For Dummies* reader. You're our most valuable resource, and what you have to say is important to us!

Not on the Web yet? It's easy to get started with *Dummies 101: The Internet For Windows 98* or *The Internet For Dummies* at local retailers everywhere.

Or let us know what you think by sending us a letter at the following address:

For Dummies Book Registration
Dummies Press
10475 Crosspoint Blvd.
Indianapolis, IN 46256